DEVELOPMENTAL MODELS
OF THINKING

DEVELOPMENTAL PSYCHOLOGY SERIES

SERIES EDITOR
Harry Beilin

Developmental Psychology Program
City University of New York Graduate School
New York, New York

LYNN S. LIBEN. *Deaf Children: Developmental Perspectives*

JONAS LANGER. *The Origins of Logic: Six to Twelve Months*

GILBERTE PIERAUT-LE BONNIEC. *The Development of Modal Reasoning: Genesis of Necessity and Possibility Notions*

TIFFANY MARTINI FIELD, SUSAN GOLDBERG, DANIEL STERN, and ANITA MILLER SOSTEK. (Editors). *High-Risk Infants and Children: Adult and Peer Interactions*

BARRY GHOLSON. *The Cognitive-Developmental Basis of Human Learning: Studies in Hypothesis Testing*

ROBERT L. SELMAN. *The Growth of Interpersonal Understanding: Developmental and Clinical Analyses*

RAINER H. KLUWE and HANS SPADA. (Editors). *Developmental Models of Thinking*

In Preparation

HARBEN BOUTOURLINE YOUNG and LUCY RAU FERGUSON. *Puberty to Manhood in Italy and America*

SARAH L. FRIEDMAN and MARIAN SIGMAN. (Editors). *Preterm Birth and Psychological Development*

LYNN S. LIBEN, ARTHUR H. PATTERSON, and NORA NEWCOMBE. (Editors). *Spatial Representation and Behavior Through The Life Span: Theory and Application*

DEVELOPMENTAL MODELS OF THINKING

Edited by

RAINER H. KLUWE
*Institut für Psychologie
der Universität München
München, West Germany*

HANS SPADA
*Lehrstuhl für Allgemeine Psychologie
Psychologisches Institut der Universität
Freiburg, West Germany*

ACADEMIC PRESS   1980
A Subsidiary of Harcourt Brace Jovanovich, Publishers
New York   London   Toronto   Sydney   San Francisco

ACADEMIC PRESS, INC.
111 Fifth Avenue, New York, New York 10003

United Kingdom Edition published by
ACADEMIC PRESS, INC. (LONDON) LTD.
24/28 Oval Road, London NW1 7DX

Library of Congress Cataloging in Publication Data
Main entry under title:

Developmental models of thinking.

(Developmental psychology series)
Based on papers presented at a conference held at
the University of Kiel (Germany) Sept. 11–14, 1977,
sponsored by the German Stiftung Volkswagenwerk and
organized by the Institute for Science Education of the
University of Kiel.
Includes bibliographies and index.
1. Thought and thinking––Congresses. 2. Cognition
in children––Congresses. 3. Human information processing
––Congresses. 4. Piaget, Jean, Date ––Congresses.
5. Cognition in children––Mathematical models––
Congresses. I. Kluwe, Rainer. II. Spada, Hans.
III. Stiftung Volkswagenwerk. IV. Kiel, Universität.
Institut für die Pädagogik der Naturwissenschaften.
V. Series·
BF723.C5D495 155.4'13 79–6780
ISBN 0–12–416450–1

PRINTED IN THE UNITED STATES OF AMERICA

80 81 82 83 9 8 7 6 5 4 3 2 1

Contents

1

Two Models of Intellectual Development and Their Reference to the Theory of Piaget

HANS SPADA AND RAINER H. KLUWE

2

Mathematical and Psychometric Models of Cognitive Development from the Viewpoint of Information-Processing Theories

GERD LÜER

v

3
A Theory of Growth
HOBEN THOMAS

4
The Study of Cognitive Development through Causal Modeling with Qualitative Data
P. M. BENTLER

5
Quantitative Changes in Cognitive Development: Description, Measurement, and Theoretical Explication
G. RUDINGER AND H. RÜPPEL

6
Information-Processing Models of Intellectual Development
DAVID KLAHR

7
Formal Precision, Where and What for, Or: The Ape Climbs the Tree
RUDOLF GRONER, BEAT KELLER, AND CHRISTINE MENZ

8
The Development of Logical Competence: A Psycholinguistic Perspective
RACHEL JOFFE FALMAGNE

9
Analysis of Understanding in Problem Solving
JAMES G. GREENO

10
The Role of Invention in the Development of Mathematical Competence
LAUREN B. RESNICK

11

Piaget's Theory: Refinement, Revision, or Rejection?
HARRY BEILIN

12

Constructive Problems for Constructive Theories: The Current Relevance of Piaget's Work and a Critique of Information-Processing Simulation Psychology
J. PASCUAL-LEONE

List of Contributors

Numbers in parentheses indicate the pages on which the authors' contributions begin.

HARRY BEILIN (245), Graduate School and University Center, City University of New York, New York, New York 10036

P. M. BENTLER (77), Department of Psychology, University of California, Los Angeles, Los Angeles, California 90024

JAMES G. GREENO (199), Department of Psychology and Learning Research and Development Center, University of Pittsburgh, Pittsburgh, Pennsylvania 15260

RUDOLF GRONER (163), Psychologisches Institut der Universität Bern, Gesellschaftsstrasse 49, CH-3012 Bern, Switzerland

RACHEL JOFFE FALMAGNE (171), Department of Psychology, Clark University, Worcester, Massachusetts 01610

BEAT KELLER (163), Psychologisches Institut der Universität Bern, Gesellschaftsstrasse 49, CH-3012 Bern, Switzerland

DAVID KLAHR (127), Department of Psychology, Carnegie-Mellon University, Schenley Park, Pittsburgh, Pennsylvania 15213

RAINER H. KLUWE (1), Institut für Psychologie der Universität München, Geschwister-Scholl-Platz 1, 8000 München 22, West Germany

GERD LÜER (33), Institut für Psychologie der Technischen Hochschule Aachen, Krämerstrasse 20-34, 5100 Aachen, West Germany

CHRISTINE MENZ (163), Psychologisches Institut der Universität Bern, Gesellschaftsstrasse 49, CH-3012 Bern, Switzerland

J. PASCUAL-LEONE (263), Department of Psychology, York University, Downsview, Ontario M3J 1P3, Canada

LAUREN B. RESNICK (213), Department of Psychology and Learning Research and Development Center, University of Pittsburgh, Pittsburgh, Pennsylvania 15260

G. RUDINGER (107), Psychologisches Institut der Universität Bonn, An der Schlosskirche 1, 5300 Bonn, West Germany

H. RÜPPELL (107), Psychologisches Institut der Universität Bonn, An der Schlosskirche 1, 5300 Bonn, West Germany

HANS SPADA (1), Lehrstuhl für Allgemeine Psychologie, Psychologisches Institut der Universität, Niemenstrasse 10 (Peterhof), D-7800 Freiburg, West Germany

HOBEN THOMAS (43), Department of Psychology, Pennsylvania State University, University Park, Pennsylvania 16802

Preface

This volume presents detailed views of the state of the art in the field of developmental models of thinking. These views, generally divisible into mathematical and psychometric models, information processing models, and Piaget-centered models are provided by outstanding researchers in the field.

The problem of how intellectual abilities evolve during human ontogenesis is central to psychological research. Because of the relevance of this question for diagnostic purposes and for the improvement of instruction, further progress is strongly demanded from psychologists in the field. The present state of theory construction in developmental psychology is considered to be insufficient, despite the extensive work of Piaget and his group, which dominates the area and leads to a steadily growing number of studies. However, there do exist some new formalized developmental theories of thinking. Many of these theories show a high degree of precision and testability. Furthermore, they capture some of the essentials of Piaget's theory and, more importantly, overcome some of its insufficiencies. Moreover, there are experimental approaches that are explicitly guided by theoretical models of cognitive development. These theories focus more on the empirical examination of derived hypotheses and the refinement of models, and are less guided by Piaget's theory.

These new lines of research were the basis for a conference entitled "Developmental Models of Thinking," held at the University of Kiel (Germany) from September 11–14, 1977. The Kiel conference enabled for the first time a fruitful and critical comparison of all three major approaches—Piagetian, measurement, and information processing. The so-called measurement approach is based on mathematical and psychometric models of intellectual development. The information processing approach is best described by the work of the Carnegie-Mellon group.

However, as this volume shows, research not relying on computer simulation is also included.

The selection of participants was made primarily with respect to our goal to invite psychologists who contribute through their work to the construction of models in the field of cognitive development. Theoretical models were to be discussed, as well as the corresponding empirical results. These results provided a concrete basis for the comparison of different approaches because, in some cases, the empirical studies were based on the same problems. The contributions for this volume are based on some of the presentations during the conference. They have been considerably revised and rewritten for this volume in order to fit into an integrated, edited treatise.

The volume contains 12 chapters which form three subsets. Chapters 1–5 address the description of cognitive development through the use of mathematical and psychometric models. One characteristic of these contributions is the explicit consideration of interindividual differences. Chapters 6–10 represent variants of the information processing approach. And Chapters 11–12, provide an evaluation of the Genevan approach and of some recent directions taken by this type of research on cognitive development.

The book provides an extensive and integrative overview of the variety of ongoing theoretical and empirical research aiming at developmental models of thinking. This makes it of general interest to psychologists in all fields. It is of particular interest to workers in the fields of developmental, cognitive, and instructional psychology and to educators.

We wish to thank all of the authors for their readiness to follow our requests for revisions and modifications. Without this cooperation, this comprehensive volume would not have been possible. Furthermore, we are grateful to all the participants of the Kiel Conference in September 1977 for their contributions. This conference was sponsored by the German Stiftung Volkswagenwerk (Az. 34 314). The support of Urs Baumann and Hermann Wegener, faculty members of the Department of Psychology at Kiel University, enabled us to hold the conference. Mrs. Sinn provided invaluable assistance in taking care of all administrative problems.

We want to thank the Institute for Science Education at the University of Kiel and its managing director, Karl Frey.[1] The Institute was especially helpful in organizing the conference. We also wish to acknowledge the assistance of Aida Starke, Ute Kühl, Petra Möller, and Monika Wenhart in preparing this volume.

---

[1] The IPN is a research institute financed by Schleswig-Holstein and by the German federal government. The institute's function is a national one. Through its research work, it aims to further develop and promote science education.

Overview

The contributions to this volume address the question of how to model cognitive development. The authors who have been brought together here are proponents of different research approaches. As a consequence, the answers vary considerably. A common feature, however, is the explicit search for theory-guided hypotheses about cognitive development and the goal of empirical studies in order to improve the theory.

Spada and Kluwe (Chapter 1) point out that the construction of formal models should be a central goal for developmental psychology. They review studies of two different models of thinking and intellectual development. These models are based on hypotheses about cognitive operations used by children of different ages to solve certain problems. They are also based on psychometric assumptions, and allow the specification and testing of hypotheses about quantitative and structural cognitive developmental changes in problem-solving processes. One model is based on assumptions of the deterministic model of structural learning (Scandura 1973) and corresponds to the findings of Inhelder and Piaget (1958). The second model is a generalization of the probabilistic latent trait model of Rasch (1966). Both models are compared on the basis of data that have been collected under different experimental conditions.

Lüer (Chapter 2), in his evaluation of mathematical models as a possible means for describing cognitive development, addresses the work done by Spada and Kluwe. His criticism focuses on restrictions and assumptions connected with some mathematical models. Favoring the information processing approach himself, Lüer claims that some mathematical models simplify the understanding of cognitive development. However, he shows connections between the mathematical approach and the information processing approach that probably make the distinction an arbitrary one.

The contribution of Thomas (Chapter 3) represents a theory of developmental growth that focuses on the functional relationship between means and standard deviations at various age levels.[1] Referring to early work of Thurstone, Thomas discusses the high sample correlation coefficients (e.g., for cognitive measures) computed on pairs of sample means and standard deviations obtained at each of the varying age points. He is able to show that analysis of variance as a model for developmental growth is readily falsified. He concludes that viewing growth phenomena within additive structures is inappropriate. Instead, Thomas proposes a multiplicative model in which the growth process is presented as a product of an age-specific growth parameter and random variables.

Bentler (Chapter 4) gives an extensive outline of the possibilities of studying cognitive development through causal modeling with qualitative data. Starting from a detailed discussion of the problems of description and explanation in developmental research, he presents a non-technical overview of latent attribute models (latent structure model, scalability model, latent trait model, factor analysis model), description models (dichotomous regression model, structural equation model), and multinomial response models (log-linear model, cross-classification with errors model).

Rudinger and Rüppell (Chapter 5) discuss the description of quantitative changes in cognitive development, taking into account the question of interindividual differences. Their main goal is to show the relationship between the quantitative approach and the qualitative–structural approach to cognitive development; they are considered to be complementary. Sternberg's componential analysis is discussed as a possible paradigm for combining the psychometric tradition and the qualitative–structural approach. However, the authors' evaluation of this paradigm lead them to a related model of mental abilities proposed earlier by Selz (1935). His model of intelligence and his method of training defined cognitive processes are considered to be promising with regard to the quantification of intellectual development.

Following this group of contributions, which deals predominantly with questions of the quantitative description and mathematical modeling of cognitive development, Klahr (Chapter 6) gives an outline of the information processing approach to research on cognitive development as it is followed at Carnegie-Mellon University. He focuses on computer simulation of different levels of cognitive competence as a method to elaborate a model of cognitive development. Basically Klahr aims at task-specific information processing models to account for learning and performance. Several empirical paradigms provide a good illustration of how a system

[1] This contribution was not originally included in the Kiel Conference since Professor Thomas was not able to accept an invitation due to previous commitments.

of production rules solves a central problem of information processing models, that is, what knowledge is available at different age levels. Klahr also discusses the advantages of self-modifying production systems.

Groner (Chapter 7), known for his work in mathematical learning theories, is an expert in mathematical psychology as well as in computer simulation. He and his coauthors, Keller and Menz, give a detailed criticism of the computer simulation approach to cognitive development.

The next three chapters by Joffe Falmagne, Greeno, and Resnick represent different examples of the information processing approach to cognitive development. The chapter by Joffe Falmagne (Chapter 8) aims at a theoretical framework for propositional reasoning and its development during childhood. The discussion of differences between her approach and the Piagetian approach leads to the tentative conclusion that young children do master some pattern of inductive inference at a fairly abstract level. Joffe Falmagne elaborates a theoretical framework that assumes that logical competence may develop in part as a result of a concept learning process: The structural concept being learned is a given rule of inference. A central part of the theoretical framework is obviously the changing availability of alternative modes of representation for verbally given information during the course of cognitive development.

The basic problem emphasized by Greeno (Chapter 9) is related to Joffe Falmagne's introductory discussion of the differences between the Genevan and the "propositional" approaches: the understanding of tasks. Greeno's chapter focuses on two forms of conceptual understanding: semantic interpretations of arithmetic, and arithmetic as a semantic model of a more abstract formal language. With respect to the first form, Greeno attempts a detailed description of how children generate a semantic interpretation of a given problem and of how they identify the appropriate relationship in the formal language of arithmetic. With respect to the second form of conceptual understanding, Greeno introduces an important distinction between implicit and explicit understanding. Unlike explicit understanding, an implicit conceptual understanding of arithmetic does not require knowledge of a formal language. However, the procedures that are used for reasoning in a given domain like arithmetic should follow the properties specified by a formal language. This distinction is important in light of the question of what children acquire during development. Referring to Piaget and his work on class inclusion, Greeno points out that Piaget did not assert that children acquire explicit understanding of a formal language of logic and set theory. As a consequence, Greeno claims a theory of procedures is necessary in order to analyze children's acquisition of general cognitive principles by studying their cognitive procedures.

Resnick's empirical and rational task analysis (Chapter 10) presents a way to analyze how children detect and solve problems. From her empirical and theoretical work, she concludes that stimulation of the development of task-oriented sequences of cognitive states will improve intellectual abilities. This development leads to an increasingly comprehensive understanding of the tasks and enables the children to reach the originally formulated objectives. It is of interest that careful experimental research on arithmetic and instruction led Resnick to study the role of invention in the process of the learning of thinking.

The last two chapters center on questions and problems connected with new research based on the theory of Piaget. Beilin (Chapter 11) ponders the alternative "revision or refinement of Piaget's theory," discussing the role of transformations and correspondences in cognition, the problem of decalage, and the interrelations between learning and development and between language and thought. Beilin, one of the American experts on Piaget-centered research, gives an integrative overview of the present state of the field.

Pascual-Leone (Chapter 12) critically examines Piaget's data base and methodology in order to illustrate the empirical invariances underlying the Piagetian notions of stage and equilibration. He also compares Piaget's data base and methodology with those of information processing approaches—in particular that at Carnegie-Mellon University. Of special interest is his discussion of the method of "metasubjective task analysis" and of the problem of "truly novel" performances.

1

Two Models of Intellectual Development and Their Reference to the Theory of Piaget

HANS SPADA AND RAINER H. KLUWE

Introduction

The Perspective

Mathematical models based on (a) hypotheses about cognitive operations used by children of different ages to solve individual problems; and (b) psychometric assumptions are, in our opinion, valuable tools in the analysis of cognitive development. They allow precise specification and testing of hypotheses about quantitative and structural cognitive developmental changes in problem-solving processes. By means of these models we attempt to bridge the gap between developmental information-processing approaches and psychometric procedures used to assess intellectual development.

In two empirical studies in which students aged 9–16 solved balance scale problems, preexperimental hypotheses concerning their cognitive operations, deduced partly on the basis of the work by Inhelder and Piaget (1958) and partly by observing children solving such problems, were specified and tested through the use of two mathematical models of this type:

1. A deterministic model of cognitive development which is a special case of the model of Scandura (1973, 1977) and corresponds with assumptions of a qualitative developmental change in the sense of Piaget (cf. Spada, 1976; Groner & Spada, 1977).
2. A probabilistic model, the linear logistic model of thinking (Scheiblechner, 1972; Fischer, 1974, 1977; Spada, 1976, 1977), which is a variant of the latent trait model of Rasch (1966).

In the latter model, intellectual development is described as the quantitative change of problem-solving abilities, but it also allows us to test some restrictive hypotheses about structural changes.

By working with these models it is feasible to test assumptions about cognitive development so long as it is possible to specify those assumptions in the context of specific solutions to specific problems obtained by students with differing developmental levels.

In this chapter the deterministic model of qualitative developmental change and the logistic model of quantitative change are compared on the basis of plausibility, theoretical relevance, and empirical validity. Some implications for assessment and teaching are then drawn.

A General Remark

This study is based on the conviction that many questions in the areas of general psychology, developmental psychology, and differential psychology must be approached simultaneously if they are to be solved. The history of scientific psychology to date shows that the formulation of general psychological theories is often particularly fruitful if attention is paid to aspects of development. An analogous idea can also be developed for differential psychology: If one succeeds in describing how certain individual differences have arisen developmentally, then one will have taken a significant step toward their psychological explanation. We believe that general laws of behavior can be proved only by taking individual differences into account, and that one can best understand what is general and what is different by means of a developmental analysis. Furthermore, we proceed from the premise that psychological theory construction should make as much use as possible of formalization in order to arrive at precise and testable statements.

Deficiencies of a Solely Qualitative Analysis of Developmental Change

Almost no investigation of cognitive development is made without referring to or basing the work on the theory of Piaget and his Genevan collaborators. The empirical studies by these authors are unsurpassed in richness of detail and findings, and their theory is the only one that claims to explain cognitive development so completely (cf. Inhelder & Piaget, 1958; Piaget & Inhelder, 1969; Inhelder, Sinclair, & Bovet, 1974). Nevertheless, in the last decade, Piaget's theory of concrete and formal thinking has been subjected to critical attacks regarding (a) the logico-mathematical model of how cognition is structured (Osherson,

1975; Flavell, 1977; Suarez, 1977), (b) the stage concept itself (Flavell, 1971, 1977; Suppes, 1973), and (c) the difficulty in judging the validity of this theory, which seems in many aspects too vague to generate the predictions necessary to test it (Osherson, 1974).

With regard to the stage concept, Keating (in press) says: "Discontinuous and/or abrupt changes in cognitive development, perhaps especially in late childhood and beyond, are difficult to demonstrate convincingly. The cumulative evidence to date on adolescent cognitive development leaves a strong impression of continuous, quantitative and multidimensional growth in abilities. . . . Separating the insightful descriptive components . . . from the more central structural theory, we note that there appears to be no empirical test of crucial elements of the latter." Flavell (1977) puts it like this: "The stage-to-stage developmental changes [may be] not quite so exclusively qualitative if you look at underlying processes; the within-stage changes more gradual, important and long lasting than originally believed, and the same stage developments less concurrent than Piagetian theory seemed to require [p. 249]."

Deficiencies of a Solely Psychometric Analysis of Developmental Change

Psychometric analyses of developmental data often describe alterations in individual problem-solving behavior as quantitative changes in one or more latent variables. For example, changes in problem-solving capability could be represented as a quantitative increase of an ability parameter—applying the Rasch model (Spada, 1969). With such investigations and the assessment procedures deduced from them, the pitfalls of applying classical test theory and factor analysis to developmental data are avoided (Fischer, 1974; Spada, 1970). Still, the psychometric approach is deficient in at least two ways.

First, this approach neither analyzes problems psychologically nor explains why different difficulty parameters result for individual problems. The central question, that is, how differing problem difficulties can be explained from a cognitive and developmental psychological viewpoint, is not answered. Second, no analysis is carried out concerning how changes in individual ability are to be understood developmentally. In other words, a theory of problem difficulty and ability development which goes beyond the quantification of problem difficulties and personal abilities is lacking in a solely psychometric analysis.

Structural, Psychometric Models of Cognitive Development

In order to overcome the first deficiency some of the'more recent psychometric models make possible a detailed investigation of the relevant components of problem-solving processes without at the same time neglecting individual differences (Scheiblechner, 1972; Fischer, 1974; Spada, 1976, 1977). These models, while based on Rasch's model, also include hypotheses about problem structure.

By the "psychological structure" of a problem we mean the type and number of cognitive operations (or "rules") applied by persons of a certain population (e.g., students of a certain age attending a certain type of school) to solve a problem. (The term "structure" is not used in the factor analytic sense.) We use the term "solution algorithm" for that set of sequences of cognitive operations that makes possible the solution of a whole class of problems. The type of learning connected with the solution of problems is often called "structural learning" (cf. Scandura, 1973). Structural learning refers to a learning process based on the application, deduction, and acquisition of rules or—from a psychological viewpoint—of cognitive operations corresponding to these rules.

Another theoretical framework which will be used in the formulation of problem-solving hypotheses and assumptions about individual differences and developmental change is Scandura's (1973, 1977) deterministic model. This is particularly relevant with respect to a formalization and test of some of the hypotheses of the Genevan school about the correspondence between cognitive operations and problem-solving behavior.

In this chapter the application of these models of cognitive development will be restricted to one problem-solving area, namely, balance-scale problems. Hypotheses about concurrent developmental changes with regard to several classes of problems will not be discussed.

Balance-Scale Problems

The balance-scale problems used in this investigation are in some ways analogous to those analyzed by Piaget and his co-workers. In Piagetian theory, great significance is attributed to the development of the concept of proportion. A full understanding of this development would be of practical relevance, for example, for teaching physics, since proportional relations represent a simple quantitative functional law that is frequently treated in introductory physics. For diagnostic questions (cf. various tests for the assessment of mechanical–technical understanding), a usable theory of the development of proportional reasoning would also be valuable.

A detailed description of changes in problem-solving behavior in proportional tasks in the course of development can be found in Inhelder and Piaget (1958). The following quotation from Piaget and Inhelder (1969), synthesizes results of their earlier studies and provides a good basis for the formulation of problem-solving hypotheses.

> The notion of proportion appears at eleven or twelve in several different areas and always in the same initially qualitative form. . . . Concerning the balance, for example, the subject first by ordinal reasoning discovers that the greater the weight, the lower the arm. . . . Also by ordinal reasoning, he discovers that a single weight W pulls the arm down more the farther it is placed from the pivot . . . the child discovers that the result stays the same if he increases a weight without changing the distance from the center on the one side, while increasing the distance without changing the weight on the other. From this he derives the hypothesis . . . that when you begin with two equal weights at equal distances from the center, you maintain equilibrium by decreasing one weight but moving it farther away. . . . It is only then that he grasps the simple metrical proportion . . . [pp. 141–142].

By analyzing such statements and by observing children solving such problems, we deduced hypotheses about the cognitive operations that children use to find the correct solutions to problems of the type used in our investigation. The result was a sample of balance-scale problems with specified problem-solving hypotheses. Figure 1.1 shows some of these problems.

Table 1.1 gives a short description of the cognitive operations assumed to be relevant for the solutions of these problems. The operations are numbered 1–7 in order of their sequence of mastery in the course of child development assumed in the deterministic model (cf. pages 11–12). Operation 8 refers to another type of balance-scale problem used only in one of the two experiments of this investigation. It corresponds in sequence of mastery to Operation 5. This sequence is based on an analysis of the studies by Inhelder and Piaget.

Let us discuss briefly the sample of different problems shown in Figure 1.1. It is hypothesized that Problem a is solved by applying Operation 1, and Problem b by applying Operation 2. With regard to Problem d, for example, it is hypothesized that Operations 1 and 4 are relevant for the solution, which leads to the following conclusion: Because the weight on the left side is reduced, the bar is going to be unbalanced. To compensate for this change in weight, the weight on the right side has to be moved outward.

For every item i, a vector of the problem structure $\mathbf{f}_i$ is defined consisting of ones and zeros, where a one at the jth position denotes the presence of operation j in item i, and a zero denotes its absence. Thus, the structure of the example item d is (1, 0, 0, 1, 0, 0, 0, 0).

(A). PROBLEM a   Operation 1

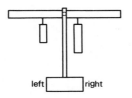 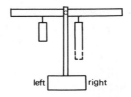

The drawing shows a balance scale with weights. The weights are hung in such a way that the scale is in equilibrium.

Now the weight is increased on the right-hand side of the bar. Will the scale

remain in equilibrium ☐
or tilt downward on the left-hand side ☐
or tilt downward on the right-hand side? ☐

If you do not know the correct answer, please mark:
I do not know ☐

(B). PROBLEM b   Operation 2

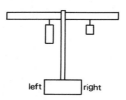 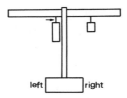

The drawing shows a balance scale with weights. The weights are hung in such a way that the scale is in equilibrium.

Now the weight on the left-hand side of the bar is hung further inward. Will the scale

remain in equilibrium ☐
or tilt downward on the left-hand side ☐
or tilt downward on the right-hand side? ☐

If you do not know the correct answer, please mark:
I do not know ☐

(C). PROBLEM c   Combination of Operations 1 and 3

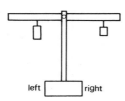 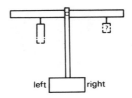

The drawing shows a balance scale with weights. The weights are hung in such a way that the scale is in equilibrium.

Now the weight on the left-hand side of the bar is increased. In order to keep the bar in equilibrium, the weight on the right side of the bar must

stay the same ☐
be decreased ☐
be increased ☐
I do not know ☐

(D). PROBLEM d   Combination of Operations 1 and 4

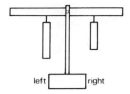

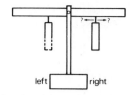

The drawing shows a balance scale with weights. The weights are hung in such a way that the scale is in equilibrium.

Now the weight on the left-hand side of the bar is decreased. In order to keep the bar in equilibrium, the weight on the right-hand side of the bar must

stay in the same position ☐
be hung further inward ☐
be hung further outward ☐
I do not know ☐

(E). PROBLEM e   Combination of Operations 1 and 5

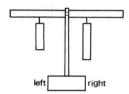

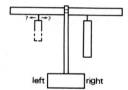

The drawing shows a balance scale with weights. The weights are hung in such a way that the scale is in equilibrium.

Now the weight on the left-hand side of the bar is reduced. In order to keep the bar in equilibrium, this weight must

stay in the same position ☐
be hung further inward ☐
be hung further outward ☐
I do not know ☐

(F). PROBLEM f   Combination of Operations 1,5 and 6

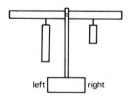

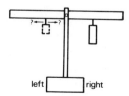

The drawing shows a balance scale with weights. The weights are hung in such a way that the scale is in equilibrium.

Now the weight on the left-hand side of the bar is reduced to a fourth. In order to keep the bar in equilibrium, this weight must be hung
- compared with previously -

four times further outward ☐
three times further outward ☐
twice as far outward ☐
stay in the same position ☐
only half as far outward ☐
only a third as far outward ☐
only a quarter as far outward ☐
I do not know ☐

(G). PROBLEM g   Combination of Operations 1,5 and 7

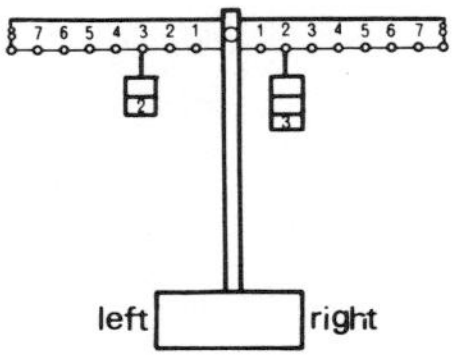

left   right

The drawing shows a balance scale with weights. The weights are hung in such a way that the scale is in equilibrium.

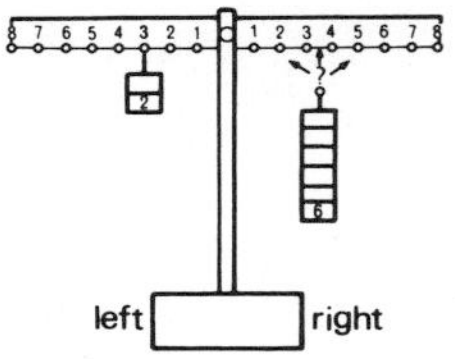

Now the weight on the right-hand side is increased to six pieces of weight. Where must this weight now be hung to keep the scale in equilibrium?

1 ☐   4 ☐   7 ☐

2 ☐   5 ☐   8 ☐

3 ☐   6 ☐   I do not know ☐

(H). PROBLEM h   Combination of Operations 2 and 8

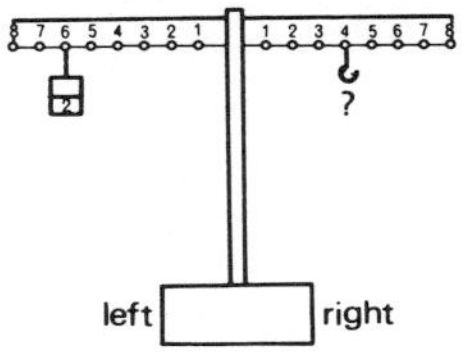

left   right

In this task the weight on the right-hand side of the bar is still missing. It is indicated where it should be hung. To establish equilibrium the weight on the right side has to be

the same ☐
lighter ☐   I do not know ☐
heavier ☐

compared to the weight on the left side.

This task represents a type of item which was only used in the first investigation.

FIGURE 1.1. *Some balance scale problems and the cognitive operations assumed to be relevant for their solution.*

We attempted to construct only those problems whose solutions demand certain subsets of the postulated cognitive operations. Thus, for example, Problems a–f do not show numbers with regard to either weights or length of the lever arms. In this way, we tried to avoid having the product rule—represented in Operation 7—be used to solve problems that can be solved without it. We avoided using numbers in some problem groups not only for experimental reasons, that is, in order to make possible a better correspondence between correct solutions and problem-solving hypotheses, but also it was our conjecture that numbers in problems—for example, in problems that are solvable with semiquantitative considerations, as in Operations 3, 4, and 5—are often manipulated arbitrarily, which inhibits the process of thinking in which we are interested (cf. Karplus & Karplus, 1973; Suarez, 1977).

Two experiments were carried out with problems of this type. In the first experiment, data were obtained from written tests given to students who were tested in groups. In the second experiment, data were

TABLE 1.1

The Eight Cognitive Operations Assumed to Be Relevant for the Solution of Balance-Scale Problems of the Type Discussed

Operation	
1	Attention to and deduction from different amounts of weights.
2	Attention to and deduction from different lengths of the lever arms.
3	Compensation of a change of the amount of one weight or the length of one lever arm in the same modality on the other side of the bar.
4	Compensation of a change in the other modality on the other side of the bar.
5	Compensation of a change in the other modality on the same side of the bar.
6	Additional consideration of the factor of change necessary for a compensation leading to equilibrium.
7	Additional deduction from the law of levers saying that the products of weight and length of the lever arm have to be equal on both sides.
8[a]	Compensation of an inequality in one modality by a reciprocal inequality in the other modality on the same side of the bar.

[a] Operation 8 refers to a type of problem used only in the first experiment (Items 1.5–1.8 and 1.21–1.24; see Table 1.2).

obtained from students who were tested individually with real balance scales. In both experiments the problems were presented in such a sequence that, with regard to their structure, the simplest ones were to be answered first and the most complex last.

The hypothetical structure of all items under study can be summarized in a problem-structure matrix $F = (\mathbf{f}_{ij})$. Table 1.2 shows the structure matrices for the problems of both experiments.

Most of the problems in the first experiment—namely, Problems 1.1–1.4 and 1.9–1.20 correspond to problems in the second experiment in such a way that pairs of problems are assumed to be structurally parallel, that is, they are described by means of the same problem-solving hypotheses. Problems 1.5–1.8 were not used in the second experiment and Problems 1.21–1.24 were replaced by Problems 2.15–2.20 because these eight problems in the first experiment are not in accordance with the general framework of the problem construction. All the other problems consist of (a) a balance scale in equilibrium as the object of comparison and (b) a second balance scale with a change in either one of the weights or in the length of one of the lever arms.

Of course, the hypotheses about the structure of the problems do not encompass all aspects of the problem-solving process. However, they encompass those characteristics that are most relevant to the prediction of individual solutions or solution probabilities. An important assumption on which such problem-solving hypotheses rest is that all the correct problem solutions are based on the same cognitive operations.

TABLE 1.2

Samples of Balance-Scale Problems Presented in the Experiments and the Corresponding Problem-solving Hypotheses[a]

		Operations							
	Problems	1	2	3	4	5	6	7	8
A. PROBLEM–SOLVING HYPOTHESES MATRIX OF EXPERIMENT II									
	1.1	1	0	0	0	0	0	0	0
	1.2	0	1	0	0	0	0	0	0
	1.3	0	1	0	0	0	0	0	0
	1.4	1	0	0	0	0	0	0	0
	1.5	0	1	0	0	0	0	0	1
	1.6	1	0	0	0	0	0	0	1
	1.7	1	0	0	0	0	0	0	1
h	1.8	0	1	0	0	0	0	0	1
c	1.9	1	0	1	0	0	0	0	0
d	1.10	1	0	0	1	0	0	0	0
	1.11	0	1	0	1	0	0	0	0
	1.12	0	1	1	0	0	0	0	0
e	1.13	1	0	0	0	1	0	0	0
	1.14	0	1	0	0	1	0	0	0
	1.15	0	1	0	0	1	1	0	0
f	1.16	1	0	0	0	1	1	0	0
	1.17	0	1	1	0	0	1	0	0
	1.18	0	1	0	1	0	1	0	0
	1.19	1	0	0	1	0	1	0	0
	1.20	1	0	1	0	0	1	0	0
	1.21	1	0	0	0	0	0	1	1
	1.22	0	1	0	0	0	0	1	1
	1.23	1	0	0	0	0	0	1	1
	1.24	0	1	0	0	0	0	1	1
B. PROBLEM–SOLVING HYPOTHESES MATRIX OF EXPERIMENT II									
a	2.1	1	0	0	0	0	0	0	
b	2.2	0	1	0	0	0	0	0	
c	2.3	1	0	1	0	0	0	0	
e	2.4	1	0	0	0	1	0	0	
d	2.5	1	0	0	1	0	0	0	
	2.6	0	1	0	1	0	0	0	
	2.7	0	1	0	0	1	0	0	
	2.8	0	1	1	0	0	0	0	
	2.9	0	1	0	0	1	1	0	
	2.10	0	1	1	0	0	1	0	
	2.11	0	1	0	1	0	1	0	
f	2.12	1	0	0	0	1	1	0	
	2.13	1	0	0	1	0	1	0	
	2.14	1	0	1	0	0	1	0	
	2.15	0	1	0	1	0	0	1	
	2.16	0	1	0	0	1	0	1	
	2.17	0	1	1	0	0	0	1	
	2.18	1	0	1	0	0	0	1	
g	2.19	1	0	0	0	1	0	1	
	2.20	1	0	0	1	0	0	1	

[a] 1 = Operation needed; 0 = Operation not needed. The letters a, b, c, d, e, f, g, and h refer to Figure 1.1. In Experiment II, however, real balance scales were used.

10

A Deterministic Model of the Development of the Concept of Proportion Based on Problem-Solving Hypotheses

The Assumptions of the Model

The first model is based on problem-solving hypotheses and on modified and more precise and restrictive assumptions derived from Inhelder and Piaget's (1958) statements about the development of reasoning with respect to balance-scale problems. According to these authors, the concept of proportion develops step by step. In the course of this development, the child builds up a more comprehensive understanding of proportional problems: With each step, further cognitive operations become available to him or her and the set of solvable problems increases. This description of the developmental process (cf. Inhelder & Piaget, 1958) not only provides information on how to formulate problem-solving hypotheses but also makes it possible to deduce assumptions about developmental regularities in the acquisition of the corresponding cognitive operations.

The deterministic model of the development of the concept of proportion is based on two central assumptions:

1. The individual operations are acquired in the course of development in a certain sequence that is the same for all children. The given numbers for Operations 1–7, listed in Table 1.1, correspond to this supposed sequence. The level of development can be assessed by determining the operation that was acquired last.

2. It is assumed that the operations are applied in a deterministic fashion. A child who has learned a certain operation will apply it correctly to all problems that require this operation. The problem-solving behavior is, therefore, assumed to be deterministic in the following sense: A child, under the appropriate testing conditions, can solve all those problems correctly for which he or she has acquired the necessary operations. The child is not, however, capable of solving any of the other problems.

Figure 1.2 shows the functional relationship to be expected, on the basis of these two assumptions, between problem-solving probabilities and individual level of development. Functions that describe the relation between solution probability and latent variable are denoted as item characteristic curves in latent trait theory. The form of these item characteristic curves is that of scalogram analysis (Guttman, 1950).

A procedure used in this investigation to test the validity of the deterministic developmental model also shows this correspondence to scalogram analysis. The method is illustrated in detail in Table 1.3 for a

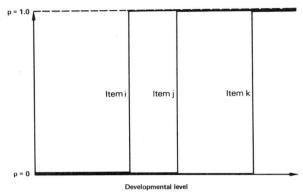

FIGURE 1.2. *The relationship between problem-solving probabilities and developmental level postulated in the deterministic model. The item characteristic curves of three problems with the following problem-solving vectors* $\mathbf{f_i} = (0,1,0,0,0,0,0,0)$, $\mathbf{f_j} = (0,1,1,0,0,0,0,0)$ *and* $\mathbf{f_k} = (0,-1,1,0,0,1,0,0)$ *are given (cf. also Figure 1.4). The abscissa distances between the inflection points of the three item characteristic curves are chosen arbitrarily because the latent variable "level of development" is —on the basis of the assumptions of this model—only accessable on an ordinal scale level.*

small sample. It should be mentioned that both model assumptions (*a*) and (*b*) *and* the problem-solving hypotheses are tested simultaneously by this procedure. Therefore, deviations indicate that these assumptions *and/or* the problem-solving hypotheses are incorrect.

Results of Validity Tests for the Deterministic Model: Experiment I

In the following we refer to the data of Experiment I, that is, the written test with multiple-choice items. Twenty-four balance-scale problems, like those in Figure 1.1, were given (cf. the corresponding problem-solving matrix in Table 1.2) to 949 pupils, aged 10–16, of both sexes. The students were attending Realschul- and Gymnasium-classes of the fifth, sixth, eighth, and ninth grades. We recorded cross-sectional data about the correctness of the solutions.

The results of the validity test, illustrated in Table 1.3 for a small sample of items, were very negative. Almost none of the 949 answer vectors was admissible with regard to the model assumptions. The same was true even when only the data of subsamples of items were analyzed.

Another analysis of the data, in which pairs of problems were studied, equally demonstrated the inadequacy of the model. Table 1.4 illustrates the procedure for a small sample of items and gives their results. The frequencies n_{iu} at the top of each cell of the matrix show how many pupils solved problem *i* correctly and problem *u* incorrectly. Let us single out some of the results:

TABLE 1.3
A Validity Test for the Deterministic Developmental Model Illustrated on the Basis of a Subset of Balance-Scale Problems of Experiment II

A. PROBLEM–SOLVING HYPOTHESES MATRIX[a]

Problems	Operations					
	1	2	3	4	5	6
2.1	1	0	0	0	0	0
2.2	0	1	0	0	0	0
2.3	1	0	1	0	0	0
2.5	1	0	0	1	0	0
2.4	1	0	0	0	1	0
2.14	1	0	1	0	0	1
2.13	1	0	0	1	0	1
2.12	1	0	0	0	1	1

[a]1 = Operation needed; 0 = operation not needed.

B. VARIANTS OF MASTERY OF INDIVIDUAL OPERATIONS IF THE THEORY IS VALID[a]

Variants	Operations					
	1	2	3	4	5	6
1	0	0	0	0	0	0
2	1	0	0	0	0	0
3	1	1	0	0	0	0
4	1	1	1	0	0	0
5	1	1	1	1	0	0
6	1	1	1	1	1	0
7	1	1	1	1	1	1

[a]1 = Operation mastered; 0 = operation not mastered.

C. ADMISSIBLE ANSWER VECTORS IF THE DETERMINISTIC MODEL HOLDS. THE OCCURRENCE OF OTHER ANSWER VECTORS FALSIFIES THE MODEL[a]

Problems							
2.1	2.2	2.3	2.5	2.4	2.14	2.13	2.12
0	0	0	0	0	0	0	0
1	0	0	0	0	0	0	0
1	1	0	0	0	0	0	0
1	1	1	0	0	0	0	0
1	1	1	1	0	0	0	0
1	1	1	1	1	0	0	0
1	1	1	1	1	1	1	1

[a] 1 = Problem correctly solved; 0 = Problem not correctly solved.

TABLE 1.4
A Validity Test for the Deterministic Developmental Model and for Some Assumptions of the Probabilistic Latent Trait Model Illustrated on the Basis of a Subset of Problems of Experiment I [a]

	Problem not solved						
Problem solved	1.2 (1,0,0) −.9	1.3 (1,0,0) −1.3	1.5 (1,0,1) −.9	1.8 (1,0,1) −.3	1.22 (1,1,1) .9	1.24 (1,1,1) .8	Problem numbers Problem structures f_i Difficulty parameters $\hat{\sigma}_i$
1.2	×	26 2.38 1.49	88 .92 1.00	144 .44 .55	331 .15 .17	325 .18 .18	
1.3	62	×	98 .56 .67	169 .30 .37	355 .10 .11	352 .14 .12	
1.5	81	55	×	157 .53 .55	333 .17 .17	315 .18 .18	
1.8	63	52	83	×	291 .31 .30	280 .34 .33	
1.22	48	36	57	89	×	144 1.12 1.10	
1.24	59	50	56	95	161	×	

[a] The frequencies n_{iu} at the top of each cell of the matrix show how many pupils solved problem i correctly and problem u incorrectly. The next numbers correspond to the ratios n_{ui}/n_{iu}. The numbers at the bottom show the ratios $e^{(\hat{\sigma}_i)}/e^{(\hat{\sigma}_u)}$. With regard to problem structure, only the operations 2, 7, and 8 which are relevant for these problems are given.

According to the problem-solving hypotheses, Problems 1.22 and 1.24, for example, should be solvable by means of the same operations. If one also considers the assumption of a deterministic solution behavior, there should be zero frequencies in the corresponding cells instead of the frequencies 161 and 144. Perhaps even more contradictory are deviations in the problems with a different problem structure. Thus, for example, 89 children did not solve the structurally more simple Problem 1.8 correctly, but solved the structurally more complex Problem 1.22 correctly. As such, the data show that the deterministic model (which rests on the assumptions formulated above and on the discussed problem-solving hypotheses) is inaccurate at least with regard to the testing procedure used in Experiment I.

Hofer (1977) who worked with related problems, arrived at a similar conclusion: "It is striking that the tasks were solved with great irregularity. The assumption that mastered operations will generally always be recognized and correctly applied, does not seem to be correct [p. 39]."

However, it is not clear from these analyses whether the deviations are due to a violation of the problem-solving hypotheses or of the two central assumptions of the deterministic developmental model. Further, the deviations (cf. for a comprehensive survey of corresponding results, Wohlwill, 1973) are so extensive that one should try, for example, to

1. Revise the deterministic model (e.g., by incorporating assumptions about learning during the problem-solving process),
2. Compare the results of the written test with an analysis of data from carefully planned and executed individual sessions with actual balance scales, and
3. Describe the data within the framework of a latent trait model based on the same problem-solving hypotheses.

A Markovian Learning Model Based on the Deterministic Developmental Model

Let us first discuss a deterministic model that includes learning assumptions. Such a model, a Markovian model for structural learning, was formulated by Groner and Spada (1977). They assumed an experimental setting in which each student independently solved a series of problems of the type discussed and, after every item, was given feedback only about the correct solution. The model features a hierarchical sequence of operations that corresponds to the assumed developmental sequence. There are six assumptions in this model (for details, cf. Groner & Spada, 1977, pp. 140–145):

1. For every operation j, there is a probability s_j expressing the relative frequency of children who are able to apply operation j and all lower operations of the ordered sequence correctly, but do not master operation $j + 1$ or any other higher operation at the beginning of the problem series.
2. An operation j will be learned with probability γ_j in a trial with a problem involving this operation. Maximally, one operation is learned in a single trial.
3. For every operation j, either the child is able to apply it correctly or he is incapable of performing it.
4. A learned operation is assumed to be one which is applied correctly in all consecutive trials.
5. Operation j can only be learned if the child is already able to apply

the lower operation $j - 1$ correctly. For $j = 1$, no knowledge of a preceding operation is assumed.

6. A problem will be solved correctly if, and only if, the child is able to apply all of the relevant operations defined by the problem-solving hypotheses vector $\mathbf{f}_i$, correctly.

These assumptions generate a matrix of transition probabilities with as many states (plus one) as there are relevant operations for the problem domain under study. There are only transitions to higher operations, with the highest operation in ordered sequence corresponding to an absorbing state.

This Markovian model was applied to the data of Experiment I (Groner & Spada, 1977) but the results did not answer the question of model validity since the experimental conditions did not really correspond to the assumptions of the model. Insufficient data were obtained in the second experiment—discussed on pages 16–20—to test this model sufficiently. Therefore, a real test of the usefulness of the model is still pending, although some of the analyses carried out with regard to the deterministic developmental model also indicated problems with the Markovian model.

Results of Validity Tests for the Deterministic
Model: Experiment II

The form of problem-solving tests in Experiment I naturally places other demands on the students than the test situation used by Inhelder and Piaget. The Genevan assessment procedure gives the children the opportunity to experiment with the balance scale and with the weights, as well as to test their own assumptions directly. The children are invited to give judgments about phenomena they can produce themselves with objects they are allowed to handle. "The child is given the opportunity of comparing what he has predicted will happen with what actually happens in certain situations [Inhelder, Sinclair, & Bovet, 1974, p.20]."

In Experiment I, it is possible that the internal tests of the adequacy of the cognitive operations that are required could make this test situation more difficult for the children. For example, the relatively simple cognitive operations needed for comprehending semiquantitative relations have a different character and are more difficult in the written test version. Furthermore, despite the "I do not know" category, there is a possibility that the correct answer is arrived at through guessing.

To check these possibilities (cf. Aebli in Lüer & Spada, 1977), in Experiment II a sample of problems analogous to those given in Experiment I was compiled but presented by means of real balance scales in individual sessions, with feedback in half of the cases. In addition to the choice of one answer from various given possibilities, the children were asked to give the reasons for their choice and to explain the situation and their observations.

The main question in this second experiment was whether the data would better fit the deterministic developmental model in this test situation. A second question was whether feedback about the correctness of the given answers had an effect on the solution and whether this effect in turn depended on the structure of the problems and the developmental level of the children. Therefore, the outcome of the answer chosen by the child was demonstrated on the balance scale in half of the sessions.

One fundamental feature of the Genevan school's "critical exploration method" is "that the experimenters constantly formulate hypotheses about the children's reactions from the cognitive point of view, and then devise ways of immediately checking these suppositions in the experimental situation [Inhelder, Sinclair, & Bovet, 1974, p. 22]." In contrast to this procedure, in Experiment II, the problem-solving hypotheses and model assumptions were stated prior to running the experiment and were tested by means of a fixed sequence of problems.

The subjects were 32 pupils from one primary (Grades 3 and 4) and one secondary (Grades 5 and 7) school (16 male and 16 female; 8 third grade, mean CA = 113 months; 8 fourth grade, mean CA = 124 months; 8 fifth grade, mean CA = 138 months; 8 seventh grade, mean CA = 157 months) ranging in age from 8 to 13 years.

The duration of the individual sessions was approximately 60 min, during which 20 balance scale problems were presented. Table 1.2, which has already been discussed, contains the problem-solving hypotheses matrix of these problems. The problems were worked on in numerical order.

As in most of the problems in Experiment I, two balance scales were used to present the problem situation. In Experiment II we used balance scales which were readily available on the market. For Problems 2.1–2.14, the weights were made of wood and differed in size relative to their weight. The balance scales had no units. Only for Problems 2.15–2.20 were brass disks used that had to be added to each other in order to obtain different weights. These balance scales did have units.

Two matrices were analyzed more closely:

1. A 20 × 32 data matrix A (1 = pass, 0 = fail) on the basis of the choice of one of the provided response possibilities (cf. Figure 1.1).
2. A 20 × 32 data matrix B (1 = pass, 0 = fail) on the basis of the given explanations and reasons.

A comparison of the matrices shows that, in the majority of cases, *both* the choice of a response and the given explanation were correct (361 cases) or *both* were wrong (198 cases). Still, in 60 cases the choice of a response was correct, but the explanation was wrong. The relative frequency of such reactions was very different in the four grade levels (third grade, 14%; fourth grade, 16%; fifth grade, 5%; seventh grade, 2%; which can be traced in part to differences in verbalization ability) and with regard to the different problems, grouped according to their structure (Problems 2.1–2.2, 2%; Problems 2.3–2.8, 2%; Problems 2.9–2.20, 17%; the problem structure of the last group is characterized by the "quantitative" Operations 6 and 7). In 21 cases the child himself corrected a wrong response in connection with a correct explanation. No systematic differences were found with regard to these cases.

These results indicate that error in the first testing procedure, namely the much less time-consuming multiple-choice technique, is relatively small. Here one must bear in mind that the problems were constructed in such a way that the given set of response alternatives in each case comprised the total number of possible answers. Nevertheless, nearly all the analyses to be discussed are based on matrix B, that is, the data on the correctness of the given explanations and reasons.

An analysis of the data of this matrix—applying the model validity test illustrated in Table 1.3—almost always resulted, even when analyzing smaller subsets of problems, in deviations. Even if one drops the assumption that the operations were acquired in a certain sequence, deviations are obtained. The results are thus in agreement with those obtained from the written test data, although the relative frequency of deviations for data from individual sessions is somewhat smaller.

It is interesting that the number of deviations is smaller for the matrix B data than for the matrix A data. The variable "correctness of explanations given" corresponds to the assumptions of the deterministic developmental model somewhat better than the "correctness of selected response possibility variable" even if the fit is not sufficient in either case.

Possible causes for these deviations include:

1. It was possible to answer Problem 2.15, for example, correctly—contrary to our problem-solving hypotheses—with a very simple semiquantitative consideration. The weight on the right side of the second balance scale hung farther out than the weight on the left side. The weight on the left side was composed of two brass disks. If one considers that the weight on the right side must be less, only Weight 1 remains the response possibility.
2. Operation 6, "consideration of the factor of change," is, depending on the type of factor to be considered (twice, four times, a third, etc.), of varying difficulty.
3. As far as Problems 2.15–2.20 are concerned, Operation 6 could also replace Operation 7 presumed in the solution process.

These few examples show that at least some of the problem-solving hypotheses do not describe the solution process sufficiently. We shall have to consider this fact also when testing the validity of the probabilistic latent trait developmental model. But let us first look at the results of the feedback condition in the second experiment.

The Effects of Feedback in Experiment II

Half of the children in each age group were given feedback, that is, the outcome of their answers was demonstrated for them on the balance scale; the other half received no feedback.

To test the statistical significance of the effects of the different factors —factor A, grade levels; factor B, feedback conditions; factor C, groups of structurally similar tasks—an analysis of variance was calculated on the basis of data from matrix B (correctness of explanations and reasons given). The dependent variable was the number of correct solutions per child and problem group, with repeated measurements for factor C. There were statistically significant effects for factors A (grade levels) and C (groups of structurally similar tasks) and for the interaction between them. These results, represented graphically in Figure 1.5, will be discussed on pages 22–25 in connection with assumptions about the probabilistic developmental model.

Surprisingly enough, no statistically significant effects resulted from the feedback factor or any of the interactions connected with it. Most obvious—though not statistically significant—is the interaction between feedback and grade level. Older children profited more than younger ones from the feedback (Figure 1.3). This finding which we in-

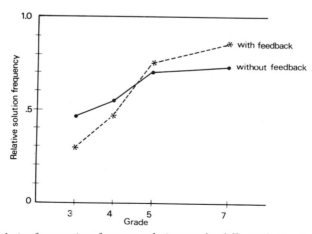

FIGURE 1.3. *Relative frequencies of correct solutions under different feedback conditions and grade levels. The results are based on data matrix B (explanations) from Experiment II.*

terpret only with reservation may, among other things, be traced back to the fact that the number of correct—and thus, reinforced—responses was higher for the older children.

A Latent Trait Model of the Development of the Ability to Solve Proportional Tasks

The Assumptions of the Model

The deterministic model of qualitative developmental change was shown to be inadequate by the data from both experiments. In the following, a model is discussed in which intellectual development is described as a quantitative change in problem-solving abilities. This linear logistic test model (Fischer, 1974, 1977; Scheiblechner, 1972), which is a variant of the Rasch model (1966; cf. pages 91–94 in this volume for a discussion of latent trait models), is also discussed in detail by Spada (1976, 1977) in connection with other logistic models of learning and thought.

The model is characterized by the following equation

$$p \left\{ \begin{array}{l} \text{student } v \\ \text{solves} \\ \text{item } i \end{array} \right\} = p_{vi}$$

$$= \underbrace{\frac{\exp(\xi_v - \sigma_i)}{1 + \exp(\xi_v - \sigma_i)}}_{\text{Rasch model}} = \underbrace{\frac{\exp(\xi_v - \sum_{j=1}^{m} f_{ij}\eta_j + c)}{1 + \exp(\xi_v - \sum_{j=1}^{m} f_{ij}\eta_j + c)}}_{\text{Linear logistic model}} \quad (1)$$

The probability that student v solves problem i correctly is, according to the Rasch model, understood as the logistic function of two parameters, namely, ξ_v characterizing the ability of the student to solve problems of this kind, and σ_i characterizing the difficulty of the problem. The item parameter σ_i itself is seen as a linear function of the number and difficulty of the necessary operations; f_{ij} denotes the hypothetical frequency with which operation j is needed (f_{ij} is an element of the problem–solving matrix; for the item samples of Experiments I and II, cf. Table 1.2). The parameter η_j denotes the difficulty of operation j; c is a normalizing constant. The resulting model is a Rasch model with a linear marginal condition (for an introduction to some of the psychometric aspects of Rasch's model, cf. Rost & Spada, 1978).

On the basis of this model, the development of the ability to solve proportional problems can be described as follows:

1. Developmental changes in problem-solving behavior can be represented as changes in the person parameters ξ. These parameters reflect children's ability to solve problems of this type. Inter- and in-

traindividual differences in problem-solving ability can be interpreted to some extent as differences in the degree of mastery of the solution algorithm.

2. For all children in a specified age range (with regard to this investigation, the age range between 8 and 16 years), the rank order of the difficulties of the cognitive operations that are relevant for proportional problems is the same; or to be more precise: For all children of this age range the relations of the operation difficulties remain constant, that is, the operation parameters—scaled on the basis of the logistic model—are invariant with regard to age. During a relatively large phase of the development of children and adolescents, the problem structure also remains constant. That is, correct solutions are based on the same cognitive operations.

Figure 1.4 shows the functional relationship that is expected on the basis of the model equation between problem-solving probabilities and children's problem-solving ability, which itself corresponds with the developmental level. The figure shows that the relationship corresponds to intuitive expectations within the range of medium and higher developmental levels. Given a person of average ability, the probability of a correct solution of the structurally most complex of the three problems is very small. For a person with higher ability, the solution probabilities of the three problems approach each other and become approximately one for very high values. In the medium and upper range of the latent variable, the functional relationship that is shown in Figure 1.4 can be understood to be a more precise version of model (1c) proposed by Flavell (1971, p. 426) to describe the development of intellectual abilities. For the lowest performance range, that is, for younger children than those studied in this investigation, the assumed relation does not ap-

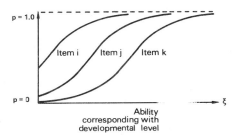

FIGURE 1.4. *The functional relationship postulated in the linear logistic model between problem-solving probabilities and the ability that corresponds with the developmental level. The item characteristic curves of three problems with the following problem-solving vectors* $\mathbf{f}_i = (0,1,0,0,0,0,0,0)$, $\mathbf{f}_j = (0,1,1,0,0,0,0,0)$ *and* $\mathbf{f}_k = (0,1,1,0,0,1,0,0)$ *are shown. The abscissa distances between the three item characteristic curves —which are parallel to one another— were computed by means of data from Experiment I and reflect the differences in problem-solving difficulty.*

TABLE 1.5
A Test of the Rasch Model with Regard to Its Probabilistic Nature Based on Data Matrix B
(Explanations) from Experiment II

Problems		2.1	2.2	2.3	2.4	2.5	2.6	2.7	2.8	2.9
Item difficulty parameter estimates	$\hat{\sigma}_i{}^a$	−3.5	−1.8	.3	−1.9	−1.6	−.5	−1.7	−.9	.5
	$\hat{\sigma}_i{}^b$	−3.5	−1.9	.3	−1.9	−1.9	−.5	−2.3	−1.1	.7

[a] $\hat{\sigma}_i$ = Estimates based on the n_{iu} frequencies (number of subjects solving problem i correctly, but problem u incorrectly)

[b] $\hat{\sigma}_i$ = Estimates based on the item scores (number of subjects solving the individual problems correctly)

pear very plausible. This is that area of the latent variable for which we obtained no data from both experiments. Therefore, it was possible to test the validity of the model only for children with average and high abilities.

For reasons of simplicity, in this section, the concepts of ability and developmental level are used more or less synonymously. Neither of the two terms should, of course, disguise the fact that the variable that they denote is influenced by a multitude of factors.

Results of Validity Tests for the Probabilistic Model: Experiments I and II

The linear logistic model is a Rasch model with a linear marginal condition that represents the problem-solving hypotheses. Therefore, the model is applicable only if the assumptions of the Rasch model are not violated by the data. The validity of the Rasch model can be tested in several ways (cf. Fischer, 1974). One possibility is conditional likelihood ratio tests (Andersen, 1973) that enable us to analyze a central assumption of the Rasch model: that of sample free parameter estimates. These tests—applied to data from different samples of subjects who took part in the first experiment—showed a sufficient fit, although, because there was a large body of data (949 subjects), the deviations turned out to be statistically significant in some cases (for details, cf. Spada, 1976). With regard to Experiment II, analogous tests did not yield significant results. But in this case, the number of subjects was extremely small (32).

By means of another type of model control, the "probabilistic" aspect of the latent trait developmental model can be tested more directly against the assumptions of the deterministic model. Table 1.4, discussed on pages 12–15 in connection with a test of the deterministic model and based on some data of Experiment I, can also be used to test

TABLE 1.5 (*Continued*)

2.10	2.11	2.12	2.13	2.14	2.15	2.16	2.17	2.18	2.19	2.20
1.5	1.7	.5	0	1.5	−.4	1.3	1.0	.6	.8	2.8
1.6	1.8	.7	.1	1.6	−.7	1.3	1.1	.7	.9	3.3

this aspect of the probabilistic model. The frequencies n_{iu} at the top of each cell of the matrix show how many pupils solved problem i correctly, but problem u incorrectly. According to the deterministic model, many of the cells of this matrix should contain zero frequencies. According to Rasch's model, the following equation should hold:

$$n_{ui}/n_{iu} \approx \exp(\hat{\sigma}_i)/\exp(\hat{\sigma}_u) \tag{2}$$

This equation can be used for a model control if the item parameters σ_i are estimated by means of a procedure based not on the n_{iu} frequencies, but on the item scores (= number of subjects who solved the individual items correctly). A procedure of this type is the conditional maximum-likelihood parameter estimation method, based on item and person scores, and used very frequently in applications of Rasch's model (Fischer, 1974, pp. 230–239).

A test of Eq. (2), carried out in this way, shows that in many cases the ratios are nearly equal (cf. the second and the third numbers in the cells of the matrix in Table 1.4). Small deviations were obtained when Problems 1.2 or 1.3 and 1.5 or 1.8 were compared. In these cases, the difficulty of the structurally more complex problems was overestimated if the computation is based on the n_{iu} frequencies. This means, however, that the deviations go in the direction one would expect on the basis of the deterministic model. In the case of Problems 1.2 and 1.3, the ratios differ markedly.

A similar test was applied to the data of Experiment II. The results of the analysis, based on the data of all children and problems, are given in Table 1.5. A comparison of the item parameters estimates—computed in one case by means of the n_{iu} frequencies, in the other case on the basis of the item scores—shows a very good fit.

Figure 1.5, which also refers to the data of Experiment II, shows how the relative frequency of correct solutions depends on grade level and the structural complexity of the problems. Even though Figure 1.5 and Figure 1.4 are *not* comparable directly (because Figure 1.5 shows the relation between relative solution frequency, grade level, and problem complexity, and Figure 1.4 represents the relation between solution

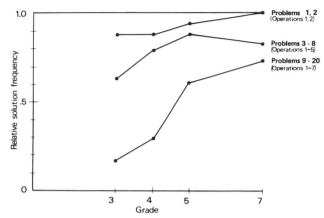

FIGURE 1.5. *Relative frequencies of correct solutions with regard to three subsets of problems and four grade levels. The results are based on data matrix* B (*explanations*) *from Experiment II.*

probability, Rasch-scaled ability, and problem difficulty), the similarity is striking anyway.

It seems justifiable to conclude from these different tests that the probabilistic latent trait model describes quite well the increase of solution probabilities of problems of different structural complexity at least for the higher developmental age range.

Tests of the validity of the problem-solving hypotheses carried out on the basis of the linear logistic model with data from both experiments yielded differing results. We found statistically significant differences between the following two sets of estimates of the item difficulty parameters σ_i:

1. Estimates computed—according to the linear marginal condition of the model—on the basis of the problem-solving hypotheses and the estimates of the operation difficulty parameters η_j, which themselves were calculated by means of an algorithm for the linear logistic model (cf. Fischer, 1974, pp. 348–359).
2. Estimates computed without taking into account this linear marginal condition but instead applying an algorithm for the Rasch model.

These two sets of parameter estimates differ if it is not possible to explain the difficulty of the individual problems by means of the problem-solving hypotheses. For the purpose of this statistical control, we used conditional likelihood ratio tests and analyzed the validity of the linear marginal condition (cf. Fischer, 1974, pp. 359–360).

Graphical controls indicate that the correspondence between these two different sets of parameter estimates is not so bad. This is in accordance with the following results. The two sets of parameter estimates are correlated in Experiment I with $r = .94$ and in Experiment II with $r = .85$. (The precision of the estimates is much less in Experiment II.)

In addition to the statistical significance of the differences, another fact reminds us to be very cautious about attaching importance to and interpreting the difficulty parameters of the different operations addressed in these problem-solving hypotheses: The estimates of these parameters differ markedly in the two experiments (high parameter estimates indicate high operation difficulties: for a description of the eight operations, cf. Table 1.1; for an interpretation of the results with regard to Experiment I, cf. Spada, 1976):

(a) Experiment I (data on correctness of solution):

$$\hat{\eta}_2 - \hat{\eta}_1 = .4, \qquad \hat{\eta}_3 = .6, \qquad \hat{\eta}_4 = 1.4, \qquad \hat{\eta}_5 = 1.2,$$
$$\hat{\eta}_6 = 1.6, \qquad \hat{\eta}_7 = 1.4, \qquad \hat{\eta}_8 = .6$$

(b) Experiment II (data on correctness of explanations):

$$\hat{\eta}_2 - \hat{\eta}_1 = .8, \qquad \hat{\eta}_3 = 1.7, \qquad \hat{\eta}_4 = 1.3,$$
$$\hat{\eta}_5 = 1.0, \qquad \hat{\eta}_6 = 2.1, \qquad \hat{\eta}_7 = 2.0$$

We conclude from these data that the validity of the problem-solving hypotheses cannot be regarded as definitively substantiated in the framework of the probabilistic latent trait model.

Inferences for Diagnostic Questions and for Instruction

Given that one of the two models holds for some specified problem-solving area—which, strictly speaking, was not the case in our investigation with regard to the deterministic model and doubtful with regard to the probabilistic one—what are the inferences that could be made (a) for diagnostic questions, and (b) for teaching?

Diagnostic Questions

The different theoretical assumptions about intellectual development on which the deterministic developmental model and the probabilistic latent trait model rest also imply a different concept concerning the diagnostic assessment of this process. The deterministic model requires the determination of the operation that was acquired last for the assessment of intellectual development. This can be ascertained easily on the basis of the child's answer vector, if the model is valid and if the selection of items is appropriate.

On the other hand, with regard to the probabilistic model which describes intellectual development as the quantitative change of problem-solving abilities, the assessment of the extent of the ability in question —acquired by a certain time—is of interest. Both, inter- and intraindividual differences in developmental changes can be assessed if they are reflected in the degree of problem-solving ability. It should be mentioned that the validity of the problem-solving hypotheses is not a precondition for diagnostic assessment by means of the probabilistic model if we are only interested in quantitative changes. The model must only fit the data with regard to the assumptions of Rasch's model (cf. Fischer, 1974; Wright, 1977).

From the viewpoint of information processing theories, the question may be asked whether measuring intellectual development by means of "abilities" reflected in quantitative person parameters is not deficient with regard to "what" develops—even when the construct "ability" can be related to the degree of mastery of a certain solution algorithm with defined cognitive operations. It is also questionable whether it is useful to use this model to assess the different effects, for example, of various socialization conditions, when on the basis of this approach, model–immanent explanations for possible differences are not given. And it is often argued, with good reason, that psychologically relevant aspects of learning, of restructuring of knowledge, etc. cannot be captured by measuring changes in latent variables reflecting problem-solving ability.

Teaching

With regard to the deterministic developmental model, the Markovian learning model—which was discussed on pages 15–16—provides a basis for drawing some consequences for teaching (cf. Groner & Spada, 1977). If the model holds, the learning process in any given problem-solving area can be optimized by a suitable sequencing of the problems such that a problem is given as subsequent instructional trial with one additional operation—namely, the next one in the ordered sequence of operations not yet mastered by the student. The model would predict that items corresponding only with operations already learned or with operations further up in the sequence of operations not yet acquired will be completely ineffective. Different optimization problems could be studied—for example, the problem of minimizing the number of trials necessary to satisfy a specified learning criterion.

Let us now consider what inferences can be drawn from the probabilistic model for improving the ability of children to solve certain problems. If both the model and the problem-solving hypotheses are valid, the difficulty of the operations can be measured by means of the parameters η_j. Proceeding from both the problem-solving matrix, which specifies which operations are needed to solve which problems, and from estimations of the operation difficulty parameters, one can again deduce consequences for the selection and sequential order of contents in teaching. The sequence of teaching cognitive operations can be oriented on an operational hierarchy. In a hierarchy of operations (cf. Spada, 1976, p. 173) the operations are classified according to whether they occur alone or whether they occur together with one or several other operations in the problem-solving processes. Proceeding from the simple operations at the base of the hierarchy, one can go either to the more difficult operations or to the ones that only occur in combination with other ones. Operations at higher levels in the hierarchy are only treated when the operations with which they are needed in solution processes have already been taught and practiced sufficiently. The problem-solving matrix shows which problems could be used to practice the relevant operations and combinations of operations.

Aside from such structural considerations—which do not differ too much with regard to either model, that is, the deterministic or the probabilistic one—the latent trait model makes it possible to estimate the efficiency of certain teaching methods by means of assessing the change of person parameters—that is, the degree of the problem-solving ability in question. A precondition is that the effects are quantitative in nature and not qualitative.

In the field of physics education, Häussler (1978) made use of both the structural aspect of basing teaching on problem-solving hypotheses and the assessment aspect. He analyzed two different strategies to improve the ability of adolescents to solve problems of the type "recognizing functional relationships." The subjects of the investigation were 1037 students, aged 12–16. Häussler worked with the linear logistic model (a) to measure the effects of the instructional strategies, and (b) to describe, by means of problem-solving hypotheses, the constituents of the solution algorithms used by the students to solve the problems. This description formed the basis for developing and formulating two different instructional strategies. One of them was based on so-called "spontaneous" algorithms; these were the operations used when students were able to solve individual problems correctly before any training in this special field was provided. As part of the second instructional strategy, "synthetic" algorithms were taught; these were more comprehensive, theoretically superior, higher order algorithms. Häussler ascertained that both strategies yielded statistically significant, substantial, and relatively long-lasting positive effects. With regard to a transfer to new problems—that is, problems that could not be solved directly by means of the algorithms taught—the teaching of the spontaneous algorithms turned out to be more effective. Presumably, this strategy had forced the students at the onset to consider the possibility of being confronted with new problems and to develop solution algorithms on their own—along the lines of the learned spontaneous algorithms—in order to cope with these problems.

A Summary and Some Critical Conclusions

This line of research is one of the few examples of a numerical, mathematical approach for formulating and testing theories in the field of cognitive development.

Children of various ages are given problems from one problem-solving area in a preexperimentally determined sequence. Testing is done in either group or individual settings and the problems are presented in either written form or with the aid of concrete experimental arrangements. The problems are solved by the children with or without feedback about the correct answer. Data pertaining to the variables "correctness of the solution" and/or "correctness of the explanations and reasons given" are gathered.

More characteristic of this approach than the particular experimental setup is the necessity of formulating hypotheses, before the data are analyzed statistically, about steps in the problem-solving process that enable children (e.g., of different age and educational background) to solve the individual problems. These assumptions—called problem-solving hypotheses—about children's thought processes when solving problems can be tested empirically because they are formulated with regard to a numerical, mathematical model. This is done by integrating them within a model such as that of Scandura or of Rasch. The resulting model describes the dependency of the problem-solving behavior of a child on the difficulty of the problem—corresponding with the problem-solving hypotheses—and on the individual's ability to solve problems of this type—which can be interpreted to some extent as the degree of availability of the necessary solution algorithms.

The formulation of such a model has invariance assumptions as a prerequisite, that is, the model has restrictive assumptions about the determinants of the observed phenomena. For example, the problem-solving process of all children of a specified group is assumed to be formed by the same cognitive operations if the problem is solved correctly. It is also typical of this research approach that the empirical application of the models, besides testing individual assumptions, also allows for the (quantitative) assessment of properties of the problems and/or cognitive operations and properties of the individuals.

Reviewing the results of an application of the two models in both experiments with balance scale problems, it can generally be said that neither the deterministic developmental model, nor the probabilistic linear logistic model can be used to describe completely all of the findings:

1. The assumptions of deterministic problem-solving behavior, and of a certain sequence in which the operations become applicable in the course of development and that this sequence is the same for all children are presumably too restrictive.

2. The Rasch model describes the differing increase of solution probabilities of problems of varying complexity in the higher developmental range quite well, but makes rather implausible assumptions concerning developmental changes in the lower range. Nevertheless, at the moment, this model seems to be one of the best possible choices to *qualify* intellectual development.

3. The linear logistic model cannot provide an incontestable basis for formulating and testing psychological problem-solving hypotheses. Some of the results of validity tests showed that the fit is not really satisfactory. In addition, it is impossible to use this type of model or the Rasch model to describe a dynamic qualitative change, which is a central and intuitively convincing concept in many psychological theories of cognitive development and learning (cf. Kluwe, 1979).

4. The problem-solving hypotheses formulated for balance scale problems in the framework of the deterministic, respectively, the probabilistic model (cf. Table 1.1 and Table 1.2) are not fully sufficient to explain the differences in the difficulty of the individual balance scale problems. They do not capture all of the factors that are relevant with regard to the difficulty or psychological complexity of the problems.

A general question in this context might be whether the contentual/psychological contribution of investigations of this type has as yet become truly significant in terms of our understanding of cognitive development. As far as the work we have done is concerned, an important reason for a negative answer is that we paid much less attention to the derivation of the problem-solving hypotheses than we did to the question of testing them. It might be asked: What good is a good test of bad hypotheses? We conclude from this criticism that:

5. Much more attention has to be paid to methods for generating better and more differentiated hypotheses about the problem-solving processes.

Such hypotheses should include encoding and decoding operations. They should also take into account the difference between utilization and evocation discussed by Flavell (1971), to name only two directions for extending these hypotheses.

The detailed records of the explanations given by the children in the second experiment could be one source for modifying and deepening the problem-solving hypotheses although it must be doubted whether these explanations reflect directly some of the components of the problem-solving processes. Recordings of eye movements could provide another interesting data base because we observed remarkable differences in this respect in the second experiment with two actual balance scales. Seesaw problems—to address a quite different experimental setting for balance problems—could enrich the data base in another way.

Let us summarize by changing somewhat the first statement in this chapter. Models based on problem-solving hypotheses are interesting tools for analyzing cognitive development. They will become truly valuable tools if it is possible to improve the problem-solving hypotheses and to develop less restrictive models to specify and test them.

Acknowledgments

The authors thank Mrs. Lilli Maass for her assistance in planning, realizing, and analyzing the individual testing sessions.

References

Andersen, E. B. A goodness of fit test for the RASCH model. *Psychometrica*, 1973, *38*, 123–140.

Fischer, G. H. *Einführung in die Theorie psychologischer Tests*. Bern: Huber, 1974.

Fischer, G. H. Linear logistic test models: Theory and application. In H. Spada & W. F. Kempf (Eds.), *Structural models of thinking and learning. Proceedings of the IPN —Symposium 7. Kiel 1975*. Bern: Huber, 1977. Pp. 203–225.

Flavell, J. Stage–related properties of cognitive development. *Cognitive Psychology*, 1971, *2*, 421–453.

Flavell, J. *Cognitive development*. Englewood Cliffs, N.J.: Prentice Hall, 1977.

Groner, R. & Spada, H. Some markovian models for structural learning. In H. Spada & W. F. Kempf (Eds.), *Structural models of thinking and learning. Proceedings of the IPN — Symposium 7. Kiel 1975*. Bern: Huber, 1977. Pp. 131–159.

Guttman, L. The basis of scalogram analysis. In S. A. Stouffer *et al*. (Eds.), *Studies in social psychology in World War II*. Vol. IV. Princeton, N.J.: Princeton University Press, 1950.

Häussler, P. Evaluation of two teaching programs based on structural learning principles. *Studies in Educational Evaluation*, 1978, *4* (3), 145–161.

Hofer, A. *Die Auswirkungen des Feedback und der Reihenfolge der Aufgabenverteilung auf das Problemlösungsverhalten von Kindern bei Proportionalitätsaufgaben*. Unpublished (Institute for Psychology at the University of Bern, 1977).

Inhelder, B. & Piaget, J. *The growth of logical thinking from childhood to adolescence*. New York: Basic Books, 1958.

Inhelder, B., Sinclair, H., & Bovet, M. *Learning and the development of cognition*. London: Routledge & Kegan Paul, 1974.

Karplus, R. & Karplus, E. F. Ratio: A longitudinal study. In K. Frey & M. Lang (Eds.), *Kognitionspsychologie und naturwissenschaftlicher Unterricht —Cognitive processes and science instruction*. Bern: Huber, 1973. Pp. 305–313.

Keating, D. P. Adolescent thinking. In J. P. Adelson (Ed.), *Handbook of Adolescence*. New York: Wiley, in press.

Kluwe, R. *Wissen und Denken*. Stuttgart: Kohlhammer, 1979.

Lüer, G., & Spada, H. Denken lernen. In W. Tack (Ed.), *Bericht über den 30. Kongress der Deutschen Gesellschaft für Psychologie in Regensburg 1976*. Bd. 1. Göttingen: Hogrefe, 1976. Pp. 133–154.

Osherson, D. *Logical abilities in children, Vol. 1. Organization of length class concepts: Empirical consequences of a Piagetian formalism*. New York: Wiley, 1974.

Osherson, D. *Logical abilities in children. Vol. 3. Reasoning in adolescence: Deductive inference*. New York: Wiley, 1975.

Piaget, J. & Inhelder, B. *The psychology of the child*. London: Routledge & Kegan Paul, 1969.

Rasch, G. An item analysis which takes individual differences into account. *Brit. J. math. statist. Psychol.*, 1966, *19*, 49–57.

Rost, J. & Spada, H. Probabilistische Testtheorie. In K. J. Klauer (Ed.), *Handbuch der Pädagogischen Diagnostik*. Bd. 1. Düsseldorf: Schwann, 1978. Pp. 59–97.

Scandura, J. M. *Structural learning I. Theory and research*. New York: Gordon & Breach, 1973.

Scandura, J. M. A deterministic theory of learning and teaching. In H. Spada & W. F. Kempf (Eds.), *Structural models of thinking and learning*. Bern: Huber, 1977. Pp. 345–382.

Scheiblechner, H. Das Lernen und Lösen komplexer Denkaufgaben. *Z.f. exp. u. angew. Psychol.*, 1972, *19*, 476–505.

Spada, H. Invariante Intelligenzdimensionen als Basis für Selektion und Klassifikation. In M. Irle (Ed.), *Bericht über den 26. Kongress der Deutschen Gesellschaft für Psychologie in Tübingen 1968*. Göttingen: Hogrefe, 1969. Pp. 166–175.

Spada, H. Intelligenztheorie und Intelligenzmessung. *Psychol. Beiträge*, 1970, *12*, 83–96.

Spada, H. *Modelle des Denkens und Lernens*. Bern: Huber, 1976.

Spada, H. Logistic models of learning and thought. In H. Spada & W. F. Kempf (Eds.), *Structural models of thinking and learning*. Bern: Huber, 1977. Pp. 227–262.

Suarez, A. *Formales Denken und Funktionsbegriff bei Jugendlichen*. Bern: Huber, 1977.

Suppes, P. Facts and fantasies of education. In M. C. Wittrock (Ed.), *Changing education: Alternatives from educational research*. Englewoods Cliffs, N.J.: Prentice Hall, 1973. Pp. 6–45.

Wohlwill, J. *The study of behavioral development*. New York: Academic Press, 1973.

Wright, B. D. Solving measurement problems with the Rasch model. *Journal of Educational Measurement*, 1977, *14*, 97–116.

2

Mathematical and Psychometric Models of Cognitive Development from the Viewpoint of Information-Processing Theories

GERD LÜER

Introduction

The title of this contribution describes the task I faced preparing this chapter: I was asked to present a critical comment on the approach to the psychology of thinking that makes use of psychometric models as its main mode of research. The task was given to a psychologist who is labeled a follower of the information-processing approach. (In the following I shall use the term "information processor" to indicate someone in this position.)

It is my goal to demonstrate that there is no sense in a comparison of research on thought processes based on psychometric models versus information processing theories. It is my opinion that this confrontation is not justified, because we are dealing with two research paradigms that are not comparable and that are not rivals of each other. It seems to me necessary to start with some clarifications.

Clarifications of Some Methodological Misunderstandings

Quite frequently one encounters the opinion that cognitive psychologists using psychometric models are applying high-brow mathematical methods of data representation and analysis. By contrast, "information processors" are psychologists who consider "thinking aloud" or even introspection as an appropriate method of doing research on thinking; if they retain a vestige of concern for formalization, they do computer simulation. Naturally, such a comparison does not make any sense. It confuses different methodologies and compares things that are not comparable: procedures of data *collection* and procedures of data *analysis*. This misunderstanding is probably the origin of the opinion (or maybe the prejudice) that one group of scientists consists of accurate experimentalists with sophisticated research designs, handling complex formal models that appear quite impressive to the mathematical layman, whereas the other group of psychologists is not doing experimental research in the strict sense of the term. The latter evaluate only "soft" data with "soft" methods of analysis. Although such attributions obviously are not true, these associations remain a persistent part of the opinion within the scientific community.

Those who view thinking as a process of creating a solution, step by step, by means of the reception, coding, processing, and reorganization of information are trying to find out what happens while human beings are thinking. The processes involved can take place at different levels, and the processing can be organized either in a parallel or in a sequential fashion.

By analyzing empirical data, one can obtain evidence for every step of this complex process. This body of empirical evidence will be the basis for the derivation of principles that (supposedly) guide human problem-solving. Since nobody is likely to share the opinion that this can be accomplished by employing only one method (one form of data representation and analysis), what does this imply for our discussion concerning the adequacy of applied methods?

One must make a comparison between, on the one hand, a way to comprehend problem-solving processes (which are made up of many individual subprocesses) and, on the other hand, a certain class of mathematical models of data representation and analysis, for example, deterministic and probabilistic models. To view problem solving as information processing is a fundamental concept that, I believe, best allows one to understand and to explain the cognitive processes investigated. Therefore, this point of view does not predetermine which methods of data collection, representation, and analysis are best suited to the investigation and evaluation of the problems in question. In principle, the whole range of known methods and techniques is applicable. This principle is as valid for introspection as it is for psychophysiological measurements, so far as data collection is concerned. It applies equally to the whole spectrum of data-analysis techniques, ranging from the four-field chi-square test to highly complex mathematical models. There should be only one criterion for deciding which methods to use: the extent of their expected contribution to answering the question, What is going on during human thinking?

It is possible that the renunciation that causes information processors to claim only one method as theirs and thereby makes the weal and woe of their research approach dependent on it led to the notion that "information processors" are unpretentious in their choice of methods. The record of published counterexamples proves that this opinion is not valid at all and makes a lengthy discussion of this topic superfluous.

We do not have to stress the point that the research goals put forward by Spada and Kluwe, Chapter 1 in this volume, are also valid for information-processing theories: Formalization, accuracy, and the possibility of rigorous examination are general scientific principles. Everyone —not only psychometricians—strives to observe them. However, it has to be admitted that in some areas there are no appropriate research methods available that are powerful enough to meet these requirements. The creation and application of problem-solving heuristics is such an area, especially since heuristics are often modified in important ways during the problem-solving process itself. To conclude from this that these areas of research do not exist is, in my opinion, as wrong as to abandon the application of soft methods to these problem areas (keeping in mind that the objective is to obtain only "soft" results).

I would like to add a few illustrative examples to support the preceding statements. Some time ago, psychometric methods of investigation, based on an information-processing point of view, were already being employed as part of the analysis of problem-solving processes. The work of Sydow (1970) concerning goal distance represents a classic example of how results obtained by psychological scaling can advance our understanding of certain aspects of the thinking process. On the other hand, Spada and Kluwe (Chapter 1) describe their procedure for stating hypotheses about the structure of the investigated tasks: ". . . by observing children solving such problems" (see page 5). Subsequently, they propose to make use of more detailed protocol analyses to examine hypotheses that could not be verified by their initial data.

The work of Sydow (1970) is an example of the investigation of specific hypotheses about the processing of information by means of psychometric methods and their formal representation. Complementarily, the chapter by Spada and Kluwe shows how methods such as observation and protocol analysis, conventionally assigned to information-processing theories, are necessary prerequisites for a meaningful application of a mathematical model. Both approaches reveal a strong interaction of the research concepts discussed previously, although one should not fail to notice that the focal points of these investigations are very different. But are these differences evidence enough to justify a division of the research community into information processors and psychometricians? My answer to this question is a distinct no.

Discussion of the Presented
Psychometric Models

It would be a mistake to assume from the preceding remarks that the problem of the choice and the application of methods of data collection methods and analysis in the psychology of thinking is completely insignificant. It may be the case that some approaches are based on specific assumptions of a model that are not appropriate for the investigation of the thinking process. I would now like to review the psychometric models presented by Spada and Kluwe (Chapter 1) with these considerations in mind. In doing so, I will focus on methods of data collection, problem structure, and prerequisites for the application of psychometric models.

Methods of Data Collection

It is hard for an information processor to believe that it is possible to infer, solely from the information that someone did or did not solve a problem, how and by which principles he or she found the solution. This scepticism is fostered by data on detailed solution paths, which are again and again full of surprises, and which show that problem-solving behavior is extremely variable and flexible (Simon, 1975). In addition, experiences with factor analyses of IQ tests are not encouraging in overcoming this scepticism. Today, it is very doubtful whether dimensions of intelligent behavior derived by factor analysis can contribute to the advancement of our understanding of intelligent performance. Moreover, the attentive reader observes with interest the development of the data collection in those two experiments reported by Spada and Kluwe:

Experiment I. Data from pencil-and-paper tests in terms of multiple-choice answers—group experiment.

Experiment II. Data from investigations of individuals; problem solutions were recorded in more detailed protocols (i.e., not only right-or-wrong answers).

Obviously, the expectation was that a subject is a source of more information than just right or wrong answers. Finally, a comment on the presented choice of the right answer among a complete set of possible alternative answers: The representatives of the traditional German psychology of memory already knew about the difference between reproduction and recognition. Therefore, it is only fair to ask whether recognition ability has anything in common with problem solving.

Problem Structure

It has been noted that the analysis of problem structure (i.e., determining the sequence of operations required for the solution) emerged from the personal observations of the authors and from the findings of Inhelder and Piaget (1958). Strictly speaking, the analysis is therefore a matter of reexamining an already known context, so far as the hypotheses of Inhelder and Piaget are concerned. There is nothing to be said against such a procedure, but it does demonstrate the extent of dependence on data sources other than those of the authors!

But I have more momentous reservations about the completeness of describing a problem structure in this way. It seems inconsistent with an interest in stable and long-lasting, problem-solving processes that tasks or even problems are analyzed solely in terms of the application of rules and that, in addition, a rigid hierarchy of operations is the only basis for solution. It scarcely seems plausible that thinking follows a rigid algorithm in the case of complex problems in the same way that mental arithmetic is based on a known sequence of operations.

If, in fact, my expressed reservations are incorrect, the following questions must still be answered: Do the subjects make no use of more comprehensive operations (e.g., meta-operators, heuristics) such as have been observed with numerous other problems? Which additional cognitive processes are part of the difference between problem solving and mere applications of operations?

Prerequisites for the Application of Psychometric Models

This section deals with some of the logical requirements that must be met while applying the above-mentioned methods. First, I discuss the deterministic model. In this case, a quasi-Guttman scale is necessary to establish a hierarchy of operations. According to this model, a subject must be able to execute all operations that are ranked below a certain operation that he or she has mastered. This implies, for instance, a complete mastery of physics problems in a certain domain up to a point beyond which the subject is no longer able to produce solutions. This point is also interpreted as a developmental level of the subject. From known difficulties with Guttman scaling, it does not come as a surprise that such restrictive requirements cannot be met. Practically all questions concerning the usefulness of the model remain unanswered, because there is no way to determine whether the choice of operations or their ranking within the hierarchy, or both, are responsible for the failure of the evaluation. This, of course, does not affect the general doubt that such an approach is at all able to cast light on the nature of cognitive processes.

Similar, although not identical objections have to be made about the application of the Rasch model to the analysis of cognitive processes. In this case, too, only sequences of operations, such as algorithms, are the subject of the investigation. This leads to the problematic interpretation of inter- and intraindividual differences of development as different levels of mastery of the algorithm.

Considerations for a Research Concept of the Development of Cognitive Processes

No one doubts that human thought is exceptionally complex. It follows that we are dealing with a large number of variables that determine this cognitive process. Because of this, it is not meaningful to pick out a few of these variables and then to treat them individually. Furthermore, we know from empirically proven facts that we are not only dealing with a highly complex process but also with a partially unstable occurrence that varies greatly among individuals and situations. For this reason, we have to set aside the idea that thought is a product of a psychical apparatus that deals with a limited number of variables functioning similarly in every situation.

It appears necessary to me to describe the problem-solving process on various levels. McCarthy and Hayes (1969) (cf. also Dörner, 1976) took this consideration into account by postulating an epistemic and a heuristic structure. It is possible that in the area of the epistemic structure we are dealing with variables that can be researched in a classical framework, as for example in the case of concept formation or the psychology of memory. On the other hand, the important heuristic structure of the thought process is dominated primarily by extremely variable and flexible connections in terms of organizational principles.

To get a picture of how humans reorganize their knowledge when solving problems, it is necessary to describe the process. To do this, one cannot simply ask subjects how they will proceed. It is more important to determine which way, and by which means, they really try to reach a solution. For this reason, the psychology of problem solving is the science of following the search for the solution and describing as correctly as possible how it happened—not how it should or could have occurred. We thus have two essential demands for a research strategy for the problem-solving process:

1. The study of problem solving cannot stop with the demonstration that subjects have applied the rules correctly or incorrectly. More important are what separate transformation steps in the problem-solving process have been used and to what result they have led. We had to learn from our own studies that correct results can be attained by the application of incorrect rules, and vice versa.

2. The real task is to discover which combinations of the elements in the problem-solving process lead to the *formation of new rules*. Principles of organization play an important role here. They are the interface between the knowledge at hand and the heuristics with which solutions are to be framed. Simplifications and abstract reduction of aspects of the problem-solving structure which would not have been accessible by mere logical analysis reflect the existence of such principles.

From the above considerations it is possible to derive certain requirements for the data that must be obtained from empirical study of the problem-solving process. A number of consequences for experimental design also arise automatically as a result of this.

It is not sufficient, in my opinion, to analyze the products and results of the thought process without taking into account how they came about. The years of research on human intelligence with factor analysis show us very clearly where this leads. The research done by Putz-Osterloh and Lüer (1975) and Putz-Osterloh (1977) shows that this can lead to grave misinterpretations of the spatial abilities factor. If we also take into account developmental psychological changes in intelligence achievement, we have to take an even more pessimistic stance with regard to this static approach.

Added to the difficulty concerning the interpretation of the basic dimensions and their value for explanation is a further difficulty, which arises from the mathematical analysis methods associated with factor analysis. This does not mean that psychological data can never be adequately represented in mathematical models. However, in the field of the psychology of thought, and especially in the field of the development of such cognitive processes, it appears to me that there is still a gap to be filled between the psychological contents to be researched and the mathematical models representing them. Mathematical models force us to accept so many restrictions and simplifications that a complete understanding of the cognitive process is complicated rather than simplified.

From the preceding arguments, one could get the misimpression that I believe that no experiments should be carried out in the field of problem-solving psychology. The focal point of this argument is just the opposite: It is a plea for the most wide-ranging collection of data on problem solving in order to enlarge our state of knowledge about this cognitive occurrence. Such data can be gathered from observation, or obtained from thinking-aloud protocols, video recordings, or from eye movement registration. These data provide us with an indication of how subjects arrive at solutions—a data base that is unbiased and perhaps full of surprises. It is very inconvenient to gather data in this way. Out of necessity, the samples for these experiments must be smaller than those where test scores in terms of 1 or 0 are analyzed. Such data are not as handy as multiple-choice data. At the same time, my plea is to avoid restrictions and simplifications under all circumstances because of the complexity of the material in the field of cognitive psychology. A possible loss of precision of the information-processing data can be accepted, so long as the data responds to needs that cannot be met by methods of higher precision.

Conclusions

The principle question as to whether in research on cognitive processes we should or should not attempt psychometric measurements has to be decided in favor of such research strategies. Once we are in a position of being able to define a process so precisely that we can account for it in terms of valid, describable variables, we should of course follow the goal of precise measurement. However, we should not forget the importance of a single, or perhaps a few variables in the total structure of a complex occurrence.

I hope that Spada (1977) will be proved right in his claim that psychology which views problem solving as the processing of information can produce many theoretical assessments and hypotheses that can be proved and refined with appropriate mathematical methods. However, above all, we must avoid allowing mathematical models to determine what we should or should not measure. Research methods must be adapted to suit the contents of the research, not the opposite.

The mathematician Lichtenberg (1742–1799) once said that there are many phenomena under the sun for which there are no theories or explanations in our textbooks. In the same vein, there are many theories in our textbooks for which there are no phenomena under the sun. We should, above all, preserve ourselves from the latter danger in cognitive psychology.

References

Dörner, D. *Problemlösen als Informationsverarbeitung.* Stuttgart: Kohlhammer, 1976.

Inhelder, B., & Piaget, J. *The growth of logical thinking from childhood to adolescence.* New York: Basic Books, 1958.

McCarthy, J., & Hayes, P. J. Some philosophical problems from the standpoint of artificial intelligence. In B. Meltzer & D. Michie (Eds.), *Machine intelligence 4*. Edinburgh: University Press, 1969. Pp. 463–502.

Putz-Osterloh, W. Über Problemlöseprozesse bei dem Test Würfelaufgaben aus dem Intelligenztest IST und IST-70 von Amthauer. *Diagnostica*, 1977, *23*, 252–265.

Putz-Osterloh, W., & Lüer, G. Informationsverarbeitung bei einem Test zur Erfassung der Raumvorstellung. *Diagnostica*, 1975, *21*, 166–181.

Simon, H. A. The functional equivalence of problem solving skills. *Cognitive Psychology*, 1975, *7*, 268–288.

Spada, H. Die Förderung strukturellen Lernens anhand formalisierter Theorien. In W. H. Tack (Ed.), *Ber. 30. Kongr. DGP in Regensburg 1976*. Göttingen: Hogrefe, 1977. Pp. 135–138.

Sydow, H. Zur metrischen Erfassung von subjektiven Problemzuständen und zu deren Veränderung im Denkprozeß (Parts I and II). *Zeitschrift für Psychologie*, 1970, *177*, 145–198 (I); 1970, *178*, 1–50 (II).

3

A Theory of Growth[1]

HOBEN THOMAS

Introduction

Primitive man certainly must have made some simple observations about growth processes. Surely the following two must have been among them. First, older persons are, on the average, bigger than children. Second, older individuals show greater variability in their physical characteristics than do their younger peers. This second observation is so fundamental to growth that Thorndike has regarded it as the very essence of growth itself. "Imagine," he suggests, "a group of adults whose heights and weights showed no greater standard deviations than those of newborn babies! [Thorndike, 1966, p. 126]."

What is central to this chapter is the interrelationship between averages and standard deviations when viewed from a developmental perspective. Probably every developmental psychologist has observed data in which the means and standard deviations, computed at varying age points, march along together in a regular and orderly fashion. Indeed, evidence for such covariation can be found in the earliest writings. In 1935, Lambert A. J. Quetelet first reported average heights and range of heights for Belgian boys and girls from birth to age 17 (Quetelet, 1835, 1842/1969). [Almost 60 years would pass before Pearson would define, in 1894, what is now termed the standard deviation (Walker, 1931).] In

[1] Much of the research reported here was done at the Institut für Psychologie, der Christian Albrechts-Universität Kiel, West Germany, during 1975–1976 while supported by a Fulbright–Hays research award and by der Kultusminister des Landes Schleswig–Holstein.

Figure 3.1 are graphed Quetelet's data for girls. It shows a strong linear pattern well reflected in the .90 correlation for the 18 pairs of means and ranges. The corresponding value for boys is .86.

Ninety years later, Thurstone (1925) noted that the absolutely scaled means and standard deviations of mental test scores, obtained from children of varying ages, were highly correlated and that both increased with age. This observation led to his 1928 paper in which he assumed the absolutely scaled means and standard deviations were linearly related. This assumption enabled Thurstone to estimate what he felt was the age at which zero intelligence occurs. What may be most interesting is not Thurstone's perhaps dubious claim to having found intelligence to be zero in the fetus; rather, in a manner highly unlike Thurstone's efforts in so many areas of psychology, his approach was strictly empirical: He had no theory to account for the observed correlations.

It is the central thesis of this chapter that the functional relationship between means and standard deviations, widely observed in both physical and psychological growth data, has important theoretical and methodological implications. There appears to be no theory that can adequately account for the empirical facts. Indeed, it will be shown that a very large class of models utilized for both data analysis and as theories of growth can be readily falsified. An alternative theory will be proposed that appears to capture the empirical facts more satisfactorily.

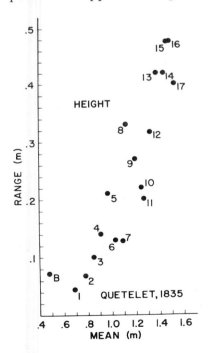

FIGURE 3.1. *Sample means and ranges of height in meters (m) at yearly ages from birth (B) through 16 years for Belgian girls.*

Some implications of the model, both theoretical and methodological, will be considered. The parameter estimation problem will have to await detailed treatment elsewhere, but will be considered for certain cases.

Data with Correlated Means and Standard Deviations

It is not necessary to search very far in the developmental literature to find instances where the means and standard deviations are correlated. Denney and Moulton's (1976) data are fairly typical. They were interested in children's reasons for judging objects as similar. Their children were 3, 4, 5, and 9 years old, and their sample sizes ranged from 22 to 49. For six of their eight measures, the means and standard deviations were given for each of their four age groups. Four of these mean–standard-deviation correlation coefficients were .78 or higher; one was −.828, another −.0244.[2]

It is in the literature concerned with cognitive processes, such as Denney and Mouton's, that such patterns of relations are most likely to be observed. And when within the same article or, even better, across different articles on the same general topic, similar patterns of statistical values are observed, there is increasing confidence that the reason for the observed relationship is something other than chance, especially if several as opposed to just three different age groups are utilized. Elkind (1964) studied children's ability to recognize ambiguous figures, counting the number of cards each child recognized. For the six age groups of children, (6½– 12 years old) and for two different stimuli sets, the correlations between the statistics for the two stimulus sets were .85 and .89; Santostefano and Paley (1964) studied cognitive control in tasks somewhat similar to Elkind's. For their three age groups (6, 9, and 12 years), the coefficients were, for each cognitive control measure, .81, .86, and .98. Thomas and Jamison (1975) investigated the beliefs children hold regarding the slope the surface of still water assumes in vessels oriented at different angles. Their dependent variable was the child's adjusted angular setting produced on an apparatus. For either 9 or 12 different age groups, using 6-year-old children through college-age adults, and for each sex separately, the 10 correlation coefficients computed from

[2] Conventional hypothesis testing procedures for evaluation of the observed correlations are useless in this situation as will be clarified in sequel. If desired the standard deviation of r may be taken as $(m-1)^{-1/2}$, a value that will be clarified below. The data suggest a discontinuity between 5 and 9 years; if the oldest group is excluded, these correlations are not lower than $|.97|$ a result not obtained if any of the other age group is similarly deleted.

their data ranged from .72 to .97. Wohlwill (1973, p. 338), one of the few writers to comment on the mean and standard deviation correlation in developmental data, culled data from Witkin *et al.* (1954). Wohlwill reports three measures of field dependency for five age groups of children, 8–17 years old, plus an adult group. For each sex separately, and for each task, the six coefficients (each computed from six mean–standard-deviation pairs) ranged from .66 to .96.

It is important to emphasize that simply knowing that the means and standard deviations covary does not imply how they will be correlated with age or development. Older children, as would be expected, recognized more ambiguous pictures in Elkind's (1964) task than did younger children. Thus, the higher the scores, the better the children's performance and both the means and standard deviations increased with age. For Witkin *et al.* (1954), and for Thomas and Jamison (1975), the reverse was true. For example, Witkin *et al.* measured error scores. In the rod-and-frame task, the smaller the angular deviation of the rod from the correct vertical position, the better the performance. Thus, both the average error and the standard deviations decreased toward zero as age increased. Whether means and standard deviations increase or decrease with age is to be determined by how the dependent variable is defined, but, as has been seen, the relationship between the means and standard deviations can be similar, regardless of how such statistics may covary with age.

Given the arbitrary way in which dependent variables may be defined in psychology, negative correlation coefficients between means and standard deviations can be observed that, with slight dependent variable redefinition, may become positive coefficients. For example, Witkin *et al.* (1954) defined angular error in the rod-and-frame task to be referenced from the vertical axis, defined as 0°. The better the performance, the smaller the angular deviation. Perfect performance would be 0°. Had Witkin instead referenced errors from the horizontal axis defined as zero, perfect performance would be 90° (from the horizontal axis) and poorer performance would have deviations less than 90°. Thus, the better the performance, the larger the angular deviation. As such, changing the reference axis would result in a change of *sign* of the observed mean–standard-deviation correlation coefficient.

The research area in which the mean standard deviation correlations are most consistent and most striking is that in which Thurstone was working over 50 years ago. Thurstone (1928) examined six cross-sectional growth studied of children within the age range from 21 months to 15½ years. The correlation coefficients for absolutely scaled means and standard deviations were never lower than .97. Each coefficient is based on from 6 to 12 age groups. Of course, absolutely scaled means and standard deviations are not the same as sample means and standard deviations computed at each age. However, there are abundant data published since Thurstone's paper that indicate that the correlation coefficients computed on sample means and standard deviations are almost as high as those based on the absolutely scaled values Thurstone reported.

Table 3.1 provides a representative but not exhaustive summary of data obtained from many well-known growth studies in which the dependent variables are, with one exception, mental age or point-scale scores. Data using age-relative IQ scores are similar—as will be noted momentarily.

Table 3.1 indicates that regardless of the methodology, whether it is cross-sectional or longitudinal, from roughly 1 year through adolescence the correlation coefficients between the means and standard deviations are uniformly high. Most coefficients are in the 90s, with higher coefficients associated with longitudinal studies. The fact that the coefficients are similar, regardless of method, suggests that the results are not cohort-specific, but rather reflect a general property of intellectual development. Even for crude indices, such as the Goodenough Draw-a-Person test, the coefficients are still high (see also Laosa, Swartz, & Holtzman, 1973). But correlation coefficients can be misleading. In Figure 3.2a are graphed the point-scale means and standard deviations from Nancy Bayley's (1933) longitudinal Berkeley Growth study group for ages 1–36 months. The configuration is N-shaped, with two discontinuities: one at about 6 months and another around 1 year. This configuration is no sampling artifact. It is also to be found in Wilson's (1972) large-scale longitudinal study of twins, also shown in Figure 3.2a. The same general configuration is evident, but less strikingly so, in Bayley's (1965) cross-sectional study. Because of these two obvious discontinuities, the means and standard deviations for Bayley's point-scale scores obtained before 9 months were not included in the computation of the correlation coefficients reported in Table 3.1.

By examining Figure 3.2b it is clear that the mean and standard deviation values do not covary over the entire 10–59 year age-span Jones and Conrad (1933) tested, as the .86 correlation coefficient in Table 3.1 might suggest. The only reasonably linear portion is to be found for those subjects 10–21 years or so; for these age groups the correlation coefficient is .95. Notice in Figure 3.2b the standard deviations are concave and increasing against the means through the growth years. This finding is not unique to this cross-sectional study. It is also found in longitudinal studies. As one example, consider the longitudinal Brush study (Ebert & Simmons, 1943) data for boys shown parallel to Jones and Conrad's data (1933) in Figure 3.2b. This nonlinear curvature will be of concern later.

In most mental growth studies, as Table 3.1 suggests, the dependent

TABLE 3.1

Correlation Coefficients Computed between Sample Means and Standard Deviations for Mental Test Scores from Selected Studies

Variable	r(m)[a]	SD(r)[b]	Subjects and ages	Range of n's	Method[c]	Reference
Bayley Point Scale	.92(13)	.30	Boys and girls, 9–36 mo	46–71	LS	Bayley, 1933
Bayley Point Scale	.94(4)	.57	Twins, boys and girls, 9–24 mo	298–400	LS	Wilson, 1972
Bayley Point Scale	.42(7)	.41	Girls, 9–15 mo	39–53	CS	Bayley, 1965
Bayley Point Scale	.88(7)	.41	Boys, 9–15 mo	41–53	CS	Bayley, 1965
Army Alpha Raw Scores	.87(18)	.24	Boys and girls, 10–59 yr	34–106	CS	Jones & Conrad, 1933
Army Alpha Raw Scores	.95(10)	.33	Boys and girls, 10–21 yr	34–87	CS	Jones & Conrad, 1933
'37 Binet MA	.93(10)	.33	Girls, 6–15 yr	13–165	CS	Ebert & Simmons, 1943
'37 Binet MA	.78(10)	.33	Boys, 6–15 yr	27–134	CS	Ebert & Simmons, 1943
'16 & '37 Binet MA	.97(10)	.33	Girls, 3–10 yr	100	LS	Ebert & Simmons, 1943
'16 & '37 Binet MA	.97(10)	.33	Boys, 3–10 yr	81	LS	Ebert & Simmons, 1943
Varying tests, MA	.91(10)	.33	Girls, 7–16 yr	130	LS	Anderson, 1939
Varying Tests, MA	.88(10)	.33	Boys, 7–16 yr	135	LS	Anderson, 1939
Goodenough IQ	.95(6)	.45	Black children, Grades 1–6	30	CS	Kennedy & Linder, 1964

[a] r(m) denotes the number of pairs of means and standard deviations on which r is based.

[b] SD(r) denotes the standard deviation, $(m - 1)^{-1/2}$, computed under model assumptions discussed in text.

[c] L denotes longitudinal, CS cross sectional.

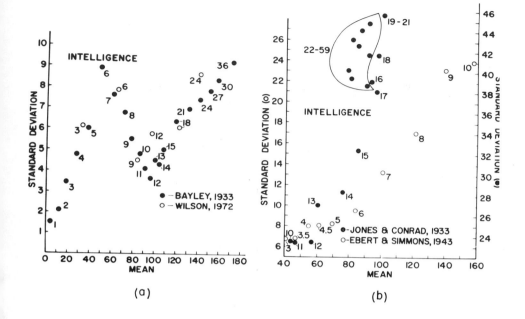

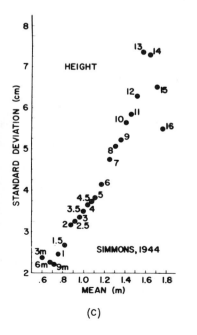

FIGURE 3.2. *Means and standard deviations for intelligence or height of individuals for ages indicated. (a) Longitudinal data for boys and girls with ages in months. (b) Cross-sectional data for boys and girls are from Jones and Conrad (1933). Cross-sectional data from Ebert and Simmons (1943) are for boys. (c) Three joined longitudinal height sequences for boys 3 months–7 years, 6–12 years, and 11–16 years.*

variable is not measured on an age-relative scale; mental age units or point scale scores are provided. However, in some studies of mental development only age-relative IQ scores are given. The Fels study (Sontag, Baker, & Nelson, 1958) is one example. In longitudinal investigations, but not consistently in cross-sectional data, where age-relative IQ is the dependent variable, the same mean–standard-deviation pattern is evident, although the magnitudes of the correlations are, not surprisingly, smaller. For example, in the Fels data, for children aged 2½–12 years, the correlation coefficients ranged from .66 to .90, where each coefficient was based on from 10 to 14 pairs of values.

Are there physical growth data that display similar mean and standard deviation relationships? An affirmative answer would seem warranted based upon an examination of Quetelet's height data in Figure 3.1. There are, however, reasons for checking further. First, a similar finding in physical growth data, while not implying that physical and psychological processes have uniquely common causal factors, would at least allow for the possibility that a common model might be used to account for both psychological and physical growth data. Such a suggestion is not new. For example, Galton's (1889) general nature–nurture model for height is essentially the same model (albeit recast in modern language) that underlies current nature–nurture discussions of intelligence. Second, and more important, in the assessment of physical growth via measures such as height or weight, there are no severe measurement-theoretical concerns. The measurement model underlying physical measurement is well-known and was formalized as early as 1901 by Hölder; height measurement is measurement on a ratio scale, and such scales have well-known properties. In psychology, the situation is often much less satisfactory. Particularly in the case of mental test scores, no measurement model exists (cf., e.g., Suppes & Zinnes, 1963) so it is not clear what the uniqueness properties are that underlie the numerical mental test scores. Thus, although there appear to be sufficient data to strongly suggest otherwise, it could nonetheless be argued that the observed statistical relations are simply artifacts of the psychological measurement process. Parallel findings in physical growth data would argue against such an interpretation.

Table 3.2 shows representative findings for five different physical measures: breathing capacity, standing height (or length in the case of infants), ramus height (a measure of dental development), weight, and strength. Height has been extensively studied; for some longitudinal studies the mean standard deviation correlation coefficients are essentially 1, as Table 3.2 indicates. When comparisons between longitudinal and cross-sectional methods are possible, as they are with height, longitudinal studies reveal somewhat higher correlation coefficients, a finding consistent with the psychological data reported earlier. Figure

TABLE 3.2
Correlation Coefficients Computed between Sample Means and Standard Deviations for Selected Physical Measures

Variable	$r(m)$[a]	$SD(r)$[b]	Subjects and ages	Range of n's	Method[c]	Reference
Breathing Capacity	.97(14)	.27	Boys, 6–18 yr	64–410	CS	Meredith, 1935
Height	.99(14)	.27	Girls, 3 mo–7 yr	85	L	Simmons, 1944
Height	.98(14)	.27	Boys, 3 mo–7 yr	81	L	Simmons, 1944
Height[d]	.90(18)	.24	Girls, birth–17 yr	Unknown	CS	Quetelet, 1969
Height[d]	.86(18)	.24	Boys, birth–17 yr	Unknown	CS	Quetelet, 1969
Ramus Height	.96(4)	.57	Boys, 8–9½ yr	20	L	Grizzle & Allen, 1969
Weight	.83(11)	.32	Ghananian girls, 5–15 yr	25–272	CS	Fiawoo, 1976
Weight	.92(11)	.32	Ghananian boys, 5–15 yr	27–261	CS	Fiawoo, 1976
Strength	.95(9)	.35	Boys 7–15 yr	19–109	CS	Cureton, 1964

[a] $r(m)$ denotes the number of pairs of means and standard deviations on which r is based.
[b] $SD(r)$ denotes the standard deviation, $(m - 1)^{-1/2}$, computed under model assumptions discussed in text.
[c] L denotes longitudinal, CS cross sectional.
[d] Range used as measure of variation.

3.2c reveals certain relationships not captured by the correlation coefficients reported in Table 3.2. Three longitudinal sequences from the same Brush study (Simmons, 1944) have been joined together to reveal the pattern of mean and standard deviation changes from infancy through adolescence for boys' height. In the case of mental test scores, a linear relationship is not a meaningful description of the pattern of mean–standard-deviation relationships over the entire growth sequence, but it may be a useful reflection of the pattern of relationship in the postinfancy through early adolescent period. This statement appears to be true of certain physical measures as well. Note in Figure 3.2c that whereas the means increase monotonically with age, the standard deviations do not. They reach a minimum around 9 months or so, after which they increase until adolescence. Even Quetelet's data (Figure 3.1) indicate that the minimum range is about 1 year. This marked curvilinear pattern is also evident in other height data (e.g., Meredith, 1935). It is interesting that a similar minimum also occurs in infant mental test data such as in Bayley's (1933) and Wilson's (1972) shown in Figure 3.2a.

Note also in Figure 3.2c the standard deviations are concave up against the means from about 1 year through adolescence. The standard deviations do not continually increase, however, and at some point in adolescence, the slight increase in means is associated with decreasing standard deviations resulting in a striking downturn of the graph, as in Figure 3.2c.

In many respects, the findings from certain physical growth data parallel data on psychological growth. But not all psychological growth data reveal mean–standard-deviation correlations. This is true of physical growth data as well. However, there are many other physical measures where high positive mean and standard deviation correlations are evident. For instance, Cureton (1964) reported 36 different physical measures and included means and standard deviations for each age from boys usually within the age range of 6–15 years; the median of the 36 mean–standard-deviation correlation coefficients is .60. All except eight are positive.

In summary, an examination of both the psychological and physical growth literature for both longitudinal and cross-sectional methodologies, and for a variety of dependent variables, pairs of sample means and sample standard deviations computed at varying age points often show similar relationships. Particularly for the postinfancy through early adolescent years, the means and standard deviations are often highly positively correlated. Thus, it does not seem unreasonable to suggest that a common model may be useful for characterizing much psychological and physical growth data. But first consider how familiar models might characterize such correlations.

Analysis of Variance Models as Theories of Growth[3]

The place to start when atttempting to assess the theoretical significance of the observed mean–standard-deviation correlations is to evaluate the expected value of the mean and standard deviation random variable, denoted $R(\overline{X}_i, S_i)$, under statistical models that are candidates for models of growth. The expected values may then be compared with the observed values, $r(\bar{x}_i, s_i)$, such as those reported in the preceding section.

It seems appropriate, for two related reasons, to begin with analysis of variance (ANOVA) models. First, ANOVA is widely employed in psychology generally, and, as a result, it has shaped both theory and methodology. Second, ANOVA models resemble a large class of statistical models including, for example, regression and factor analysis. One important way in which such models are similar is that the hypothesized components are assumed to combine by an additive operation. A number of critically important analytical reasons, but not psychological reasons, have dictated why statistical theory has focused almost exclusively on additive combinations. The consequence has been that such additive models have tended to become reified as psychological models; this point will be expanded upon momentarily. Of course, most of the physical and psychological growth data just reviewed have never been analyzed with an eye toward making inferences or testing hypotheses about factors responsible for the growth changes observed. Most classical growth studies are largely descriptive; this fact, however, does not prevent the data from being used to evaluate statistical models that also are candidates for growth models.

Analysis of variance is used in growth studies for a variety of different reasons. Consequently, the implications derived from its use are likely to be different. As one illustration, consider again Denney and Moulton's (1976) interest in the child's changing bases for classifying objects as alike. From an ANOVA viewpoint, differences among their growth groups are to be viewed as differences in means; thus, age (or treatment) differences are expressible as additive constant differences influencing means and nothing else. I regard Denney and Moulton's use of ANOVA as an implicit growth theory because their use of it is not conceptually

[3] A more appropriate title might be Linear Models as Theories of Growth; by linear model is meant any additive combination of random variables and constants in which the components have the coefficient one. With such a distinction, analysis of variance would be regarded as a data analysis framework for estimating and evaluating hypotheses concerning the components. Here, this distinction will be slurred somewhat in keeping with general usage in the psychological literature and the model and method will occasionally carry the same name.

tied to their explanations concerning the nature of how the observed growth changes occurred. Thus, there are no obvious psychological reasons, and they provide none, why they should have chosen to view age differences as being represented as additive mean differences, except perhaps that it is the conventional thing to do. They might, perhaps just as plausibly, have considered changes in variance or skew. Perhaps their primary interest was not to assess average age differences per se, but rather to demonstrate that *some* change occurred in the dependent variable. Such a strategy translates into statistical tests against a class of "omnibus alternatives," a term Lehmann (1975) has used to characterize procedures, like the Kolmogorov–Smirnov, that specifically test for various changes in distribution and are not intended to focus, as is ANOVA, on specific parameter differences.

In situations where some change in the dependent variable seems clear, as in Denney and Moulton's study, neither the data analysis nor the implicit underlying theory implied by the analysis seems terribly important. If any study is apt to be an influential one, it will probably not be because of the particular data analysis used anyway.

The situation is different, however, when ANOVA becomes what I would term an explicit growth theory. Here the model structure underlying ANOVA takes on added psychological significance, and there is a close affinity between ANOVA as a statistical inferential model and as a model for psychological inference. Important uses of ANOVA in this way include, for example, Anderson's (1962) functional measurement theory and Sternberg's (1969) memory model. In developmental psychology, Schaie's (1965) general developmental model is a good example. Schaie noted, importantly, that in growth studies it was not always clear from observed score changes over age, what conditions produced the observed changes. For example, an old problem is to account for the decline in mental test scores observed in cross-sectional aging studies (e.g., Jones & Conrad, 1933) while increases in adult mental test scores are sometimes observed in longitudinal studies (e.g., Bayley, 1955). Schaie proposed that observed or phenotypic scores should be viewed as having three latent components; first, a cohort effect, denoting year or generation of birth; second, an age effect, reflecting age influences on test scores, and third, influences surrounding the time of testing. Although modifications have been proposed to Schaie's original formulation (e.g., Baltes, 1968), within the present context, none of these proposed changes is important. What is critical to Schaie's model and modifications of it, is that treatment effects are viewed as additive constant effects and, equally important, inferences about the relative importance of such effects are inferences made through an ANOVA framework. Clearly central to the whole enterprise is the acceptance of the ANOVA model as an appropriate structural model for the characterization of growth.

Most growth studies, however, do not yield neatly to a simple binary implicit–explicit classification. However, there are clear hallmarks that, when jointly in evidence, strongly suggest that use of ANOVA might be regarded as an explict growth theory. For example, when the analysis becomes complex, when interaction terms seem necessary to characterize the data, and when the statistical significance of certain effects specifically alters the nature of the psychological discourse, then such analyses should be regarded as an explicit growth theory framework. Certainly, a large number of psychological growth studies may be so viewed since complex analyses with significant interaction terms are often present, and such statistical significance seems so often to call forth the need for psychological explanation.

It will be useful in sequel to distinguish three classes of assumptions when viewing models, including ANOVA models. First, there are *operational* assumptions, which refer to how the components, either random variables or fixed constants, combine. For all commonly utilized ANOVA models, the components add. Second, there are *parameter value* assumptions. Depending on the nature of model, parameters are typically fixed by hypothesis (e.g., the mean of the error random variable is zero) or viewed as estimable from data (e.g., estimating a treatment effect). Finally, there are *distributional* assumptions, that is, how the random variables are distributed.

These different classes of assumptions are not all of equal importance. Operational assumptions are at the core of most models, including ANOVA models, and were the first and primary concern of Sir Ronald A. Fisher (Plackett, 1960). His first model called for all fixed constants with an additive structure. Interestingly enough, apparently ill at ease with an additive structure, Fisher first tried a product structure (Plackett, 1960, p. 212). On the other hand, distributional assumptions are probably least important. They did not concern Fisher initially (Plackett, 1960) and, in fact, would not be as important today for many applications of ANOVA if interest focused on descriptive estimation and not on hypothesis testing. Furthermore, as is well-known from Monte Carlo studies, for many ANOVA applications neither certain (hypothesized) parameter values nor distributional assumptions may be critical (cf., e.g., Gaito & Wiley, 1963).

Expectations of $R(\overline{X}_i, S_i)$ under Analysis of Variance Models

It is sufficient to consider the simplest ANOVA model represented by the right-hand terms of Eq. (1). Certainly

$$X_i = \mu + \alpha_i + E_i \tag{1}$$

is a familiar structure.[4] Consider Denney and Moulton's (1976) study again. Here $i = 1, 2, 3$, and 4 and denotes their 3-, 4-, 5-, and 9-year-old children. Observations of their 3-year-old children would be observations on the random variable X_1 for example. In Eq. (1) μ is the grand mean selected such that $\Sigma \alpha_i = 0$, and α_i are the age-specific (treatment) constants. The model has one random variable E_i that reflects all within-age variation, including true individual differences as well as assessment or measurement error.[5]

If interest focuses on estimation of the unknown parameters, it is sufficient to assume that E_i has 0 mean and variance σ_i^2. For hypothesis testing, each E_i is usually assumed to be normally distributed and all $\sigma_i^2 = \sigma^2$ (cf., e.g., Gaito & Wiley, 1963). Consider the standard deviation and expectation of X_i: $\text{Var}(X_i) = \sigma_i^2 = \sigma^2$, so the standard deviation of X_i is $[\text{Var}(X_i)]^{1/2} = \sigma$. Similarly, $E(X_i) = \mu_i = \mu + \alpha_i$.

Now the graph of the model parameters $\sigma_i = \sigma$ against μ_i is a horizontal line of 0 slope (assuming $\mu_i \neq \mu_j$ somewhere), and the immediate issue concerns what the graph of the estimates of these parameters, or alternatively, what the corresponding correlation computed from these estimates should be. For example, for Denney and Moulton's (1976) functional category the sample estimates for their 3-year-old children were $\bar{x}_1 = \hat{\mu}_1 = \hat{\mu} + \hat{\alpha}_1 = 2.65 - 2.42 = .23$, where $\hat{\mu} = 2.65$, and $\hat{\sigma}_1 = s_1 = .75$. The pairs (x_i, s_i) for their four age groups were (.23, .75), (.81, 1.47), (2.54, 3.40), and (7.02, 3.56). While $r = .83$ for these pairs, the expected value of R under their ANOVA model is quite different: It is zero. This result may be stated as a theorem.

THEOREM

Let $(\overline{X}_i, S_i)$, $i = 1, \ldots; m$, denote sample means and sample standard deviations computed from m random samples from distributions that are normal, mean μ_i, variance σ^2, that is, $n(\mu_i, \sigma^2)$. When the observations on sample i are not independent from the observations on sample j, as in longitudinal studies, assume $n(\mu_i, \sigma^2)$ and $n(\mu_j, \sigma^2)$ are bivariate normal. Then the sample correlation coefficient R computed from the m pairs has expectation 0 and variance $(m-1)^{-1}$.

Space limitations preclude the proof from being given here, but for the case when observations are independent, as in cross-sectional studies, the argument follows directly from a theorem by Huber (1977, p. 46), once it is recalled that the vector of sample means and sample stan-

---

[4] Throughout this chapter, italic capital letters will denote random variables, lowercase letters the values they take-on. Greek letters will denote fixed constants.

[5] Denney and Moulton (1976) initially assumed a model that included a sex variable and an interaction term. Since neither was significant, the assumed model may be reduced to Eq. (1).

dard deviations in the normal case (Anderson, 1958, p. 53) are independent vectors.

This result may be regarded as a direct test of the appropriateness of viewing growth phenomena within additive structures such as analysis of variance. And given the magnitude of many observed mean–standard-deviation correlation coefficients, it suggests that ANOVA may be a very inappropriate model within which to view growth phenomena.

This problem may not be too serious for what I term implicit uses of ANOVA, such as Denney and Moulton's (1976), but it is troublesome when ANOVA is clearly used as an explicit growth theory, as in Schaie's (1972) effort to assess cohort, age, and testing time effects on the mental age changes of children in the Harvard Growth Study. While Schaie did not report the means and standard deviations for the children he selected, Anderson (1939) also made use of the Harvard Growth Study data in his analyses. The correlation coefficients computed from Anderson's means and standard deviations are reported in Table 3.1. These coefficients, .91 and .88, place into question the meaning to be associated with Schaie's inferences.

It might be proposed that a way out of the dilemma is for developmental psychology to employ multivariate ANOVA procedures, and this avenue is certainly one possible alternative. The advantages of such an approach appear to be that one can relax certain restrictive variance and covariance assumptions. Multivariate ANOVA models still maintain additive operational assumptions, but more restrictive distributional assumptions are required, typically multivariate normality (cf., e.g., Morrison, 1967). However, to elect this option, it is argued, represents a serious misreading of the data. The consistently high correlation coefficients observed between the standard deviations and the means in many growth studies appears to be no haphazard affair. The coefficients are typically closer to one than to zero, and this fact should tell us something about appropriate models for characterizing growth and analyzing growth data.

What is suggested by the empirical facts is that an appropriate model should conceptually link the parameter means and standard deviations within the model structure, so that these parameters are functionally related and vary together, just as the corresponding sample estimates covary. Conventional multivariate ANOVA models do not provide this option, although perhaps such a model might be developed. These models simply allow the elements of the mean and standard deviation vectors to be different; generally, any particular pattern of means and standard deviations is as admissible as any other. Thus, these models cannot account for the observed relations between sample means and standard deviations, and thus by implication they may be the wrong models.

The above results suggest that inferences have been made under models which appear to be clearly wrong models. This interpretation stimulates a number of questions. Among them, how should growth be characterized? This question is tackled next.

A Proposed Model Structure

Consider the model

$$X_i = \nu_i G_i + I, \tag{2}$$

where X_i, G_i, and I are random variables and $\nu_i > 0$ is a fixed parameter. Only observations of values of X_i are possible, so that right-hand members represent the assumed underlying model structure. Although it is not necessary, it will be notationally convenient and intuitively useful to view increasingly larger values of the index i as denoting increasingly older age groups that will typically be viewed as having increasingly larger means and standard deviations.

Consider $\nu_i G_i$ to be the heart of the model, and momentarily disregard I. $\nu_i G_i$ is viewed as an age or maturational specific growth random variable. At each age, there is an identically distributed G_i random variable with $E(G_i) = \mu > 0$, $\mathrm{Var}(G_i) = \sigma^2$. In the case of cross-sectional studies at ages i and j, G_i and G_j are independent. For longitudinal studies G_i and G_j are correlated. Each $\nu_i > 0$ may be viewed as a growth rate parameter such that at ages $i < j$, usually $\nu_i < \nu_j$. Suppose height is of interest. Through the growth years certainly $0 < E(X_1) < E(X_2) < \cdots < E(X_m)$, which simply reflects the observation that average height increases. This fact is accounted for by assuming that $\nu_i < \nu_j$ when $i < j$ with the result that $0 < E(\nu_i G_i) < E(\nu_j G_j)$ or $0 < \nu_i \mu < \nu_j \mu$. Since $\nu_i < \nu_j$ $\mathrm{Var}(\nu_i G_i) = \nu_i^2 \sigma^2 < \mathrm{Var}(\nu_j G_j) = \nu_j^2 \sigma^2$, which implies that $\nu_i \sigma < \nu_j \sigma$ and so on when $i < j$. Thus, the increases in means and corresponding increases in standard deviations are accounted for by the age-specific multiplicative contant ν_i, regardless of whether longitudinal or cross-sectional situations are of concern. Figure 3.3 illustrates pictorially the ideas involved. Here each G_i is assumed to be normal $n(6, 1)$. The varying values of the ν_i are given by the set N. In the figure, since each G_i is pictured as normal, so is each $\nu_i G_i$. The corresponding parameters for each distribution are also given in the figure.

As an alternative viewpoint, consider three individuals with values on G_i of 4, 5, and 6. Suppose $\nu_i = 2$. Then the observed values on X_i, assuming the effects of I are ignored, would be 8, 10, and 12. Thus, ν_i effects each individual's score differentially in the sense that it spreads out the scores. Here $\nu_i G_i$ may be viewed as a kind of individual specific interaction, but not an interaction in the conventional analysis of variance

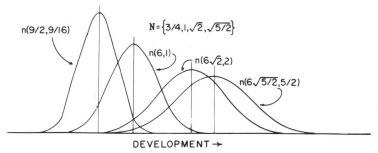

FIGURE 3.3. *Pictorial characterization of growth model* $X_i = \nu_i G_i$ *where* X_i *is normal. The increasing growth parameters,* ν_i, *are given by the set* N. $n(6\nu_i, 1\nu_i^2)$ *denotes a normal distribution with mean* $6\nu_i$, *and variance* $1\nu_i^2$, *so* $n(\frac{9}{2}, \frac{9}{16}) = n(6\nu_i, \nu_i^2)$ *where* $\nu_i = \frac{3}{4}$.

sense. Of course $\nu_i G_i$ is simply a multiplicative effect; but it is intended to reflect an interaction in a more biological sense.

Now consider the interpretation of the random variable I. I reflects those characteristics displayed at birth and in early development that are to a large extent influenced by innate biological factors. Physical characteristics including birth length are examples. Behavioral examples include the complex coordinated reflexive involuntary swimming responses (McGraw, 1943). Gradually, with brain development and experience, such involuntary reflexes give way later in the first year to more learned swimming responses. For Piaget, early reflexive responses define intelligence. It is the modification of these reflexes by learning and maturation that signals for Piaget maturing sensorimotor intelligence.

Within the context of the model of Eq. (2), these changes are assumed to reflect the increasingly important role of $\nu_i G_i$ relative to I. Initially at birth and in the early months of development, I is more important than $\nu_i G_i$; later the reverse is true. The particular value of I each individual takes on is assumed to reflect largely biologically determined components. It is the variability of I, σ_I^2, that reflects this individual variation. For example, if i denotes the first month and j the tenth year, first-month variability in height is largely variability determined by σ_I^2, and $\nu_i^2 \sigma^2$ is assumed to be small. Similarly, variability in sensorimotor intelligence is viewed as being represented largely as σ_I^2. However, variability of concrete operational intelligence and variability of height at 10 years is likely to be negligibly determined by variability in I, so $\nu_j^2 \sigma^2$ dominates σ_I^2. Thus, early in life σ_I^2 is much larger than $\nu_i^2 \sigma^2$ but, beyond infancy, it is likely that $\nu_j^2 \sigma^2$ is very much larger than σ_I^2. The expectation of I, $E(I) = \tau$, would be a positive constant because it is a major component of for example average neonatal birth length.[6]

[6] In an effort to focus on the substantive components of Eq. (2), an error random variable is not parameterized. A discussion of how error might be viewed appears below.

The empirical justification for the above scenario will be clearer following a more formal consideration of Eq. (2). The expectation of Eq. (2) is

$$\mu_{x_i} = \nu_i \mu + \tau, \tag{3}$$

where typically all the parameters of Eq. (3) are positive.

The standard deviation of Eq. (2) is

$$\sigma_{x_i} = (\nu_i^2 \sigma^2 + 2\rho\nu_i\sigma\sigma_I + \sigma_I^2)^{1/2}, \tag{4}$$

where ρ denotes the correlation between G_i and I. The "working" component of Eq. (3) and Eq. (4) is ν_i. Regardless of the value of the remaining parameters the components, $\nu_i\mu$ and $\nu_i^2\sigma^2$ become increasingly important as ν_i increases. Now the mean and standard deviation are conceptually linked in the model of Eq. (2) through the growth parameter ν_i. Solving for ν_i in Eq. (3) gives $\nu_i = (\mu_{x_i} - \tau)/\mu$ which can replace ν_i in Eq. (4). Then letting $d = (\sigma/\mu)(\mu_{x_i} - \tau)$, the standard deviation of X_i may be written as

$$\sigma_{x_i} = (d^2 + 2d\rho\sigma_I + \sigma_I^2)^{1/2}. \tag{5}$$

Note that $\sigma_{x_i}^2$ is quadratic in d.

Equation (5), it is proposed, is the equation that functionally relates the parameter means μ_{x_i} and standard deviations σ_{x_i} and that underlies the many observed sample mean and sample standard deviation covariations.

Let us assume that σ_{x_i} and μ_{x_i} in Eq. (5) may be regarded in reality as being continuous variables, which is equivalent to viewing growth as a continuous process with the point-value parameters at each age being but convenient approximations to reality. Assume further that the first two derivatives of σ_x with respect to μ_x exist (the index i is suppressed to denote continuity). Then, an examination of these derivatives will reveal, together with Figure 3.4, how the function graphs and thus will allow for a comparison between model and data. Note that the only components in Eq. (5) that change with age are σ_x and μ_x.

The first derivative test implies that when:

$$\rho > -d/\sigma_I, \qquad \sigma_x \text{ increases as } \mu_x \text{ increases,}$$

and when

$$\rho < -d/\sigma_I, \qquad \sigma_x \text{ decreases as } \mu_x \text{ increases.} \tag{6}$$

Here $\tau \geq 0$ and all other parameters are assumed to be positive. Thus, for a range of values of ρ, σ_x in Eq. (5) increases as μ_x increases. σ_x is minimum when $\rho = -d/\sigma_I$ or equivalently when $d + \rho\sigma_I = 0$. The second derivative of Eq. (5) is positive when $|\rho| < 1$, which is true unless I and G_i are perfectly correlated. This fact reveals that σ_x graphed against μ_x will be concave upward. From inequalities (6) it is clear that there is a point in Eq. (5) where σ_x is minimum. Consider where this minimum

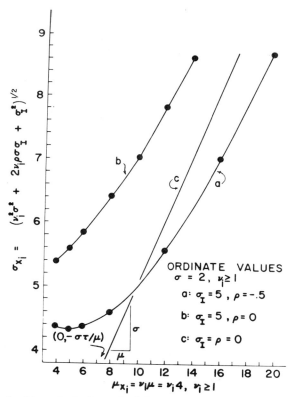

FIGURE 3.4. *Graph of hypothetical standard deviation and mean parameters for three cases based on the model of Eq. (2). Function shown is Eq. (5) which is identically Eq. (4) against Eq. (3), with parameters and curves as specified for a, b and c. τ is assumed to be zero.*

is likely to be located. Suppose ρ is negative such that $\rho < -d/\sigma_I < 0$. Since $\mu_x - \tau = \nu\mu > 0$, $\mu_x - \tau$ is always positive. With growth, $\mu_x - \tau$ must become larger. Now $\mu_x - \tau$ can be a small positive number but only when μ_x is small. In the case of height, for example, μ_x is smallest at birth. If $\rho < -d/\sigma_I < 0$, σ_x will initially decrease as μ_x increases, ultimately achieving a minimum. Further increases in μ_x will cause the inequality to reverse making $\rho > -d/\sigma_I$; thus, σ_x will increase with additional increases in μ_x. Figure 3.4, curve a, illustrates this trend.

The preceding discussion thus provides a possible explanation for the initial decrease in standard deviations observed in mental test and height data, Figure 3.2b and c. The model cannot account for the more complicated N-shaped function in Figure 3.2a nor can it account for decreases in observed standard deviations shown in later adolescence, as seen for example in mental growth and height data. It is not critical to argue that $\rho < -d/\sigma_I$; rather, it is simply noted that with this assumption, the model of Eq. (2) can account for an interesting characteristic of data. It should be noted that even if $\rho < -d/\sigma_I$, the theory does not imply that the correlations among the same individuals measured at different age points will be negative.

A consistently observed feature of growth data is that, through the growth years, the standard deviations graph concave upward and are increasing against the means. Quetelet's data for height (where range is the measure of spread) in Figure 3.1, and other physical and intellectual growth data shown in Figures 3.2b and c reveal this pattern. Thus, it would seem important that the proposed model be consistent with this empirical fact. As noted earlier, σ_x against μ_x is precisely of this form for all $|\rho| < 1$, so the model accounts well for this feature of the data. In Figure 3.4, curves a and b show this curvature for hypothetical model parameter values. Finally, if the variance of I is regarded as negligible but I has constant influence τ, then σ_x of Eq. (5) is linearly related to μ_x as Figure 3.4, curve c illustrates.

The preceding graphic development may naturally suggest a regression approach to the problem of parameter estimation. This possibility will be briefly considered here because it will be possible at the same time to suggest some model simplifications.

Focusing attention on the growth years after infancy, a linear relation between the means and standard deviations might be a reasonable first approximation. For many of the data sets, the mean and standard-deviation correlation coefficients are already close to 1, and as Figure 3.2 suggests, a straight line might describe some of the data rather well, at least for some growth periods during the childhood years.

The primary component of Eq. (5) which makes the function nonlinear is σ_I^2. In fact, the degree of concavity observed in the data may well reflect the size of the unknown constant variance σ_I^2. For example, if σ_I^2 is large s_i against $\bar{x}_i$ will be quite concave, while if it is negligible so that it may be assumed to be zero, then $\rho = 0$, and the mean and standard–deviation parameters are linearly related as noted previously. With $\sigma_I^2 = 0$, the model of Eq. (2) could be reduced to

$$X_i = \nu_i G_i + \tau, \tag{7}$$

where I is assumed to have constant influence τ. Similarily, Eq. (5) becomes

$$\sigma_{x_i} = d = (\sigma/\mu)\mu_{x_i} - \sigma\tau/\mu. \tag{8}$$

Given that Eq. (7) seems reasonable, it is tempting to estimate σ/μ and τ by regressing s_i on $\bar{x}_i$. The slope coefficient estimates σ/μ, and $-\tau$ is estimated by the intercept divided by the slope. However, the usual linear regression theory collapses here, so caution is necessary. For one, the predictor variables in standard regression models are fixed constants.

Here they are observations on random variables. For another, the joint distribution of the set of pairs $(\overline{X}_i, S_i)$ is not known; worse, the pairs are not even identically distributed. All may not be lost, however. Perhaps forming the regression of s_i on the $\bar{x}_i$, then $\bar{x}_i$ on the s_i, and then averaging the appropriate estimates may be more sensible.

Consider again the ν_i growth parameters which were literally parameterized out of existence in Eq. (5), and consider again the full model of Eq. (2). Return, too, to a view of growth which says that at each age, ν_i may be regarded as a fixed parameter. Here the goal is to explore the expectation of $R(\overline{X}_i, S_i)$ under the model of Eq. (2). Suppose $\mu_{x_i} < \mu_{x_j}$; this condition implies $\nu_i < \nu_j$ and it can be shown that this result implies $[\mathrm{Var}(X_i)]^{1/2} < [\mathrm{Var}(X_j)]^{1/2}$ when $\rho \geq 0 > - \sigma(\nu_i + \nu_j) (2\sigma_I)^{-1}$. Thus, not surprisingly, for the means and standard deviations to be properly ordered requires a condition that can be defined on ρ and that is also implied by the condition $\rho > - d/\sigma_I$ of Eq. (6). Thus, a perfect Spearman *rank order* correlation is assured on the pairs $(\mu_{x_i}, \sigma_{x_i})$ when the condition on ρ holds for all pairs i and j. Now let the sample pairs $(\bar{x}_i, s_i)$ replace their parameter values; then by Chebyschev's theorem (e.g., Cramér, 1946, p. 253), each sample statistic converges in probability to its parameter value as sample size becomes large. Thus, the *rank order* correlation between sample means and sample standard deviations will be 1 in the limit under the model of Eq. (2) provided the condition on ρ, noted above, holds. Figure 3.4, curves a and b intuitively suggest that even if the set of parameter pairs μ_{x_i} and σ_{x_i} are perfectly rank ordered, the product–moment correlation computed on the parameter pairs should be bounded away from 1 by an amount that depends on the size of σ_I^2. (This is based on the fact that σ_I^2 induces curvature in the graph and the pairs μ_{x_i} and σ_{x_i} are linearly related only when σ_I^2 is zero [if $|\rho| < 1$].) This intuition is correct. Under the model of Eq. (2), $E[R(\overline{X}_i, S_i)] > 0$ given certain normality assumptions and that the condition on ρ holds. So a point-value expectation cannot be given for the model of Eq. (2) unless unknown parameters are specified. However, it is important to observe and easy to show that $R(\overline{X}_i, S_i)$ converges in probability to 1 as sample size at each age point i increases and as σ_I^2 approaches zero.

These results have some practical implications for using data to evaluate models. First, if the sample size at each age is moderately large, any rank-order correlation computed from the sample means and standard deviations should be large. If it is not, the proposed model in Eq. (2) is invalidated. Second, if the computed product–moment correlation among the m sample pairs is high, and particularly when an interval constructed around $r(\bar{x}_i, s_i)$ using $\pm 2(m - 1)^{1/2}$ does not cover zero, the models underlying analysis of variance may be rejected. Third, a positive correlation which is too high to be consistent with ANOVA models but which departs substantially from one suggests that under Eq. (2), a constant variance term, σ_I^2, (which might also reflect an error component) is large and should not be ignored.

Estimating Parameters

Let $\beta = \sigma/\mu$. Then from the simple model $X_i = \nu_i G_i$ can be written $\beta\mu_{x_i} = \sigma_{x_i}$, where β is called the coefficient of variation. A number of papers have been concerned with estimating σ and μ under similar models (see, e.g., Gleser and Healy's, 1976). One might hope that the research literature would offer some leverage for the problem of estimating the parameters of Eq. (2), all of which are unknown. But unfortunately this does not appear to be the case. Progress within these frameworks requires β to be known (see also Khan, 1968), and there is little help for the problem of estimating ν_i, the most interesting parameter.

It should come as no surprise that the estimation problem for models of the form of Eq. (2) is no picnic. Even in "simple" cases where there are three independent, equally sized samples from random variables distributed as $n(\nu_i\mu, \nu_i^2\sigma^2)$, $i = 1, 2, 3$, all parameters unknown, a conventional maximum likelihood approach appears to yield no simple solution. Properties often associated with maximum likelihood solutions, such as uniqueness, are no longer achievable. So, as a general approach, maximum likelihood estimation appears, unhappily, to have little to recommend it.

The general estimation strategy has been a varied one. For instance, for some parameters, maximum likelihood estimates have been obtained under closely related distributions that would follow from similar models, with least squares approaches being used to estimate the remaining parameters.

To illustrate the approach assume the model of Eq. (7), which is $X_i = \nu_i G_i + \tau$, and has one random variable, G_i. The parameters to be estimated are ν_i, μ, τ, and σ. Assume X_i is normal, so there are n_i observations from distributions $i = 1, 2, \ldots, m$ of the form $n(\nu_i\mu + \tau, \nu_i^2\sigma^2)$. A standard piece of theory is that for each sample the maximum likelihood estimates of $\nu_i\mu + \tau$ and $\nu_i\sigma$ are $\bar{x}_i$ and s_i, respectively. The desired estimates will be functions of these statistics.

Intuition would suggest the ratio s_1/s_2 would estimate ν_1/ν_2, since $\nu_1\sigma/\nu_2\sigma = \nu_1/\nu_2$. In fact, this ratio is a solution to the likelihood equations for samples from $n(\mu_i, \nu_i^2\sigma^2)$, $i = 1, 2$, and similarly for the more general case. For the situation at hand, this distribution is the closely related one. Since, for any pair, s_i/s_j will estimate the ratio ν_i/ν_j it is convenient to express the desired ratios in terms of a common value. One possibility is to select the smallest sample standard deviation. Let $\min(s_i, i = 1, \ldots, m) = \min s$. Often $s_1 = \min s$. Then define

$$r_i = s_i/\min s, \qquad i = 1, 2, \ldots, m. \qquad (9)$$

Thus, $r_i \geq 1$ is an estimate of ν_i scaled by a positive multiplicative constant. Suppose $\min s = s_k$. Then let s_k be taken as an estimate of σ, with the estimate denoted σ^*, where $\nu_k = 1$. Next, define

$$Q = \Sigma(\bar{x}_i - \nu_i\mu - \tau)^2,$$

and solve $\partial Q/\partial\mu$, $\partial Q/\partial\tau$ in terms of $\bar{x}_i$ and ν_i. Then

$$\hat{\tau} = \frac{(\Sigma\nu_i)(\Sigma\nu_i\bar{x}_i) - (\Sigma\nu_i{}^2)(\Sigma\bar{x}_i)}{(\Sigma\nu_i)^2 - m\Sigma\nu_i{}^2} \qquad (10)$$

and

$$\hat{\mu} = (\Sigma\bar{x}_i - m\hat{\tau})/\Sigma\nu_i \qquad (11)$$

are least squares estimates of τ and μ with ν_i known. Define estimate $\bar{\tau}$ as Eq. (10) but where r_i replaces ν_i. And define estimate μ^* as Eq. (11) where $\bar{\tau}$ and r_i replace $\hat{\tau}$ and ν_i.

The estimates of σ^* and μ^* are unique within a multiplicative constant, and both are dependent on the choice of $\min s$. Another way of viewing σ^* and μ^* is to say that for some $\nu_k\sigma$ and $\nu_k\mu$, set $\nu_k = 1$ so that the population parameters σ and μ are taken as these values. Then the population parameters $\nu_i\sigma$ and $\nu_i\mu$ at each of the varying ages are viewed as products involving the age k constants. Lack of uniqueness except within a multiplicative constant is not a happy situation. It seems common in models like Eq. (2) and Eq. (7), which have multiplicative structures, to obtain ratio estimates that often lack uniqueness. In practical applications this problem may not be too serious, since all estimates can be easily rescaled if desired. Note that $\bar{\tau}$ is, however, not dependent on the choice of $\min s$. This fact is easily seen by replacing r_i for each ν_i in Eq. (10).

This simple approach to estimation appears in simulation studies to be quite satisfactory when sample size at each age is moderate, about 30 or so. Since the procedure utilizes sample means and standard deviations, estimates under the model of Eq. (7) can be produced from published statistics with little additional computation. Furthermore, a partial check on the adequacy of the model can be obtained by computing

$$m^{-1}\Sigma(\bar{x}_i - r_i\mu^* - \bar{\tau})^2, \qquad (12)$$

which measures the average squared deviations of the estimated values from the observed values. This average is independent of the choice of the scaling constant $\min s$ from Eq. (9). If the model of Eq. (7) is appropriate, certainly the number from Eq. (12) should be small.

To illustrate the procedure, consider again Denney and Moulton's (1976) study and focus on their 3-, 4-, and 5-year-old age groups. For their functional concept category data (letting subscripts denote age groups), $r_3 = 1, r_4 = 1.96, r_5 = 4.53, \bar{\tau} = -.449, \mu^* = .65, \sigma^* = .75 = s_3$. The average of the summed residuals defined by Eq. (12) was .0014, which suggests a good fit of the model to the data, and the model of Eq. (7) fit quite well for their remaining five data sets. The r_i values may be viewed as growth rate parameter estimates, which suggests that the magnitude of change for the function concept category performance between 4 and 5 years is much more rapid than between 3 and 4 years. Growth for some other categories is quite different. For example, $r_3 = 1.06, r_4 = 1$, and $r_5 = 1.40$ for their perceptible concept category. The τ estimate seems best viewed, in these data, as a measurement constant, in much the same way, the grand mean in analysis of variance may be so viewed.

In data under the models of Eqs. (2) and (7), the sample means and sample standard deviations may not be perfectly rank ordered, owing to variability of the estimators. Since the estimates of r_i are defined by the sample standard deviations alone, it is from the ordering of the standard deviations that primary information about growth processes is inferred, and not from the sample means, as is typically the case. There is safety in proceeding this way. It is interesting to observe that 95% confidence intervals about σ_{x_i} are shorter than confidence intervals about μ_{x_i} in the normal case, for $n \geq 4$, which can be revealed by constructing the intervals.[7] (For a discussion of these constructions, see Johnson and Kotz, 1970, p. 66).

General Discussion

George E. P. Box (1976) has reminded us that our conceptual models of phenomena are at best only approximations of reality. Life being as it is, the best that might be hoped for is that the models guiding our thinking will not lead us far astray.

Developmental psychology is as healthy as it is in part because many of the questions we wish to answer have to do with orderings. For example, does the development of mass conservation precede weight conservation? Is the left side of the infant's brain more sensitive to speech sounds than the right side? Is, as Denney and Moulton (1976) asked, functional category usage by 5-year-olds greater than that by 3-year-

---

[7] Let $L(\mu)$ and $L'(\sigma)$ denote the lengths of the 95% confidence intervals for μ and σ. Then $L(\mu) = 2st(n - 1, .025)/(n - 1)^{1/2}$ and $L'(\sigma) = n^{1/2}s\{[\chi^2(n - 1, .975)]^{-1/2} - [\chi^2(n - 1, .025)]^{-1/2}\}$, where $t(\cdot)$ and $\chi^2(\cdot)$ are the corresponding t and x^2 distribution cutting points. Then $L(\mu) > L'(\sigma)$ when $n \geq 4$.

olds? If we are willing to regard as evidence that A precedes (or dominates, is more useful than, etc.) B as equivalent to an ordering of means
say $\mu_A < \mu_B$, it may make little difference how our theory of growth
characterizes such orderings as having come about. Thus, it might be
that $\mu_A + \alpha = \mu_B$, or $2 \log \mu_A = \log \mu_B$. Since for any distribution, the
sample mean is an unbiased estimate, our simple test can be

A precedes B if and only if $\bar{x}_A < \bar{x}_B$.

If the number of observations is moderately large, our simple decision
rule will be the correct one most of the time. Although not stated in this
way, many of the earlier (e.g., Barker, Kounin, & Wright, 1943) and
more recent research issues can often be reduced to these terms. The
order question pervades Piaget's theory and is in part the reason for our
recent preoccupation with it. For many order questions there may be
little reason to do differently what has been done for years.

   If, however, a goal is to construct theories that attempt to unravel the
structural basis of the growth process and perhaps push us a bit closer
to answering Anastasi's (1958) question of how certain factors affect
growth, the model structure through which our quesses are made will
likely be taxed when required to produce such inferences. We must
therefore be more alert to model difficulties.

   The proposed theory does suggest a different viewpoint regarding
growth. It can also provide a different and possibly useful orientation to
certain situations, as the following three examples attempt to illustrate.

Interaction

   Consider groups of children denoted as c_p, $p = 1,2$, and treatment
conditions d_q, $q = 1,2$. The group differences might be sex differences
and the treatments might be experimental manipulations or measurements at two age points. Suppose the four observed means were

	d_1	d_2
c_1	2	4
c_2	3	6.

For simplicity, assume the sample values coincide with their parameter
points. It is natural to "think interaction" when viewing the above
values since neither the columns nor the rows differ by an additive constant. Assume a conventional linear model analysis of variance structure with normally distributed errors with zero means. The expectation
for such a model would be

$$\mu_{pq} = \mu + \alpha_p + \beta_q + \gamma_{pq}, \tag{13}$$

where α_p, β_q and γ_{pq} denote the row, column, and cell interaction effects, and μ is the grand mean. The corresponding estimates are, respectively, for one cell $\mu_{11} = 2 = 3.75 - .75 - 1.25 + .25$, and the μ estimate is chosen so that the estimates of $\Sigma\alpha_p = \Sigma\beta_q = \Sigma\gamma_{pq} = 0$.

Usually, little interest is paid to the corresponding cell standard deviations; if $r(s_i, \bar{x}_i)$ for the four pairs is negligible, conventional additive theory would not be rejected and would probably provide a quite plausible characterization. Suppose (for simplicity) the sample standard deviations coincided with the corresponding means. Then $r(s_i, \bar{x}_i) = 1$ suggesting that the conventional model structure underlying the expectation, Eq. (13) is the wrong model.

When these data are viewed within the framework of the model of Eq. (7), there is a choice. If it seemed sensible to obtain a single μ^* and $\bar{\tau}$ from the four samples, this could be done. On the other hand, if c_1 were boys and c_2 were girls measured at two ages d_1 and d_2, it might be more sensible to represent sex differences in the μ parameter. Then μ^* for boys would be 2, and for girls it would be 3. The growth rate parameter indexed by r would be 1 for age d_1 and 2 for age d_2, and $\bar{\tau} = 0$.

This approach yields a different view of the group–treatment effects. There is no interaction in the conventional sense because there is no departure from additivity of the group and treatment effects to worry about. It is the value of each individual's score on G that is multiplied by the v_i growth parameter that represents the individual–treatment interaction. In this sense there is always an interaction in the proposed theory.

It is important to note that the issue is not simply one of removing an additive interaction; it is a question of how treatment effects on individuals are to be viewed. If the goal is simply to remove an additive interaction and perhaps at the same time alter $r(\bar{x}_i, s_i)$, certainly Tukey (1977) has the techniques for doing just that. But to proceed in this way implies a desire to maintain a view that growth is an additive affair. Clearly there are many times when additivity is a very sensible viewpoint, but a hint is provided about its sensibility when $r(\bar{x}_i, s_i)$ is examined.

Correlational Analyses

Suppose, for instance, the task is to estimate the correlation coefficient parameter between heights of fraternal twins—an apparently simple problem. Pairs of twins are measured; either the Pearson or intraclass coefficient is computed to provide an estimate of the unknown correlation parameter. As Kowalski (1972) has demonstrated, it is important to assume the observations have been sampled from a bivariate normal distribution. But there is a critical rub: The pairs of observations must be a random sample, which means that the observations must all come from the *same* bivariate normal density.

Suppose it is not possible to find in sufficient numbers same-aged pairs of twins, and instead $n/2$ 5-year-old pairs and $n/2$ 10-year-old pairs of twins are sampled. It is obvious that neither the height means nor height variances for these two age groups are the same, which implies the n pairs are not a random sample from the same bivariate normal density. What meaning would a computed correlation coefficient have when based on all n pairs? The question has no simple answer, as can be seen by examining the expectation of the sample covariance, the numerator of the sample correlation coefficient for a correlation computed from such data. This turns out to be

$$[((n - 1)/n) (\rho_{(X_1, Y_1)}\sigma_{X_1}\sigma_{Y_1} + \rho_{(X_2, Y_2)}\sigma_{X_2}\sigma_{Y_2})$$
$$+ (\tfrac{1}{2})(\mu_{X_1}\mu_{Y_1} + \mu_{X_2}\mu_{Y_2} - \mu_{X_2}\mu_{Y_1} - \mu_{X_1}\mu_{Y_2})]/2$$

where X_1, Y_1 and X_2, Y_2 denote the pairs of marginally normal random variables for each of the two age groups, and the subscripts on the parameters denote their corresponding marginal means and variances. The situation is not at all what we have come to expect; for example, depending on the marginal means and standard deviations the two bivariate correlations $\rho_{(.)}$ can vanish, but the expected covariance can be far from zero, which means that the expected value of the correlation coefficient can also be far from zero! With real data, the situation may be much more complicated than in this hypothetical example, and the implications for theory, heritability theory as one example, may be disturbing.

For example, it is common to use mental tests of monozygotic twins to estimate the heritability of IQ, given certain nature–nurture assumptions (Thomas, 1975). Such analyses presuppose that the twins so measured may be viewed as being samples from a common bivariate normal population, which suggests the twins when measured should be about the same age since IQ means and standard deviations like mental age score means and standard deviations may increase over age, as was noted earlier. An examination of the well-known twin studies indicates the twins have often not been of similar age when tested. Take, for example, the results of Newman, Freeman, and Holzinger (1937). Is it sensible to assume that twins Ruth and Betty, $12\tfrac{1}{2}$ years old, are from the same bivariate normal population as Gladys and Helen, 35 years old? Unless the answer is yes, and for all twin pairs varying in age from $11\tfrac{1}{2}$ to 59 years, it is not clear how the computed correlations should be interpreted.

In the statistical literature, this problem refers to sampling from contaminated distributions or from population mixtures. And the problem is generally difficult. To my knowledge it has not been considered in the statistical literature for the correlational problem. How serious it may be for developmental research is difficult to say without further study. But certainly it is common to combine children of different ages for purposes of computing a common correlation coefficient. The model proposed here, which might be denoted the ν-model, offers no solution to the problem; its role was largely in calling attention to what could be a problem that may have gone unrecognized before.

Racial Differences in Intelligence

Comparisons between black children and white children on standard intelligence tests have sometimes revealed that sample means and sample standard deviations for blacks are smaller than for whites (Kennedy, van de Riet, & White, 1963). Myriad explanations have been offered for such differences, but typically the differences considered refer to mean differences, and not standard deviation differences. So far as is known there has never been any explanation that accounts jointly for these mean and standard deviation differences. The ν-model does provide an accounting. For example, if the black mean is taken as 80, with standard deviation 12, and the white mean 100 with standard deviation 16 which, in round numbers, is what Kennedy $et\ al.$ (1963) reported, then under the model of Eq. (7) $\mu^* = 60$, $\bar{\tau} = 20$, $r_{\text{black}} = 1$, $r_{\text{white}} = 1.33$, and $\sigma^* = 12$, suggesting that differences in the ν_i parameters, as indexed by differences in r_i, distinguish between the groups. While the origin of the possible differences is not clear, this interpretation may help refocus the problem.

It is worth observing the conventional additive nature–nurture models (e.g., Jensen, 1969), within which black–white IQ differences are often viewed (e.g., Jensen, 1973), do not explicitly consider developmental processes. Thus, heritability and model parameters are viewed as age-invariant constants. It may well be that an understanding of the factors influencing intellectual growth will come about only when current age-static, nature–nurture models are replaced by models that explicitly consider growth processes.

Individual Growth Patterns and Between-Age Correlations

In longitudinal studies the pattern of between-age correlations for a variety of variables including height and intelligence has a structure familiar to any developmentalist; the more proximal the ages at which the observations occur the higher the correlations, and between-age correlations for tests equally spaced are higher for older children than for younger children (e.g., Bloom, 1964). Guttman (1954) has termed such patterns a simplex. So far as is known there has never been an entirely satisfactory explanation for such patterns. The most popular explanation is probably still Anderson's (1939) overlap hypothesis. But the fit of the overlap hypothesis to height data, for example, does not appear to be good (cf. Bloom, 1964, p. 28), a difficulty Anderson himself was first to recognize.

Within the ν-model such correlations can be accounted for by considering the correlations between G_i and G_j from the model of Eq. (7) at ages i and j, but this approach is hardly inspiring, and without considering other factors, it is not particularly interesting. I would guess these between-age correlations will be understood in a satisfactory way only after the growth patterns for different individuals are properly understood. So let us take a somewhat different approach by considering a related issue.

Let $x' = \nu_i g' + \tau$ and $x = \nu_i g + \tau$ be two observations on X_i under the model of Eq. (7). Here g' and g denote the corresonding values on G_i for the two observations. These might be, for example, heights or mental test scores of two children at some common age i. Without loss of generally, assume $\tau = 0$, since this constant simply carries through all that follows. Consider what a child's expected score at age j should be given his score at age i, $i < j$. Assume X_i and X_j and thus G_i and G_j and bivariate normal. The expected score at age j is

$$E(\nu_j G_j | \nu_i g) = \nu_j \mu + \rho_{G_{ij}} \nu_j (g - \mu), \tag{14}$$

and similarly for the second child. Here $\rho_{G_{ij}}$ denotes the correlation between G_i and G_j and is independent of ν_i and ν_j. Note in Eq. (14) that the amount of growth from i to j depends on the initial value of g or g' for each individual, provided $\rho_{G_{ij}} \neq 0$. Clearly under the model of Eq. (7) the increment from one age to the next is not a constant for all individuals. When will a child's expected score at age j be larger than at age i? Certainly it will be when $\rho_{G_{ij}} = 1$, and since $\nu_i < \nu_j$ then $\nu_i g < \nu_j g$. Less obvious perhaps is that if $\rho_{G_{ij}} > \nu_i / \nu_j > 0$ then the individual's expected score at age j will be larger than the score at age i, provided that g is positive.[8] That is,

$$\nu_i g < \nu_j \mu + \rho_{G_{ij}} \nu_j (g - \mu) = E(\nu_j G_j | \nu_i g). \tag{15}$$

Finally, consider how longitudinal growth curves for different individuals should appear under the ν-model of Eq. (7). It is common to observe that, with development, growth curves for different individuals

---

[8] (i) $0 < \nu_i / \nu_j < \rho_{G_{ij}} \Rightarrow \nu_i - \nu_j \rho_{G_{ij}} < 0 \Rightarrow g(\nu_i - \nu_j \rho_{G_{ij}}) < 0, \quad g > 0$.

   (ii) $0 \leq \nu_j \mu (1 - \rho_{G_{ij}}), \quad \nu_j \mu > 0$.

   (iii) From (i) and (ii), $g(\nu_i - \nu_j \rho_{G_{ij}}) < \nu_j \mu (1 - \rho_{G_{ij}})$ which when rearranged yields Eq. (15).

often spread apart or "fan out." Suppose for our two children at age i that $0 < x' < x$ or equivalently $0 < g' < g$, and $\rho_{G_{ij}} > \nu_i/\nu_j > 0$, so that each child's expected score at some older age j will be larger than for age i. Then with these conditions, it is true that

$$\nu_i g - \nu_i g' < E(\nu_j G_j \nu_i g) - E(\nu_j G_j | \nu_i g'). \tag{16}$$

Thus, the scores will be expected to "fan out." Equation (16) follows directly from Eqs. (14) and (15). Hence, the conditions sufficient for Eq. (15) to hold are sufficient for the "fan spread" hypothesis, represented in Eq. (16), to hold. This model implication can be tested in data, with $\rho_{G_{ij}}$ easily estimated from the between–age correlations. The prediction assumes the model of Eq. (7); if the prediction is falsified, a second random variable may need to be introduced as in the model of Eq. (2).

Some Remaining Problems

Many problems remain. Here I will note briefly those I view as most important.

To be useful in a broader context, the proposed model would need to be developed so that it can include more parameters and thus reflect the realities of a larger variety of situations in much the same way analysis of variance may be expanded. To do so increases the difficulty of the parameter estimation problem, but the problem does not seem unapproachable. Nor does the problem of testing hypotheses or setting confidence intervals seem impossible provided one stays within a normal theory framework.

Perhaps an ideal solution, if it could be achieved, would be to reformulate the ν-model within a rank theory framework. There are two important reasons for this suggestion. First, statistical models based on ranks have simplified assumptions compared to their normal theory or parametric versions as Lehmann (1975), among others, has been quick to point out. Thus, they are applicable to a wider variety of situations. Second, in developmental psychology particularly, observations are too often given arbitrary numerical assignments, assignments that are treated as if the numbers have additive properties. More realistically, the measurement structure is probably more ordinal than additive. As such, rank-based procedures may be more sensible from this standpoint as well.

In conventional analyses of variance models like Eq. (1), the random components E_i might, from a developmental psychological viewpoint, be more charitably regarded as individual differences random variables, since they probably reflect, in many studies, more real differences among people than observational or measurement errors. I have not explicitly considered the problem of how random error (which here means measurement or observational error) should be viewed since I wished to stress the importance of the more substantive model components. Some might prefer to view G_i in Eq. (7) as an error variable since it does, in real data, reflect any measurement and observational error components as well as real human differences.

If an additional random variable were parameterized to reflect measurement or observational errors, it is interesting to consider how it might be characterized. In many developmental studies of cognition, for example, older children typically receive more items than younger children, thus providing more opportunity for observational and judgmental errors. The implication of this fact is that observational error variance, as with organismic variance, may also increase with age. Even for something as easily measured as height, measurement variability may increase with age. My son, several years older and much taller than his younger sister, shows considerably more variation in his height when measured at varying times during the day. Part of the reason may be that with sleep the human body lengthens, and with activity it shortens—and for him, there is more to "grow" during the night and "shrink" during the day than for his sister. In any event, the typical assumption that errors are constant over age or treatment groups may, sometimes, be quite inappropriate.[9]

Although the discussion has viewed growth as a relatively gradual and continuous affair, there is little in the above development to restrict its application to certain processes viewed as more stage–like than continuous in character. For example, the estimation procedures should still be sensible ones for certain discrete processes. From a psychological standpoint, the critical issue is whether the particular growth process under consideration has changed so much in a qualitative sense as to preclude meaningful comparisons of the scalar values obtained at each stage or age. If so, the proposed v-model is clearly the wrong one.

Acknowledgments

I am most grateful to a number of colleagues who have provided helpful criticisms of an earlier version of this paper, but particular thanks should go to G. Pollicello, II and T. P. Hettmansperger.

References

Adams, W. J. *The life and times of the central limit theorem.* New York: Kaedmon, 1974.
Anastasi, A. Heredity, environment, and the question "How?" *Psychological Review,* 1958, 65, 197–208.

[9] An interesting historical discussion of how errors of observation were interpreted is provided by Adams (1974).

Anderson, J. E. The limitations of infant and preschool tests in the measurement of intelligence. *Journal of Psychology*, 1939, *8*, 351–379.

Anderson, N. H. On the quantification of Miller's conflict theory. *Psychological Review*, 1962, *69*, 400–414.

Anderson, T. W. *An introduction to multivariate statistical analysis.* New York: Wiley, 1958.

Baltes, P. B. Longitudinal and cross-sectional sequences in the study of age and generation effects. *Human Development*, 1968, *11*, 145–171.

Barker, R. G., Kounin, J. S., & Wright, H. F. (Eds.). *Child behavior and development: A course of representative studies.* New York: McGraw–Hill, 1943.

Bayley, N. Mental growth during the first three years. *Genetic Psychology Monographs*, 1933, *14*, 1–92.

Bayley, N. On the growth of intelligence. *American Psychologist*, 1955, *10*, 805–818.

Bayley, N. Comparisons of mental and motor test scores for ages 1–15 months by sex, birth order, race, geographical location, and education of parents. *Child Development*, 1965, *36*, 379–411.

Bloom, B. S. *Stability and change in human characteristics.* New York: Wiley, 1964.

Box, G. E. P. Science and statistics. *Journal of the American Statistical Association*, 1976, *71*, 791–799.

Cramér, H. *Mathematical methods of statistics.* Princeton, New Jersey: Princeton University Press, 1946.

Cureton, T. K. Improving the physical fitness of youth. *Monographs of the Society for Research in Child Development*, 1964, *29*, No. 4 (Serial No. 95).

Denney, D. R., & Moulton, P. A. Conceptual preferences among preschool children. *Developmental Psychology*, 1976, *12*, 509–513.

Ebert, E., & Simmons, K. The Brush Foundation Study of child growth and development I. Psychometric tests. *Monographs of the Society for Research in Child Development*, 1943, *8*, No. 2 (Serial No. 35).

Elkind, D. Ambiguous pictures for study of perceptual development and learning. *Child Development*, 1964, *35*, 1391–1396.

Fiawoo, D. K. Physical growth and social environment: A West African example. In E. Fuchs (Eds.), *Youth in a changing world: Cross-cultural perspectives on adolescence.* The Hague: Mouton, 1976. Pp. 79–92.

Gaito, J., & Wiley, D. E. Univariate analysis of variance procedures in the measurement of change. In C. W. Harris (Ed.) *Problems in measuring change.* Madison, Wisconsin: University of Wisconsin Press, 1963. Pp. 60–84.

Galton, F. *Natural inheritance.* New York: Macmillan, 1889.

Gleser, L. J., & Healy, J. D. Estimating the mean of a normal distribution with known coefficient of variation. *Journal of the American Statistical Association*, 1976, *71*, 977–981.

Grizzle, J. E., & Allen, D. M. Analysis of growth and dose response curves. *Biometrics*, 1969, *25*, 357–381.

Guttman, L. A new approach to factor analysis: The radex. In P. F. Lazarsfeld (Ed.), *Mathematical thinking in the social sciences.* Glencoe, Illinois: Free Press, 1954. Pp. 258–348.

Hölder, O. Die Axiome der Quantität und die Lehre vom Mass. *Berichte über Verhandlungen der Königlich Sächsischen Gesellschaft der Wissenschaften zu Leipzig, Mathematisch–Physische Classe*, 1901, *53*, 1–64.

Huber, P. J. *Robust statistical procedures.* Philadelphia: SIAM, 1977.

Jensen, A. R. How much can we boost IQ and scholastic achievement? *Harvard Education Review*, 1969, *39*, 1–123.

Jensen, A. R. *Educability and group differences.* New York: Harper & Row, 1973.

Johnson, N. L., & Kotz, S. *Distributions in statistics: Continuous univariate distributions —1.* Boston: Houghton Mifflin, 1970.

Jones, H. E., & Conrad, H. S. The growth and decline of intelligence: A study of a homogeneous group between the ages of ten and sixty. *Genetic Psychology Monographs*, 1933, *13*, 223–298.

Kennedy, W. A., & Linder, R. S. A normative study of the Goodenough Draw-a-Man Test on Southeastern Negro elementary school children. *Child Development*, 1964, *35*, 33–62.

Kennedy, W. A., van de Riet, V., & White, J. C., Jr. A normative sample of intelligence and achievement of Negro elementary school children in the Southeastern United States. *Monographs of the Society for Research in Child Development*, 1963, *28*, No. 6 (Serial No. 90).

Khan, R. A. A note on estimating the mean of a normal distribution with known coefficient of variation. *Journal of the American Statistical Association*, 1968, *63*, 1039–1041.

Kowalski, C. J. On the effects of non-normality on the distribution of the sample product–moment correlation coefficient. *Journal of the Royal Statistical Society* [Series C (Applied Statistics)], 1972, *21*, 1–12.

Laosa, L. M., Swartz, J. D., & Holtzman, W. H. Human figure drawings by normal children: A longitudinal study of perceptual–cognitive and personality development. *Developmental Psychology*, 1973, *8*, 350–356.

Lehmann, E. I. *Nonparametrics: Statistical methods based on ranks.* San Francisco: Holden-Day, 1975.

McGraw, M. B. *The neuromuscular maturation of the human infant.* New York: Columbia University Press, 1943.

Meredith, H. V. The rhythm of physical growth: A study of eighteen anthropometric measurements on Iowa City white males ranging in age between birth and eighteen years. *University of Iowa Studies in Child Welfare*, 1935, *11*, No. 3.

Morrison, D. F. *Multivariate statistical methods.* New York: McGraw Hill, 1967.

Newman, H. H., Freeman, F. N., & Holzinger, K. J. *Twins: A study of heredity and environment.* Chicago: University of Chicago Press, 1937.

Plackett, R. L. Models in the analysis of variance (with discussion). *Journal of the Royal Statistical Society* (Series B), 1960, *22*, 195–215.

Quetelet, L. A. J. *A treatise on man and the development of his faculties.* Gainesville, Florida: Scholars Facsimiles & Reprints, 1969. [Originally published in French in 1835 and in English in 1842.]

Santostefano, S., & Paley, E. Development of cognitive controls in children. *Child Development*, 1964, *35*, 939–949.

Schaie, K. W. A general model for the study of developmental problems. *Psychological Bulletin*, 1965, *64*, 92–107.

Schaie, K. W. Limitations on the generalizability of growth curves of intelligence. A reanalysis of some data from the Harvard Growth Study. *Human Development*, 1972, *15*, 141–152.

Simmons, K. The Brush Foundation study of child growth and development II. Physical growth and development. *Monographs of the Society for Research in Child Development*, 1944, *9*, No. 1 (Serial No. 37).

Sontag, L. W., Baker, C. T., & Nelson, V. L. Mental growth and personality development: A longitudinal study. *Monographs of the Society for Research in Child Development*, 1958, *23*, No. 2 (Serial No. 68).

Sternberg, S. Memory-scanning: Mental processes revealed by reaction–time experiments. *American Scientist*, 1969, *57*, 421–457.

Suppes, P., & Zinnes, J. L. Basic measurement theory. In R. D. Luce, R. R. Bush, & E. Galanter (Eds.), *Handbook of mathematical psychology.* Vol. 1. New York: Wiley, 1963. Pp. 1–76.

Thomas, H., & Jamison, W. On the acquisition of understanding that still water is horizontal. *Merrill–Palmer Quarterly*, 1975, *21*, 31–44.

Thomas, H. A model for interpreting genetic correlations with estimates of parameters. *Psychological Bulletin*, 1975, *82*, 711–719.

Thorndike, R. L. Intellectual status and intellectual growth. *Journal of Educational Psychology*, 1966, *57*, 121–127.

Thurstone, L. L. A method of scaling psychological and educational tests. *Journal of Educational Psychology*, 1925, *26*, 433–451.

Thurstone, L. L. The absolute zero in intelligence measurement. *Psychological Review*, 1928, *35*, 175–197.

Tukey, J. W. *Exploratory data analysis*. Reading, Massachusetts: Addison–Wesley, 1977.

Walker, H. J. *Studies in the history of statistical method*. Baltimore: Williams & Wilkins, 1931.

Wilson, R. S. Twins: Early mental development. *Science*, 1972, *175*, 914–917.

Witkin, H. A., Lewis, H. B., Hertzman, M., Machover, K., Meissner, P. B., & Wapner, S. *Personality through perception*. New York: Harper, 1954.

Wohlwill, J. F. *The study of behavioral development*. New York: Academic Press, 1973.

4

The Study of Cognitive Development through Causal Modeling with Qualitative Data[1]

P. M. BENTLER

Introduction

This chapter will review some recent developments in methods used to analyze qualitative data as they pertain to the study of cognitive development. Cognitive development can, of course, be studied with a variety of methodological tools: the safest, from an inferential point of view, being pure experimentation; hypothesis-testing via quantitative and qualitative methodologies applied to nonexperimental data representing a second-best, but still valuable, tool for theory testing; and exploratory data analysis of response–response relations representing the weakest form of investigation. Realizing full well the importance of moving toward true experimentation, particular attention is focused upon the more frequently encountered situation of nonexperimental data, and even here, where quantitative methodologies have been growing particularly rapidly, the discussion is limited to some observations on new developments for the analysis of nonquantitative data that seem to be quite promising to research on cognitive growth. Because of the importance of psychological theory to the methods to be discussed, these newer methodologies will be incorporated into the framework of construct validation and social science theory. Without such a framework, they seem to hold little promise for developmental psychology, and to the study of cognitive development in particular. After all, a fundamental interdependence exists between substantive social science

[1] This investigation was supported in part by a Research Scientist Development Award (KO1-DA00017) and a research grant (DA01070) from the U.S. Public Health Service.

theory, the theory of methodology and statistics, and empirical data: Each realizes its fullest potential by incorporating the best of the other. Substantive theory remains little more than speculation without sound data gathered in the context of an appropriate methodology to exploit both theory and data. Theoretical development in methodology, mathematical modeling, or statistics cannot rise above purely formal development, however elegant such development may be, without an important problem to tackle or without substantive theory to guide analyses of viable empirical data. And even the best empirical data cannot reveal its secrets without a scientist's careful attention to its inherent methodological and theoretical deficiencies as well as to its strengths.

The interrelations among theory, methodology, and data have been pointed out many times previously. In this chapter the theme is pursued in the context of construct validation, an idea developed by Cronbach and Meehl (1955). Construct validation refers to the scientific confirmation of tests and measures as indices of postulated attributes or qualities. I propose that construct validation can be operationalized and assessed by some recent developments in causal modeling. This newly developed set of methodological tools can help to foster and evaluate substantive theory as it is applied to appropriately gathered empirical data (Bentler, 1978).

While construct validation via causal modeling represents a potentially fruitful approach to a variety of empirical data, it is also relevant to the understanding of repeated measurements of data such as those that are encountered in the study of cognitive growth. In such research, one typically deals with multiple indicators of various important constructs, measured sequentially, to be understood in the context of various background or control variables. Meaningful analysis of the research data requires evaluating the causal influences of the background variables on the constructs at various time points, the effects of various constructs on each other, the effects of a construct on itself across time, as well as such potential effects as indicator errors correlated across time. Not all of these effects can as yet be studied with qualitative data. Repeated measurements automatically generate nonexperimental data, so that methods for drawing causal inferences from such data immediately become relevant to research on cognitive development. Although a variety of analytic strategies can be employed to deal with various aspects of such longitudinal data, the causal modeling approach allows the entire system to be analyzed simultaneously in the context of theory.

Before proceeding to explicate construct validation and how it can be operationalized, the roles of description and explanation in developmental research are reviewed. Next, the concept of construct validity is reviewed and a causal modeling approach to implement it is proposed. Some recent developments in the analysis of latent attribute models, prediction models, and multinomial response models are also described. Finally, the generality and scope of mathematical models as they interrelate with social science theory and data are discussed.

A short review of traditional thinking will create an appropriate perspective on what may reasonably be expected from the newer methods, as well as reinforce the virtues of some older ways when considered in relation to research goals. The belief that a new concept or procedure will have momentous impact, finally making social and behavioral research truly scientific in molds approved by philosophers of science or practitioners of the successful physical sciences, must be resisted. Seldom are such expectations realized. The concept of construct validity, for example, was heralded as a useful advance over previous concepts of validity (APA, 1954), but its novelty, usefulness, and clarity were soon considered controversial (e.g., Bechtold, 1959; Cronbach, 1971, pp. 480–484), and its potential contributions were reformulated (e.g., Campbell, 1960; Loevinger, 1957). Thus, I do not propose a revolutionary methodological panacea for the social sciences; rather, I suggest the importance of combining tried and novel methods according to the goals of an investigation.

Description and Explanation in Developmental Research

Describing a phenomenon or an effect is a task that generally precedes the theoretical understanding or explanation of the phenomenon or effect. In the earliest stages of investigation, the description itself may be quite crude and unsophisticated, using neither elegant research methods nor constructs in approaching the problem. Clinical observation might provide an important example of the initial stages of description. Adequate description, carried out with due regard for methodological issues such as sampling, measurement, artifacts, and the like, will generally replace unsystematic description, but even at this stage, substantive knowledge must be consulted for hypotheses or partial theories of the phenomenon. This consultation is necessary, at the very least, to define the domain of relevance of the phenomenon and to identify both variables that might be measured and environmental conditions that might be necessary to observing the phenomenon. Statistical methods that might be consulted are descriptive in nature, and statistical inference may be limited to the problem of drawing specialized parametric inferences about a subject population from the given sample.

Explanation of a phenomenon is a step further removed from description. Certainly, adequate description is a necessary precursor to the development of effective or useful explanations of the phenomenon. Explanation typically involves going beyond the data: drawing deductions from a model, making predictions based on prior experience and theory, and testing hypotheses. While it can be argued that complete and thorough description may suffice in some domains of inquiry (e.g., history, anatomy), the development of principles that can be applied to changing circumstances typically involves going beyond the data. Similar considerations make it obvious that there are levels of explanation, from simple, highly specific hypotheses that may have received thorough empirical support, to complex and elaborate theoretical systems that interrelate and explain numerous specific phenomena in various contexts. Certainly, explanation at any level represents an important goal of science.

The Role of Experimentation

An ideal method of going from description to explanation involves experimentally manipulating independent variables, randomly assigning subjects to treatment conditions, and observing the outcome on univariate or multivariate dependent variables. Through confirmation and rejection of hypotheses, true experiments provide the surest means to develop theory, since potentially confounding extraneous variables will, via randomization, be uncorrelated with treatment outcome in large samples (e.g., Fisher, 1935). Obviously there must be a continuous interchange between substantive theory and experimentation, for the choice of independent variables to be manipulated must be dictated by substantive knowledge; similarly, the choice of appropriate dependent variables depends upon substantive theory and prior empirical results. As model building proceeds through a variety of manipulations and observations of effects, substantive theory can gain in effectiveness and range.

It is possible for substantive theory to play a relatively minor role in experimentation when rather arbitrary values are chosen for independent variables and when only single dependent variables are measured. In such simple univariate analysis of variance situations, the role of theory may be limited to defining the manipulations and the relevance of a given observed dependent variable to that manipulation. Because of the inherent virtues of the experimental method, any relation between independent and dependent variables will become empirically verified or disconfirmed, thus providing an impetus to the revision of substantive theory if wrong and confirmation of theory, if right. When several independent variables have been manipulated simultaneously, their interaction can be investigated by exploratory means even in the absence of theory, but theory can focus upon the relevant analyses to the exclusion of the irrelevant ones.

There is of necessity a stronger interrelationship between theory and empirical data via quantitative techniques when experimentation is concerned either with the manipulation of variables that are themselves parametrized and embedded within a theory, or with the measurement of multiple dependent variables. In such situations there must be a greater reliance on theory to develop the data-analytic strategy. The data provide feedback for the modification and further development of theory. Thus, with dozens of dependent variables in an experiment, it will be desirable to develop a model of the relationship of these variables to the constructs being experimentally modified in the experiment, since it is unlikely that the variables will reflect the treatment equally.

In the area of cognitive development, unfortunately, true experimentation cannot always be implemented. Consequently, moving from description to explanation remains difficult at best. A large class of data that are obtained is nonexperimental in nature, obtained perhaps under a variety of nonexperimental conditions.

Causal Inferences from Nonexperimental Data

Every researcher who has studied methodology in science or statistical methods has learned that correlation does not imply causation. Are there any methods for making causal statements from associative, correlational data? The specific idea of analyzing causation by analysis of correlations was introduced years ago via path analysis (Wright, 1921), but the best single general source on inference in nonexperimental research remains the work of Campbell and Stanley (1963), who discuss a variety of alternative quasi-experimental designs for data gathering as well as their associated strengths and weaknesses. Clearly, different data-gathering methods will yield results with different attributes, and none approaches the virtues of the true experiment. The possibilities for alternative explanations of given results are immense in naturalistic settings, since confounding cannot be unraveled through control variables when there is an absence of theory and knowledge of sampling conditions. There is no point to repeating the Campbell–Stanley discussion here, although it should be noted that the literature on nonexperimental designs is growing rapidly (e.g., Cook & Campbell, 1976; Kenny, 1975; Linn & Werts, 1977).

It is often stated that the associational nature of correlational data, being concerned with the measurement of response–response interrelations rather than stimulus–response relationships (Bergmann &

Spence, 1944), is its fatal flaw. However, it can be proposed that there is a different, but equally severe problem with nonexperimental techniques as traditionally developed: They are simply descriptive and exploratory in nature rather than hypothesis-testing or confirmatory. Although it is possible to test hypotheses about population values of observed correlations, or sets of such correlations with quantitative data (e.g., Larzelere & Mulaik, 1977), for example, such tests are only rarely incorporated into a reasonably developed theoretical framework, and the information gleaned from such simple tests represents a rather minor improvement beyond the data themselves. Correlational results, like psychological tests, are hardly ever used as instruments of social science theory (e.g., Loevinger, 1957; Underwood, 1975). This is not a necessary state of affairs, and it is changing.

Methodologists have recently introduced mathematical models and methods of statistical analysis, such as causal modeling, which have made it possible to test relatively complex theories that could be actualized in nonexperimental data. For introductory discussions of causal modeling, see Duncan (1975), Heise (1975), Kenny (1979), or Bentler (1980a). The most widely known among hypothesis-testing models for quantitative data is Jöreskog's (1977) LISREL model, which is a special case of Bentler's (1976a) general structural model (see Bentler & Woodward, 1978, for a proof as well as an illustration with Head Start data). Interrelations among a variety of models for quantitative data are given by Bentler and Weeks (1979), who also introduce a simple, general model. Hypothesis-testing models of a quite different sort are being developed for qualitative data, as will be shown later. Nonexperimental data can be inspected with these techniques to determine if they are consistent with a given theory, or whether the theory must be inadequate, given the data. While there is no methodology for proving a theory to be correct, and while multiple theories may equally well describe the data, an incorrect theory can be rejected if the data logically (theoretically) provide a reasonable test of the theory.

In the ideal situation, correlational data as well as experimental data would be relevant to the building and testing of substantive theory. However, despite Cronbach's (1957) two-decade-old plea for the integration of these two "disciplines," their integration remains a task for the future (Cronbach, 1975). It seems that the methodology for integration may finally be developing in the form of nonexperimental hypothesis-testing procedures about data structures.

The Role of Longitudinal Methods

In the absence of true experimentation, researchers have turned to longitudinal methods in an attempt to eliminate certain explanations for given data. In contrast to cross-sectional research, longitudinal research involves the passage of time, and since Western philosophy has almost universally agreed that causal processes must work forward in time, not backward, time-dependent events can help to eliminate otherwise plausible explanations of data. Of course, longitudinal research is a natural component of developmental psychology.

While repeated measurement of a set of subjects provides potentially important information that simply cannot be obtained any other way (namely, intraindividual change and individual differences therein, or information about the stability of attributes) and while it eliminates potential bias problems associated with retrospective recall, simple longitudinal designs—without appropriate control groups—leave much to be desired in the way of internal and external validity (e.g., Labouvie, 1976; Labouvie, Bartsch, Nesselroade, & Baltes, 1974). Even with such controls, implicit assumptions regarding relevant a priori substantive knowledge are required, assumptions whose utilization may make causal interpretation rest upon a shaky base. For example, in order to obtain a reasonable causal model to test longitudinally, one must be measuring all relevant causal variables and be assessing their effects at appropriate rather than arbitrary times (e.g., Heise, 1975). One must know the causal lag (i.e., the time required for an influence to occur) quite accurately. As Davis (1976) states, "If weather influences one's mood, the influence probably occurs the same day; but if a college degree influences income, the effect cannot be detected the evening of Commencement [p. 3]." Substantive theory is clearly called for, but even reasonably well-developed theory may be unable to exclude alternative explanations as reasonable. Of course, longitudinal research itself may be necessary to help determine the information on lag time that may be required for effective use of longitudinal methods (i.e., use that increases the scope and power of a substantive theory).

The Role of Causal Modeling

The phrase "causal modeling" is used here as a shorthand to denote hypothesis testing in the context of the analysis of an entire system of nonexperimental data. The word "modeling" refers to the fact that the data analysis will have to be guided by theoretical specification, and the word "causal" refers to the fact that such a specification is typically intended to explain, rather than describe, the data. The causal model, in essence, serves as a guide to data analysis of a rather complete sort; for example, the interrelations among all variables are accounted for (rather than searching for a few significant associations, as in typical data analysis). In this context, of course, lack of association can be as meaningful as association.

Causal modeling cannot be applied easily to domains of inquiry that are still purely descriptive in nature and whose research has not progressed beyond data exploration. Some preliminary theory building, of a sort potentially translatable into testable propositions, must exist.

When substantive theory can be translated into an appropriate mathematical model and reasonable assumptions can be made regarding measurement level and distributions of the variables, strict model evaluation through hypothesis-testing statistical procedures is made possible. Substantive theory or prior model building must have developed to the point that explicit expectations regarding the data can be formulated, and null hypotheses tested. In the ideal case, competing models and explanations would be pitted against each other regarding their ability to explain the very same data. The "crucial experiment" idea represents this concept: One theory will receive support, the others will be rejected. However, social science seems to have great difficulty in formulating theories that are sufficiently explicit to yield contradictory predictions that can be tested in given situations.

In the absence of competing models, the adequacy of a given model might be evaluated by its ability to account for a significant amount of variance in some dependent variable. This might be exemplified by a significantly nonzero multiple correlation coefficient or discriminant function, for example. A more stringent test of a model might lie in the use of specific coefficients (such as beta weights) in a statistical method, with verification of reliable prediction. A still more stringent test of a model would lie in its ability to account for essentially all of the relevant data. This is the goal of causal modeling. It might be noted that the goal here is often not one of rejecting a null hypothesis, but rather accepting it; then the model is plausible, since it cannot be rejected. Of course, as in traditional methods of statistical hypothesis-testing, if a given model does not fit the data, the model would be rejected as inadequate. See Bentler (1980a), Bentler and Bonett (in press), and Zahn and Fein (1979) for further discussion of goodness of fit and statistical hypothesis-testing in models for quantitative and qualitative data.

A Causal Modeling Approach to Construct Validation

The idea of construct validation, as introduced by Cronbach and Meehl (1955), represented an attempt to broaden the conceptualization of the validation process for psychological tests and measures. Cronbach and Meehl proposed that measurement instruments would have to be evaluated with regard to such data as group differences, correlational results, evidence on the internal structure of measures, studies of change over occasion, and studies of process. In addition, since instruments are typically designed to reflect a given construct, or postulated attribute, whose meaning must be determined according to its relationship to other theoretical constructs and observable variables, construct validation was construed to represent a process of a continuing sort that would ultimately tie down the given construct in a more complete "nomological network." The construct validation concept provided a useful antidote to the simplistic view of validation as represented by a correlation coefficient. It reinforced the importance of separating statements about theoretical relationships from statements about measurement operations. This very same distinction was to be picked up years later in the causal modeling literature, without any reference to the important prior history of this idea.

Cronbach and Meehl (1955) did not provide a formal definition of construct validity. Thus, researchers have some freedom to propose their own definition. I shall try to be explicit in this chapter regarding all terms, but propose that the phrase "substantive theory" be left undefined, to be supplied by the knowledgeable researcher. However, the following definitions are proposed with the intention of their being reasonably consistent with previous writings on construct validity as well as the burgeoning literature on quantitative structural equation models in the social sciences.

1. The construct validity of a substantive theory refers to the empirical adequacy of a causal model, evaluated on relevant data by appropriate statistical methods.
2. A causal model is the representation of a substantive theory by a structural model and a measurement model.
3. A structural model is a representation of the interrelations among constructs through mathematical equations.
4. A measurement model is a representation of the interrelations between constructs and variables through mathematical equations.
5. A construct is a postulated attribute of a measured object.

These definitions are also applicable in the context of qualitative data, but it must be acknowledged that error theories are much more advanced for quantitative models. As a result, the distinction between a structural model and a measurement model is more difficult to implement with qualitative data analytic methods. Nonetheless, these definitions represent a bridge between traditional and more modern methodological concerns. A construct can typically be represented mathematically as a latent (unobserved) random variable, while the manifest data on the measured object can be represented as observed random variables. In quantitative models, the latent variables are considered to be continuous, and in qualitative models, discrete. As such, the construct validity of a substantive theory refers to the adequacy of the model that interrelates various latent random variables to each other as well as to observed random variables, the entire representation for the population being evaluated in a sample by statistical means. In a given application, the researcher must be able to specify the causal model and determine which mathematical aspects of the model need to be determined from the data (parameter estimation) and which aspects are to be given in mathematical form by the substantive theory (fixed, known parameters).

The current approach to construct validation is different from the Cronbach–Meehl (1955) approach in that it is concerned with the construct validity of a substantive theory, focusing immediate attention on the entire nomological network of associations of a given construct to other constructs and manifest variables. The goal is to evaluate a theory. The Cronbach–Meehl approach, on the other hand, focuses greater attention on the problem of understanding a given test or measure. Their primary goal is to evaluate the construct validity of a test.

The causal modeling literature has been strongly oriented to the statistical testing of the adequacy of a proposed model. Can the causal modeling approach to construct validation help improve inadequate theories? I propose that it can be an effective aid to theory building in ways not derivable from previous discussions of construct validity: through an analysis of the "identification" problem, through relaxation and alternative imposition of parametric constraints, and through analysis of lack of fit of the model.

The identification problem is not easy to explain in nontechnical terms, and it is difficult to find technical generalizations that hold for a wide variety of circumstances and models. The idea is as follows. A given causal model includes, as part of its specification, a set of parameters that governs the structural and measurement models. These parameters may be known or unknown; in the latter case, they must be estimated from the data. Under a given specification, the parameters— along with the random variables—will generate one and only one observed data structure (e.g., means and covariance matrices in the case of quantitative data, or cross-classification frequencies in the case of qualitative data). If there are two or more different structures generating the same data structure, the structures are equivalent. If a parameter has the same value in all equivalent structures, the parameter is identified, and if all parameters are identified the whole model is said to be identified. The model must be identified in order for statistical estimation to be successful.

If a causal model has deficiencies in identification, it cannot be evaluated empirically. The possibility and problems of empirically evaluating a theory were discussed by Cronbach and Meehl (1955) and Torgerson (1958). They emphasized the fact that a sufficient number of constructs must be appropriately defined operationally for a theory to have empirical meaning. Evaluating the identification of a specific causal model provides a test as to the possibilities for its empirical evaluation. If the model is "overidentified," meaning, loosely speaking, that there are fewer parameters than data points (e.g., means and covariances), the model is scientifically useful because it can be rejected by the data. If the model is "just identified," meaning, loosely speaking, that there is a one-to-one transformation possible between the data and the parameters, the model is not scientifically interesting since it can never be rejected (no matter what the data). If some parameters of the model are "underidentified," meaning, loosely speaking, that they can take on many values rather than be uniquely defined, the model is not statistically testable. This also makes the model useless. A technical analysis of underidentification may provide clues as to various methods for improving the model so as to make it testable. Sometimes, such an analysis may not be practically feasible; however, some methods of causal modeling provide an index consequent to a computer analysis that informs the user whether the model was in fact statistically testable. Thus, the concept of identification and its application in a given situation provides insights to construct validity that were not previously available.

The causal modeling procedures described below allow one to choose quite freely which parameters of the model are to be treated as known and which must be estimated from the data. Such a decision can be modified in accordance with the results of data analysis. For example, if parameters that were thought to be quite different turn out to be almost identical the model could be reestimated, subject to the constraint that the parameters be exactly the same. Another illustration might involve modifying the nomological network itself (i.e., setting some parameters to a known zero and testing the adequacy of such a restriction). Obviously, causal modeling makes it possible to improve theories because it allows alternatives to be compared. In some situations, such model comparisons are completely legitimate and open to a statistical test that compares the two models and has its own chi-square fit value. In other circumstances, the statistical assumptions may no longer be met, and cross-validation becomes essential.

If a proposed causal model does not fit the data, one has the possibility of evaluating alternative ways of modifying the model. For example, the measurement model may need refinement, or the fault may lie with the structural model. It may be possible to obtain clues about lack of fit by examining the residuals. Clearly, any ability to favorably modify one's initial causal model represents an improvement over previous approaches to construct validity.

The following section gives a short, nontechnical overview of some recent developments in the analysis of nonexperimental qualitative data. It is highly selective, ignoring very old methods that have recently been rediscovered (e.g., the 16-fold table, Kenny, 1976; Kessler, 1977), newer methods that do not, as yet, have a solid statistical basis (e.g., graph theory, Roberts, 1976), and highly specialized models (e.g., structural models of organization in free recall, Rotondo, 1977).

Causal Models for Qualitative Data

There are a variety of models available for hypothesis-testing analyses of cognitive and developmental data. Unfortunately, there is no agreed-upon classification of methods for the analysis of qualitative data, and, because of the relative newness of the statistical methods involved, there is little experience regarding the specific methodologies that might prove most relevant to the analysis of data in the field of cognitive development. Consequently, I have developed my own typology of methods, and selected within each of these types of techniques some statistical tools that seem to offer promise for developmental researchers; however, knowledgeable methodologists may disagree with my selection of topics. Specifically, I shall discuss prediction models, latent attribute models, and multinomial response models. Although these models are discussed separately and sequentially, it should not be assumed that the statistical and mathematical foundation of the methods is completely different. In a chapter such as this one, technical details cannot be emphasized—what is important is that the substantive researcher gain some understanding of the purposes and applications of a given method. If the technique sounds relevant to a research problem, the researcher will have to obtain more specific information from the cited sources in order to be able to apply the technique.

It must also be explicitly mentioned that the methods to be discussed require the assistance of a computer. The methods of estimation are sufficiently complicated that it is simply not practical to use these techniques without "canned" programs. In most cases, the sources cited in the references provide computer programs to perform the analyses, or indicate where such programs might be available.

Latent Attribute Models

One of the most typical questions to be asked regarding a set of qualitative data, including dichotomous variables in particular, involves the measurement structure of such data: Are there any underlying attributes that might be able to explain the observed data? If so, their elimination would drastically modify the interrelationships among the data, usually to such an extent that the variables would be independent in their absence. If such latent attributes exist, it becomes important to understand their operation, particularly through the parameters that relate the latent data to the manifest, observed data. It may even be important to estimate various aspects of these latent attributes, such as an individual subject's value of the latent attribute.

There are a wide variety of latent attribute models including latent structure, scalability, latent trait, and factor analysis models. They differ in the kind of assumptions they make about the overt data, in the assumptions they make about the latent attributes, and in the relation between these two aspects of the data. Some models make very weak assumptions; others, quite strong assumptions. If strong assumptions can be tested, then models making strong assumptions may be preferred. This would also be true if given models were quite robust with respect to violation of such assumptions.

LATENT STRUCTURE MODEL

The topic of latent structure analysis, introduced by Lazarsfeld (1959) and studied most extensively by Lazarsfeld and Henry (1968), is an extremely broad one. The specific model that might be of interest to developmental researchers is the latent class model as developed by Goodman (1974). The type of data to which this model is applicable involves a number of polytomous variables, such as might be found in a multidimensional contingency table. Each individual in a sample is observed to fall in a given manifest class of each variable. The problem posed by the latent structure analysis is whether there is a latent, unobserved variable that itself consists of a number of latent classes. More specifically, the model relates the probability of an individual's falling into a given combination of manifest classes as the sum of probabilities associated with being in each of the given number of latent classes. Within a given latent class, the manifest variables are mutually independent. Consequently, any association between the manifest variables is due to the variation of individuals across latent classes.

One way to think of this model—without equations—is as a type of factor analysis. The overt data consist of variables that happen not to be continuous, but rather are dichotomous or polytomous, with no particular ordering being associated with the classes of each variable. The problem of analysis is to find a latent "factor" that accounts for the observed data. The factor, however, unlike traditional factor analysis, is not continuous: Rather, the factor itself is a nominal variable consisting of a number of classes. The classes are latent because they must be deduced from the data.

Actually, although the statistical development is in terms of a single latent variable consisting of a number of latent classes that are deduced to account for the observed data, the latent variable may be considered to represent a cross-classification of a number of latent variables (rather than just one). In other words, the model is flexible enough to allow for the existence of a complicated latent structure, which can be obtained from the analysis by appropriately setting constraints on the parameters. However, because the technique is developed solely on the information in the data, one should not consider the resulting latent classes to represent continua, or the latent space as being a dimensional space. Rather, it remains a nominally measured space.

The parameters of the model are estimated by the method of maximum likelihood, and a chi-square test assesses the goodness of fit of the model to data. A chi-square that is too large, relative to degrees of freedom, indicates that a given model is not consistent with the data. It may become necessary to modify the model, for example, by increasing the number of latent classes or by imposing restrictions on various parameters. As a consequence, with enough diligence it typically becomes possible to find a model that fits the data. As mentioned previously, however, there is no guarantee that a model that fits truly represents "the causal structure" of the data; there may be several alternative models that fit equally well.

The latent structure model is particularly interesting because it makes very few assumptions about the data. On the other hand, for this very reason it may yield conclusions that are too weak. In developmental research, for example, one may inquire about the latent classes that represent the process of cognitive growth, say, in the area of conservation of quantity. While the latent classes which can be recovered from the analysis of passing and failing a variety of test items may indeed reproduce the data, it may be desirable to obtain more information from the data than the number of latent classes and the distribution of subjects across them. It may be desirable to place the latent classes onto a continuum representing cognitive growth. Such an analysis is possible with the next method.

SCALABILITY MODEL

The Guttman (1950) scaling model is well known, and has been studied in a variety of contexts (e.g., Bentler, 1971; Mokken, 1971; Proctor, 1970; Wohlwill, 1973). It is known that the model represents the qualitative prototype for quantitative measurement, but that it can yield, by itself, only an ordinal scale of development. However, when compared to unordered latent classes, it may be desirable to obtain a typology of subjects that is ordered.

Goodman's (1975a) basic contribution to the analysis of Guttman scales lies in a probabilistic formulation of the problem that avoids the problem of response error by incorporating it into the scaling scheme. Specifically, an individual is either intrinsically scalable, or is not. The problem of the analysis is to determine the proportion of intrinsically scalable individuals as well as the proportion of unscalable individuals. No continuum can be obtained for the unscalable individuals. However, among the scalable individuals, there is a distribution of scale types that can be ordered in the well-known Guttman fashion. Given a particular distribution of scale types, one can estimate the frequencies of various response patterns that should be observed in the data. Observed data are compared to expected data by a chi-square test under the model. One desires to find a model that can fit the data with a nonsignificant value for chi-square.

In addition to the fundamental model just described, Goodman's system of analysis allows one to vary the number of scale types in a given analysis. In a developmental context, this variation might correspond to asking whether there are only "nonconservers," with respect to a given class of Piagetian tasks, or whether there are also "transitional" individuals. In addition, of course, the procedure determines the proportion of individuals for whom the scaling model cannot be applied. In the ideal situation, this number will be very small. The method also allows some flexibility in the number of latent dimensions. Thus, not only can one consider scalable and unscalable individuals, but one might posit two different orderings of individuals and variables. Such scales, called "biform" by Goodman, represent extensions of the uniform Guttman scales as they are typically considered. It would take a reasonable theory, however, to propose various biform scales that might be considered.

Goodman's method for scaling response patterns is closely related to the method described above for latent structure analysis. In fact, it is possible to obtain the uniform scales quite easily as restricted latent structure models.

LATENT TRAIT MODEL

Latent trait models are concerned with transforming information obtained on a nominal scale into a latent scale that is interval in nature (i.e., defined up to a linear transformation of scale and origin, Lord, 1975). While in principle such latent traits can be considered to be multidimensional, practical procedures have been developed only for the case of a single latent dimension, that is, a unidimensional latent continuum. Of course, in order to draw strong conclusions about a latent trait, either stronger assumptions or a more complicated model must be entertained than was described previously. The basic mechanism for defining a strong scale lies in the item-characteristic curve, which represents a mathematical function that relates the probability of a given response to an item (e.g., a correct response on a cognitive task) to the ability or other characteristic measured by all the items. This curve represents the regression of item response on the latent trait. In the general case, it is assumed that this regression function is nonlinear, although there are actually a variety of specific models that make different assumptions about this regression. In the pure Guttman scale, if measured without error, it is assumed that this regression is a step function, that is, going from zero to one (fail to pass) at a given point on the latent continuum, with different items, of course, having this transition occurring at different values of the latent continuum. Such a step-function, however, seems unrealistic to many psychometricians, and the linearity assumption associated with another simple model seems implausible.

The most widely studied and successfully developed latent trait model is, at the moment, the Rasch (1966) model (e.g., Andersen, 1973; Fischer, 1976; Hambleton & Cook, 1977; Whitely & Dawis, 1974; Wright, 1977). This model supposes that a single item is associated with a given parameter that describes the nonlinear item characteristic curve. Similarly, as in a one-factor model of factor analysis, each individual is assumed to have a given parameter representing his standing on the latent trait. However, the relation of observed response to the latent trait is not given by the simple linear model of factor analysis, but rather by a nonlinear function known as the one-parameter logistic function. This logistic function is quite similar to the normal curve, so that the item characteristic curve for each item looks very similar to the S-shaped curve of the cumulative normal distribution. Items vary in terms of what aspects of the latent continuum they cover most adequately (i.e., where they are best able to discriminate the trait). The Rasch model is particularly inviting because the problem of estimation of parameters is essentially resolved, making it possible for it to be applied in a large variety of circumstances. Once having estimated the parameters, it becomes possible to test the model for goodness of fit (e.g., Andersen, 1973).

The Rasch version of the logistic model has a number of interesting attributes that make it particularly attractive for work in developmental psychology (see, e.g., pages 20–24 by Spada and Kluwe for a discussion of its role in modeling intellectual growth). In the first place, it is possible to obtain estimates of the latent trait that are essentially independent of any particular choice of items (variables, tasks) that subjects encounter, provided that the items have been appropriately calibrated. This makes it possible, for example, for older subjects to be tested on completely different items or tasks as compared to younger subjects, but still allows reference of all responses to a single underlying continuum. Furthermore, it is possible to equate two different tests, such as parallel forms, to yield measures of the same latent trait. Item calibration is also made more general with the Rasch model, since item parameters should be invariant across subgroups, such as age groups, chosen for analysis. Furthermore, this model does not assume that measurement precision is equal at all points on the latent continuum, and provides indices to evaluate the goodness of subjects' parameter estimates. Most importantly, for rather technical reasons, total scores obtained as simple unit-weighted sums of the number of items passed, represent adequate measures of the unknown latent trait: This is because these scores are sufficient estimators of the latent trait.

As might be expected from its various positive features mentioned above, the Rasch model is becoming ever more popular in educational research, which faces many of the same problems as developmental research (namely, wide age ranges under study, dichotomous indicators, and potent single latent traits). An introduction to an application of this model to an educational setting involving test equating can be found in Rentz and Bashaw (1977). The model is discussed in the context of item banking by Wood (1976).

It must be mentioned that, just as the Guttman scale is a special case of item characteristic curve theory, so is the Rasch scale. As pointed out previously, it is a one-parameter logistic model. There are also two- and three-parameter logistic models (e.g., Birnbaum, 1968; Lord, 1977; Marco, 1977). In these models, all items are not equivalent except for their projection onto the latent continuum. In the two-parameter models, various items can have different item-characteristic curve shapes, but the latent trait is still assumed to map onto the observed continuum defined by the probability of emitting a correct response (i.e., the continuum of zero to one). In the three-parameter logistic model, an item may be answered correctly with nonzero probability at all levels of ability. Unfortunately, these more complex (and, hence, more realistic) models are as yet incomplete in all aspects of the theory of statistical estimation; thus, they cannot always be counted on to be applicable in practical situations. However, when they do apply, they are extremely powerful. For example, the three-parameter model appears to be essential to applications of tailored testing, a computer-interactive method for providing subjects with the specific tasks that are optimally suited to estimate their standing on the latent trait (e.g., Urry, 1977).

There exist still more complicated versions of latent trait models than the various logistic models already mentioned. In particular, the previously mentioned models can be applied only in circumstances in which items are dichotomous. When an item or variable consists of a number of response categories, it is possible to consider each response alternative as being represented by an item characteristic curve, with the correct alternative being represented by a monotonically increasing function of ability (e.g., Bock, 1972; Fischer, 1977; Samejima, 1972). When the response categories are themselves ordered with respect to the latent trait, a still more refined model can be utilized (Samejima, 1969, 1977a, 1977b). However, the latter models would currently seem to be of greater interest to educational and psychological test specialists than to developmental psychologists, whose primary interest is in studying cognitive growth. A latent trait model of relevance to individual growth can be found in Bock (1976).

FACTOR ANALYSIS MODEL

A generalization of latent trait models is to be found in the recent developments of factor analysis models for dichotomous variables (Christoffersson, 1975; Muthén, 1978). The Christoffersson and Muthén models are essentially the same, but Muthén has developed a more efficient method of estimating the parameters of the model. In these models, it is assumed that each observed dichotomous variable is simply a manifestation of an underlying, latent continuous variable, with these two variables being related by a threshold parameter that maps the observed dichotomous response to the latent variable in a step fashion. If the response strength of the latent variable is above a given point, a "correct" response is made by the subject; otherwise, an incorrect response is made. The latent continuous variable is assumed to have an ordinary factor-analytic representation. That is, it represents a weighted combination of latent common factors and uniqueness. In this way, the ordinary factor-analytic model is made relevant to the analysis of binary data. The model is fit to the data using a generalized least squares approach, using information in the first and second-order proportions to fit the model to data. A chi-square test can assess the goodness of fit of the model to the data.

Because of its attention to underlying multidimensional representations, the factor model is applicable in a greater variety of circumstances than are unidimensional latent trait models. On the other hand, the model makes the rather strong assumption of multivariate normality of the underlying latent variables. This assumption does not provide a hindrance to analysis if, in fact, the model does fit given sets of data, but in the absence of an adequate fit of the model, it is difficult to know whether the fault lies in the assumption of the factor model or, rather, with the distribution assumed for the variables. In developmental research, the assumption of normality would seem to be a reasonable one for many variables when obtaining data within narrow age ranges, but it is clearly possible to imagine situations where such an assumption would seem to be questionable. For example, in a study of Piaget's concept of conservation, it might be quite unreasonable to assume normal distributions on the latent trait of "conservation" unless an appropriate mix of ages were represented. Nonetheless, because evidence seems to indicate the possibility of at least two dimensions of conservation (e.g., Goldschmid & Bentler, 1968; Goldschmid et al.,1973), a method such as the one currently being described would be directly relevant for evaluating such a hypothesis in acceptable statistical terms. Monotonicity analysis (Bentler, 1970a), on the other hand, which we have used extensively in the past, clearly does not possess this statistical virtue.

The factor model for dichotomous variables can be treated like other, more ordinary, factor models, in both exploratory and confirmatory contexts (e.g., Bentler, 1976b). That is, it is possible simply to determine the dimensionality of the latent space; the number of factors is varied until the model fits a given set of data (e.g., Zelniker, Bentler, & Renan, 1977). On the other hand, the model can also be used in confirmatory contexts, in which one has a theory about the space. Such a theory could demand that certain parameters be equal to one another, or that some parameters be set at zero. In this way, more complicated measurement models could be entertained. The ability to evaluate competing models would seem to represent a necessary condition for the effective utilization of causal modeling.

Prediction Models

In the qualitative models, the primary aim of the analysis is to relate the observed data to underlying attributes that are presumably more important, since the manifest variables are simply considered to be realizations of the latent variables under the various specific models. In other instances, attention is given not so much to understanding the structure that generates the data, but rather to prediction. In the context of quantitative continuous variables, the prediction problem is one of multiple regression or canonical correlation, while the structural problem is one of factor analysis. In the analysis of dichotomous variables, there exists a potentially useful regression model to predict a single dependent variable from a set of independent variables, as well as a more complicated model that relates dichotomous dependent variables to quantitative and qualitative independent variables through a structural measurement model, as described above.

DICHOTOMOUS REGRESSION MODEL

When the variables in regression are all dichotomous, including predictor and criterion variables, the ordinary linear least-squares model is not appropriate to the analysis. The ordinary model requires, when used in a statistical context, that the criterion variable be normally distributed, with constant variance across variation in the predictors (i.e., homoscedasticity). These conditions are not met with binary variables, and, in addition, predicted values under the model could fall outside the 0–1 range. Consequently, an alternative methodology would seem desirable. One such alternative is the logit model, as developed by Grizzle, Starmer, and Koch (1969), Theil (1970), Goodman (1972a, 1975b), and others. This model can be written in a general form that allows the predictors and criterion variables to relate through higher order "interactions" in addition to the simple main effects of predictor variables.

In the logit model, a multiplicative version of the "log-linear" model is written to represent the probability of an observation associated with a given response on the criterion (such as, "yes" or "correct") being associated with a particular pattern of responses to all other variables. This probability is, of course, a given entry in the multidimensional contingency table relating all variables to each other; the entry associated with a given criterion response is analyzed. The model that is written to express this probability, or frequency, is like a multiplicative version of an analysis of variance model. That is, the model contains the products (rather than sums) of terms representing the marginal distributions (main effects) of all variables, as well as various levels of interactions, from two-way interactions to extremely high-order interactions. (In practice, as in very complex analysis of variance designs, only the lowest level interactions are typically required; but far more than only main effects are needed to fit most models.) A second, similar multiplicative equation is written for the other response to the criterion variable ("no," "wrong," etc.). The ratio of the two criterion probabilities can then be expressed as ratios of only certain terms in the very complete multiplicative model previously written; the remaining terms simply cancel. This ratio of criterion probabilities is thus itself expressed as a product of terms that can similarly be interpreted as main effects and interactions. Now, taking logarithms of this ratio of probabilities, we obtain a logit. Since the logit equals the log of the product of various multiplicative parameters, the logit also equals the simple sum of the logs of those parameters. Thus, we have an additive model for the logit as a dependent variable. This dependent variable can be regressed on the various predictor terms. As might be expected, in many circumstances only several predictor terms or parameters are needed to account for the observed data within statistical accuracy, and various terms can be dropped. Goodman (1972a) suggests that the complete logit regression equation can be estimated for data (but not tested, since it has no remaining degrees of freedom), and the size of the parameters may provide a clue as to which terms seem to be insignificant and could be dropped from the analysis without significant loss of predictive accuracy. There is an overall test of significance of a logit model, based upon the chi-square test. Various competing models that contain only specified interaction terms can be compared for adequacy of fit.

There are a variety of approaches to obtaining statistical estimates of the parameters of these models. Grizzle *et al.* (1969), for example, favor the method of weighted least squares, while Goodman (1972a) favors a method based on maximum likelihood. Goodman suggests that his methods are asymptotically more efficient, but this is not a well-established result. His computerized implementation of the method, however, appears to be more rapid and, consequently, less expensive.

There is an alternative approach to regression with dichotomous variables, as outlined by Goodman (1975b). It involves writing an additive (rather than multiplicative) model for the probabilities of criterion class versus response pattern, and estimating the parameters in the additive model. This approach is not particularly recommended, although when all variables have marginal probabilities in the .25–.75 range, there appears to be little practical difference between the two approaches.

Because of the bewildering number of possible higher order effects when dealing with a large number of variables (these effects grow exponentially with the number of variables), it is necessary in these models to deal with a relatively small number of variables on the one hand, and with relatively explicit causal models on the other. The more explicit the various possible causal models, the greater the number of variables that can be accommodated, in principle. This is because only a certain set of models can be evaluated statistically. There is simply no way to use these regression models in exploratory ways to find the optimal regression model, with the fewest number of parameters, and with the most explanatory power. Nonetheless, such an exploratory methodology is possible when considering only three, four, or maybe five variables. Goodman provides some guidelines in such a situation.

STRUCTURAL EQUATION MODEL

The dichotomous factor analysis model of Christoffersson (1975) and Muthén (1978) was discussed on pages 94–95. In this model, binary manifest variables are related to latent continuous factors. Muthén (1976) has extended this general model by including a structural equation component, namely, an additional set of equations that considers the latent quantitative variable to itself be a dependent variable in its regression on a set of known, manifest variables. These manifest independent variables can be qualitative or quantitative in nature. Thus, the ultimate effect of the combined model is to consider the dichotomous dependent variables to be related, as a set, to several independent predictor variables (through the latent variable as a mediator of the regression). Thus, the model can be considered to represent an interesting generalization of a regression model with multiple dependent variables.

Of course, as was pointed out previously, the factor-analytic model for dichotomous data allows for the existence of multiple quantitative latent variables. The structural equation model does not single out only one latent variable as an intermediary in the regression. Rather, it uses all the latent variables that might exist simultaneously. In addition, it is possible to investigate the causal effects of various latent variables on each other. However, it must be reiterated that it is extremely helpful to have a causal model to test, rather than to hope that the method will find "the" causal structure through exploration. At best, data can be considered to be consistent with a causal hypothesis, but not proof of it. Those hypotheses that must be implausible, given the data, can be rejected in accordance with a statistical test.

Multinomial Response Models

One of the most popular approaches to the analysis of unordered categorical data is the linear logistic model, or the log-linear model, as it is popularly known. An entire class of data-analytic procedures has been developed based on this and similar models (e.g., Bishop, Fienberg, & Holland, 1975; Davis, 1975; Goodman, 1972b; Haberman, 1974; Nerlove & Press, 1973; Plackett, 1974). One of the more relevant techniques involves fitting data to multiway contingency tables. Bock (1975) refers to the statistical problem involved as one of estimating multinomial response relations, based upon the sampling distribution that appears most relevant to such tables and to more general qualitative data situations. A more specialized problem in contingency tables is the analysis of a single cross-classification, where the observations may be misclassified. Such a model is presented by Thomas (1977).

LOG-LINEAR MODEL

See pages 95–96 for a discussion of the dichotomous regression model that results when writing the two criterion-predictor response pattern probabilities as a multiplicative function of main effects and various levels of interaction, taking their ratio, and obtaining logarithms (a linear predictive model results). In the analysis of general categorical data that can be cross-classified, the distinction between predictors and criterion variables does not make sense, but it is still possible to write the probability or frequency associated with a given cell in a multiway contingency table as a multiplicative function of various types of parameters. When natural logarithms are taken of these frequencies, the model is decomposed into linearly additive components (hence, the name log-linear model). The problem in the analysis of such data lies in obtaining a model that accounts for the observed probabilities or frequencies within statistical accuracy. For example, if the categorizations were completely independent, then knowing the marginal distributions on each nominal, unordered variable would make it possible to estimate the probability of its being in a given joint cell of the table as a simple product of marginal probabilities, as is well-known from principles of statistical independence applied to the two-by-two contingency table. As is also known from such tables, the hypothesis of independence can be tested by chi-square, which represents an indication of closeness of the observed frequencies to those that would be obtained under the model of independence. The log-linear model takes the simple idea of hypothesis-testing associated with the two-by-two table and generalizes it to multiway, larger tables.

When the probability that a nominal, unordered variable will fall in a given joint cell of a multiway table cannot be simply predicted from the marginals of the table, the task of finding a model that can predict this probability for each and every cell of the table becomes quite complicated. As pointed out previously, there is an extremely large class of potential models that grows exponentially with the number of variables and number of categories on a variable. Goodman (1972b) suggests that in small tables it is possible to fit a "saturated" model, which can be considered to be a nontestable model that includes all possible parameters from the lowest order to the highest order. The presence of apparently powerful and trivial effects in such an analysis can be a clue to the elimination of parameters associated with given effects, and to a concentration on others. Typically, for example, very high-way interactions turn out to be quite small and can be discarded. As was pointed out previously, however, it certainly helps to have a causal model to test in these situations, since the number of potential exploratory models quickly becomes too large to consider as the number of variables increases. To provide a specific idea, the reader is no doubt familiar with two-by-two versus two-by-two-by-two factorial designs in analysis of variance (e.g., Thompson & Bentler, 1971). As the design increases from only two binary cross-classified variables to three, the number of analytic parameters and effects to be interpreted grows substantially. Consider the case of the 2^{10} contingency table, however. Data associated with such a table become totally incomprehensible unless higher order effects can be ignored; indeed the computations become prohibitively expensive as well.

CROSS-CLASSIFICATION WITH ERRORS MODEL

General models for the analysis of contingency tables do not always provide the same insight into a research area as may be possible in the analysis of a specific model. Such is the case when considering the quite narrow problem recently addressed by Thomas (1977), involving the problem of stages in cognitive development (e.g., Bentler, 1970b). He considers the case of a single cross-classification, in which subjects have given two behavioral responses, each of which is classified into ordered categories. For example, there may be two conservation tasks, and on each task a subject is considered to be an "early," "intermediate," or "late" conserver. In Wohlwill's (1973) terminology, three plausible models could explain the observed data in such a developmental situation. For example, in Model I, a model for synchronous progression, a child should be classified at an equal level for each of the two variables; for example, he might be an "early" conserver on both tasks. In Model II, a decalage model, one type of conservation might precede the development of the other type. Consequently, only certain patterns of cross-classification responses should be evident in the data; for example, the child may be an early conserver on one task, but may be anywhere in the sequence on the other task, or an intermediate conserver on one task, but either intermediate or late on the other task. Wohlwill has also discussed a reciprocal interaction model, a Model III, in which there is a cyclic process in which one task leads first, and the other leads later. The statistical problem is to decide among these models with given data, when certain of the cells of the cross-classification may be presumed by theory to be empty, and when a certain level of error of classification of subjects to cells may be present. Thomas presents a method for performing this analysis, and choosing among models. Although there is no specifically justifiable basis for choosing "the" correct model from such a comparison, it may become clear from the chi-square as to which model must be rejected and which may be plausible. Thomas presents two examples from the developmental literature, finding his techniques to be applicable to practical developmental contexts.

Generality and Scope of Theory, Methods, and Data

This concludes the survey of descriptive, exploratory, and hypothesis-testing uses of data, as integrated into substantive theory, and potentially evaluated by a causal modeling approach to construct validity. The methods of qualitative data analysis reviewed above are obviously growing very rapidly, and potentially, they have a lot to offer social science research. However, I would like to remind the reader that causal modeling as a hypothesis-testing approach to research is not necessarily superior to alternative approaches to research. It may be that data description or exploratory model building is more appropriate to the level of theoretical sophistication of a given research area and to its data base.

Nonetheless, when a research area is mature enough so that it is possible to formulate a fairly complete nomological network that relates constructs to each other and to observed variables, the causal modeling approach to hypothesis-testing, with its ability to analyze even nonexperimental, response–response relationships, has great potential. Not the least of its benefits might be that researchers will be stimulated into developing substantive theory, with a goal of making it amenable to evaluation by causal modeling.

Although causal modeling appears to have a useful future in social science research, the causal modeling methodology itself will need further research and improvement. It is clear that both substantive theory and empirical data make demands on this methodology that it cannot currently meet. For example, it is still difficult to deal effectively with ordered variables rather than purely qualitative or quantitative data. Yet, most psychological data fall into such an intermediate status. As another example, latent trait models such as the logistic, Rasch model, can as yet only handle unidimensional special cases. Yet, most psychological data are intrinsically multidimensional. Finally, models for qualitative data analysis are only slowly able to deal with the distinction between manifest and latent variables, a distinction shown in quantitative models to be of fundamental importance (e.g., Bentler, 1980a,b). Certainly more investigation of this problem is called for.

If causal modeling becomes integrated into social science research, the issue of comparing competing causal models will certainly arise: Which theory has the highest construct validity? When competing models are being evaluated on a given set of data, the comparison may be relatively easy, but when the data bases are different the problem is much more complicated. In the context of two competing theories attempting to explain the same data, the causal model that fits more adequately would be superior; if two models happen to account for the data equally well, in the absence of other considerations, one could consider the more parsimonious model—the one with the fewest number of parameters—as the superior model. It might be tempting to utilize the chi-square test or a similar index derivable from causal models when comparing models across differing data bases, even when the data are only minimally different (as when certain manifest variables are substituted for others). While such an approach may sometimes work, particularly when the manifest variables are extremely well understood as manifestations of latent constructs, a fit index cannot, in general, provide a sufficient rationale for comparing the maturity and scope of alternative theories. Everything else being equal, including ability to account for data, the theory whose nomological network is richer would seem to be more mature. The richness of the network would be difficult to quantify, however, because at issue would be such considerations as the total number of variables, the number of parameters, the ratio of variables to parameters, the ratio of known to estimated parameters, the richness of the structural model (evaluated perhaps by the number of parameters or the number of dimensions), and richness of the measurement model (similarly evaluated). In view of the likelihood of disagreement about the necessary tradeoffs involved, however, it might be impossible to find a general formula for combining such information. How might one weight, for example, the value of adding a variety of methods of measurement (in the sense of Campbell & Fiske, 1959; Bentler & McClain, 1976; Bentler & Lee, 1979) to a given structural model, as compared to increasing the number of parameters in a measurement model by increasing the number of monomethod (single data –source) variables measuring a given construct? Clearly one might more easily be able to increase the number of parameters in a model by adding, say, additional self-report variables, but many researchers would feel that greater true understanding might be obtained by adding the more remote heteromethod (multiple data-source) variables. Unfortunately, there is no general solution to the quandry of comparing causal models so as to determine in some abstract way whether one is superior to another. We would propose, however, that a certain degree of skepticism regarding causal modeling reports might be in order: It is entirely possible for statistically acceptable causal models to represent theoretical trivia. The substantively meaningful use of such models must incorporate theoretical sophistication as well as high quality empirical data.

References

Andersen, E. B. A goodness of fit test for the Rasch model. *Psychometrika*, 1973, *38*, 123–140.

APA Committee on Psychological Tests. *Technical recommendations for psychological tests and diagnostic techniques.* Washington, D.C.: American Psychological Association, 1954.

Bechtold, H. P. Construct validity: A critique. *American Psychologist*, 1959, *14*, 619–629.

Bentler, P. M. A comparison of monotonicity analysis with factor analysis. *Educational and Psychological Measurement*, 1970, *30*, 241–250. (a)

Bentler, P. M. Evidence regarding stages in the development of conservation. *Perceptual and Motor Skills*, 1970, *31*, 855–859. (b)

Bentler, P. M. An implicit metric for ordinal scales: Implications for assessment of cognitive growth. In D. R. Green, M. P. Ford., & G. B. Flamer (Eds.), *Measurement and Piaget.* New York: McGraw-Hill, 1971. Pp. 34–63.

Bentler, P. M. Multistructure statistical model applied to factor analysis. *Multivariate Behavioral Research*, 1976, *11*, 3–25. (a)

Bentler, P. M. Factor analysis. In P. M. Bentler, D. J. Lettieri, & G. A. Austin (Eds.), *Data analysis strategies and designs for substance abuse research.* Washington, D.C.: U.S. Government Printing Office, 1976. Pp. 139–158. (b)

Bentler, P. M. The interdependence of theory, methodology, and empirical data: Causal modeling as an approach to construct validation. In D. B. Kandel (Ed.), *Longitudinal research on drug use: Empirical findings and methodological issues.* New York: Wiley, 1978. Pp. 267–302.

Bentler, P. M. Multivariate analysis with latent variables: Causal modeling. *Annual Review of Psychology,* 1980, *31,* 419–456.

Bentler, P. M. Linear systems with multiple levels and types of latent variables. In K. G. Jöreskog & H. Wold (Eds.), *Systems under indirect observation: Causality, structure, prediction.* Amsterdam: North-Holland, 1980, in press.

Bentler, P. M., & Bonett, D. G. Significance tests and goodness of fit in the analysis of covariance structures. *Psychological Bulletin,* in press.

Bentler, P. M., & Lee, S. Y. A statistical development of three-mode factor analysis. *British Journal of Mathematical and Statistical Psychology,* 1979, *32,* 87–104.

Bentler, P. M., & McClain, J. A multitrait–multimethod analysis of reflection–impulsivity. *Child Development,* 1976, *47,* 218–226.

Bentler, P. M., & Weeks, D. G. Interrelations among models for the analysis of moment structures. *Multivariate Behavioral Research,* 1979, *14,* 169–185.

Bentler, P. M., & Woodward, J. A. A Head Start re-evaluation: Positive effects are not yet demonstrable. *Evaluation Quarterly,* 1978, *2,* 493–510.

Bergmann, G., & Spence, K. W. The logic of psychophysical measurement. *Psychological Review,* 1944, *51,* 1–24.

Birnbaum, A. Some latent trait models and their use in inferring an examinee's ability. In F. M. Lord & M. R. Novick (Eds.), *Statistical theories of mental test scores.* Reading, Massachusetts: Addison–Wesley, 1968. P. 568.

Bishop, Y. M. M., Fienberg, S. E., & Holland, P. W. *Discrete multivariate analysis: Theory and practice.* Cambridge, Massachusetts: MIT Press, 1975.

Bock, R. D. Estimating item parameters and latent ability when responses are scored in two or more nominal categories. *Psychometrika,* 1972, *37,* 29–51.

Bock, R. D. *Multivariate statistical methods in behavioral research.* New York: McGraw-Hill, 1975.

Bock, R. D. Basic issues in the measurement of change. In D. N. M. De Gruijter & L. J. Th. van der Kamp (Eds.), *Advances in psychological and educational measurement.* New York: Wiley, 1976. Pp. 75–96.

Campbell, D. T. Recommendations for APA test standards regarding construct, trait, or discriminant validity. *American Psychologist,* 1960, *15,* 546–553.

Campbell, D. T., & Fiske, D. W. Convergent and discriminant validation by the multitrait–multimethod matrix. *Psychological Bulletin,* 1959, *56,* 81–105.

Campbell, D. T., & Stanley, J. C. Experimental and quasi-experimental designs for research on teaching. In N. L. Gage (Ed.), *Handbook of research on teaching.* Chicago: Rand McNally, 1963. Pp. 171–246.

Christoffersson, A. Factor analysis of dichotomized variables. *Psychometrika,* 1975, *40,* 5–32.

Cook, T. D., & Campbell, D. T. The design and conduct of quasi-experiments and true experiments in field settings. In M. D. Dunnette (Ed.), *Handbook of industrial and organizational research.* Chicago: Rand McNally, 1976.

Cronbach, L. J. The two disciplines of scientific psychology. *American Psychologist,* 1957, *12,* 671–684.

Cronbach, L. J. Test validation. In R. L. Thorndike (Ed.), *Educational measurement.* Washington, D.C.: American Council on Education, 1971. Pp. 443–507.

Cronbach, L. J. Beyond the two disciplines of scientific psychology. *American Psychologist,* 1975, *30,* 116–127.

Cronbach, L. J., & Meehl, P. E. Construct validity in psychological tests. *Psychological Bulletin,* 1955, *52,* 281–302.

Davis, J. A. Analyzing contingency tables with linear flow graphs: D Systems. In D. R. Heise (Ed.), *Sociological methodology, 1976*. San Francisco: Jossey-Bass, 1975. Pp. 111–145.

Davis, J. A. Studying categorical data over time. Mimeograph, Dartmouth College, Hanover, New Hampshire, 1976.

Duncan, O. D. *Introduction to structural equation models*. New York: Academic Press, 1975.

Fischer, G. H. Some probabilistic models for measuring change. In D. N. M. De Gruijter & L. J. Th. van der Kamp (Eds.), *Advances in psychological and educational measurement*. New York: Wiley, 1976. Pp. 97–110.

Fischer, G. H. Some probabilistic models for the description of attitudinal and behavioral changes under the influence of mass communication. In W. F. Kempf & B. H. Repp (Eds.), *Mathematical models for social psychology*. Bern: Huber, 1977.

Fisher, R. A. *The design of experiments*. Edinburgh: Oliver and Boyd, 1935.

Goldschmid, M., & Bentler, P. M. *Concept assessment kit —conservation*. San Diego: Educational and Industrial Testing Service, 1968.

Goldschmid, M., Bentler, P. M., Debus, R. L., Kohnstamm, G. A., Modgil, S., Nicholls, J. G., Reykowski, J., & Warren, N. A cross-cultural investigation of conservation. *Journal of Cross-Cultural Psychology*, 1973, *4*, 75–88.

Goodman, L. A. A modified multiple regression approach to the analysis of dichotomous variables. *American Sociological Review*, 1972, *37*, 28–46. (a)

Goodman, L. A. A general model for the analysis of surveys. *American Journal of Sociology*, 1972, *77*, 1035–1086. (b)

Goodman, L. A. Exploratory latent structure analysis using both identifiable and unidentifiable models. *Biometrika*, 1974, *61*, 215–231.

Goodman, L. A. A new model for scaling response patterns: An application of the quasi-independence concept. *Journal of the American Statistical Association*, 1975, *70*, 755–768. (a)

Goodman, L. A. The relationship between modified and usual multiple-regression approaches to the analysis of dichotomous variables. In D. R. Heise (Ed.), *Sociological methodology, 1976*. San Francisco: Jossey-Bass, 1975. Pp. 83–110. (b)

Grizzle, J. E., Starmer, C. F., & Koch, G. G. Analysis of categorical data by linear models. *Biometrics*, 1969, *25*, 489–504.

Guttman, L. The basis for scalogram analysis. In S. A. Stouffer *et al.* (Eds.), *Measurement and prediction*. Princeton, New Jersey: Princeton University Press, 1950. Pp. 60–90.

Haberman, S. J. *The analysis of frequency data*. Chicago: University of Chicago Press, 1974.

Hambleton, R. K., & Cook, L. L. Latent trait models and their use in the analysis of educational test data. *Journal of Educational Measurement*, 1977, *14*, 75–96.

Heise, D. R. *Causal analysis*. New York: Wiley, 1975.

Jöreskog, K. G. Structural equation models in the social sciences: Specification, estimation and testing. In P. R. Krishnaiah (Ed.), *Proceedings of the symposium on applications of statistics*. Amsterdam: North Holland, 1977. Pp. 265–287.

Kenny, D. A. A quasi-experimental approach to assessing treatment effects in the nonequivalent control group design. *Psychological Bulletin*, 1975, *82*, 345–362.

Kenny, D. A. A cross–lagged panel correlation approach to the sixteen–fold table. Mimeograph, Harvard University, Cambridge, Massachusetts, 1976.

Kenny, D. A. *Correlation and causality*. New York: Wiley, 1979. pp. 288.

Kessler, R. C. Rethinking the 16-fold table problem. *Social Science Research*, 1977, *6*, 84–107.

Labouvie, E. W. Longitudinal designs. In P. M. Bentler, D. J. Lettieri, & G. A. Austin (Eds.), *Data analysis strategies and designs for substance abuse research*. Washington, D.C.: U.S. Government Printing Office, 1976. Pp. 45–60.

Labouvie, E. W., Bartsch, T. W., Nesselroade, J. R., & Baltes, P. B. On the internal and external validity of simple longitudinal designs. *Child Development*, 1974, *45*, 282–290.

Larzelere, R. F., & Mulaik, S. A. Single sample tests for many correlations. *Psychological Bulletin*, 1977, *84*, 557–569.

Lazarsfeld, P. F. Latent structure analysis. In S. Koch (Ed.), *Psychology: A study of a science*, Vol. 3. New York: McGraw-Hill, 1959. Pp. 476–542.

Lazarsfeld, P. F., & Henry, N. W. *Latent structure analysis*. Boston: Houghton Mifflin, 1968.

Linn, R. L., & Werts, C. E. Analysis implications of the choice of a structural model in the nonequivalent control group design. *Psychological Bulletin*, 1977, *84*, 229–234.

Loevinger, J. Objective tests as instruments of psychological theory. *Psychological Reports*, 1957, *3*, 635–694.

Lord, F. M. The "ability" scale in item characteristic curve theory. *Psychometrika*, 1975, *44*, 205–217.

Lord, F. M. Practical applications of item characteristic curve theory. *Journal of Educational Measurement*, 1977, *14*, 117–138.

Marco, G. L. Item characteristic curve solutions to three intractible testing problems. *Journal of Educational Measurement*, 1977, *14*, 139–160.

Mokken, R. J. *A theory and procedures of scale analysis*. The Hague: Mouton, 1971.

Muthén, B. Structural equation models with dichotomous dependent variables. Mimeograph, University of Uppsala, Uppsala, Sweden, 1976.

Muthén, B. Contributions to factor analysis of dichotomous variables. *Psychometrika*, 1978, *43*, 551–560.

Nerlove, M., & Press, S. J. *Univariate and multivariate log linear and logistic models*. Santa Monica: RAND Corporation, 1973.

Plackett, R. L. *The analysis of categorical data*. London: Griffin, 1974.

Proctor, C. H. A probabilistic formulation and statistical analysis of Guttman scaling. *Psychometrika*, 1970, *35*, 73–78.

Rasch, G. An item analysis which takes individual differences into account. *British Journal of Mathematical and Statistical Psychology*, 1966, *19*, 49–57.

Rentz, R. R., & Bashaw, W. L. The national reference scale for reading: An application of the Rasch model. *Journal of Educational Measurement*, 1977, *14*, 161–179.

Roberts, F. S. *Discrete mathematical models*. Englewood Cliffs, New Jersey: Prentice-Hall, 1976.

Rotondo, J. A. Discrete structural models of organization in free recall. *Journal of Mathematical Psychology*, 1977, *16*, 95–120.

Samejima, F. Estimation of latent ability using a response pattern of graded scores. *Psychometric Monographs*, 1969, No. 17.

Samejima, F. A general model for free-response data. *Psychometric Monographs*, 1972, No. 18.

Samejima, F. A method of estimating item characteristic functions using the maximum likelihood estimate of ability. *Psychometrika*, 1977, *42*, 163–191. (a)

Samejima, F. Weakly parallel tests in latent trait theory with some criticisms of classical test theory. *Psychometrika*, 1977, *42*, 193–198. (b)

Theil, H. On the estimation of relationships involving qualitative variables. *American Journal of Sociology*, 1970, *76*, 103–154.

Thomas, H. Fitting cross-classification table data to models when observations are subject to classification error. *Psychometrika*, 1977, *42*, 199–206.

Thompson, S. K., & Bentler, P. M. The priority of cues in sex discrimination by children and adults. *Developmental Psychology*, 1971, *5*, 181–185.

Torgerson, W. S. *Theory and methods of scaling*. New York: Wiley, 1958.

Underwood, B. J. Individual differences as a crucible in theory construction. *American Psychologist*, 1975, *30*, 128–134.

Urry, V. W. Tailored testing: A successful application of latent trait theory. *Journal of Educational Measurement*, 1977, *14*, 181–196.

Whitely, S., & Dawis, R. V. The nature of objectivity with the Rasch model. *Journal of Educational Measurement*, 1974, *11*, 163–178.

Wohlwill, J. F. *The study of behavioral development*. New York: Academic Press, 1973.

Wood, R. Trait measurement and item banks. In D. N. M. De Gruijter & L. J. Th. van der Kamp (Eds.), *Advances in psychological and educational measurement*. New York: Wiley, 1976. Pp. 247–263.

Wright, B. D. Solving measurement problems with the Rasch model. *Journal of Educational Measurement*, 1977, *14*, 97–116.

Wright, S. Correlation and causation. *Journal of Agricultural Research*, 1921, *20*, 557–585.

Zahn, D. A., & Fein, S. B. Large contingency tables with large cell frequencies: A model search algorithm and alternative measures of fit. *Psychological Bulletin*, 1978, *86*, 1189–1200.

Zelniker, T., Bentler, P. M., & Renan, A. Speed vs. accuracy as a measure of cognitive style: Internal consistency and factor analysis. *Child Development*, 1977, *48*, 301–304.

5

Quantitative Changes in Cognitive Development: Description, Measurement, and Theoretical Explication

G. RUDINGER AND H. RÜPPEL

Quantitative Changes in Cognitive Development: The Psychometric Assessment

The emphasis on the words "quantitative" and "cognitive" in this chapter indicates its focus on the psychometric approach to cognitive functions. That is, the accent is placed principally on "intelligence," as defined psychometrically. Elkind (1971) differentiates between two traditions in the measurement of cognitive ability: the so-called psychometric tradition and the Piagetian tradition. Both traditions have unique attributes, some of which are briefly mentioned here (cf. Elkind, 1971; Furth, 1973).

The psychometric tradition takes only the products or results of cognitive processes into consideration; the number of actual answers to cognitive tasks is taken as a quantitative indicator (in the form of sum values) of achievement or ability level. Although this paradigm views the development of intelligence as a quantitative change in test achievement, the Piagetian paradigm conceives of intelligence as the emergence of new mental structures. Traditionally, interindividual differences have been of particular interest to psychometricians. While developmental psychologists have been more interested in intraindividual structural changes, it must be pointed out that the concept of structure also has its place in psychometric paradigms, especially in connection with multivariate procedures. In addition, psychometrically oriented researchers interested in developmental phenomena also attempt to combine interindividual and intraindividual aspects in the description and analysis of change.

Elkind sees these two traditions, qualitative–structural and quantitative–psychometric, not as competing with one another but as complementary. Nevertheless, attempts have been made either to combine the two approaches (e.g., Piagetian tasks are "made psychometric") or to call the processes involved in solving cognitive problems either Piagetian tasks or psychometric intelligence test items (Carroll, 1974; Hunt, 1974; Putz-Osterloh & Lüer, 1975; Royer, 1977; Warburton, 1969; Whiteley, 1977). We will return to these approaches later in this chapter when Sternberg's (1977) component theory is discussed as a research paradigm.

Elkind argues that the quantitative approach is of great practical value in the prediction of scholastic achievement, etc. This chapter attempts to show that the utility of the quantitative approach must not be limited to the prediction of achievement if one wishes to suceed either in evaluating cognitive processes and structures quantitatively and/or in logically identifying cognitive tasks and the extent of transfer between them.

Quantitative Changes in Cognitive Development

A Concept of Development

This section is concerned with the description of tasks from the standpoint of a developmental psychology that is also interested in the measurement of quantitative changes in cognitive development. "Developmental psychology concerns itself with the description, explanation and modification of interindividual differences (and similarities) in intraindividual change [Baltes, Reese, & Nesselroade, 1977, p. 7]." Not only does this most recent definition of the life-span group lend support to the "changes-within-the-individual approach," it is also a clear affirmation that there are differences in individual patterns of change. This broad concept can be operationalized in a number of ways.

The Taxonomy of Change: The Buss Model

This section presents a possible operationalization of the concept of a taxonomy of change. From the viewpoint of a psychometrician, the model proposed by Buss (1974) develops a unified conceptual framework of change (and stability). The Buss model should not be confused with the well-known Schaie (1965; 1977) model with Baltes' (1968) "Age × Cohort plan," or with the multivariate models recently com-

piled by Nesselroade (1977) in the context of the Age × Cohort plan."
Based on Cattell's (1966) three-dimensional "Person × Variable × Occasion box," the model orders and defines interindividual differences,
intraindividual differences, and intraindividual change as well as their
relationships. A comparison of each of these three dimensions to the
other two, which remain constant, results in the following six cases (see
Figure 5.1):

1. Interindividual differences in intraindividual differences. Individuals are compared at one point of measurement across different
   variables.
2. "Intervariable" differences in interindividual differences. Variables are compared for individuals at one point of measurement.
3. Intraindividual differences at different points of measurement. Occasions are compared for all variables for one individual.
4. "Intervariable" differences (or intraindividual differences) in intraindividual change. Variables are compared for all occasions for
   one individual.
5. Interindividual differences in intraindividual changes. Individuals
   are compared for all occasions in one variable.
6. Differences in interindividual differences at different points of
   measurement. Occasions are compared for all individuals in one
   variable.

In each case, the dimension mentioned first is the point of interest and is
compared with samples taken from the elements of the second dimen-

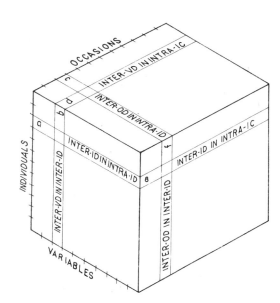

FIGURE 5.1. Six cases that result from comparison of each of the dimensions to the other two, which remain constant. ID = individual differences; IC = individual changes; VD = variable differences; OD = occasion differences. (From Buss, 1977.)

sion. Cases 3–6 are useful approaches to developmental psychology because they contain, in part, independent measurements or changes in the values of variables over time.

It would, of course, be possible to expand each of the six methods of data collection in such a way that for purposes of comparison a sample would also be taken from the third dimension, which, up to now, has remained constant, for example:

> 3'. Changes in interindividual differences versus changes in intraindividual differences. The variance for different individuals would be compared. These variances reflect the degree of individual differences for each point of measurement.

This strategy results in 15 methods of data collection for interindividual differences, intraindividual differences, and intraindividual changes. The first three consider only one dimension at a time. The next six work with two dimensions. In the last six, all three dimensions are compared in a three-step process (see Example 3').

In addition to change and variability, stability has also proved to be a central concept in the description of development. According to Buss, the multivariate developmental situation can mean stability of differences either between or within subjects over time. An excellent discussion of the various meanings of stability can be found in Wohlwill (1973a): for example, stability as predictability, as invariance, as regularity, as consensus, as the constancy of the relative position within a group, and as the preservation of individual differences. The numerous attempts to establish "developmental functions" and growth curves, especially in the area of cognitive functions (stability as regularity and predictability) make clear the dominance of this concept (e.g., Bloom, 1964; Horn & Cattell, 1966; Thomae, 1961).

This model, however, has certain weaknesses. For example, there is the problematic assumption of the invariance of developmental dimensions, or rather the problem of the validity of using a measurement instrument for all age groups, cohorts, and points of measurement in the Schaie–Baltes paradigm (Baltes & Schaie, 1973b). As Buss (1977) expresses it, "It is quantitative rather than qualitative or structural change, which the model is capable of addressing and it is therefore confined to slices of the life-span where the invariance of one's constructs has been demonstrated [p. 14]."

Information about the invariance of the meaning of the dimension in question can be obtained through multitrait–multimethod analysis, or, more generally, through the use of the structural-equation approach, which provides information regarding measurement models and construct-related structural models (Bentler, 1978; Jöreskog, 1977).

Problems in the Measurement of Intelligence

A detailed discussion of the classical processes used in the measurement of intelligence is not necessary within the context of this chapter. Only certain points will be considered that might be relevant for quantification approaches.

The classical (factor analytic) models of intelligence are not theoretical outlines of cognitive structures. Rather, they are classification systems for items that are supposed to measure intelligence. However, without a psychological theory of intelligence, the universe of either intelligence test items in the sense of Cronbach (1972), or of theoretically relevant facets in the sense of Guttman (1953), is undefined (Evans, 1969). An exception is Guilford's (1967) structure of intellect model. Shortcomings in these theories cannot be compensated for by taking recourse in classical models of test theory or in elaborate probabilistic measurement models (e.g., Birnbaum, 1968; Rasch, 1960). A psychological theory of intelligence would allow the formation of hypotheses about the abilities, components, operations, or microprocesses necessary and sufficient for the solution of problems. The absence of such a theory, however, leads to representation difficulties in the context of a theory of measurement. In this case, there is no firm basis for clear, significant quantification (cf. Hunt, 1974).

The explicit formulation of rules that regulate the linking of components and which can be empirically examined (cf. Spada & Kluwe, this volume; Sternberg, 1977) seems to be the first step in this direction. At present, however, the procedures for the measurement of intelligence that have their origins in the psychometric tradition attain, at best, the dignity of index measurements (Dawes, 1972). Such indices have pragmatic value but their theoretical force is minimal. In such cases, one cannot speak of the existence of a quantitative dimension of development in which the changes take place.

Developmental Aspects of Theories of Intelligence

The Concept of Ability

Invariant (developmental) dimensions for the description of cognitive development are often introduced from the standpoint of the concept of ability. According to Fleishman and Bartlett (1969), abilities are the product of maturing and learning, and are characterized by stability in adulthood. Through transfer, abilities facilitate a multiplicity of specific learning tasks and can be seen as the general basis of skills. The term "skill" refers to the quick, exact performance of a sequence of activities in one homogeneous task area. Ferguson (1956) offers a definition of abilities similar to that of Fleishman and Bartlett. For him, abilities are attributes of behavior which, through learning, have attained a crude stability or invariance in the adult and which, as they develop in the child, exhibit considerable stability over limited periods of time at particular age levels. Operationally defined, the term "ability" refers to asymptotic measures of achievement; learning is considered to be a specific form of transfer, which in this case, is seen as a mathematical function that specifies how a dependent variable will change relative to a change in an independent variable. Abilities become apparent and distinct through a process of differential transfer. They are differentially effective in learning situations in which two different processes can be distinguished: positive transfer in the development of abilities, and task-specific learning processes in the differentiation of abilities.

Cultural factors prescribe what should be learned at a given age; as a result, different cultural environments lead to the development of different patterns of abilities. Those abilities which are culturally valid and which correlate with numerous achievements (accomplishments) required by the culture are those which exhibit an increase with age. A quantification of the development of intelligence based on Ferguson's (1956) theory involves various difficulties due to the large number of cultural learning processes and the resulting complex network of differential transfer effects. For this reason, it is virtually impossible to estimate the total differential transfer potential of a given period of development. Theoretically, however, such a quantification would seem conceivable for segments of the development of abilities through the use of training studies. In a 1975 study, Rüppell had children overlearn selected information-processing strategies, and the extent of transfer to other cognitive learning processes was quantified. The extent of transfer was employed in the quantitative evaluation of development. The objection that Ferguson's transfer model is not capable of explaining the large number of adult skills is not sustainable in view of the probability that an even greater number of possible differential transfer effects exists.

The principal difficulty involved with developmental transfer models is that too little research has been done on transfer mechanisms. Gagné (1968), in connection with cumulative learning models, indicated some of the difficulties involved in such research. He pointed out that transfer in very simple problems is often studied in laboratory situations but that very little is known about cumulative effects of transfer in complex learning processes over a longer period of time.

Cattell's Theory of Intelligence

Ferguson's (1956) model can be compared with Cattell's (1971) model of intelligence. In Cattell's model "fluid intelligence," takes the place of Ferguson's differential transfer. Fluid intelligence facilitates learning in all complex situations. In addition, Cattell postulates "crystallized intelligence," which facilitates transfer effects. Cattell's "investment" theory of fluid and crystallized intelligence offers some possible explanations of changes in cognitive development (Cattell, 1971; Horn & Cattell, 1966) in that it makes it possible to predict differential quantitative changes over an entire life span. Crystallized intelligence increases even after the age of 20—the achievement level depends on environmental influences and experience (upbringing, education, etc.). Fluid intelligence diminishes after age 20 as a result of changes in basic neurological structures. Fluid intelligence is not exclusively hereditary. It can be seen as a product of the neurological capacity in interaction with subjectively and culturally invariant experience processes. Evidence of these different quantitative developmental functions could be found in cross-sectional studies and, although somewhat less clearly, in life-span developmental studies and longitudinal studies of subjects at advanced ages (Rudinger, 1976).

Cattell's theory has led many researchers to seek parallels to Piaget's concept of the development of cognitive processes. Clayton and Overton (1976), for example, concluded that there is a relationship between fluid intelligence and concrete operations and that the attainment of the stage of formal operations is dependent on qualitative aspects of the educational experience. Several attempts have also been made to expand Piaget's theory of cognitive development to cover the entire life span (Arlin, 1976; Piaget, 1972; Riegel, 1973).

From a developmentally oriented standpoint, Cattell's theory has several reference points to offer, since it gives explicit information about the requirements and the development of quantitative dimensions of intelligence. Within the theoretical framework, there are instruments of measurement related to a network of theoretical constructs. Three questions arise in this context:

1. What kind of environmental conditions would lead to the optimal development of these dimensions of intelligence?
2. Which processes in fluid intelligence and which in crystallized intelligence are involved in the solution of problems? (See Dörner, 1976.)
3. Is there a change in these processes corresponding to a developmentally determined change of level?

METATHEORY: NATURE–NURTURE

The first question leads directly to a discussion of the metatheoretical problem known as the nature–nurture controversy. However, we wish to refrain from going into this problem in this chapter (cf., e.g., Cancro, 1971; Heckhausen, 1974).

Precisely how the assumed interactions between heredity and environment take place is also unclear since both constructs (heredity factors–environment) are too complex. There is neither a clear picture of the relationship between genetic factors and intelligence (cf. Hirsch, 1971; Rainer, 1976), nor a sufficient taxonomy of relevant environmental aspects (Wohlwill, 1973b). At the moment, however, there is increased interest in uncovering those relevant environmental aspects that would be of help in explaining intellectual development and achievement. As an example, consider some of the principal categories of Marjoribanks' (1972) taxonomy: standards for achievement, activity etc., maternal and paternal dominance. With the use of a path-analytic procedure, we were able to show that, in the case of the elderly, 38% of the variance of intellectual performance can be explained by the conditions under which the subjects live (Rudinger & Lantermann, 1978). Similarly, Rees and Palmer (1970) presented a reanalysis of compiled data from five well-known American longitudinal studies with children and adolescents (Fels, Denver, Berkeley studies, Oakland).

ENVIRONMENTAL TAXONOMIES AND INTERVENTION

Some recent work in this area has been done by Walberg and Marjoribanks (1976). Their taxonomy is composed of 12 different models in which the variables of family background, stimulation conditions, etc. are represented and tested for their effects on cognitive development. This and other studies show the considerable influence that environmental influences have on the quantitative development of cognitive abilities (Trudewind, 1975). As a consequence, intervention programs have been suggested which seek to provide a more stimulating environment and thus accelerate the development of cognitive abilities (e.g., Labouvie & Gonda, 1976; Robertson-Tschabo et al. 1976).

From a theoretical standpoint, one can consider such studies as "quasi-experiments" or training studies for the information that they provide about cognitive development (Baltes & Goulet, 1971). Here, however, there are two problems: that of external validity (e.g., Hultsch & Hickey, 1977) and that of inferring underlying cognitive processes (and how they can be influenced).

Intelligence and Cognitive Processes

With the so-called training studies, evidence has been sought for the "trainability" of fluid intelligence (Plemons *et al.*, 1977). According to Cattell, the basic elements of a given group of tasks must be overlearned in order to eliminate the variance due to environmental factors. Cattell maintains that such overlearning exists in the area of spatial abilities. French (1965), however, using the method of thinking aloud in combination with questioning of subjects, was able to show that the performance in the space test "cubes" is largely a product of analytic strategies. These and comparable findings (e.g., Hunt, 1974) have brought to light the fact that it is still unclear which cognitive abilities are necessary to solve which test tasks. One of the consequences of this realization could be to shift the quantitative description of cognitive development either to a more general level or to a more specific level. Hunt (1975) worked with the first possibility within the conceptual framework of cognitive styles and made it more tangible through the so-called "conceptual complexity" construct. The problem here is that, with this kind of generalization, the boundaries dissolve between the cognitive, social and emotional spheres of development. Furthermore, in this case, quantitative measurement is difficult. Hunt's attempt to measure "cognitive complexity" with short essays on topics such as "legislation," "parents," and "insecurity" is not very convincing.

The second possibility for relating intelligence and cognitive processes stems from various authors' use of theories of human information-processing. The approach that we consider to be the most extensively developed is Sternberg's (1977) component theory of intelligence. At the same time, this approach is closely related to the psychometric tradition.

STERNBERG'S COMPONENT THEORY OF INTELLIGENCE

According to Sternberg, components are the elementary units of information processing. The component theory specifies the nature of these components, the rules governing the combination of components, the sequence in which the components appear, a pattern of the parallel or serial application of single components, and the speed and ease of the components' performance.

These theoretical elements have led to five contributions to the explication of cognitive development:

1. New components are acquired, or one learns how to apply already acquired components to new situations.
2. New rules of combination are acquired, or one learns to apply already acquired rules to new situations.

3. The sequence in which components appear is restructured, or one learns to apply stable, already existing sequences to new tasks.
4. The pattern of parallel or serial application of single components is changed, or one learns to apply already existing patterns to new tasks.
5. Components are executed more quickly and with greater ease.

Sternberg's (1977) description of cognitive development leads to a strong knotting of qualitative and quantitative changes. The specifically quantitative changes are particularly obvious in the expanded range of application of the existing components, rules governing their combination, component sequences, patterns of parallel and serial application, and in the increasing speed and ease of the components' performance.

Sternberg developed concrete models of solution processes for "analogical reasoning." By means of a painstaking, creative, intensive, and extensive task analysis, he looked at the appropriateness and adequacy of these models. The intensive task analysis consisted of internal and external validation. Internal validation is the decomposition of the given task into its components. External validation is the estimation of the significance of the components for the occurrence of interindividual differences in external tasks. In our opinion, Sternberg's quantitative–qualitative procedure is, at present, the most complex and most well-thought-out approach to research in intelligence that links the psychometric tradition to that of information processing.

If Sternberg's approach (or a comparable model, e.g., Spada, 1976) should prove to be successful and should determine stable, empirically tested components, then the problems involved in measuring intelligence (discussed on page 111) will have been brought one step closer to a solution. However, the chances of success with this approach are not too great. Sternberg himself sees the limits of his approach in the following problems:

1. Parameters are often confounded.
2. A decision between alternative models is often not possible.
3. Components are not always clearly identifiable since it is not always possible to decide whether the same components are repeated or whether different components come into play. "If the component scores are very highly correlated across subjects (after correlation for attenuation) then there is a good chance that the component scores are actually measures of the same component. One cannot be certain however, since distinct components may be correlated [Sternberg, 1977, p. 76]."
4. It is unclear whether the mathematical description of models is

suitable for the examination of complex processes or whether their usefulness extends only to a middle level of complexity.

This last point is particularly significant for questions in developmental psychology, since it is concerned with long-term processes in a natural environment.

INVARIANCE OF COMPONENTS

A general aspect, which may argue against the existence of uniform, stable intelligence components, is the great difference in individual learning environments and the mental ability to adapt to them. Neisser (1976) and others (cf. Posner *et al.*, 1977) argue that the chief task of intelligence research is not the analysis of intelligence, but the analysis of environment. Posner *et al.* summarize this position as follows: "The human information processing system is so adaptable that its mechanisms cannot be specified by empirical study, at least with the methods available in psychology. Instead, one might assume that the system has adapted by evolution to perform in a way that is optimal for the particular environments that have exerted selective pressure [p. 482]."

General doubt as to the existence of stable components of information processing and problem-solving methods can be derived from Frederiksen's (1969) and Aebli's (1970) approaches. Frederiksen argues for the empirically confirmed hypothesis that solution methods or cognitive strategies are functions of ability and the given task structure. Abilities facilitate the formation of task-specific strategies that function as transfer mechanisms. In this case, the quantitative measurement of these strategies is not directly possible but can be accomplished, for instance, with Frederiksen's "strategy assessment tests." Aebli places special emphasis on the possibility of a temporary formation of task-specific solution strategies. Instead of trying to explain cognitive achievement with stable structures, Aebli speaks in terms of ephemeral products of elaboration, which are not directly connected with one another, but which all grow out of a basic cognitive repertoire. It is assumed that the basic repertoire becomes more elaborate in the course of development, thus increasing interindividual differences.

Miller (1965) described the dynamics of the intellect similarly but included "chaotic" elements:

1. Thinking consists of a mixture of images, ideas, and symbols for these ideas.
2. Thinking is not necessarily logical.
3. Details, facts and symbol relations are selectively and unreliably stored in the memory and are subject to the changing influences of personality variables.

4. Thinking requires the contiguity of goal formation, the setting of alternatives and their implications.
5. Thinking is subject to influences of negative transfer.

Such concepts hardly offer a means of quantifying cognitive development, perhaps because they are too closely oriented to reality.

AN ALTERNATIVE? SELZ'S MODEL

A model that could possibly mediate between the models already mentioned is, paradoxically enough, one of the oldest empirically supported models of intelligence: Selz's (1935) model. For Selz, intelligence is a system of generalized operations of thought for the acquisition and utilization of knowledge that is built up in a step-by-step process in the course of its development. Parallel to this system, a network of rules is developed that regulate the application of certain operations of thought to the solution of certain kinds of tasks. Selz found support for his concept in findings from experiments on inductive and deductive thinking. In one pedagogical program of acceleration based on a process analysis, evidence was found of significant transfer effects. The development of the network of rules described by Selz can perhaps be seen as an anticipated specification of what Bruner (1964) maintains to be the chief characteristic of cognitive development: "Maturation consists of an orchestration of these [simpler] components in an integrated sequence [p. 2]."

With regard to the quantification of intellectual development, various possibilities result from Selz's approach. On the one hand, it seems possible to measure the generalized operations of thought by the amount of transfer they produce in a training experiment in which a specified information processing strategy is to be learned. On the other hand, the quality of the network of rules could be evaluated by the number of already learned operations the child transfers to the solution of a new task.

However, before such attempts at quantification are made, it seems necessary to clarify the developmental prerequisites for the origination of the processes mentioned by Selz and Bruner. Evidence of the existence of such prerequisites can be found in work done by Case (1975) who questioned Gagné's (1968) cumulative learning model in its function as a developmental model. He showed that intellectual development results not only from a hierarchy of increasingly complex skills, but also from the maturationally determined emergence of general competence such as: (a) the development of the ability to coordinate information, defined by the number of skills that a subject is able to use in a coordinate way in a learning situation; and (b) the development of the ability to control the natural reactions in problem situations and to regulate better the use of unsuitable skills.

A "TRAINING EXPERIMENT"

Selz's procedure of teaching defined cognitive processes and making inferences about the adequacy of the theory of intelligence from observed transfer effects is also interesting with regard to studying developmental processes in "training experiments." Such experiments, proposed by Bronfenbrenner (1977) and carried out under the motto: "If you want to understand something, try to change it [p. 517]", have been conducted primarily by Soviet developmental psychologists. On a more general level, the "training studies" mentioned previously could also be considered as belonging to this group. A project conducted by Rüppell, Rüppell, and Böker (1974), mentioned earlier in connection with Ferguson's transfer theory, is a training experiment more extended in time and with greater emphasis on the mediation of cognitive processes. This research project was designed to develop a learning environment that mediates the overlearning of information processing strategies which characterize selected structure-of-intelligence abilities (Guilford, 1967). In accordance with Ferguson's theory, it is assumed that these overlearned strategies will directly promote the development of the abilities so that they become stable elements of the intelligence of an individual.

These directly promoted abilities were selected with the intent of facilitating the development of all the other nonselected structure-of-intelligence abilities by means of transfer of training. The rationale behind selecting a strategy is based on the functional organization of abilities. Because this functional organization is still unknown, the empirical factors of intelligence (Royce, 1973) are taken as a first approximation of this organization. The problem with this approximation lies in the inference of causal transfer relations from correlations (Pawlik, 1973). Functional organization of abilities can only be inferred when correlations are mainly due to transfer relations between abilities. One cannot exclude the possibility that cognitive abilities correlate only because of correlating environmental learning conditions. It follows that when the number of empirically stated intelligence factors is taken as an estimate of the number of functionally unrelated dimensions of intelligence, the latter is underestimated. This danger can be reduced by using Royce's (1973) redundant compilation of intelligence factors. The danger can be further reduced when these factors are supplemented by additional dimensions that are useful in the construction of a complete learning hierarchy. The supplemented dimensions were selected in such a way that the final set of directly promoted abilities provides for the formation of (a) the problem-solving sequence "cognition–convergent or divergent production–evaluation"; (b) the developmental sequence "figural–semantic–symbolic contents"; and (c) the sequence "units or relations or classes–systems–implications." Using this strategy, 33 structure-of-intelligence abilities were selected and hierarchically ordered. The development of a learning environment that enables the overlearning of the abilities was based on principles for clarifying educational environments (Moore & Anderson, 1969) and on principles of instructional psychology. It was shown that these principles can be implemented in a coordinated manner by means of *n*-person games. Such a game was designed for every ability selected. The designing process began with an analysis of a large number of cultural games and the information processing strategies that they involve. Figure 5.2 shows the game hierarchy.

The evaluation of the first level of this game hierarchy shows that the intended learning processes effectuate no immediate gains in the underlying abilities. However, it was shown that learning of the information-processing strategy of one game facilitated the learning of the more complex information processing strategy of a related game. These results led to the evaluation of cognitive development by measuring the ability to learn specified information processing strategies under con-

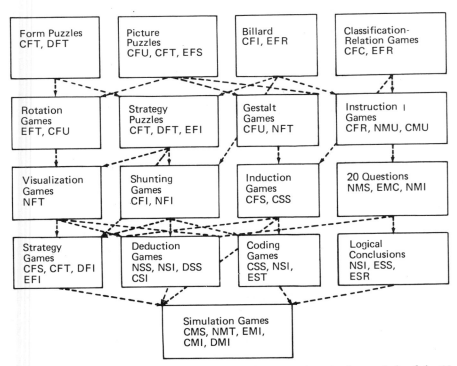

FIGURE 5.2. *The game hierarchy. The logical validities are given in the symbols of the SI-model. The arrows show the directions of the assumed transfer effects.*

trolled conditions. This ability is quantified by a two-step sequential testing procedure. In the first step, the child has to solve a problem that is more difficult than the ones in the preceding games. With the help of a standardized interview, the experimenter evaluates how many already-learned elements of the information processing strategies are applied in solving the problem. In the second step, the child has to learn an information-processing strategy that enables him to solve the problem optimally. This learning process is characterized by modeling cycles in which the experimenter demonstrates the strategy and the child imitates his behavior. The number of modeling trials the child needs before he or she is able to perform the strategy is taken as the child's developmental score in the underlying abilities.

The first step provides a measure of the quality of Selz's network of rules for the regulation of the application of thought operations. The score obtained from the second step reflects the transfer potential of the cognitive processes that have been learned up to that point. This potential is interpreted as a developmental measure of the underlying ability. These abilities are identified with the help of Guilford's SI-model. It has been suggested that flow charts be used in the logical analysis of test problems (cf. Fleishman, 1975; Meeker, 1969) because they make possible, through a series of binary decisions, the successive limitation of the abilities in Guilford's SI-model. The attempt to determine the abilities empirically by factor analysis has led to no clear factor solution. Furthermore, the use of such training experiments presents one difficulty when attempting to gain knowledge about the sequence of partial processes that can then be fitted into a theoretical framework: Trained or learned processes and strategies are modified and transformed by the individual (Glaser, 1976; Putz-Osterloh, 1974).

References

Aebli, H. Kognitive Entwicklung als Aufbau in einem soziokulturellen Kontext. *Schweizerische Zeitschrift für Psychologie*, 1970, *29*, 389–471.
Arlin, P. K. Toward a metatheoretical model of cognitive development. *International Journal of Aging and Human Development*, 1976, *7*, 247–253.
Baltes, P. B. Longitudinal and cross-sectional sequences in the study of age and generation effects. *Human Development*, 1968, *11*, 145–171.
Baltes, P. B. & Goulet, L. R. Exploration of development variables by manipulation and simulation of age differences in behavior. *Human Development*, 1971, *14*, 149–170.
Baltes, P. B. & Labouvie, G. V. Adult development of intellectual performance: Description, explanation, modification. In G. Eisdorfer & P. L. Lawton (Eds.), *The psychology of adult development and aging*. Washington: APA, 1973. Pp. 157–220.
Baltes, P. B., Reese, H. W. & Nesselroade, J. R. *Life-span developmental psychology: Introduction to research methods*. Monterey, CA: Brooks-Cole, 1977.

Baltes, P. B. & Schaie, K. W. On life-span developmental paradigms. In P. B. Baltes & K. W. Schaie (Eds.), *Life-span developmental psychology: Personality and socialization.* New York: Academic Press, 1973.

Bentler, P. M. Theory testing via causal modeling in developmental psychology. In G. Rudinger (Ed.), *Entwicklungs-psychologische Methoden.* Stuttgart: Kohlhammer, 1978. in press.

Birnbaum, A. Some latent trait models and their use in inferring an examinee's ability. In F. M. Lord & M. R. Novick (Eds.), *Statistical theories mental test scores.* Reading, Mass.: Addison-Wesley, 1968. Pp. 397–472.

Bloom, B. S. *Stability and change in human characteristics.* New York: Wiley, 1964.

Bronfenbrenner, U. Toward an experimental ecology of human development. *American Psychologist*, 1977, *32*, 513–531.

Bruner, J. S. The course of cognitive development. *American Psychologist*, 1964, *19*, 1–15.

Buss, A. R. A general developmental model for interindividual differences, intraindividual differences, and intraindividual changes. *Developmental Psychology*, 1974, *10*, 70–78.

Buss, A. R. Toward a unified framework for psychometric concepts in the multivariate developmental situation: Intraindividual change and inter- and intraindividual differences. In J. R. Nesselroade & P. B. Baltes (Eds.), *Longitudinal research in the behavioral sciences: design and analysis.* Final Report, Pennsylvania State University, 1977. Pp. 2–35.

Cancro, R. Genetic contributions to individual differences in intelligence: an introduction. In R. Cancro (Ed.), *Intelligence, genetic and environmental influences.* New York: Grune & Stratton, 1971. Pp. 59–65.

Case, R. Gearing the demands of instruction to the developmental capacities of the learner. *Review of Educational Research*, 1975, *45*, 59–87.

Carroll, J. B. Psychometric tests as cognitive tasks: A new "structure of intellect". *ETS Bulletin*, RB-74-16, Princeton, N.J., 1974.

Cattell, R. B. (Ed.). *Handbook of multivariate experimental psychology.* Chicago: Rand McNally, 1966.

Cattell, R. B. *Abilities: Their structure, growth and action.* New York: Houghton Mifflin, 1971.

Clayton, V. & Overton, W. F. Concrete and formal operational thought processes in young adulthood and old age. *International Journal of Aging and Human Development*, 1976, *7*, 237–245.

Cronbach, L. J., Gleser, Goldine C., Nanda, H. & Rajaratnam, N. *The dependability of behavioral measurements.* New York: Wiley, 1972.

Dawes, R. D. *Fundamentals of attitude measurement.* New York: Wiley, 1972.

Dörner, D. *Problemlösen als Informationsverarbeitung.* Stuttgart: Kohlhammer, 1976.

Elkind, D. Two approaches to intelligence: Piagetian and psychometric. In D. R. Green, M. P. Ford & G. B. Flamer (Eds.), *Measurement and Piaget.* New York: McGraw-Hill, 1971. Pp. 12–28.

Evans, G. T. Intelligence, transfer and problem-solving. In W. B. Dockrell (Ed.), *On intelligence. The Toronto Symposium.* London: Methuen, 1969. Pp. 191–233.

Ferguson, G. A. On transfer and the abilities of man. *Canadian Journal of Psychology*, 1956, *10*, 121–131.

Fleishman, E. A. Toward a taxonomy of human performance. *American Psychologist*, 1975, *30*, 1127–1149.

Fleishman, E. A. & Bartlett, C. J. Human abilities. In P. H. Mussen & M. R. Rosenzweig (Eds.), *Annual Review of Psychology*, 1969, *20*. Pp. 349–380.

Frederiksen, C. H. Abilities, transfer and information retrieval in verbal learning. *Multivariate Behavioral Research Monograph*, 1969, *2*.

French, J. W. The relation of problem-solving styles to the factor composition of tests. *Educational and psychological measurement*, 1965, *1*, 9–28.

Furth, H. G. Piaget, J. IQ and the nature-nurture controversy. In K. F. Riegel (Ed.), *Intelligence: Alternative views of a paradigm.* Basel: Karger, 1973. Pp. 61–74.

Gagné, Contributions of learning to human development. *Psychological Review,* 1968, *75,* 177–191.

Glaser, R. Components of a psychology of instruction: toward a science of design. *Review of Educational Research,* 1976, *46,* 1–24.

Guilford, J. P. *The nature of human intelligence.* New York: McGraw-Hill, 1967.

Guttman, L. A special Review of Harold Gulliksen. *Theory of Mental Tests, Psychometrika,* 1953, *18,* 123–130.

Heckhausen, H. Anlage und Umwelt als Ursache von Intelligenzunterschieden. In F. E. Weinert *et al.* (Eds.), *Funkkolleg Pädagogische Psychologie.* Bd. 1, Frankfurt: Fischer, 1974. Pp. 277–312.

Hirsch, J. Behavior-genetic analysis and its biosocial consequences. In R. Cancro (Ed.), *Intelligence, genetic and environmental influences.* New York: Grune & Stratton, 1971. Pp. 88–107.

Horn, J. G., Cattell, R. B. Age differences in primary mental ability factors. *Journal of Gerontology,* 1966, *21,* 210–220.

Hultsch, D. F. & Hickey, T. *External validity in the study of human development: Theoretical and methodological issues.* Draft, Pennsylvania State University, 1977.

Hunt, D. E. Person–environment interaction: A challenge found wanting before it was tried. *Review of Educational Research,* 1975, *45,* 209–230.

Hunt, E. B. Quote the Raven? Nevermore! In L. W. Gregg (Ed.), *Knowledge and cognition.* Hillsdale, N.J.: Lawrence Erlbaum, 1974. Pp. 129–159.

Jöreskog, K. G.: Statistical estimation of structure models in longitudinal– developmental investigation. In J. R. Nesselroade & P. B. Baltes (Eds.), *Longitudinal research in the behavioral sciences: design and analysis.* Final Report, Pennsylvania State University, 1977. Pp. 309–410.

Labouvie-Vief, G. & Gonda, J. Cognitive strategy training and intellectual performance in the elderly. *Journal of Gerontology,* 1976, *31,* 327–332.

Marjoribanks, K. Environment, social class and mental abilities. *Educational Psychology,* 1973, *63,* 103–109.

Meeker, M. N. The structure of intellect. *Its interpretation and uses.* Columbus: Merrill, 1969.

Merz, F. & Stelzl, I. Modellvorstellungen über die Entwicklung der Intelligenz in Kindheit und Jugend. *Zeitschrift für Entwicklungspsychologie und Pädagogische Psychologie,* 1973, *5,* 153–166.

Miller, R. B. Psychology for man–machine problem-solving system. Poughkeepsie, N.Y.: *IBM Technical Report* oo.1246 (AD 640 283), 1965.

Moore, O. K. & Anderson, A. R. Some principles for the design of clarifying educational environments. In D. A. Goslin (Ed.), *Handbook of socialization theory and research.* Chicago: Rand McNally, 1969. Pp. 571–614.

Neisser, U. *Cognition and reality: principles and implications of cognitive psychology.* San Francisco: Freeman, 1976.

Nesselroade, J. R. Issues in studying developmental change in adults from multivariate perspective. In J. E. Birren & K. W. Schaie (Eds.), *Handbook of the psychology of aging.* New York: Van Nostrand, 1977. Pp. 59–69.

Nesselroade, J. R. & Baltes, P. B. (Eds.) *Longitudinal research in the behavioral sciences: design and analysis.* Final Report, Pennsylvania State University, 1977.

Nesselroade, J. R., Schaie, K. W., & Baltes, P. B. Ontogenetic and generational components of structural and quantitative change in adult cognitive behavior. *Journal of Genetic Psychology,* 1972, *27,* 222–228.

Newell, A. & Simon, H. A. *Human problem solving.* Englewood Cliffs, N.J.: Prentice-Hall, 1972.

Overton, W. F. & Reese, H. W. Models of development: Methodological implications. In J. R. Nesselroade & H. W. Reese (Eds.), *Life-span developmental psychology: methodological issues.* New York: Academic Press, 1973. Pp. 65–86.

Pask, G. *Conversation, cognition and learning: a cybernetic theory and methodology.* Amsterdam: Elsevier, 1975.

Pawlik, K. Zur Frage der psychologischen Interpretation von Persönlichkeits-fragebogen. *Bericht aus dem Psychologischen Institut der Universität Hamburg,* 1973, *22.*

Piaget, J. Intellectual evolution from adolescence to adulthood. *Human Development,* 1972, *15,* 1–12.

Plemons, J. L., Willis, S. L. & Baltes, P. B. Modificability of fluid intelligence in aging: a short-term longitudinal training approach. *Journal of Gerontology,* 1977, in press.

Posner, M. I., McLean, J. P., & Weimer, W. B. Cognition: forwards or backwards? *Contemporary Psychology,* 1977, *22,* 481–484.

Putz-Osterloh, W. Über die Effektivität von Problemlösungs-training. *Zeitschrift für Psychologie,* 1974, *182,* 253–373.

Putz-Osterloh, W. & Lüer, G. Informationsverarbeitung bei einem Test zur Erfassung der Raumvorstellung. *Diagnostica,* 1975, *XXI/4,* 166–181.

Rainer, I. D. Genetics of intelligence: current issues and unsolved questions. *Research Communications in Psychology, Psychiatry and Behavior,* 1976, *1,* 607–618.

Rasch, G. *Probabilistic models for some intelligence and attainment tests.* Copenhagen: The Danish Institute for Educational Research, 1960.

Rees, A. H. & Palmer, F. H. Factors related to change in mental test performance. *Developmental Psychological Monograph* 1970, No. 2.

Riegel, K. F. (Ed.) *Intelligence: alternative views of a paradigm.* Basel: Karger, 1973.

Robertson-Tschabo, E. A., Hausmann, C. B., & Arenberg, D. A. A classical mnemonic for older learners: a trip that works! *Educational Gerontology,* 1976, *1,* 215–226.

Royce, J. R. The conceptual framework for a multi-factor theory of individuality. In J. R. Royce (Ed.), *Multivariate analysis and psychological theory.* New York: Academic Press, 1973. Pp. 305–380.

Royer, F. L. Information processing in the block design task. *Intelligence,* 1977, *1,* 32–50.

Rudinger, G. Correlates of changes in cognitive functioning. In: Thomae, H. (Ed.) *Patterns of aging, contributions to human development.* Vol. 3, Basel: Karger, 1976. Pp. 20–35.

Rudinger, G. & Lantermann, E. D. Soziale Bedingungen der Intelligenz in Alter, *ISSBD Journal,* 1978, in press.

Rüppell, H. Optimierung kognitiver Lernprozesse durch Spiele. *Zeitschrift für Pädagogik,* 1975, *21,* 403–405.

Rüppell, H., Rüppell, M., & Böker, H. D. *Intelligenzförderung durch Spiele.* Hamburg: Unveröffentlichter Forschungsbericht, 1974.

Schaie, K. W. A general model for the study of developmental problems. *Psychological Bulletin,* 1965, *64,* 92–107.

Schaie, K. W. Limitations on generalizability of growth curves of intelligence. A reanalysis of data from the Harvard Study. *Human Development,* 1972, *15,* 141–152.

Schaie, K. W. Quasi-experimental research designs in the psychology of aging. In J. E. Birren & K. W. Schaie (Eds.), *Handbook of the psychology of aging.* New York: Van Nostrand, 1977. Pp. 39–58.

Schaie, K. W. & Strother, C. R. A cross–sequential study of age changes in cognitive behavior. *Psychological Bulletin,* 1968, *70,* 671–680. (a)

Schaie, K. W. & Strother, C. R. The effects of time– and cohort differences on the interpretation of age changes in cognitive behavior. *Multivariate Behavioral Research,* 1968, *3,* 259–294. (b)

Selz, O. Versuche zur Hebung des Intelligenzniveaus. *Zeitschrift für Psychologie,* 1935, *134,* 236–301.

Spada, H. *Modelle des Denkens und Lernens.* Bern: Huber, 1976.

Sternberg, R. *Intelligence, information processing, and analogical reasoning: the componential analysis of human abilities.* Hillsdale, N.J.: Lawrence Erlbaum, 1977.

Thomae, H. Vorstellungsmodelle in der Entwicklungspsychologie.*Zeitschrift für Psychologie*, 1961, *165*, 41–58.

Trudewind, C. *Häusliche Umwelt und Motiventwicklung*, Göttingen: Hogrefe, 1975.

Tuddenham, R. D. A "Piagetian" test of cognitive development. In W. B. Dockrell (Ed.),*On intelligence. The Toronto symposium.* London: Methuen, 1969. Pp. 49–70.

Van De Ven, H. & Pieters, J. P. *A Poisson/Erlang model for response latency of mental tasks.* 8. Europäisches Meeting Math. Psych., 1977, Saarbrücken.

Walberg, H. J. & Marjoribanks, K. Family environment and cognitive development: twelve analytic models. *Review of Educational Research*, 1976, *46*, 527–552.

Warburton, F. W. The British Intelligence Scale. In W. B. Dockrell (Ed.), *On intelligence. The Toronto Symposium.* London: Methuen, 1969. Pp. 71–99.

Whiteley, S. E. Information-processing on intelligence test items: some response components. *Applied Psychological Measurement*, 1977, *1*, 456–476.

Wohlwill, J. F. *The study of behavioral development.* New York: Academic Press, 1973. (a)

Wohlwill, J. F. The concept of experience: S or R? In K. F. Riegel (Ed.), *Intelligence: alternative views of a paradigm.* Karger: Basel, 1973. (b) Pp. 90–108. (b)

6

Information-Processing Models of Intellectual Development

DAVID KLAHR

Introduction[1]

The purpose of this volume is to generate productive comparisons, contrasts, and criticisms of current approaches to the study of cognitive development. My own contribution to that goal will be to describe an information-processing approach to the study of cognitive development. Rather than attempt to present a broad survey of the relevant research, I will limit my remarks to a description of some features of theoretical and empirical work from my own laboratory.

What properties would an information processing theory of cognitive development possess? Ideally, such a theory would be: (a) sufficiently general to encompass a wide variety of developmental phenomena; (b) sufficiently precise and consistent to be cast as a running computer program; and (c) sufficiently operational to be subject to empirical test. Over the past several years, we have been attempting to formulate such a theory, and a progress report (Klahr & Wallace, 1976) describes our work up to around 1974. Our own evaluation of the theory proposed therein is that it satisfies the first of the three criteria above, but that it still needs to be extended to satisfy the other two.

In the next section, I will summarize some of the important features of our work as it stood when we completed work on our book. Then, on pages 132–157, I will describe my efforts to make the theory more precise and more testable. Pages 157–160, describe some of the currently

[1] Preparation of this work was supported in part by Grant BNS77-16905 from the National Science Foundation, and in part by a grant from the Sloan Foundation. This chapter appeared previously in *Structural/Process Theories of Complex Human Behavior,* edited by Joseph M. Scandura, published by Sijthoff & Noordhoff International Publishers b. v., Alphen aan den Rijn, The Netherlands. It is reprinted here by permission.

DEVELOPMENTAL MODELS
OF THINKING

ISBN 0–12–416450–1

unresolved issues in the design of self-modifying systems, and pages 160–161, contain some concluding comments.

General Orientation

Faced with the behavior of a child performing a task or learning how to perform it, we pose the question: "What processing routines and what kinds of internally stored information would a person need in order to generate the observed behavior?" The answer takes the form of a set of rules that can be interpreted by an information-processing device (i.e., a computer program). The program thus constitutes a model of the human.

One distinctive feature of this approach is its emphasis on precision. Since the models are stated in the form of running computer programs, they tend to be much more detailed and explicit than is typically the case, and their logical consistency as well as their detailed predictions of behavior in various environments can be directly tested simply by running them. However, many individual assumptions and assertions cannot be tested directly. The complete set of model statements can never be formally evaluated beyond a sufficiency criterion, although informal criteria such as plausibility and generality can be used.

Once models of different performance levels have been constructed, we can begin to examine the differences among them. Since the model for each performance level is itself quite precise, the nature of the change between one level and the next is better defined than in most other forms of modeling.

System Architecture of the Adult
Information-Processing System

Although there are still many points of disagreement, over the past 20 years there has emerged a picture of the general structure of the human information-processing system (cf. Bower, 1975; Hunt, 1971; Newell & Simon, 1972). Processing is postulated to occur in a sequence of layers, starting with environmental stimuli impinging on the senses, and continuing on to the "deeper" or "central" processes. Associated with each layer is some storage capacity (a buffer) that holds information while it is further processed by subsequent stages. The sensory processes, which receive and store all sensory information for fractions of a second are at the outer layer. Up to this point the system appears to operate in parallel and unselectively. At the next level, selected and partially encoded information is retained for further processing by modality-specific (e.g., visual or auditory) buffers, for somewhat longer periods of about 1 sec duration.

Next, information is passed through a limited capacity buffer, usually identified as short-term memory (STM). Information in STM must be attended to and retained for some period, from 5 to 10 sec, before it can be transferred to long-term memory (LTM).

Long-term memory appears to be of essentially unlimited capacity. It is organized as a network of associated concepts and propositions, and a collection of strategies and procedures. The routines in LTM control information transfer among the layers of processing, the searching of the conceptual and propositional network, and programs for the modification of LTM.

The Young Information-Processing System

So much for the adult information-processing system. How shall we characterize the child? We face one overwhelming fact: On almost every task presented to them, children's performance is poorer than adults': They are slower, they make more errors, they do not attend or remember as well. However, for children beyond the age of 5, there is no reason to believe that the system architecture just outlined—parallel sensory buffers, limited STM, and unlimited associative LTM—changes with age. An even stronger view, which we entertain as a working hypothesis, is that there is no substantial change in the parameters, that is, the capacities and rates, of the components of this system architecture.

The major difference between children and adults is that, rather than simply possessing "smaller" or "slower" STMs, children appear to be deficient in prior knowledge of facts, procedures, and strategies; in control of attention; and in utilization of memory processes. Evidence for this viewpoint can be found in several studies, including Chi (1976, 1977) and Huttenlocher and Burke (1976). Thus, the central focus of our theory is a representation of the knowledge in LTM, and a theory of how that representation is changed to permit increasingly powerful performance within a stable system architecture.

REPRESENTATION OF KNOWLEDGE

Our representation for knowledge in LTM takes the form of a production system. A production system is a formalism for expressing how an information-processing system might respond to the momentary state of knowledge in which it finds itself: That is, how it might determine what to do next, given what it now knows. The basic unit is a *production*. A production is a rule that consists of a *condition* and an *associated action*. The condition tests the instantaneous knowledge-state of the system (i.e., the current contents of its buffers). If a condition is satisfied, then its actions are executed, changing the state of knowledge. A collection of productions that serve some specific function is called a *produc-*

tion system. There are several ways the set of productions can be organized and coordinated to produce some purposeful piece of information processing, and some examples will be given in the next major section.

ACQUISITION OF KNOWLEDGE

We will describe several general principles that underlie self-modification. They will all involve the creation of new productions in LTM, and the central question will be, "What information source tells the system when to add these new productions?" The system must have some means of monitoring its own activity in order to answer this question. The mechanism we propose uses something we call the *time line.*

The time line contains a sequential record of the system's activity. Information about the initial and final states of the buffers involved in an episode are placed in the time line at the conclusion of each processing episode. If any regularities exist in the interaction of the system with the environment, they will be represented in the time line. Self-modification takes place through the detection of this regularity and the subsequent addition to the system of productions that will capitalize upon it.

We postulate a kernel of innate productions that includes a set of self-modification productions. One general principle governs the operation of the self-modification productions. The principle is a least-effort or "processing-economy" principle. The system has such a limited-capacity workspace, and such a huge LTM, and such a complex environment, that it endeavors at all times to make the symbols with which it is dealing as information-laden as possible. Similarly, it attempts to construct programs that will minimize the amount of processing necessary to do a given task. The system achieves this goal of efficient processing through three major procedures: consistency detection, redundancy elimination, and global orientation.

By *consistency detection,* we mean the discovery by the systemic productions that a set of specific sequences can be accounted for by some higher order rule. By *redundancy elimination,* we have in mind the kind of efficiency described in Baylor's work (Baylor & Gascon, 1974) on seriation or by the discovery of shortcuts by children who repeatedly face the same set of steps in a task (cf. Resnick, 1976). By *global orientation,* we mean an initial orientation to process objects as integrated wholes. Only in the face of repeated failures does the system resort to a dimensional treatment of the stimulus materials.

Regularity Detection

In the next few paragraphs, we will summarize the nature of the mechanism that implements these principles. Consider some of the current models for sequential pattern induction in which simple regularities are sought in the pattern. Once partial regularities are detected, the system attempts to work on the fine-structure of the relationships among elements in the pattern. The simplest case consists of a single dimension, and no external system of orderings (e.g., color sequences: R, Y, Y, R, Y, _, _). Additional complexity in patterns (and in the induction rules) comes from either multidimensional objects (e.g., color and orientation: RU, YD, YU, RU, YD, _, _) where orientation is up or down, or external alphabets (e.g., the English alphabet), or number systems that have sets of rules for complex relations associated with them. Even more complexity comes from a relaxation of the requirements for identity, so that systems can now find "sames" that are really equivalence classes (e.g., letter series in different typefaces) or partial matches.

Now view the symbols in the time-line as a sequence in which the system is attempting to detect some consistencies. In general, all the complications just mentioned will occur, as well as conflict between the frequency of near matches and the degree of fit (e.g., many poor fits versus few good ones). In a system that is attempting to form a new production that says, in effect, "whenever you know X do Y," the determination of what constitutes an appropriate X or Y depends upon a precise model of how abstraction and generalization take place. In our theory we attempt to spell out some of the properties of this model of abstraction.[2]

The theory has been built upon and influenced by, running models, written as production systems, of performance on the classic Genevan problems: class inclusion, conservation, transitivity, as well as detailed models of elementary quantification problems. Thus, there are pieces of performance models for different levels of performance on different problems. We have not yet created a running program for our model of self-modification. (For a discussion of recent developments in self-modifying systems, see Klahr, in press.)

Summary

A few years ago, I began to approach the task of taking the current theory of self-modification and recasting it as a running simulation model, that is, to move it from the metaphorical to the concrete level. The success of such an effort rests on the solution of two subproblems, which we can call the *formal* and the *empirical*. The formal problem consists of several unresolved issues in the design of self-modifying production systems, a few of which will be described on pages 157–160. The empirical problem arises when we attempt to evaluate the model (as-

[2] Extended examples of this consistency detection procedure are presented in Chapters 5 and 6 of Klahr and Wallace (1976).

suming we can get it to run and develop). While a running model will demonstrate the logical consistency of the theory, such a model also needs to be subjected to empirical testing. The empirical base that was used in formulating the initial theory came from several sources, including the vast literature on Piagetian problems as well as from studies of the development of number concepts (Gelman, 1972a,b; Schaeffer, Eggleston, & Scott, 1974), and from the literature on language acquisition. However, the mapping between such evidence and a running model is necessarily loose, since none of the evidence was gathered with the intention of testing the particular model under consideration.

What is needed is a domain of thought that is amenable to modeling in terms of progressive improvements in competence; that is, a domain where we can see many forms of observable behavior in which the proposed regularity-detection mechanisms can function. One such area, language acquisition, clearly provides such phenomena, and some progress in attempts to build an information-processing theory of language acquisition is reported by Anderson (1976). Another candidate, and the one that I have chosen, is the development of general problem-solving skills.

Studies of Children's Problem Solving

I want to understand the mechanisms of cognitive development that underlie children's continually improving ability to solve problems. Thus I have begun to explore, within the framework of the developmental theory outlined in the preceding section, the effects of variations in instructional procedures on children's learning of, and performance on, different kinds of problems. Based on the empirical evidence obtained during these explorations, we will construct task-specific information-processing models to account for learning and performance in each situation. Drawing upon the commonalities in these models, we will then initiate a second round of model building in which we will attempt to construct a more general system that can learn from instruction in any of the problem-solving areas. Both the general model and its task-specific precursors will be written as self-modifying production systems.

Much of what we observe when people solve problems is a direct consequence of the task environment rather than of any deep psychological properties of the human information processing system. Thus it is difficult to draw conclusions of broad generality from the study of a *single* task. For this reason, we have chosen a collection of tasks with rather varied properties. In the following section I will describe just two of the tasks that we have used to assess children's developing problem-solving abilities. Tasks will be described in decreasing order with respect to the extent to which formal analysis has been completed. None of the models yet contains developmental components.[3]

The Balance Scale

In this task, subjects are asked to predict which way a two-arm balance will tip when various configurations of weights are placed on the arms. It was first introduced by Inhelder and Piaget (1958) to assess levels of formal operational thinking, and interesting variants of it are still being devised by the Genevans (Karmiloff-Smith & Inhelder, 1976). My attention was drawn to it when my colleague Robert Siegler modified the task and introduced a procedure that enabled him to make extremely precise assessments of what children know about this device (Siegler, 1976). The apparatus consists of a two-arm balance with pegs placed at equal intervals along the arms. From 0 to 4 disks of equal weight are placed on the arms. Siegler's procedure enabled him to characterize the kind of decision-rules the children use when making their predictions. The four decision models used by almost all subjects are shown in Figure 6.1. The youngest children (Model I) attend only to the total amount of weight on each side of the fulcrum, and they ignore distance completely. The most advanced children use the correct rule: multiplying the distance from the fulcrum by the number of weights on that peg, summing if more than one peg is used and then comparing the sums of the cross products (Model IV).

The configurations for this problem are classified as shown under "Problem type" in Table 6.1.[4]

The problem types are labeled according to the factor that determines the outcome. Balance problems balance; on weight problems, only the weight on each arm differs, "distance"–actually the pegs occupied–is the same, so the scale tips toward the side with more weight; on distance problems weight is the same and the side with "more distance" goes down.

On all conflict problems both weight and distance differ, but either their effect balances (conflict–balance), or the side with more weight dominates (conflict–weight), or the side with more distance dominates (conflict–distance). For a problem of any given type, each of the decision models in Figure 6.1 predicts an outcome that is correct with the frequency shown in Table 6.1.

This type of analysis can accurately classify what model a subject is using. There is a wide age range during which children acquire these rules. As shown in Table 6.2 almost all of the 5-year-olds applied the

---

[3] In describing these two tasks, I will draw heavily upon previously published reports (Klahr, 1978; Klahr & Siegler 1978). For extensions of the work described here, see Siegler and Klahr (in press).

[4] Tables 6.1 and 6.2 are reprinted from Siegler (1976).

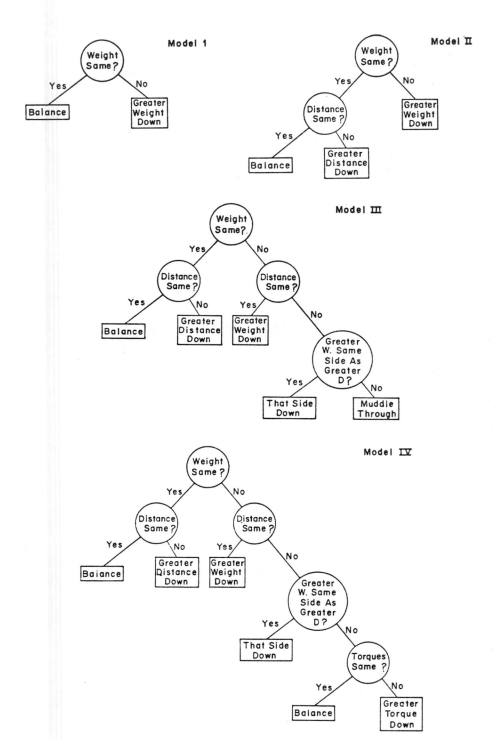

FIGURE 6.1. *Four models for balance-scale predictions.*

TABLE 6.1
Predictions for Percentage of Correct Answers and Error Patterns on Posttest for Children Using Different Models

Problem type	Models				Predicted developmental trend
	I	II	III	IV	
Balance	100	100	100	100	No change–all children at high levels
Weight	100	100	100	100	No change–all children at high levels
Distance	0 (Should say "balance")	100	100	100	Dramatic improvement with age
Conflict–weight	100	100	33 (Chance responding)	100	Decline with age Possible upturn in oldest group
Conflict–distance	0 (Should say "right down")	0 (Should say "right down")	33 (Chance responding)	100	Improvement with age
Conflict–balance	0 (Should say "right down")	0 (Should say "right down")	33 (Chance responding)	100	Improvement with age

135

TABLE 6.2
Developmental Trends Observed and Predicted on Different Problem-Types in Experiment I (Percentage of Problems Predicted Correctly)

Number of each type	Problem type	Grade, age (years), and mean age (months)					Predicted developmental trend (from Table 6.1)
		K–1st 5–6 73	4th–5th 9–10 120	8th–9th 13–14 169	11th–12th 16–17 207		
4	Balance	94	99	99	100		No change–All children at high level
4	Weight	88	98	98	98		No change–All children at high level
4	Distance	9	78	81	95		Dramatic improvement with age
6	Conflict–weight	86	74	53	51		Decline with age–Possible upturn for older children
6	Conflict–distance	11	32	48	50		Improvement with age
6	Conflict–balance	7	17	26	40		Improvement with age
	Weighted mean percentage	46	61	62	67		

weight rule, and less than 17% of the 17-year-olds knew the sum of cross-products rule.

In the testing phase just described, the subject makes a prediction about which way the balance scale will tip, but it is not actually allowed to tip. In the training phase, subjects receive feedback on the correctness of their predictions simply by observing the scale actually tip. Using training schedules composed of different problem types, Siegler (1976) was able to move 8-year-old children from Model I to Models II and III.

Although we know that we can train children to become better problem solvers on this task, we do not yet have a model of what is taking place during the instruction. In order to achieve this goal, it is first necessary to improve the way in which we describe—or represent—the decision rules used by children in each stage. We need a representation that can account not only for the logical form of the decision rules used to make predictions, but also for the psychological properties of the rules. That is, we need a representation that enables us to indicate clearly the perceptual and mnemonic demands of actually using the decision rules, as well as how those rules are organized and accessed. In the next section I will introduce such a representation for children's knowledge about this task. (An extended discussion of representational issues can be found in Klahr and Siegler, 1978.)

PRODUCTION SYSTEM REPRESENTATIONS FOR BALANCE-SCALE RULES

Figure 6.2 restates the four models of Figure 6.1 as production systems. A production system consists of a set of rules—called *productions* —written in the form of *condition–action* pairs. The conditions are symbolic expressions for elements of knowledge that might be present at some instant. A production system operates via a *recognition–action* cycle. During the recognition phase, all the condition sides of all the productions are compared with the current contents of the knowledge state. The knowledge state can be viewed as STM, or the currently activated portion of LTM, or simply as the current state of awareness of the system. The productions whose conditions are true of the knowledge state are placed into the conflict set, a conflict-resolution principle is applied, and one production fires. The action phase of the cycle executes the actions that are associated with the fired production. Then the next recognition–action cycle commences.

A sequence of condition elements on the left side of a production is interpreted as a test for the simultaneous existence of the conjunction of the individual knowledge elements. If, for a given production, all the condition elements happen to be true at some instant, we say that the production is "satisfied." If only one production is satisfied, then it

Model I
  P1:((Same W) --> (Say "balance"))
  P2:((Side X more W) --> (Say "X down"))

Model II
  P1:((Same W) --> (Say "balance"))
  P2:((Side X more W) --> (Say "X down"))
  P3:((Same W) (Side X more D) --> (Say "X down"))

Model III
  P1:((Same W) --> (Say "balance"))
  P2:((Side X more W) --> (Say "X down"))
  P3:((Same W) (Side X more D) --> (Say "X down"))
  P4:((Side X more W) (Side X less D) --> muddle through)
  P5:((Side X more W) (Side X more D) --> (Say "X down"))

Model IV
  P1:((Same W) --> (Say "balance"))
  P2:((Side X more W) --> (Say "X down"))
  P3:((Same W) (Sido X more D) --> (Say "X down"))
  P4':((Side X more W) (Side X less D) --> (get Torques))
  P5:((Side X more W) (Side X more D) --> (Say "X down"))
  P6:((Same Torque) --> (Say "balance"))
  P7:((Side X more Torque) --> (say "X down"))

FIGURE 6.2. *Production systems for four models.*

"fires": The actions associated with it, written to the right of the arrow (see Figure 6.2) are taken. These actions can modify the knowledge state by adding, deleting, or changing existing elements in it, or they can correspond to interactions with the environment—either perceptual or motor. If more than one production is satisfied, then the system needs to invoke some conflict-resolution principles in order to decide which production to fire. There are, at present, many unanswered questions about the possible types of conflict-resolution principles and their effects on the functioning of large scale production systems. We will return to this issue on pages 157–160.

Consider, for example, Model II in Figure 6.2. It is a production system consisting of three productions. The condition elements in this system are all tests for sameness or difference in weight or distance. The actions all refer to behavioral responses. None of the models in Figure 6.2 contains a representation for any finer grain knowledge, such as the actual amount of weight or distance, or the means used to encode that information. Nor is there any explicit representation of how the system actually produces the final verbal output. It is simply assumed that the system has access to encoded representations of the relational information stated in the conditions.

Returning to Model II, notice that on any recognize cycle, only one production will fire. If the weights are unequal, then P2 will fire. If the weights are equal and the distances are not, then both P1 and P3 will be satisfied, and the system needs to resolve the conflict in order to decide which production to fire. In this system we use a conflict-resolution principle in which "special cases" have priority over general cases. Since the conditions of P3 are a special case of those in P1, the conflict resolution principle will choose P3 to fire. Finally, if both weights and distances are equal, then only P1 will be satisfied and it will fire.

The production system versions of the other three models are also shown in Figure 6.2.[5]

A comparison among the four models clarifies the task facing a transition model. At the level of productions, the requisite modifications are straightforward: A transition from Model I to Model II requires the addition of P3; from II to III, the addition of P4 and P5; and from III to IV, the addition of P6 and P7, and the modification of P4 to P4' (this modification changes the action side from random muddling through to "get torque").

We can compare the four models at a finer level of analysis by looking at the implicit requirements for encoding and comparing the important quantities in the environment. Model I tests for sameness or difference in weight. Thus, it requires an encoding process that either directly encodes relative weight, or encodes an absolute amount of each and then inputs those representation into a comparison process. Whatever the form of the comparison process, it must be able to produce not only a same-or-different symbol; but if there is a difference, it must be able to keep track of which side is greater. Model II requires the additional capacity to make these decisions about distance as well as weight. This might constitute a completely separate encoding and comparison system for distance representations, or it might be the same system except for the interface with the environment.

Model III needs no additional operators at this level. Thus it differs from Model II only in the way it utilizes information that is already accessible to Model II. Model IV requires a much more powerful set of quantitative operators than any of the preceding models. In order to determine relative torque, it must first determine the absolute torque on each side of the scale, and this in turn requires exact numerical representation of weight and distance. In addition, the torque computation would require access to the necessary arithmetic production systems to actually do the sum of products calculations.

---

[5] The numbers attached to the productions (e.g., P1, P2, etc.) are not supposed to have any psychological meaning. They serve simply as labels for the reader; note that a production maintains its label across the four models.

EVALUATION OF THE PRODUCTION SYSTEM REPRESENTATION

Why use production systems? Since each of the four production-system models in Figure 6.2 makes precisely the same prediction as its counterpart in the decision-tree representation of Figure 6.1, they are equally able to account for behavior. One advantage of the production systems is that they are somewhat more explicit than the decision trees about the requirements for both the encoding operations and the rules (i.e., productions) that utilize the symbolic elements produced by the operators. They also clarify the developmental differences between models in terms of these two kinds of entities.

However, a much more important feature of the production-system representation lies in its integration of general psychological principles. Production systems of the type used here incorporate a theory of the control structure and general representation that underlies a broad range of human problem-solving ability (Newell & Simon, 1972). As Newell (1973) put it: "The production system itself has become the carrier of the basic psychological assumptions—the system architecture [the production system] is taken to be the system architecture of the human information processing system [p. 516]." Thus, models written in this form can be viewed as variants within a general psychological theory, and, to the extent that such a general theory is consistent with the empirical results from experimental psychology, these models are also consistent with them.

Another advantage of the production systems is that they force us as model builders to be very explicit in stating our assumptions about how the child encodes the environment. Such attention to encoding processes led us to the discovery of some interesting deficiencies in children's ability to learn about the balance scale.[6]

Yet another relative merit of the production systems lies in the ease with which they enable us to begin to model the self-modification process itself. In the next section we describe a procedure in which our goal was to gain a better understanding of both the encoding processes and some internal changes during a training study. We will describe a production system that can account for a series of responses during an entire training session. Then we will return to the evaluation issue (see page 150).

REVISED PRODUCTION SYSTEM FOR A "MODEL III" CHILD

Thus far, the production-system representation has been used only to suggest some of the complexities of learning about the task. In this section we will work toward the creation of a production-system model of a

---

[6] See Klahr and Siegler (1978) and Siegler (1976) for details.

single child's behavior during a training sequence. The representation will be more than suggestive, for it will be specific enough to run as a computer simulation. The simulation will serve two purposes. First, it will demonstrate the sufficiency of the model. Second, since the simulation language in which the model is stated is based upon specific assumptions about the nature of the human information-processing system, the model can be viewed as a specific instance of a much broader theory.

Our subject—Jan—was a female second-grader, 8 years old. Her performance on an 8-item pretest and a 16-item training series is shown in Table 6.3, in which, each row corresponds to a problem. The columns indicate, respectively, problem number, problem configuration, problem type (distance, balance, conflict–weight, weight, etc.), Jan's response (left down, right down, or balance), feedback from the scale (if the subject's prediction was inconsistent with what the scale did, it is

TABLE 6.3
Jan on Training Sequence, and Predictions from Four Models

Problem					Prediction				
Number	Configuration	Type	S2	Feedback	IV	II	I	IIIA	Criterion
Pretest									
1	100|100	D	L			L			
2	010|300	CW	R			R			
3	100|200	CD	R			R			
4	010|020	W	R			R			
5	020|002	D	R			R			
6	200|400	CD	R			R			
7	100|200	CD	R			R			
8	030|020	W	L			L			
Training series									
1	0200|0200	D	L	+	L	L	B	L	w
2	0020|0200	B	B	+	B	B	B	B	
3	0020|3000	CD	R	−	L	R	R	R	
4	0003|0100	CW	L	+	L	L	L	L	d
5	0200|0400	CW	L	−	R	R	R	L	
6	0102|2010	B	B	+	B	B	B	B	w
7	0003|0020	CD	L	−	R	L	L	L	
8	0100|0200	CW	L	−	R	R	R	L	d
9	0040|1020	CW	L	+	L	L	L	L	w
11	0001|2000	W	R	+	R	R	R	R	
12	0013|1020	CD	L	−	R	L	L	L	
13	0120|2200	CD	L	+	L	R	R	L	d
14	0200|1300	CW	L	−	R	R	R	L	
15	0002|0010	CD	R	+	R	L	L	R	w
16	0023|1110	CW	R	−	L	L	L	L	
					7	6	7	1	

indicated by a "– "), predictions from three of the previously described models (IV, II, and I), and finally, two columns corresponding to the model to be described in this section. The first of these columns—IIIA—contains the model's prediction, and the second contains the value of a variable criterion that is used to make the prediction. For example, Problem 7 in the training series has three weights on the first peg on the left and two weights on the third peg on the right (indicated by: 0003|0020); it is a conflict–distance problem. Jan predicted that the left side would go down, but as Model IV (which is always correct) predicted, the right side went down, so the Jan got negative feedback. The other three models shown here (II, I, and IIIA) all make the same prediction as the subject: left–down. The number at the bottom of each of the four model columns shows the number of mismatches between Jan's predictions and the model's.

Jan's responses to the pretest make her a perfect Model II subject. Her responses during the training sequence provide a poor fit to Models I, II, and IV. Recall that the criterion for fitting Model III was that the responses be essentially random for conflict problems. Thus, although the "muddle through" prediction of Model III does not make an exact prediction on any trial, it predicts the absence of a consistent pattern over the set of conflict problems. And indeed, this is what we find in Table 6.3: On 5 of the 11 conflict problems Jan responds as if she were relying on the weight cue, and on the other 6, she conforms to the distance cue. Thus, we could simply classify Jan as a Model III subject and leave it at that.

Such an interpretation has several deficiencies. First, the classification scheme itself is unsatisfactory when compared to the others. Model III subjects get so classified as a residual category—by the absence of any pattern in their responses to conflict problems—whereas all other classification is based on the occurrence of things that were predicted to happen, rather than the absence of things that should not. In addition to this "taxonomic" weakness, Model III's "muddle through" prediction tells us nothing about the psychological processes that actually operate when subjects detect conflict but do not yet know how to deal with it correctly. Finally, it is important to emphasize that Table 6.3 represents responses during a training sequence, a situation in which the child was presumably attempting to integrate the feedback from the actual behavior of the balance scale with her current hypothesis about how it worked. None of the four models described thus far has any mechanism to represent and utilize such information. The model to be described represents first steps in remedying these deficiencies.

On each trial, Jan was asked to justify her prediction, and then to explain what actually happened when the scale was allowed to tip. An analysis of her trial-by-trial explanations provided the initial evidence for the model that we eventually formulated. The most striking feature of her comments was the way she appeared to represent distance and weight on conflict problems. Both of them were treated as dichotomous: More than two weights was treated as "big"; otherwise weight was "little." And if the third or fourth peg was occupied, then distance was "big"; otherwise it was "little." Rather than present a lengthy protocol analysis here, we will show just two examples of this dichotomous encoding of distance.

On Problem 12 (0013|1020), the child predicts left down; upon seeing the result, she says:

Oh, now I think I know why. . . . I think I know because . . . it's supposed to be a rule that they usually go down more if they're on that side . . . [pointing to the extreme right of the balance scale]. *So that one went down 'cause it's two there* [pointing far right] *and none there* [pointing far left].

If we encode each arm of the balance scale into a near segment (Pegs 1 and 2) and a far segment (Pegs 3 and 4), then this protocol is easily interpreted. *They usually go down more if they're on that side* means that if the far segment is occupied ("big distance"), then the scale will tip in that direction. *Two there and none there* means that the far segment on the right is occupied by two weights, whereas the far segment on the left is unoccupied.

The second example comes from Problem 14 (0200|1300), just before the child gets feedback. She says:

This side's gonna go down [pointing left]. . . . *Even though this one has four* [pointing right] *and this one only has two* [pointing left]. . . . *Even though this one has* [pointing right] *twice as much as this* [pointing left], *that means that because this one's more* [waves to far left] *over, and that's* [pointing right] *all on that side.*

In this case, we garner support for the dichotomous distance encoding from the comment that the weights on the right arm of the scale are "all on that side." "That side" of what? By our interpetation, they are on "that side" of the midpoint of the right arm, thus making distance "little," rather than "big" on the right.

In order to determine whether this interpretation of the protocols is valid, we need to construct a model that is consistent with Jan's actual predictions on each trial, as well as her explanations. Based upon many such comments and our interpretations of them, we constructed the model whose predictions are shown in Table 6.3. In order to provide a clear overview of the model, we will describe it first in terms of a binary decision tree, plus a few ad hoc mechanisms. Then we will present a running production system for a more complete model based on the same underlying logic.

Figure 6.3 shows the binary decision-tree representation for Model

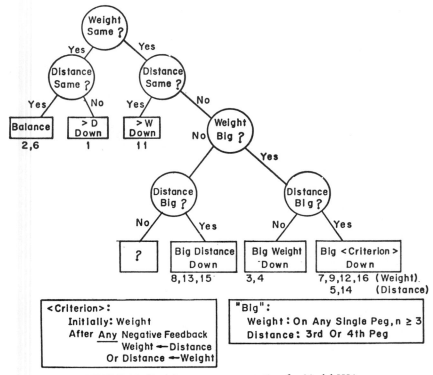

FIGURE 6.3. *Decision-tree representation for Model IIIA.*

IIIA; Jan's performance on the training sequence is shown in Table 6.3. The numbers under the terminal nodes correspond to the problems from Table 6.3 that are sorted to those nodes. The first three tests are the same as those in Model III (Figure 6.1), and they account for balance, weight, and distance problems. If neither weight nor distance is "same," then the model begins to test for "big" values. If either weight or distance—but not both—is big, then the side with the big value determines the prediction. If both are big, then Model IIIA favors whichever one is currently its criterion value. The criterion value starts as weight, but whenever negative feedback is received the criterion switches from one value to the other. The state of the criterion value is indicated in the last column in Table 6.3. Note that it changes after any negative feedback, not just on conflict trials with negative feedback.[7]

---

[7] The terminal node labeled "?" in Figure 6.3 is never reached by the set of problems in Table 6.3. Such a problem would be a conflict problem with neither weight nor distance "big." We have no evidence upon which to base a prediction about what the subject would do with such a problem.

A PRODUCTION SYSTEM FOR MODEL IIIA

The production system for Jan is shown in Figure 6.4. The representation contains the actual computer listing (with a few inessential details not shown) for the production system, which is written in a language called PSG (Newell & McDermott, 1975). Figure 6.5 contains a trace of this model running on Problem 7 from Table 6.3. Before I embark on a detailed description of the model, I will make a few comments about the properties of this rather complex representation of knowledge about the balance-scale problem.

This model represents, in addition to the child's knowledge about how the balance scale operates, her knowledge about the immediate experimental context in which she is functioning. The trial-by-trial cycle during the training phase comprises (a) observation of the static display; (b) prediction of the outcome; (c) observation of the outcome; (d) comparison of the outcome with the prediction; and (e) and revision—if necessary—of the criterion. The production systems shown previously (Figure 6.2) represented knowledge sufficient to execute only the second

```
<dimension 1>:(CLASS weight distance)    <dimension 2>:(CLASS weight distance)
<side.1>:(CLASS left right both)         <side.2>:(CLASS left right both)
<direction>:(CLASS up down level)

P1:((predict) (weight same) --> (made **)  (expect both level) say.b)
P2:((predict) (weight more <side.1>) --> (made **)  (expect <side.1> down) say.d)
P3:((predict) (weight same) (distance more <side.1>) --> (made **)  (expect <side.1> down) say.d)
P4:((predict) (weight more)(distance more) --> find.big)
P5:((predict) (criterion <dimension.1>)(<dimension.1> big <side.1>)
               (<dimension.2> big <side.2>) --> (made **) (expect <side.1> down)say.d)
P6:((predict) (weight big <side.1>) --> (made **)  (expect <side.1> down) say.d)
P7:((predict) (distance big <side.1>) --> (made **)  (expect <side.1> down) say.d)
P8:((predict)(<dimension.1>) abs --> ATTEND)

E1:((expect) --> look)
E2:((expect <side.1> <direction>)(see <side.1> <direction>) --> (did **)(see ===> saw)(result correct))
E3:((expect <side.1> <direction>)(see <side.1> <direction>) abs (see) --> (did **)(see ===> saw)
                                                                (result wrong))

SW1:((result wrong)(criterion distance) --> (old **)(distance ===> weight))
SW2:((result wrong)(criterion weight) --> (old **)(weight ===> distance))
SW3:((result correct)(criterion) --> (old **))

find.big:(OPR CALL) ;returns (weight|distance big left|right), one or two such.

look:(OPR CALL)     ; looks for result of balance tipping.
                    ; returns (see left|right down)

attend:(OPR CALL) ; initial encoding of same or difference on distance & weight
                  ;returns (weight|distance same|more left|right)
```

FIGURE 6.4. *Production system for Model IIIA.*

of these five steps, while the present model (Figure 6.4) explicitly represents all of this task-relevant knowledge in a homogeneous and integrated manner. This model utilizes, in one way or another, representations of knowledge about when and how to encode the environment, which side has *more* weight or distance, which side has a *big* weight or distance, what the current criterion value is, what the scale is expected to do, what the scale actually did, whether the prediction is yet to be made or has been made, and whether it is correct or incorrect.

PRODUCTION SYSTEM INTERPRETATION

Some general properties of production systems were described earlier. In this section we will add a few more details about how the model in Figure 6.4 operates. Recall that the basic cycle for a production system is recognize–act. During a recognition cycle, all the productions compare their condition elements with an ordered list of elements in working memory. The trace in Figure 6.4 shows the state of working memory after each cycle. For example, at the beginning of the second cycle in Figure 6.4, we see that working memory has four elements in it: (DISTANCE MORE RIGHT), (WEIGHT MORE LEFT), (PREDICT), and (CRITERION WEIGHT). An examination of the productions in Figure 6.4 reveals that P1 is the only production whose condition elements are completely matched by working memory elements, so in this case, it fires.

There are two conflict resolution principles. The first one to be applied—special case order—has already been described. If, after applying special case order, there are still two or more productions in the conflict set, then a second resolution principle—working memory order—is applied. This principle chooses the productions with the frontmost element in working memory. New information always enters the "front" of working memory, pushing all else down a "notch." Furthermore, when a production fires, its evoking elements are moved to the front of working memory (automatic rehearsal). Thus, the working-memory order, conflict-resolution principle says, in effect, "when in doubt, respond to the most recently important information."

There are several different types of actions:

1. *Working-Memory Additions.* These simply add new elements to the front of working memory. For example, if E3 fired, (result wrong) would be added to the front of working memory. Other sources of new information are the encoding operators (described below).
2. *Working-Memory Modifications.* Elements in working memory can be altered directly. The action (A $\Rightarrow$ B) changes symbol A to symbol B in the second element in working memory. The action (X **

(0003|0020)
Cycle 1
  WM: ((PREDICT) (CRITERION WEIGHT))

  Fire P8: ((PREDICT) (<DIMENSION.1>) ABS --> ATTEND)
      Output from ATTEND (input to WM) ::> (weight more left)(distance more right)

Cycle 2
  WM: ((DISTANCE MORE RIGHT) (WEIGHT MORE LEFT) (PREDICT) (CRITERION WEIGHT))
      CONFLICT.SET: (P2 P4)
  Fire P4: ((PREDICT) (WEIGHT MORE) (DISTANCE MORE) --> FIND.BIG)
      Output from FIND.BIG (input to WM) ::> (distance big right)(weight big left)

Cycle 3
  WM: ((WEIGHT BIG LEFT) (DISTANCE BIG RIGHT) (PREDICT) (WEIGHT MORE LEFT)
      (DISTANCE MORE RIGHT) (CRITERION WEIGHT))
      CONFLICT.SET: (P2 P4 P5 P6 P7)
      CONFLICT.SET: (P4 P5) AFTER SPECIAL.CASE.ORDER
      CONFLICT.SET: (P5) AFTER WM.ORDER
  Fire P5: ((PREDICT) (CRITERION <DIMENSION.1>)(<DIMENSION.1> BIG.<SIDE.1>)
      (<DIMENSION.2> BIG <SIDE.2.) --> (MADE **) (EXPECT <SIDE.1> DOWN) SAY.D)

********** LEFT down

Cycle 4
  WM: ((EXPECT LEFT DOWN) (MADE (PREDICT)) (CRITERION WEIGHT) (WEIGHT BIG LEFT)
      (DISTANCE BIG RIGHT) (WEIGHT MORE LEFT) (DISTANCE MORE RIGHT))
  Fire E1: ((EXPECT) --> LOOK)
      Output from LOOK (input to WM) ::> (see right down)

Cycle 5
  WM: ((SEE RIGHT DOWN) (EXPECT LEFT DOWN) (MADE (PREDICT)) (CRITERION WEIGHT)
      (WEIGHT BIG LEFT) (DISTANCE BIG RIGHT) (WEIGHT MORE LEFT).(DISTANCE MORE RIGHT))
      CONFLICT.SET: (E1,E3)
  Fire E3: ((EXPECT <SIDE.1> <DIRECTION>)
              (SEE <SIDE.1> <DIRECTION>) ABS (SEE) --> (DID **) (SEE ===> SAW)
(RESULT WRONG))

Cycle 6
  WM: ((RESULT WRONG) (DID (EXPECT LEFT DOWN)) (SAW RIGHT DOWN) (MADE (PREDICT))
      (CRITERION WEIGHT) (WEIGHT BIG LEFT) (DISTANCE BIG RIGHT) (WEIGHT MORE LEFT)
      (DISTANCE MORE RIGHT))
  Fire SW2: ((RESULT WRONG) (CRITERION WEIGHT) --> (OLD **) (WEIGHT ===> DISTANCE))

Cycle 7
  WM: ((OLD (RESULT WRONG)) (CRITERION DISTANCE) (DID (EXPECT LEFT DOWN))
      (SAW RIGHT DOWN) (MADE (PREDICT)) (WEIGHT BIG LEFT) (DISTANCE BIG RIGHT)
      (WEIGHT MORE LEFT) (DISTANCE MORE RIGHT))

FIGURE 6.5. *Trace of production system (Fig. 6.4) working on conflict–distance problem.*

changes the first element in working memory from A to (X (A))
[e.g., (OLD **) would change (DOG) to (OLD (DOG))].
3. *Output.* These actions are surrogates for action on the external environment. The only ones used here are say.b (say "balance") and
say.d (say "left [or right] down").

Description of Model (*Figure 6.4*). There are three major functional groups of productions:

1. *Pn*. These correspond to the major nodes in the decision tree representation. P1–P4 are essentially the same as P1–P4 in Figure 6.2. P5, P6, and P7 correspond to the tests for big things in Figure 6.3. Some of the productions use variables that can be matched by specific values in working memory elements. These variables are defined in the first three lines of Figure 6.4 in terms of the members of the class of values that the variable can take on. Thus, ⟨dimension.1⟩ and ⟨dimension.2⟩ can take on the values "weight" or "distance"; ⟨side.1⟩ and ⟨side.2⟩ can take on values of "left," "right," or "both"; and ⟨direction⟩ can take on the value "up," "down," or "level."

2. *En*. These control the model's viewing of the balance scale after it tips, and compare what it expected to see with what it actually sees.

3. *SWn*. These change the criterion whenever the system determines (via the E productions) that it has made an incorrect prediction.

There are three encoding operators. None are modeled, but their conditions of evocation are explicit, as is the form of the encoding they produce.

4. *Attend*. "Attend" does initial encoding of weight and distance. This operator can detect sameness or difference of weight or distance and can indicate the side on which weight or distance is greater. Thus, it is only an encoding of relative quantity. The model assumes that in the first instance this is all that is encoded.

5. *Findbig*. "Findbig" encodes big weight or big distance and side on which they occur (if they occur).

6. *Look*. "Look" encodes direction of tipping of scale.

Dynamics of the Model. The general procedure is as follows. First weight and distance differences, if any, are encoded. If there is no conflict, then a prediction is made, an expectation is formed, and the scale's actual behavior is observed. If it is inconsistent with the prediction, then the criterion is changed. If initial encoding reveals no clear prediction, then a second encoding is effected, this time in terms of big distance or weight. Then the rest of the process follows exactly as in the case of a single encoding.

Figure 6.5 contains a trace of the model working on one of the problems from Table 6.3. The trace shows the state of working memory at the start of each cycle, as well as which production fired. Conflicts are shown when they occur, as are the results of the encoding operators.

The system starts with an element in working memory (PREDICT) indicating that it has a goal of making a prediction, and another element representing the current value of the criterion. Since there is no element representing weight or distance, the only production whose conditions are completely satisfied is P8, which tests for (PREDICT) and the absence (ABS) of a weight or distance element ⟨DIMENSION.1⟩. ATTEND, P8's only action, is an encoding operator that is modeled only up to the point of its input–output specifications. In this case the input is presumed to be the physical arrangement of disks on pegs in the configuration (0003|0020), and the outputs, as shown in the trace, are two comparative symbols indicating more weight on the left and more distance on the right. They are directly provided by the model builder.

Thus, at the beginning of Cycle 2, working memory contains four elements, and these elements satisfy both P4 and P2 (see Figure 6.4). P4 is a special case of P2, so it fires. It recognizes that neither weights nor distances are equal, so it attempts a second encoding (FIND.BIG) to determine some absolute amounts of distance and/or weight. Once again, an unmodeled encoding operator is assumed to produce two elements, indicating a big distance on the right and a big weight on the left. The results are shown at the start of the third cycle.

Five productions are satisfied by the elements now in working memory. P2 and P4 are still satisfied since none of the elements that satisfied them on the previous cycle have been changed. P5, P6, and P7 are satisfied because they test for either big weight or big distance. Since P4 is a special case of P2 and P5 of P6 and P7, the special case order principle leaves P4 and P5 in the conflict set. But the elements that match P5 are newer than those that match P4, so working-memory order selects P5 to fire.

P5 matches whatever the current value of the criterion is (in this case, it is weight) with the corresponding "big" element [in this case (WEIGHT BIG LEFT)] and then uses the value of the directional variable (LEFT) to form its expectation (EXPECT LEFT DOWN) and to "say" its prediction.

What the system knows at this particular moment is revealed by the contents of working memory at the start of the fourth cycle. It knows that: It expects the left side to go down (EXPECT LEFT DOWN); It already made a prediction (MADE (PREDICT)); The current criterion is weight (CRITERION WEIGHT); And it knows the encodings (WEIGHT BIG LEFT), (DISTANCE BIG RIGHT), (WEIGHT MORE LEFT), and (DISTANCE MORE RIGHT).

The rest of the trace is straightforward. During Cycle 4, the system seeks an encoding of what the scale actually did, and it sees that the right side went down. On Cycle 5 it recognizes that what it saw is discrepant with what it expected (E3), so it knows that it got the problem wrong. Finally, on Cycle 6, it recognizes that it was wrong while using the weight criterion, so it changes it to distance.

EVALUATION OF REPRESENTATIONS FOR JAN'S
KNOWLEDGE

The decision tree in Figure 6.3 and the production system in Figure 6.4 are logically equivalent: Both account for all but the last of Jan's predictions during the training series. As described earlier, they differ from the representations in Figure 6.1 and 6.2 in that they model the subject's response to feedback, and because they both represent idiosyncratic encodings of the stimulus. Thus, both models have certain advantages over the previous ones.

However, the models are not equivalent in all respects, and the psychological properties of the production system—properties previously just alluded to—can now be clarified. The production system, since it embodies a general model of the human information-processing system, forces us to form very explicit hypotheses about things that the decision tree lets us finesse. There is no separation of control information from data in a production system. Every relevant piece of information is explicitly represented in working memory, and all task-specific knowledge for acting on that information is represented by productions. As indicated by the final list of elements, we are postulating a sizable amount of material floating around in working memory. It is clear that the size of working memory is well beyond the estimated STM capacity of from seven (Miller, 1956) to as little as three or four (Broadbent, 1975) items, or the "M-space" estimates (Pascual-Leone, 1970) in the same range. However, it is unclear how a system that did not have immediate access to all of this momentary knowledge could ever do the task. Questions about the amount of control information sufficient to perform the task are not addressed by the decision-tree representation.

The tiny bit of adaptation that this model makes to environmental feedback lies entirely in the alternation of the criterion value, which is held in working memory. Thus, this model makes no use of the potential power of a self-modifying production system, since the production system itself never undergoes any change. Although it would be fairly straightforward to build such a system for this specific task, many issues that underlie the construction of a *general* self-modifying production system are still unresolved.

The Tower of Hanoi

The standard version of this problem consists of a series of three pegs, and a set of *n* disks of decreasing size. The disks initially start on one of the pegs, and the goal is to move the entire n-disk configuration to another peg, subject to two constraints. Only one disk can be moved at a time, and at no point can a disk be above a smaller disk on any given peg.[8]

The problem involves a well-defined initial state, an unambiguous desired state, and a very limited set of rules about how to change states. The difficulty lies in organizing a sequence of rule applications (making of legal moves) that ultimately transforms the initial physical configuration into the desired one. Thus, it is a good vehicle for investigating some of the characteristics of problem solving that were mentioned at the outset.

CHILDREN'S VERSION OF THE PUZZLE: MONKEY CANS

For use with young children (3– 5 years old), we modified the problem in three ways that changed its superficial appearance while maintaining its basic structure.

1. *Materials.* We use a set of nested inverted cans as shown in Figure 6.6. The cans are modified so that they fit very loosely on the pegs: When they are stacked up it is impossible to put a smaller can on top of a larger can. Even if the child forgets the relative size constraint, the materials provide an obvious physical consequence of attempted violations: Little cans simply fall off bigger cans.

2. *Externalization of Final Goal.* In addition to the current configura-

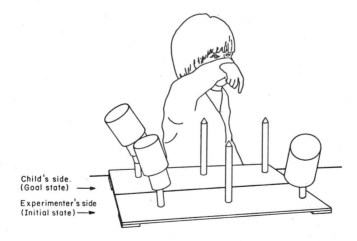

Child's side.
(Goal state) ⟶

Experimenter's side
(Initial state) ⟶

FIGURE 6.6. *Monkey-can configuration.*

[8] The many uses of this task reveal some of the changing goals and methods of experimental psychology over the last 40 years (cf. Byrnes & Spitz, 1977; Cook, 1937; Egan & Greeno, 1974; Gagné & Smith, 1962; Hormann, 1965; Klix, 1971; Neves, 1977; Piaget, 1976; Simon, 1975; Spada, 1973).

tion, the goal—or target—configuration is always physically present. We set up the child's cans in a target configuration, and the experimenter's cans in the initial configuration. Then the child is asked to tell the experimenter what to do in order to make his or her cans look just like the child's. This procedure can be used to elicit multiple-move plans: A child is asked to describe a *sequence* of moves, which the experimenter then executes.

3. *Cover Story*. The problem is presented in the context of a story in which the cans are monkeys (large daddy, medium size mommy, small baby), who jump from tree to tree (peg to peg). The child's monkeys are in some good configuration, the experimenter's monkeys are "copycat" monkeys who want to look just like the child's monkeys. The cans are redundantly classified by size, color, and family membership in order to make it easy for the child to refer to them. The subjects find the cover story easy to comprehend and remember, and they readily agree to consider the cans as monkeys.

FORMAL STATE PROPERTIES

Figure 6.7 shows all possible legal states and all legal moves for these materials. It is called the "state space." No configuration is repeated in the 27 states. The states are indicated by circled numbers, and the can that is moved is indicated by the number on the line connecting adjacent states. The solution to a problem can be represented as a path (a series of states) through the state space. For example, the minimum solution path for the problem that starts with all three cans on Peg A and ends with them on Peg C is shown along the right-hand side of the large triangle in Figure 6.7, moving from State 1 to State 8. The first move is to move the largest can (Can 3) from Peg A to Peg C, producing State 2. The next move places Can 2 on Peg B (State 3), followed by a move of Can 3 to Peg B (State 4), and so on.

There are no dead ends in this problem—any state can be reached from any other state—so that it is possible to consider very many distinct problems (702 to be exact), simply by picking an arbitrary initial and final state. However, there are no two states for which the *minimum* path requires more than seven moves.

Three pairs of special states are indicated by the large squares, circles, and hexagons: These are seven-move problems that begin and end with all pegs occupied. We call these problems "flat-ending" problems, and the "standard" seven-move problems "tower-ending" problems. As we shall see, they have somewhat different properties.

GENERAL PROCEDURE

The general procedure is designed to assess the upper limit (in terms of the length of the minimum solution path) of children's ability to solve

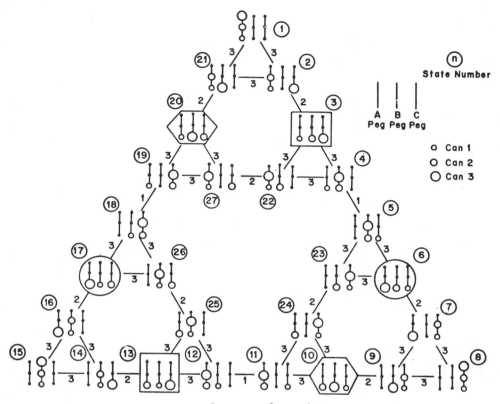

FIGURE 6.7. *State space for monkey-cans.*

this problem. The child is introduced to the materials, the rules, and the cover story, and is presented with a one-move problem (see Figure 6.6), then a two-move problem, and so on. Proceeding in this manner, we present a series of problems of increasing length until the child begins to suggest moves that are either off the minimum path, or illegal.

RESULTS

Path Length. At any point in the solution of a problem, the child can suggest either the correct move or several kinds of "incorrect" moves. These include legal moves not on the minimum path, illegal moves, and "don't knows." A global measure of the child's ability is the length of the longest problem (or subproblem) for which the child reliably stays on the minimum path.

The distribution of subjects reliably solving problems of a given length is shown in Table 6.4. The age differences are clear and striking. Consider first the 4-year-olds. None of them could solve the seven-move tower-ending problem reliably. That is, none of them could solve the

TABLE 6.4
Number of Children in Each Age Group Who Could Reliably Solve Tower-Ending
Problems Up to but Not Beyond Given Length

Age				Problem length (λ)								
Nominal	Mean	Range	N	1	2	3	4	5	6	7	λ	
3	3:10	3:8–4:4	10	0	5	1	4	0	0	0	2.9	(.99)
4	4:5	4:1–4:9	10	0	1	1	5	1	2	0	4.2	(1.2)
5	5:9	5:2–6:3	10	0	0	0	0	5	4	1	5.6	(.7)
		Total	30	0	6	2	9	6	6	1		
		Cumulative[a]		30	30	24	22	13	7	1		
	Nontransition probability			.00	.20	.08	.40	.46	.86			

[a] Total number (all groups) solving problems up to and including given problem length.

"three-disk" problem (even after experience with its subproblems). However, two of them could do the six-move problem: That is, they could solve the three-disk problem if the first move had already been made. One child could do no better than the two-move problem, and most of them could do up to four-move problems reliably before they began to err.

The fives are just about evenly divided between five- and six-move problems, and one of then could solve seven-move problems. The threes fall into two major groups: Those who cannot get beyond two moves, and those who can do four-move problems.

Planning. At times the experimenter would ask the child for not just the next move, but for the next several moves. Few of the children would verbalize multiple-move sequences beyond a few moves. Repeated prompts to do so appeared to confuse them, and had to be terminated. However, those who could and would do so showed a remarkable ability to describe a series of imagined future states and actions on those states.

The most impressive plans are shown in Figure 6.8. They came from a boy, aged 4:11.[9]

At the top of Figure 6.8, the complete five-move plan is verbalized after about 60 sec of study (Lines 209–214). The next problem for the same child has a six-move minimum path. The child starts verbalizing a move sequence after just a few seconds, (239–240), corrects himself, and then smoothly rattles off a six-move plan (241–246). Notice that when

[9] These transcriptions indicate the initial configuration (belonging to the experimenter) and the final or goal configuration (belonging to the subject) by using numbers corresponding to the can size. Thus, in Figure 6.8, "S: 321/–/–" means that the goal configuration has all the cans stacked in a tower on Peg A, and "E: 3/1/2" means that the initial configuration has Can 3 on Peg A, Can 1 on Peg B, and Can 2 on Peg C. The time (min:sec) since the session began is also shown.

```
193   P5   E: 3/1/2
194        S: 321/-/-
195
196   5:44   S: Like that, like that.
197          E: Like that, and they all want to be over here (A).
198   5:49   S: Well, that is pretty hard, but I can do it.
199          E: O.K.
200   5:57   S: Oh. Take..    I'm thinking.
202   6:10   E: What are you thinking about?
203   6:12   S: How we should do this.
204          E: Tell me what you're thinking?
205   6:15   S: About how to do this.
206          E: O.K.  What do you think?  How should we do it?
208   6:19   S: I don't know yet.
209   6:38      S: Take the yellow one (3) off and put it  on here (C),
210      and then take the red (1)  and put it on there (A), and take the..
211      and then put the yellow one and put it on here (B), and then
212      put the blue one (2)on the red, and then put the yellow one on
213      the blue one.
214   6:54  E: Let's try that.
215      What's the first thing I should do?
216      You said..
217   7:01  S: Take this one (3) and put it on there (C)..etc.


234   P6   E: 3/-/21
235        S: 321/-/-
236
237   7:26  S: Oh, that.
238   7:31      O.K.  That's easy.
239      Just take the yellow one and put it on there (B).
240   7:37      Take the (pointing to 2(C))..and take..and take, take the b..
241   7:41      No, take the blue one, put it on there (B), and then, then,
242      take the yellow and put it on the blue (points toward C, then
243      to B), and then take the red one and put it on here (A)).
244   7:51      And then take the blue one and..No, and then..and then put
245      the yellow one here (C), and then put the blue one on the
246      red one, and then put the yellow one on the blue one.
247   8:04  E: O.K.  What's first?
248   8:07  S: First, take this (3) and put it on there (B).
249          E: (3 -> B)
250   8:13  S: No, I was wrong.  Forget it.
251      (E: puts 3 back on A).
252   8:15      First take the blue one and put it on there (B).
253          E: (2 -> B)
254          S: Now take the yellow one and put it on there (B)..etc.
```

FIGURE 6.8. *Protocol from 4-year-old on five- and six-move problems.*

he starts to make actual moves, he makes the same initial error and re-
covery (248–252) that was in his verbalizations.

These protocols (as well as several others, not included here) are in
striking contrast to Piaget's results and interpretations of his investigations of the same problem (Piaget, 1976). He reports that, before the age
of 7 or 8, children did not plan, even with the *two*-disk problem. He
concludes that these children do not plan, that they cannot "combine
inversion of the order" (in our context, putting the baby under the

SOLVE.2(C, G)
    S1: Find differences (C-G). If none, then done.
    S2: n <- (Select smallest).
    S3: New.goal <- [nXY]
    S4: Move; go to S1.

SOLVE.4(C, G)
    S1: Find differences (C-G). If none, then done.
    S2: n <- (Select smallest)
    S3: New.goal <- [nXY]
    S4: culprit <- TEST.4(new.goal)
    S5: If culprit = nil, then MOVE[nXY]; go to S1.
    S6: else MOVE[culprit, current.of(culprit), empty]; go to S1.

TEST.4(nXY)
    T1: f.list <- See.from(X)
    T3: culprit <- top(f.list)/nil

SOLVE.5(C, G)
    S1: Find differences (C-G). If none, then done.
    S2: n <- (Select smallest)
    S3: New.goal <- [nXY]
    S4: culprit <- TEST.5(nXY)
    S5: If culprit = nil, then MOVE[nXY]; go to S1.
    S6: else MOVE[culprit, current.of(culprit), other.of(X, Y)]; go to S1.

TEST.5(nXY)
    T1: f.list <- See.from(X)
    T2: t.list <- See.to(Y)
    T3: if t.list = nil, then culprit <- top(f.list)/nil,
    T4: else culprit <- top.(t.list), exit.

SOLVE(C,G)   C = Current state, G = goal state
    S1: Find differences between C and G. If none, then done.
    S2: n <- (Select smallest can).
    S3: New.goal <- (Move can n from X to Y)
                      <X = current peg of n, Y = goal peg of n>.
    S4: culprit <- TEST (new.goal)
    S5: If culprit = nil, then MOVE (nXY); go to S1.
    S6: else new.goal <- (Move culprit from X' to Y'); go to S4.
                      <X' = current peg of culprit, Y' = other of (X,Y)>

TEST(nXY)
    T1: f.list <- See.from(X) <all cans above n on X>
    T2: t.list <- See.to(Y) <all cans on Y larger than n>
    T3: if f.list = nil & t.list = nil, then culprit <- nil
    T4: else culprit <- min(f.list,t.list); exit

FIGURE 6.9. *Partial models (a,b,c) and complete model (d) for sophisticated perceptual strategy.*

mommy, while it is the mommy that is moved first) with a "sort of transitivity" (using an intermediate peg to hold a can temporarily). There is, he says, "a systematic primacy of the trial-and-error procedure over any attempt at deduction, and no cognizance of any correct solution arrived at by chance [p. 291]." I find it hard to reconcile this interpretation with these protocols.

MODELS

What can children acquire on this problem? Figure 6.9 shows a series of increasingly more powerful models for performance on this problem. The weakest, SOLVE.2, can do only one- and two-move problems before it makes an error. The final model, SOLVE, corresponds to what Simon (1975) called the "sophisticated perceptual strategy [p. 272]." (The models and the predicted performance are described in detail in Klahr, 1978.) At the present stage of this project, the proposed models are but the roughest approximations to what children know when they exhibit a particular performance level on this problem. Younger children's strategies contain no tests: They are very direct in their attempt to get to the goal. Older children make tests before they move, but they still move directly, rather than generate a new goal which is further tested. Only the most advanced children have the ability both to generate subgoals and to utilize the concept of the "other" peg. For results of empirical evaluations of these and other models, see Klahr and Robinson (in press).

Production System Design Issues

I believe that production systems are a promising representation for describing distinct levels of knowledge as well as the transition between those levels. Several of the properties of production systems make them plausible models of the human information-processing system (Newell, 1973) as well as a general format for control structures in artificial intelligence systems. Their potential for modeling cognitive development and learning is suggested by Waterman's (1974) pioneering work on self-modifying production systems, and by our own account of how the development of a wide range of cognitive abilities could be viewed as the result of such a system (Klahr & Wallace, 1976). However, many questions about the nature of self-modifying production systems remain. In this section I will describe a few of them.

The broad assumptions that comprise a production system view of the human IPS were described on pages 137 and 146. Working within this framework, the model builder faces a wide range of additional design decisions before a running production system interpreter can be built. These include assumptions about short term memory management, conflict resolution principles, self-modification procedures, and the encoding of the task environment. To date, no large scale, self-modifying production system has been constructed, nor has even a modest-sized system been constructed that accounts for data of the sort we are obtaining in our studies, so it is difficult to state with certainty what the critical issues will turn out to be. However, each of the items listed in the following paragraphs appears to have potentially important implications for such systems.

Short-Term-Memory Management

The "typical" set of assumptions about STM is that it functions like a limited capacity stack, with new symbols entering the "top" or "front," and excess items being lost from the "back" or "end." Items can be rearranged by explicit actions, as well as by automatic rehearsal. In automatic rehearsal, STM elements which match a just-fired production are moved to the front of STM. The result of this set of assumptions is that there is a strong recency effect in the system's momentary knowledge state. That is, STM always has elements near the front that recently have either entered from the environment or caused a production to fire, and information that has not affected the system for a while gets pushed further and further down in STM until it is lost.

Conflict Resolution

As described earlier on page 146, it is possible that more than one production is satisfied at a time. There are several conflict-resolution principles that have been proposed, and the issue can become quite complicated (see McDermott & Forgy, 1978), so here I will try only to indicate the nature and scope of the problem. Perhaps the least well-understood resolution principle ignores the conflict by simply firing all true productions. Another, used in many of my own early models, lets the order of the productions as listed in the model determine the resolution.[10]

Another class of resolution principles is based on the logical structure of the condition elements involved in the set of true productions. The simplest one, used in the system in Figure 6.4, is "special case order." Under such an assumption, special cases have priority over general cases.

The final class of resolution principles are based on the order, in STM, of the elements that matched the satisfied productions. The simplest variant of this class is "most recent element." The production with the element closest to the front of STM is chosen.

[10] This resolution principle is implicit in any scheme that tests productions sequentially, and fires the first that is satisfied.

Typically, no one of these principles is sufficient to guarantee a unique resolution, so that some metaprinciples must be invoked to order the conflict resolution principles (McDermott & Forgy, 1978).

Interaction of Assumptions

It is very clear that the assumptions about STM management will interact with the conflict resolution principles in determining the system's behavior. What is not clear is precisely how. The only formalism we have for stating these issues and for exploring their implications are the production systems themselves.

Self-Modification

The first self-modifying production systems were written by Waterman (1974). They required a single powerful addition to the "standard" system architecture. It was a special action that assembled a production from elements in STM labeled as either conditions or actions, and then placed the newly minted production into production memory. No other important change in the system architecture was required to implement this self-modifying ability. In particular, the basic recognize–act cycle was essentially unaware of the creation of new productions, and the system never had to enter a special learning mode distinct from its performance mode. In ongoing research at Carnegie-Mellon, Newell and his colleagues have been exploring some of the properties of self-modifying production systems (Forgy & McDermott, 1977; McDermott & Forgy, 1978; Rychener & Newell, 1978). Several exploratory systems have been written in which information about the components of the production to be built is obtained by binding variable elements in the condition side of the building productions. That is, the building productions seek matches with STM elements in exactly the same fashion as any other productions, except that the information thus obtained is used to modify long term memory (the production system) rather than STM. This mechanism provides an account of STM to LTM "transfer" that is couched entirely within the conventions of production systems. (See Klahr, in press, for a further discussion of these systems.)

Theoretical Implications

The very existence of these specific questions indicates to me the relative merits of this form of theory building. My own understanding of the Piagetian notions of equilibration, assimilation, and accomodation does not lead me to well-formulated questions about the mechanisms that underlie them. The production system conceptualization admits a wide range of theoretical stances, but it demands that they be made explicit and precise. Many of the *desiderata* of a developmental theory listed by Pascual-Leone (Chapter 12 of this volume) already exist in production systems. For example, the simultaneous matching of all productions with the current contents of STM, coupled with the conflict-resolution mechanism, provides a plausible characterization of a system that can exhibit both sequentially connected, goal-directed behavior as well as interruptable, unpredictable, and "truly novel" (Pascual-Leone, Chapter 12), behavior. Assimilatory capacity of production systems is evidenced in a system that allows partially matched productions to fire, or in which variables can be satisfied by any members or partial members of their domain. Since the level of abstraction of the symbols in the condition side of productions is unlimited, a production system can range in specificity from a narrow problem– as in the balance scale productions described above—to a broad range of behavior—as in a general means–ends production system.

It is certainly the case, as Pascual-Leone points out, that we need task variations in order to determine the task-free properties of the subject, and it is also the case that there are likely to be important dimensions of individual variation. This is precisely the direction that my own work has taken (Klahr, 1978), and it is exemplified with great sophistication by the work of my colleague, Robert Siegler (1976, 1978). Indeed, much of the really exciting work in the area of individual differences is taking place within what can be broadly characterised as an information processing framework, although not necessarily with production systems (cf. Resnick, 1976; Sternberg, 1977).

Concluding Comments

In this chapter, I have attempted to convey both the style and substance of one particular approach to the study of cognitive development. The current focus is on the construction of production-system models to account for children's behavior in different problem-solving domains. It is clear that, given the fine-grained level at which we are working, the models for each stage of performance will be very much determined by task-specific details of the observed behavior. Thus, the approach has some features of a "bottom-up" attempt at theory building. On the other hand, we have adopted a set of general systemic principles, as well as a global mechanism for implementing them, that guides and constrains the model-building effort, and this gives a strong "top-down" flavor to the effort. It would seem that both approaches are necessary to make any progress in advancing our knowledge of the process of cognitive development. Even approaches that are characterized as being *either* top-down *or* bottom-up can be seen, upon careful examination, to be combinations of both (although one or the other is emphasized). In the work described here, we have attempted to be explicit and precise about both the top-level theory and the bottom-level details of human performance. The modest progress thus far encourages me in the belief that this approach will yield valuable payoffs in our search for the mechanisms of cognitive development.

References

Anderson, J. R. *Language, memory and thought.* Hillsdale, N.J.: Lawrence Erlbaum, 1976.

Baylor, G. W., & Gascon, J. An information processing theory of aspects of the development of weight seriation in children. *Cognitive Psychology,* 1974, *6,* 1–40.

Bower, G. H. Cognitive psychology: an introduction. In W. Estes (Ed.), *Handbook of learning and cognitive processes.* Hillsdale, N.J.: Lawrence Erlbaum, 1975. Pp. 25–79.

Broadbent, D. E. The magic number seven after fifteen years. In R. A. Kennedy & A. Wilkes (Eds.), *Studies in long term memory.* New York: Wiley, 1975, Pp. 3–18.

Byrnes, M. A., & Spitz, H. Performance of retarded adolescents and nonretarded children on the Tower of Hanoi problem. *American Journal of Mental Deficiency,* 1977, *81,* 561–569.

Chi, M. T. H. Short-term memory limitations in children: capacity or processing deficits?. *Memory and Cognition,* 1976, *4,* 559–572.

Chi, M. T. H. Age differences in memory span. *Journal of Experimental Child Psychology,* 1977, *23,* 266–281.

Cook, T. W. Amount of material and difficulty of problem solving: II. The disc transfer problem. *Journal of Experimental Psychology,* 1937, *20,* 288.

Egan, D. E., & Greeno, J. G. Theory of rule induction: Knowledge acquired in concept learning, serial pattern learning, and problem solving.. In L. W. Gregg (Ed.), *Knowledge and cognition.* Potomac, Maryland: 1974, Pp. 43–103.

Forgy, C., & McDermott, J. OPS, a domain-independent production system language.. *Proceedings Fifth International Joint Conference on Artificial Intelligence.* 1977, *5,* 933–939.

Gagné, R. M., & Smith, E. C., Jr. A study of effects of verbalization on problem solving. *Journal of Experimental Psychology,* 1962, *63,* 12–18.

Gelman, R. Logical capacity of very young children: Number invariance rules. *Child Development,* 1972, *43,* 75–90. (a)

Gelman, R. The nature and development of early number concepts. In H. W. Reese (Ed.), *Advances in child development* (Vol. 7). New York: Academic Press, 1972. Pp. 115–167. (b)

Hormann, A. Gaku: An artificial student. *Behavioral Science,* 1965, *10,* 88–107.

Hunt, E. What kind of computer is man? *Cognitive Psychology,* 1971, *2,* 57–98.

Huttenlocher, J., & Burke, D. Why does memory span increase with age? *Cognitive Psychology,* 1976, *8,* 1–31.

Inhelder, B., & Piaget, J. *The growth of logical thinking from childhood to adolescence.* New York: Basic Books, 1958.

Karmiloff-Smith, A., & Inhelder, B. "If you want to get ahead, get a theory." *Cognition,* 1976, *3,* 195–212.

Klahr, D. Goal formation, planning, and learning by pre-school problem solvers, or: "My socks are in the dryer." In R. S. Siegler (Ed.), *Children's thinking: What develops?* Hillsdale, New Jersey: Lawrence Erlbaum, 1978. Pp. 181–212.

Klahr, D. Non-monotone assessment of monotone development. In S. Strauss & R. Stavy (Eds.), *U-shaped behavioral growth*. New York: Academic Press (in press).

Klahr, D., & Robinson, M. Formal assessment of problem-solving and planning processes in pre-school children. *Cognitive Psychology*, in press.

Klahr, D., & Siegler, R. S. The representation of children's knowledge. In H. W. Reese & L. P. Lipsitt (Eds.), *Advances in child development* (Vol. 12). New York: Academic Press, 1978. Pp. 61–116.

Klahr, D., & Wallace, J. G. *Cognitive development: An information processing view*. Hillsdale, New Jersey: Lawrence Erlbaum, 1976.

Klix, F. *Information und Verhalten*. Berlin: VEB Deutscher, 1971.

McDermott, J., & Forgy, C. Production system conflict resolution strategies. In D. A. Waterman & F. Hayes-Roth (Eds.), *Pattern-directed inference systems*. New York: Academic Press. 1978.

Miller, G. A. The magical number seven, plus or minus two: Some limits on our capacity for processing information. *Psychological Review*, 1956, *63*, 81–97.

Neves, D. A study of strategies of the Tower of Hanoi. Paper presented at the Midwestern Psychological Association Meeting, May 1977.

Newell, A. Production systems: Models of control structures. In W. G. Chase (Ed.), *Visual information processing*. New York: Academic Press, 1973. Pp. 463–526.

Newell, A., & McDermott, J. *PSG Manual*. Pittsburgh: Carnegie-Mellon University, Department of Computer Science, 1975.

Newell, A., & Simon, H. A. *Human problem solving*. Englewood Cliffs, New Jersey: Prentice-Hall, 1972.

Pascual-Leone, J. A mathematical model for the transition rule in Piaget's developmental stages. *Acta Psychologica*, 1970, *32*, 301–345.

Piaget, J. *The grasp of consciousness*. Cambridge, Massachusetts: Harvard University Press, 1976.

Resnick, L. B. (Ed.) *The nature of intelligence*. Hillsdale, New Jersey: Lawrence Erlbaum, 1976.

Rychener, M., & Newell, A. An instructable production system: initial design issues. In D. A. Waterman & F. Hayes-Roth (Eds.), *Pattern-directed inference systems*. New York: Academic Press (1978).

Schaeffer, B., Eggleston, V. H., & Scott, J. L. Number development in young children. *Cognitive Psychology*, 1974, *6*, 357–379.

Siegler, R. S. Three aspects of cognitive development. *Cognitive Psychology*, 1976, *8*, 481–520.

Siegler, R. S. The origins of scientific reasoning. In R. S. Siegler (Ed.), *Children's thinking: What develops?* Hillsdale, New Jersey: Lawrence Erlbaum, 1978. Pp. 109–149.

Siegler, R. S., & Klahr, D. When do children learn? The relationship between existing knowledge and the acquisition of new knowledge. In R. Glaser (Ed.), *Advances in instructional psychology*, Vol. 2. Hillsdale, N.J.: Lawrence Erlbaum (in press).

Simon, H. A. The functional equivalence of problem-solving skills. *Cognitive Psychology*, 1975, *7*, 268–288.

Spada, H. Die Analyse Kognitiver Lerneffekte mit stichprobenunabhangigen Verfahren. In K. Frey & M. Lang (Eds.), *Kognitionspsychologie und naturwissenschaftlicher Unterricht*. Bern: Huber, 1973. Pp. 94–131.

Sternberg, R. *Intelligence, information processing, and analogical reasoning: The componential analysis of human abilities*. Hillsdale, New Jersey: Lawrence Erlbaum, 1977.

Waterman, D. A. *Adaptive production systems*. (CIP Working Paper 285). Pittsburgh: Carnegie-Mellon University, Department of Psychology, 1974.

7

Formal Precision,
Where and What for,
Or: The Ape Climbs the Tree

RUDOLF GRONER
BEAT KELLER
CHRISTINE MENZ

Introduction: Theoretical Analysis and Empirical Prediction

First we shall make a distinction between the two classes of models as used in this book. The label "information processing" (IP) models has been put on such different approaches as the Piagetian one (Beilin, Chapter 11; Pascual-Leone, Chapter 12), or on more recent computer representations of knowledge (Greeno, Chapter 9; Klahr, Chapter 6). If we contrast this cluster with examples from the so-called "psychometric" (PM) models, we can again find quite different approaches, such as statistical data reduction (Bentler, Chapter 4) or model-directed quantitative prediction of performance data (Spada & Kluwe, Chapter 1; Groner & Spada, 1977). Thus, the labels IP and PM are somewhat misleading, since some examples of psychometric models deal more with information processing than some examples from the other group.

It seems to us that IP models are usually more concerned with the theoretical aspect—with the attempt to arrive at a complete and general formulation. This might happen at the cost of empirical access, although not necessarily. On the other hand, PM models focus on measurement—trying to establish a clear-cut relation between theoretical entities and their operationalized empirical counterparts. Some of the complexities and intricacies of the human information-processing system might become too simplified, but this may show up later through falsification. A simple model can even be used as a minimal assumption to be tested empirically, similar to a statistical null hypothesis.

DEVELOPMENTAL MODELS
OF THINKING

However, we do not see a crucial difference between IP and PM models. Rather we see a differential weighting of preferences (i.e., theoretical analysis versus empirical prediction). Therefore, the optimal solution would be a combination of the positive features of both approaches.

The Status of Information-Processing Theories

In the following arguments, we presuppose that a computer program is a model of an underlying psychological theory. Most of the arguments would not apply to an alternative methodological stance where the program itself is the theory. Such a position, which could be maintained for research in artificial intelligence, does not seem to be really defensible in cognitive psychology.

Theoretically Precise, but . . .

We certainly must admit that the theoretical clarity of the formal precision of IP models has increased in recent years. Many prominent examples of IP models have successfully been implemented on a computer, thus demonstrating their logical sufficiency. However, such a procedure does not automatically guarantee the precise theoretical definition of the terms involved (see Point 1 in Figure 7.1). Piaget has been

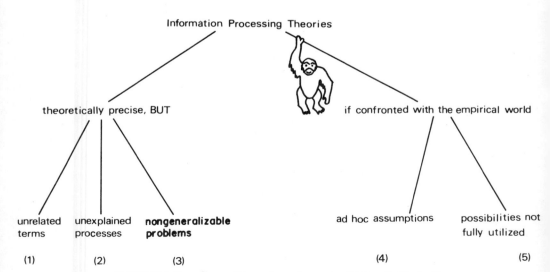

FIGURE 7.1. Tree for an IP-ape (ape drawn by Walter F. Bischof).

often criticized for using his concepts in an ambiguous way, but a similar thing can happen if a theoretical entity simply shows up in a program as a variable or a constant without any reference to the supposed meaning that could be expected from its name and its connotations in everyday language. For example, calling a list of seven elements short-term memory does not really reflect our understanding of short-term memory, yet this fact could be overlooked if one only looks at the name of the variable. (Drew McDermott, 1976, calls that "wishful mnemonics.") In our opinion, this difficulty is related to another central problem of simulation, namely that one is free to choose which aspect to implement in more detail or which one to leave out.

The same problem, of course, can arise not only with terms, but with entire processes (Point 2 in Figure 7.1). Here, the problem becomes even more serious. In principle, there is an infinite regress from complex processes to more and more elementary subprocesses where an end can only be set by an arbitrary decision not to simulate still more basic processes.

Still another problem of formal representation involves the task domain to be modeled (Point 3 in Figure 7.1). Even after very careful and subtle task analysis, there is no a priori or formal way to decide for which other task the present formalization can be generalized, or what exactly constitutes an equivalent task. An analogous issue has already been recognized in rule-learning models, where it is impossible in an open task domain to state a higher order rule as to where to apply a specific rule and where not to (see the discussion in Spada & Kempf, 1977). We are not sure to what extent this problem has been recognized on the theoretician's side in task analysis.

Empirical Validity

Referring now to the ape in the second main branch of Figure 7.1, which concerns the empirical validity of the IP models, consider Point 4. To arrive at a sufficient model formulation, many additions would have to be filled in that were not at the center of the theorist's capacity or interest. The same problem also arises if insufficient theoretical models are pressed for predictions. For instance, many models of structural representation lack performance assumptions that are needed for behavioral predictions, since not the structure itself but only its product, mediated by some unknown processes, can be observed. There are at least three strategies for getting rid of this problem:

1. Search for solutions in another field of the psychological literature, needless to say usually without success.
2. Rely on plausibility arguments, very often derived from the prescientific field.

3. Jump into ad hoc decisions; sometimes they might even become a new theory.

And now, after long efforts at theorizing, a peculiar phenomenon can be observed. The theoretician seems to be tired, and is, at any rate, very quickly satisfied with a quite modest utilization of the model or program (Point 5 in Figure 7.1). Often the theoretician restricts the model to a successful run of the whole program and maybe to some predicted failure runs. However, if the program were taken seriously as a model of human performance, it would allow for a vast number of empirical predictions. But so long as they are not followed up, logical sufficiency itself is not a sufficient property for a model of human information-processing.

Some Specific Examples Taken from Klahr's Work

In the following we will illustrate these points by specific examples taken from Klahr's (1978) work which seems to us an outstanding example of casting developmental problems in IP terms. We do not specifically wish to criticize Klahr, but would like to make our conjectures more concrete and, therefore, also more refutable. To facilitate following the main line of our arguments, a very brief recapitulation of Klahr's main points is given.

Klahr and Wallace (1976) tried to build production-system models of childrens' performance in Piagetian tasks (conservation, transitivity, etc.) at different developmental stages. Production rules are condition–action pairs operating on a "situation" in the following manner: A test is made of whether the condition of a condition–action pair is true in the given "situation". If it is not true, the next condition–action pair is tested. If it is true, the action is performed (usually resulting in a change of the "situation") and the testing cycle starts again with the first condition–action pair on the whole list which constitutes the production system. (For various extensions of this basic concept of a production system, see Anderson, 1976; Davis & King, 1975; Forgy & McDermott, 1977; Lenat & McDermott, 1977.)

Having built such models for two different stages (i.e., preoperational and concrete–operational), Klahr tries to conceive of a mechanism that would "develop" Model I into Model II, postulating that mechanism to be a model of the transition process, as the "motor" of development from stage to stage.

In later works, Klahr (1978; this volume, Chapter 6) extends the range of tasks for which he tries to provide working models of children's performance, to the balance beam problem and to the tower of Hanoi problem—a puzzle involving three pegs and a number of differently sized disks stacked in decreasing size on one peg. The goal is to transfer the whole stack onto another peg, moving only one disk at a time and never placing a larger disk on a smaller one. In experimenting with young children, Klahr uses cans instead of disks. (For details, see Klahr, 1978.)

Let us refer now to Point 1 of Figure 7.1, that is, unrelated terms. In his production-system analysis of number conservation, Klahr (1978) provides a good example of what we mean here: Performance in the conservation task directly depends on the discrimination of perceptual versus addition–subtraction transformations of a collection of elements. This discrimination depends on the establishment of a quantitative relation between two collections of elements—one collection before and one after the transformation. The quantitative relation between two collections is derived via the relation of the two corresponding quantitative symbols, and this relation in turn must be determined by a quantitative comparison system. Klahr defines quantitative symbols as ". . . semantic elements that constitute acceptable input to quantitative comparison systems. Given two such symbols, the comparison system can determine their relative magnitude [Klahr & Wallace, 1976, p. 30]." Now we seem to have a definition of "quantitative symbol." But this definition is based on the concept of a quantitative comparison system, and the concrete functioning of this system depends on what constitutes its acceptable inputs, that is, on what is to be counted as a quantitative symbol. Such a state of affairs would be formally correct, if the comparison system were implemented in a program. However, in our present example the comparison process which establishes the relation between two quantitative symbols is the OPR CALL RELATE, which means that the human operator at the computer terminal, and not the program itself, has to do the relation job.

To be concrete: If we allow only numbers to be quantitative symbols, then all the comparison system needs is an ordered list of the numbers and a process that can check which of two numbers occurs earlier in the list. Klahr also considers the possibility of quantitative symbols being lists of tokens in STM. The logic of a system that compares such quantitative symbols is essentially an internal one-to-one comparison of the tokens in the list.

These two illustrations should clarify two interrelated points:

1. The comparison system is not defined as long as its input is not defined.
2. Quantitative symbols are not defined as long as the system, to which they are input, is not defined.

This brings us to our second point: unspecified processes. To quote Klahr again: "The characterisation of any process as elementary is arbitrary and relative [Klahr & Wallace, 1976, p. 29]." Every model has to assume some processes, which are not modeled themselves, as elementary. The great danger lies in the possibility of relegating all hard problems of modeling to subelementary levels. Klahr's OPR CALLS, a prominent class of the unmodeled elementary processes, face exactly that danger. Thus, what we said in the last section could ironically be rephrased:

1. The comparison system need not be defined as long as its input is not defined.
2. Quantitative symbols need not be defined as long as the comparison system is not defined.

As an example on Point 3, nongeneralizable tasks, we take the tower of Hanoi puzzle and Klahr's distinction between "tower-ending" and "flat-ending" tasks (Klahr, Chapter 6). This distinction already alludes to the fact that the class of all possible tower of Hanoi tasks must be partitioned into different equivalence classes. A detail not mentioned explicitly by Klahr is that flat-ending tasks have two different shortest solution paths, one generated by SOLVE, his version of Simon's (1975) sophisticated perceptual strategy, and an alternative one, making the conceptual "detour" of moving the most constrained disk or can twice. In fact, tower-ending tasks are a subclass of the equivalence class of tasks optimally solved by SOLVE, and flat-ending tasks are a subclass of the equivalence class of tasks with two optimal solutions. But there is a third equivalence class containing all the tasks with the optimal solution not generated by SOLVE (Keller, 1977). What does this mean? Practically, it means that if we restrict our experiments to the first two equivalence classes described above, SOLVE generates perfect performance with which we can compare children's performances. But if we include all possible tasks, SOLVE does not generate perfect performance. Thus, not even for as simple a case as the class of Tower of Hanoi tasks do we really know what exactly constitutes an equivalence class of tasks over which we can generalize our findings.

The examples of additional ad hoc assumptions (Point 4 in Figure 7.1) are so numerous that there is no need to emphasize any single one. In fact, if serious efforts are made at all to get empirical predictions, it is hard to find any counterexample.

There seems to be a definite advantage on the side of a class of psychometric models, the Rasch-models, which clearly separate less central, so-called incidental parameters from the "structural" parameters of the model (see e.g., Spada, 1976, p. 102ff). We do not see an analogous possibility for information processing models.

We come to our last point: The precision ascribed to information processing models is certainly a virtue, but it is also an obligation for the model builder to test all empirical predictions made possible by his precise models. Klahr's production system for performance in transitivity tasks contains productions that handle the conversion of premises. Any conflict resolution principle must select one production, that is, pick up one premise for conversion, thus generating clear predictions about the relative difficulty of different tasks. Some predictions can possibly be shown as contradicting existing empirical evidence (Johnson-Laird, 1972; Groner, 1978). But the general point is that one cannot design a system for a specific range of data without paying attention to the side-effects of all assumptions on other relevant data.

The points made in the second part of this chapter all concern models of stages (and not models of the transition process), but as Klahr himself says, the latter models cannot be better than the former ones.

References

Anderson, J. R. *Language, memory and thought.* Hillsdale, New Jersey: Lawrence Erlbaum, 1976.

Davis, R., & King, J. *Overview of production systems.* Report STAN-CS-75-524, Memo AIM-271. Department of Computer Science, Stanford University, 1975.

Forgy, C., & McDermott, J. OPS, a domain-independent production system language. *Proceedings of the International Joint Conference on Artificial Intelligence,* 1977, *5,* 933–939.

Groner, R. *Hypothesen im Denkprozeß.* Grundlagen einer verallgemeinerten Theorie auf der Basis elementarer Informationsverarbeitung. Bern: Huber, 1978.

Groner, R., & Spada, H. Some markovian models for structural learning. In H. Spada & W. F. Kempf (Eds.), *Structural models of thinking and learning.* Bern: Huber, 1977. Pp. 131–159.

Johnson-Laird, P. N. The three term series problem. *Cognition,* 1972, *1,* 57–82.

Keller, B. *Eine nicht-optimale Strategie zur Lösung der erweiterten Turm von Hanoi-Aufgabe.* Unveröffentlichte Lizentiatsarbeit phil. hist. Fakultät Universität Bern, 1977.

Klahr, D. Goal formation, planning and learning by pre-school problem-solvers. In R. S. Siegler (Ed.), *Children's thinking: What develops?* Hillsdale, New Jersey: Lawrence Erlbaum, 1978.

Klahr, D., & Wallace, I. G. *Cognitive development: An information processing view.* Hillsdale, New Jersey: Lawrence Erlbaum, 1976.

Lenat, D. B., & McDermott, J. Less than general production system architectures. *Proceedings of the International Joint Conference on Artificial Intelligence,* 1977, *5,* 928–932.

McDermott, D. Artificial intelligence meets natural stupidity. *SIGART Newsletter ACM,* 1976, *57,* 4–9.

Simon, H. A. The functional equivalence of problem solving skills. *Cognitive Psychology,* 1975, *7,* 268–288.

Spada, H. *Modelle des Denkens und Lernens.* Bern: Huber, 1976.

Spada, H. Logistic models of learning and thought. In H. Spada & W. F. Kempf (Eds.), *Structural models of thinking and learning.* Bern: Huber, 1977. Pp. 227–262.

Spada, H., & Kempf, W. F. (Eds.). *Structural models of thinking and learning.* Bern: Huber, 1977.

8

The Development of Logical Competence: A Psycholinguistic Perspective

RACHEL JOFFE FALMAGNE[1]

The focus of this chapter is on logical reasoning as it is embodied in language comprehension and language use, and on the development of logical competence defined in that sense (i.e., in particular, the competence involved in reasoning with verbally stated problems of a self-contained kind, such as syllogisms). Some speculations about the way in which this competence may be presumed to develop are discussed on pages 177–186, and data are presented that provide initial support for those speculations. More specific theoretical notions about the cognitive processes involved in the reasoning situations considered are proposed on pages 186–194; this theoretical framework is then used to reformulate more clearly both the issues outlined in the previous section and the notion of logical competence itself. Before turning to these matters, a few preliminary clarifications are examined regarding the domain of discourse of the present discussion.

Preliminaries: Alternative Approaches to Logical Development

In order to bring into clearer focus the questions to be addressed here, it will be useful to distinguish between two current approaches to logi-

[1] Preparation of this contribution was supported in part by Grant SED 78-22294 from the National Science Foundation and the National Institute of Education, in part by a general research and facilities grant to Clark University from the William T. Grant Foundation and in part by Grant No. 9003-28 from the Mellon Foundation.

cal development: the Piagetian approach and the approach that takes as its object of study the competencies and processes involved in reasoning with verbal, self-contained statements. No polemical stance is implied in this distinction regarding the ultimate separateness or convergence of these approaches in terms of their focus and their findings. Rather, the aim of this section is to delineate what I see to be the domain of discourse of the two approaches as they now stand. General issues related to the philosophical context of this discussion will be examined briefly at the end of this section.

This distinction between the two approaches to logical development has been discussed elsewhere (Falmagne, 1975a, 1975c), but some of its aspects will be elaborated here more explicitly. Its essentials are best captured by saying that Inhelder and Piaget's (1958) work on logical development and the work associated with theirs, focuses on the child as a scientist, whereas the other traditional line of work, to which the discussion in the following sections pertains, focuses on the child and the adult as logicians.

The preceding contrast can be drawn at two levels: in terms of an analysis of the kinds of problems presented to the child in the two respective task domains, and in terms of the cognitive processes that can be presumed to be implicated in the respective tasks. Clearly, task analyses cannot be separated sharply from considerations about underlying processes, since a description of task requirements intrinsically relies on the operations that the subject must perform. Nevertheless, these two modes of analysis do differ in focus and emphasis, and the present section will therefore examine the comparison between Piagetian and "propositional" approaches to logical development from each of those two perspectives in turn.

Differences in Task Demands

From the point of view of a task analysis, studying the child as a logician or, alternatively, as a scientist, are two distinct endeavors. When studying the child as a logician, we focus on the child's knowledge of the formal and semantic properties of language, we keep factual biases minimal in the statement of the reasoning task, and we require the subject to disregard that factual information and to draw conclusions from the premises in much the same manner as a linguist would judge the grammaticality of a sentence. A problem presented to the child might be, "If Susan is studying, then she is not sitting in this chair. Susan is sitting in this chair. Is she studying?" The question of interest is the extent to which the child is able to base her or his answer upon the structural relations within and between the premises rather than upon (or in addition to) their empirical content. Of course, operationalizing this question is a major issue in itself; furthermore, any formulation of the question that is more specific than the deliberately rough formulation above, entails important theoretical choices and commitments. Some of these issues will be briefly discussed later in this chapter when we examine various modes of reasoning, but for the present purpose it is sufficient to say that what we are studying developmentally within such an approach is the process of gradual structuring of the linguistic environment by the child. In contrast, in the Piagetian tradition, the child is viewed as a scientist attempting to discover properties of the real world, and typically tested in situations in which he or she has to draw inferences about a natural phenomenon (as in the physics experiments described by Inhelder and Piaget, 1958). The "object of the game" is therefore different, in the same way that an empirical science differs from a formal discipline in what it aims to achieve. Piagetian studies do indeed examine children's logic to the extent that logic mediates scientific inquiry. But they also intrinsically involve other functions or task requirements, as does scientific inquiry. The first obvious feature of the "scientific" situation is that it is essentially an inductive problem, aimed at the discovery of an empirical law, in which deductive reasoning only provides segments of the overall course of reasoning. Another requirement, specific to the "scientific" task and crucial for the contrast being made here, is that the child has to generate a preliminary description or encoding of the real events themselves, that is, of the empirical premises to which inferences will be applied. Furthermore, a relevant description of real events is a prerequisite for appropriate inferences to be possible. The empirical implications of the latter point are illustrated by data from Siegler (1976) among others, demonstrating the importance of the encoding of events as a source of age-related differences in children's scientific reasoning. Similarly, a perusal of the young subjects' protocols reported in Inhelder and Piaget (1958) illustrates the same point. For example, in the billiard table experiment reported in that volume, in which children have to discover the law regarding the equality of the angle of incidence and the angle of reflection of the ball on the edge of the table, young children often mimic the trajectory of the ball as being a curve rather than two straight segments. It is clear that such an encoding, from which the crucial information—the angle—is missing, precludes making the appropriate inference and, prior to this, performing the appropriate experimental manipulation.

Clearly then, the task requirements of "scientific" and "propositional" situations are partly different: "Scientific" situations involve both the application of logical rules of inference and the encoding of factual information; while in the "propositional" situations, the information is given explicitly in verbal form and the child is asked to rely exclusively on this information. Correspondingly, the reasoning processes involved in these two respective tasks must be assumed to differ in some of their components at least, as will be discussed now.

Cognitive Processes in the Two Task Domains

Granting the qualification raised previously concerning the separability of task analyses and process considerations, one way to characterize "propositional" tasks and contrast them with "scientific" problems is to say that, in the former case, the task *can* be solved by exclusively using language comprehension, logic, and the mapping between the two, whereas the "scientific" situations require the subject to generate a description of the factual state of affairs (thereby constructing the "givens" on which reasoning subsequently operates); to generate this description from an array of nonverbal information (as opposed to the former situations in which the basic information is available in linguistic form); and to carry out inductive reasoning, for which the deductive reasoning steps are only auxiliary segments.

To further specify the exact locus of this contrast, it is important first to acknowledge that each task can be approached in a variety of ways. Thus, while "propositional" situations can be dealt with by exclusively using the propositional apparatus, as mentioned above, they clearly also allow for other modes of reasoning that involve such resources as imagery, factual biases, and analogical reasoning. The operation of such factors has been widely documented (e.g., see Henle, 1962; Wason & Johnson-Laird, 1972; Revlis, 1975, and Scribner, 1977, about reliance on factual information in reasoning; see Huttenlocher, 1968 and Shaver, Pierson & Lang, 1974, about reliance on spatial representations or imagery; and see Johnson-Laird, 1975, and Johnson-Laird & Steedman, 1978, about a prototype-based analogical mode of reasoning with quantified statements). In fact, this very issue will be focused on specifically later in this chapter. Similarly, scientific problems can be solved in a variety of ways, of which the formal approach is only one, as Inhelder and Piaget (1958) have shown.

However, even though "propositional" problems are not necessarily dealt with in a propositional way, their solution entails, minimally, the processes involved in any sentence comprehension task. Furthermore, in those cases in which the problem *is* dealt with propositionally, a representation embodying the logical form of the statements is utilized as well. (Since these notions will be developed in greater detail in a subsequent section, I will not elaborate them here.) In the "scientific" problems, some internal representation of the information must also be achieved, but this representation results from an encoding of nonlinguistic input and therefore, at the very least, is mediated by a different translation process than the one implicated in the former situation. Furthermore, for the same reason, it is not obvious that the format in which the resulting internal representation is couched, must be the same in these two cases. Specifically, for example, linguistic expressions of a state-of-affairs (such as the premises of the problem in the "propositional" tasks) may lead more easily to the formal treatment of the problem than would the "scientific" situation because the logical form of the problem is made relatively more accessible by its linguistic expression. Reciprocally, it is well established empirically that natural language connectives, such as "if . . . then," are not represented in a uniform way, but rather are given a context-dependent reading (e.g., Wason & Johnson-Laird, 1972; Staudenmayer, 1975), with a strong bias in most cases toward a biconditional ("if and only if" reading) and it is quite possible that these ambiguities and biases are idiosyncratic to the verbal situation and that a conditional (as opposed to biconditional) structuring of information may be more readily available for nonverbally given information, for example.

Thus, while both situations may involve an encoding of information in some kind of logical format, each "translation" process has its own uncertainties. It is, furthermore, not necessary to assume that information is mapped into the same representational system in both cases.

These general remarks addressed the possible differences in the process of representation of the information in the "propositional" and "scientific" situations, respectively, that clearly parallel the task analysis proposed previously. One additional, self-evident difference must be mentioned: Scientific problems, being inductive in nature, require corresponding heuristics that are not implicated in deductive "propositional" situations. This point will be discussed somewhat more specifically in the next section, with particular reference to the work of Inhelder and Piaget (1958), who have provided an extensive account of such heuristics.

Remarks on the Philosophical Context of this Discussion

The relationships between logic, language, and reality are notoriously controversial among philosophers and linguists. (See Wittgenstein, 1922/1961; Frege, 1918/1956; Russell, 1956; and Putnam, 1971, for a sample of alternative positions. See Haack, 1978, for an overview of the main issues.) Specific points of controversy concern the nature of propositions as, alternatively, empirical, linguistic, or subjective entities, and, correspondingly, whether logic is more properly seen as formalizing necessary relations in the empirical world, or analytic relations within natural language.

Although the preceding discussion has focused on the strictly psychological aspects of the logician's activity as distinct from the scientist's activity as carried out by the child, such a discussion indirectly invokes the general context of these philosophical issues, in two ways. First, examining the logician's activity entails assumptions about the nature of logical knowledge. Second, examining logical development entails assumptions about the sources from which logical knowledge is derived.

Regarding the former question, the specific issue is whether logical knowledge primarily consists of knowledge about the structure of language or of knowledge about the structure of events in the empirical world. The psychological angle on this issue highlights considerations of a somewhat different kind than those of the philosopher. The concern is not so much about the foundations of logic but rather about the way in which logical knowledge articulates with the other components of an individual's knowledge structure. The discussion in the preceding pages has remained ostensibly neutral with respect to this issue, as well as with respect to related issues concerning the relations between language and thought. In an important sense, logical knowledge is knowledge about both language and the empirical world to the extent that language itself is semantically grounded in the empirical world to which parts of it refer. When reasoning about linguistically expressed propositions, the individual acesses those relations through the linguistic medium, which is not necessarily the case in the "scientific" situations. Whether similar logical operations are deployed in those two contexts at a given point in the individual's development is, in principle, a largely empirical question but one for which the relevant data base is missing at present.

Regarding the second question raised previously, it will be assumed here that logical knowledge is derived constructively both from linguistic and nonlinguistic sources, as will be discussed on pages 180–181.

Development of Propositional Reasoning: General Considerations and Speculations

With the above distinction in mind, the working hypothesis endorsed here is that

1. Logical competence, as embodied in language comprehension and language use, develops through childhood (and indeed most probably through adulthood as well).[2]

---

[2] A comment is in order, for clarification of the perspective taken in this discussion. The notion of logical competence applied here is understood more broadly than strictly refer-

2. There are a number of important similarities between the way in which this competence develops in children and the way in which it develops in adults.
3. Young children do indeed master some patterns of deductive inference at a fairly abstract level. (For example, it seems clear that a child as young as 5 or 6 years, knows that, if a statement (p) is true, its negation (not p) is false, regardless of the content of the statement.)

On the following pages, I will qualify and discuss in more detail these views on children's logical competence and I will propose one mechanism that may contribute to its development.

Logical Competence: Conceptual Issues and Developmental Assumptions

The notion of logical competence is a complex one and can be defined in at least two ways. When defined in an operational sense, a person would be said to be logically competent if he or she is able to perform successfully in the appropriate range of logical inference tasks, without regard to the nature of the processes and operations underlying this performance. Within this conception the more competent individual is one who is able to correctly perform a wider range of logical inferences across a wider range of contexts, even though he or she might conceivably apply a variety of content-based procedures (rather than formal rules or formal procedures) to this end. An alternative notion of logical competence is one that refers to only those cases in which inferences have been conducted with reliance on some abstract mode of representation that captures the logical form of the problem in some explicit way. (See Falmagne, 1975b, for a more detailed discussion of these issues.) This distinction is not unlike the distinction drawn by Greeno (Chapter 9 of this volume) between implicit and explicit understanding, with reference to algebra. In particular, Greeno's notion of implicit understanding, as well as the former sense of competence defined here,

---

ring to formal logic. Indeed numerous results, including some mentioned earlier in this section, point to the inadequacy of formal logic as a model of human reasoning. Alternative models have been proposed (e.g., Braine, 1977) that appear to reflect natural deduction more accurately. Braine's model, however, differs from formal logic in its foundations and in the sequence of derivation leading to certain results, but not in the set of theorems it generates. In particular, the various patterns of inference are sanctioned as valid or invalid in a similar way by formal and natural logic alike so that the distinction between the two, while it defines a perspective, does not affect the status of the present discussion.

only requires the subject to apply procedures whose outcome is consistent with the properties of the formal system considered (logic or algebra), but does not require explicit use of rules of that system either in formalizing the material or in carrying out the operations leading to the response.

I would like to propose the view, only partly speculative, that logical competence in both senses of the term develops through childhood (and adulthood) and, to discuss one mechanism that may account in part for this acquisition. These matters will be dealt with in general terms in the present section. In the next section, a conceptual and theoretical framework will be outlined within which those questions can be phrased more specifically and their empirical consequence articulated.

The view that logical competence, in the weaker sense, develops through childhood, receives general support from findings which indicate that children have at least a limited ability to handle propositional reasoning. Hill (1961), Ennis (1971), Kodroff and Roberge (1975), Kuhn (1977), Peel (1967), Roberge (1970, 1972), Roberge and Paulus (1971), and Taplin, Staudenmayer, and Taddonio (1970), among others, have provided evidence of this sort regarding some patterns of conditional reasoning (i.e., involving statements of the form "if . . . then . . .") and class syllogisms (i.e., involving quantified statements of the form "All A's are B's" or "Some A's are B's") in children as young as 6 years of age. Furthermore, even though there are age-related differences, particularly in the interpretation of the logical connectives and quantifiers, studies by Suppes and Feldman (1971), Neimark and Chapman (1975), Neimark and Slotnick (1970), and Paris (1973) reveal that the patterns of differential difficulty of the various logical schemes, the kind of errors made, and the factors affecting difficulty seem highly similar in children and in adults. (See Taplin, 1971; Taplin & Staudenmayer, 1973; and Wason & Johnson-Laird, 1972, for studies about adults.)

Yet, while such findings testify to some (limited) logical competence in children, in the first sense of competence defined above, they do not elucidate the specific process underlying the subjects' responses. It is therefore not known whether children's reasoning was of a formal kind in the studies reported. Thus, the second assumption advanced here, about children's ability to deal with language at a formal level in propositional reasoning contexts, is still in need of direct empirical support.

However, this stronger assumption, that children possess and develop an ability to carry out propositional reasoning with reliance on logical form, is made plausible by the following considerations.

First, a wide range of results in the literature on adults points at the fact that, whenever it is possible to do so, adult reasoning preferentially relies on factual information about the situation described rather than on the formal properties of the premises alone.[3] What needs to be demonstrated, then, is not that children spontaneously reason at a formal level, but rather that they can do it, or do do it sometimes.

Second, let us acknowledge or remember that logic and syntax, as formal systems, have a highly similar status with respect to natural language. Although the details of the parallel, its limitations, and the resulting issues are beyond the scope of this chapter, it is enough to note (a) that the two systems are alternative formalizations of natural language into, respectively, the vocabulary of grammar, and rewrite and transformational rules in the case of syntax; and propositions, connectives, and schemas of deductive inference in the case of logic;[4] and (b) that both logic and syntax interface with semantics, in ways that are partly similar. If one recognizes this parallel, it is then natural to look at both syntactic and logical development as a process of gradual structuring of the linguistic environment. Furthermore, it is natural to speculate that, just as the child learns to structure his or her linguistic environment syntactically (presumably by exploiting the interconnections between the syntactic, semantic and contextual aspects of language) he or she may also be assumed to structure the linguistic environment in terms of what statements can be legitimately derived from what other statements, and under what conditions. Within this view, the high level of sophistication reached by young children in their syntactic development lends credibility to the preceding assumptions about the development of propositional reasoning.

Before proceeding further, it is important to recognize that the view defended here, concerning logical competence in children, is not seen as incompatible with Piaget's theory, according to which children do not reach the stage of formal operations before adolescence. This is because the notion of formal operations has several facets that are conceptually independent:

1. It provides a *structural* description of the adolescent's competence and, symmetrically, the structural limitations to the degree of complexity or type of operations that the preadolescent child is able to conduct.

---

[3] For example, see Wason and Johnson-Laird (1972) about the preponderance of "practical" over "pure" inference; Henle (1962) about data illustrating subjects' "failure to accept the logical task"; Scribner (1977) for cross-cultural findings of the same kind; and Staudenmayer (1975) and Revlis (1975) for the role of empirical information in the interpretation of logical quantifiers.

[4] In fact, an inference rule can be characterized as a particular transformational rule generating a new, equivalent statement from another, or two or more statement(s), on formal grounds.

2. It describes *heuristic* characteristics of adolescent thought, namely the hypothetico–deductive approach to understanding of and theorizing about reality and the combinatorial (experimental) approach to hypothesis testing.
3. It describes characteristics of the reasoning *process*, namely the ability to reason at a propositional level (that is to say, among other things, the ability to carry out deductions by relying on formal rather than referential properties of the statements).

This last aspect is the one that concerns us here. In Piagetian situations, the subject can use or not use propositional reasoning either in encoding the experimental outcomes or in generating hypotheses. The point here is that the child may fail to resort to propositional reasoning in Piagetian situations not because of a "process deficiency" defined as in Point 3, but because of the child's orientation at the heuristic level described in Point 2. In other words, when presented with a linguistically expressed problem, as in the "propositional" tasks, the child may well be able to deal with it propositionally (in some cases) although he or she would not tend to treat (or theorize about) factual information in that manner when reasoning about an empirical phenomenon.

Logical Development: General Perspective

A comprehensive account of logical development will have to address questions on two different scales of time and generality. At the general level, such an account has to articulate the principles underlying logical development in the context of cognitive development as a whole; it has to specify the nature of the interplay between the individual's spontaneous mechanisms for acquiring and constructing logical knowledge and the contribution of empirical experience to this knowledge; and it has to describe the control mechanisms that regulate, coordinate, and integrate the various acquisitions proceeding concurrently. At the more specific level, this account has to specify the processes underlying microdevelopmental changes, that is, the course of those specific acquisitions that proceed within the context of more general trends and reorganizations.

It is to the latter set of questions that the present section will be addressed, with a specific focus on the process whereby patterns of deductive inference may be acquired and on the different levels at which they may be mastered. However, these questions are examined in the context of more general concerns, and the following general comments will help place them in their proper theoretical perspective.

Returning for a moment to the epistemological question mentioned earlier, it seems clear that a strictly empiricist account of logical development and a strictly rationalist account are equally untenable and, furthermore, intellectually unappealing. An assumption that seems more apt, both on empirical and philosophical grounds, is that natural logic is both constrained and made possible by fundamental properties of the mind—minimally by fundamental cognitive ways of processing experience. One of these basic cognitive functions is the human capacity for abstraction, which is reflected at the early stages of development in the emergence of the symbolic function and at later stages in the formal structuring underlying advanced syntactic development, for example. This capacity provides the mechanism for qualitative discontinuities in modes of thinking and of processing language, and it has been and will be invoked in this chapter when discussing the differences between content-bound ways of carrying out deductive inferences, and formal mastery of these inferences. Clearly, these assumptions are, in a general sense, entirely congruent with the constructive epistemology represented in Piaget's theory.

Regarding the development of logical competence, a general assumption underlying the foregoing discussion is that logical knowledge is derived both from awareness of the structure of language itself and from the correspondences between linguistically expressed propositions and empirical states of affairs, with the latter source of knowledge ensuring that the resulting logical system remains semantically sound and internally consistent (though not necessarily complete).

More specifically, the initial comprehension of "logical" relations is certainly semantically based and contextually restricted, as has been shown in the language development literature for other kinds of relations. However, it seems compelling to assume that further elaboration of these logical relations involves a process of abstraction from their initial content-bound meaning and an elaboration of their linguistic properties. The development of negation may be a paradigm example of this microdevelopmental process. Negation in the early stages of language development appears to signify disappearance or nonexistence, and it only subsequently emerges as a propositional operator in children of 2–3 years of age (Pea, 1980). By age 5 or 6, it seems hardly questionable that the logical properties of negation are mastered by the child at a fairly abstract level, in the sense that the child knows that if a statement p is true, its negation is false across a wide range of contents and presumably on inferential grounds. Thus, negation initially appears to refer directly to the events or objects themselves, and its meaning is grounded in direct verification of the presence or absence of these objects. Further developments, however, are of a more syntactic kind, though presumably retaining the initial meaning as their semantic foundation.

Acquisition of Patterns of Deductive Inference

This discussion will focus primarily on the latter part of this microdevelopment—that is, on the process whereby patterns of inference that may already be used or understood in a relatively "concrete" way in some specific contexts become part of the child's formal repertoire of logical knowledge.

The hypothesis to be examined here is that competence in propositional reasoning results, at least in part, from a concept-learning process whereby the child encounters instances of a given pattern of inference in his or her linguistic environment, is given feedback either by other speakers or by reality as to the correctness or incorrectness of the particular inference, and abstracts the logical structure common to those instances. Thus the structural concept of a given rule of inference would be acquired in part by abstraction of the relevant logical form from its content-bound embodiments.

Two important qualifications are needed concerning the status of this process with respect to a comprehensive account of logical development. First, the "in part" in the preceding paragraph points to the notion that, in addition to "direct" learning and abstraction, autonomous rational constructions and regulations must be assumed to occur. For example, it is unlikely that the child who has acquired three of the four patterns of conditional inference is dependent upon environmental input for acquisition of the fourth pattern. Conversely, if a pattern of inference were contradictory with respect to a pattern previously acquired, cross-consistency checks and elimination or synthesis would presumably occur. Second, it is clear that what can be acquired at a given age (or stage) may be subject to structural constraints imposed by the level of cognitive functioning of the child. Indeed, Piaget (1970) Pascual-Leone (Chapter 12 of this volume), and Klahr and Wallace (1976), among others, have described constraints of various kinds in the second respect. Nevertheless, the development of specific logical competencies within these constraints needs to be understood. The hypothesis formulated here is an attempt to do so.

An initial test of the hypothesis just stated, was conducted in three studies (Falmagne, Thompson, & Bennett, 1977; Falmagne, Thompson, Sherwood, & Bennett, in prep.) in children from second through fifth grade, with respect to a specific pattern inference, *Modus Tollens* ("if *p*, then *q*; not *q*; therefore, not *p*", where *p* and *q* can be affirmative or negative statements). All studies used a concept-learning paradigm deemed to embody some of the main aspects of the putatively relevant experience according to the hypothesis, that is, exposure to a number of instanciations of the given pattern of inference, and feedback as to the correct response, but no direct instruction. Thus, the children underwent two training sessions consisting of a number of different "word problems," half of which were Modus Tollens in the experimental groups. For example, one problem might be, "If it is Tuesday, then Mary has gym today. Mary doesn't have gym today. Is it Tuesday?" The three response choices are "yes," "no," and "can't tell."[5] Feedback was given after each response. Whether subjects had abstracted the concept of a Modus Tollens inference, and the level of generality of the concept was then assessed in a transfer session administered 2 days later. The transfer session included several types of problems of the same logical form as those encountered during training, but differing from them in surface structure. Their purpose was to assess whether the concept attained was the relevant one and to distinguish acquisition of a specific concept tied to the surface structure of the problem, from the learning of a more general concept based on the logical form of the argument. Thus, in some transfer problems, the conditional statement in the first premise was expressed with the consequent clause preceding the antecedent clause (e.g., "Mary has gym today if it is Tuesday"), in order to differentiate attainment of the relevant concept from an improvement due to strategies based on clause order. In other transfer problems, the connective "when–then" (logically equivalent to "if–then") was used in order to assess whether the concept attained was connective-specific. Similarly, in other problems, the second premise (the "not q" clause) lexically negated the q clause in the first premise rather than negating it explicitly, (e.g., "The book is red" is denied lexically by "The book is blue" and explicitly by "The book is not red"). Finally, problems similar in form to the training problems but containing nonsense content words were also included (e.g., "If Paul fibbles, then he thabbles") in order to assess the level of abstraction of the rule. All the problems used in the study were different from each other in content.

Before proceeding further, it is important to acknowledge the exact status of these studies with respect to the hypothesis being tested. They should be conceived of as feasibility studies at the psychological level, that is, their specific import is to assess whether children are cognitively equipped for carrying out the process of abstraction that has been postulated, from content-bound reasoning experience with feedback. If they are, observations in natural linguistic environments evidently will have to be conducted in order to sustain the hypothesis, as will be discussed later.

In all three studies, the transfer data revealed a significant effect of

---

[5] The instruction made it clear that "can't tell" was used to state that the answer to a problem was indeterminate, and examples of problems of all three types were provided.

training, with performance in the experimental groups superior to a control group trained with miscellaneous irrelevant inferences.[6]

But of more importance than this general effect is the fact that the resulting improvement was largest for the nonsense problems, the error rate for which became equivalent to that of meaningful problems in the experimental group, whereas it remained close to chance for the controls. Since children had not been presented nonsense problems during training, this result strongly supports the notion that children had identified the structure of a Modus Tollens inference at an abstract level and were able to recognize it in problems ostensibly devoid of referential meaning. This result also indicates that more than improvement due to training occurred: Though Modus Tollens was certainly not an entirely novel acquisition—since children in that age range do use that pattern correctly in certain cases—the results concerning nonsense problems indicate that training resulted in at least a new level of abstraction in children's representation of that pattern. In terms of the framework outlined here, concerning changes in mental representation in the course of logical development, the interpretation would be that training perhaps led children to construct a formal representation of a Modus Tollens inference. As another result congruent with this interpretation, training primarily affected those problems involving a negation in either the p or the q clause. Since problems involving a negation are typically answered at chance level in the control group and in the literature, this again suggests that training resulted in a Modus Tollens concept more abstract than the procedure used previously. This result provides weaker support for this notion than the results on nonsense problems (since training did include problems with negations) but is congruent with it.

Another question of central importance regarding the depth (or generality) of the concept attained is whether learning is connective-specific. This was not the case: Training involving one connective transferred to logically equivalent problems formulated with the other connective, resulting in equivalent performance with both, even when the "new" connective was included in nonsense problems. These results indicate again that the learning process occurred at the level of the logical form of the problems rather than being tied to their surface form.

Finally, it is of interest to note that transfer effects extended to problems involving a lexical rather than explicit negation in the second premise (see the example on page 183), thus enduring even in the ab-

---

[6] A qualification is necessary concerning the second grade group: Most of the results to be reported also held for that group (with some differences not affecting the present points) when the procedure was modified to involve dual presentation (concurrent auditory and written presentation) instead of the written presentation used for all other groups.

sence of the syntactic cues associated with negation. Here an additional result is of interest. One of the studies compared the relative effectiveness of training with problems in which the second premise is a lexical denial of the q clause with the effectiveness of training on problems explicit negation. This comparison is of interest because ordinary discourse offers few examples of fully explicit propositional reasoning. Within the context of the general hypothesis examined here it is natural to determine whether children are able to abstract the pattern of inference from examples of its lexical realizations as well as from its fully explicit examples. Furthermore, lexical denial, being more concrete, may facilitate reasoning and perhaps the abstraction of the pattern. This expectation was indeed supported by the data, and training with lexical denial fully transferred to explicitly negated formulations.

To summarize these results indicate that training resulted in improvement based on the logical form of a Modus Tollens inference rather than on surface features (since training uniformly generalized to problems in which the antecedent and consequent clause were permuted to problems with nonsense content, to problems involving a different connective, and to problems involving lexical denial). Furthermore, training appeared to result in a new level of abstraction regarding the Modus Tollens inference, since effects were largest for nonsense problems, which became equivalent in difficulty to meaningful problems. These results thus provide support for the assumption that children are cognitively equipped to abstract patterns of deductive inference through a concept learning process of the kind described above.

Several points need to be stressed here to clarify the status of this statement. First, in some of the cases just discussed, and most probably at the fifth-grade level, children presumably did have a limited "concept" of a Modus Tollens inference initially, limited perhaps in the sense of being content-bound, perhaps in the sense of applying to affirmative sentences only, and perhaps in other ways. (The term "concept" appears between quotes because distinguishing a logical concept from a relatively general procedure is an interesting and complex issue, both conceptually and empirically.) Thus, in these cases, the appropriate interpretation of our results is that training led to a new level of abstraction regarding that pattern of inference (or, more specifically, in terms of the framework proposed earlier, that a formal representation became available through exposure to a range of exemplars of the pattern), rather than to an entirely novel acquisition of a previously nonexistent inference. Let us note, however, that the latter may well be the case in some of the second-grade subjects. Whatever interpretation is adopted, the important point is that either acquisition or improvement must have been mediated by identification of the logical form of the inference, thus supporting the notion that children can carry out and represent those kinds of abstractions. The next step, of course, is to investigate whether novel patterns can be acquired through the same process. Two obvious candidates are the indeterminate inferences associated with the conditional, which are known from previous research to be essentially absent from children's deductions.

Second, although the results appear to indicate that a logical rule of inference can be abstracted through a concept learning process, they evidently do not indicate that this is how children acquire such rules in natural circumstances. Rather, they demonstrate that children have the requisite ability for this to be possible, that is, the ability to abstract a structural concept of this kind from linguistic input, without direct instruction. If the feasibility of an acquisition process of the sort hypothesized here is demonstrated by this line of study, new data are required indicating that the natural linguistic environment does indeed provide the input and feedback that render such an acquisition mechanism possible. That is, naturalistic observations and analyses of naturally occurring verbal and nonverbal interactions of the relevant kind are needed before the results of the present studies (which presumably indicate that the child is cognitively equipped for this acquisition mechanism) can be extrapolated into a conclusive statement about logical development in natural circumstances.

Keeping these provisions in mind, let us nevertheless consider that the results reported have provided evidence in support of the microdevelopmental process discussed here and turn to a more inclusive theoretical discussion in which this process can be characterized in more detail.

A Theoretical Framework for Propositional Reasoning and Its Development

So far we have examined, in rather general terms, some issues concerning the development of logical competence and offered, with supporting data, some speculations about one of the mechanisms that may underlie this development. The aim of this section is to discuss a conceptual and theoretical framework within which substantive questions concerning the reasoning process and the development of logical competence can be formulated more clearly. I want to stress that what follows should not be seen as purporting to present a fully developed theory, but rather is best seen as the outline of a theory in need of development.

Constituents of Logical Reasoning

The process of reasoning with verbal material can be conceptualized as involving three "aspects." (The deliberately noncommittal term "aspects" is intended to indicate that the three following constituents should not be seen either as serially organized or as functionally independent).

1. The subject has a long term memory representation, which preexists the logical task itself, of all sorts of complex linguistic (and nonlinguistic) information, that is, a logico–semantic network that contains structural and logical relationships between propositions and between lexical items, as well as, more generally, all the usual ingredients of language comprehension. One part of this network is the set of patterns of deductive inference that are available to the subject and may be put to use in the reasoning task, as mentioned in 3 below.

2. When a problem is encountered and a deduction has to be carried out, a representation of the problem has to be set up in working memory. This representation, can be seen as a mapping between the input problem and the representational repertoire and structures available in LTM, which is then held in working memory for the purpose of reasoning. When this *functional representation* is formal, the mapping is between the verbal problem and the logical relationships available in LTM. This mapping relies both on surface cues in the sentences (in a vein analogous to Fodor, Bever, and Garrett's (1970) notion of perceptual strategies in sentence comprehension) and on cues in the structural representation of the sentence, or semantic representation. However, the functional representation can also be couched in media other than formal. For example, it may be of an imaginal kind, thus involving a more general knowledge of the world, or it may utilize a schematized medium, in which the information is concretized into prototypical exemplars of the situation described. (See Johnson-Laird and Steedman (1978) who use the term "analogical" for a representation of this kind in the case of quantified sentences.) Thus, the representation in working memory has structural properties given in part by the content of LTM, and a modality determined in part by the content of the problem. Speculations about this representation, in particular regarding the interplay between form and modality will be discussed in more detail on pages 189–191. For now it is enough to keep in mind the mapping process involved in constructing this functional representation. The important point for the present purpose is to distinguish between the logico–semantic network mentioned in (1) and the representational medium used in working memory to encode the problem at hand and on which the logical operations or other operations will be carried out.

3. The third aspect involved in reasoning is the patterns of deductive

inference, or other transformations, that operate on (2) to construct consequences or logical derivations from the given information. Models addressing this aspect of reasoning have been proposed by Braine (1977), Johnson-Laird (1975), and Osherson (1974, 1975) for formal modes of representation, and by Johnson-Laird and Steedman (1978) for an "analogical" representational medium. These procedures and patterns of inference are stored in LTM as part of the logico–semantic network, as mentioned previously in (1), but they are mentioned here separately in terms of their specific function during the actual reasoning process.

A few comments are in order before turning to a more detailed discussion of these various points. First, at a very general level, the notions outlined in (1), concerning the semantic network that forms the background of logical reasoning, relate to the current cognitive work on representation of knowledge in memory (e.g., Norman, Rumelhart & the LNR research group, 1975; Kintsch, 1974) that is, work focused on the representation of complex linguistic information and its integration into complex knowledge structures. These notions are also related to current work in semantics concerned with the representation of logical relationships (e.g., Katz, 1972; Lakoff, 1972; McCawley, 1971), although the latter association is only partial because these linguists would not necessarily endorse the mentalistic perspective characteristic of cognitive psychology, and also because information stored in LTM is of a more general than strictly linguistic kind.

Second, what has been outlined so far, is a conceptual framework rather than a substantive theoretical statement because, in its general form, it is invulnerable to empirical test. (This is also true of the propositional models of long term memory mentioned previously, when expressed at a general level, until they take specific commitments as to the form taken by the representation of specific kinds of information.) However, a substantive contribution of the view presented here is to distinguish the long term memory representation of logical knowledge from the functional representation of a problem, i.e. the representational medium in which the problem is encoded and operated upon, and to explicitly draw attention to the "translation" process whereby natural language expressions are formalized or otherwise represented.

Third, and most important, this functional representation should not be conceived of as resulting from some kind of automatic information processing. Rather, it is controlled by heuristic processes and logical knowledge, even when it is of a seemingly concrete nature. For example, I have argued elsewhere (Falmagne, 1975b) that in the context of linear syllogistic reasoning (e.g., "A darker than B; B darker than C; is A darker than C?"), the spatial strategies that subjects appear to adopt and which consist of placing A, B, and C in the proper order on an imaginary line before reading off the answer from this array, must indeed by mediated by abstract logical knowledge, since the choice of a straight line (as opposed to a circular array, for example) as the representational medium rests on the isomorphism between properties of the spatial relationships on this line and the comparative relationships in the problem. Thus, the point is that, even when a problem is represented imaginally, for example, the way in which this image is utilized (and perhaps even the way in which it is structured), is dependent upon the logical knowledge and the overall heuristics involved in the logical processing of the problem. This point is of course very similar to the perspective emphasized by Piaget regarding the interdependence of figurative and operative knowledge.

Finally, it is worth pointing out that this framework, however schematic it has remained so far, distinctively presents a perspective on logical reasoning as integrated with general language comprehension processes. This sets it in contrast with the perspective endorsed, provisionally or not, by models of logical reasoning in which aspect 3 is almost exclusively focused upon (Braine, 1977; Johnson-Laird, 1975; Osherson, 1975, to varying degrees).[7]

Alternative Modes of Representation

Turning now to speculations of a more detailed and more substantive kind, it is assumed that, when setting up a functional representation of the problem in working memory, various modes of representation are available to the individual and which mode is used depends upon a number of factors, as I will discuss shortly. Regarding the various modalities in which a problem can be represented, one candidate is obviously an imaginal representation. The availability of an imaginal code for representing verbal material has been well documented in the cognitive literature (e.g., see Begg & Paivio, 1969; Klee & Eysenck, 1973; Kosslyn, 1975, 1976; Kosslyn & Pomerantz, 1977, for arguments in support of the psychological reality and functional distinctiveness of imagery), although the issue is not uncontroversial (see Potter, Valian & Faulconer, 1977; Marshark & Paivio, 1977, and Pylyshyn, 1973, for alternative positions). If logical reasoning is seen as integrated with language comprehension processes, it is thus natural to assume that it may

[7] Johnson-Laird (in preparation) has proposed an account of logical reasoning based entirely on the semantics of natural language and on functional representations of a prototypical and imaginal sort. The theory discussed here is congruent with Johnson-Laird's in some respects but differs from it by the developmental dimension of the present theory and by the assumption that formal patterns of inference and logical relationships are part of the representation of knowledge and are (sometimes) singled out and highlighted in the reasoning process.

involve, in some cases, an imaginal representation of the problem. On singularity of the reasoning situation in this respect, is that informatio: from more than one sentence has to be represented so that, if an imag: nal representation is invoked, we presumably have to assume that compound image is formed, perhaps including the entire array of info: mation into a unified scene. Interesting empirical questions concernin the sequential characteristics of the formation of these representation are suggested by this view.

A mode of representation conceptually distinct (if not operationall: identifiable) from the imaginal mode, is one in which the information ii the problem is particularized into a schematized or prototypical repre sentation that embodies in its specifics the essential information in th(problem, thus performing much the same function as an imaginal rep· resentation, but without the paraphernalia of visual imagery. Such a mode of representation has sometimes been argued for in the cognitive literature as a conceptual alternative to imagery. Apparently the repre- sentations invoked by Johnson-Laird (1975) and Johnson-Laird and Steedman (1978) are of this sort, and concretize quantified statements (e.q., "All beekeepers are artists") into prototypical exemplars of the sit- uation described (i.e., the notion of a particular beekeeper who is also an artist and the notion of a particular artist who may or may not be a beekeeper).

Another possible modality is a formal representation whereby the logical form of the problem is abstracted (or rather, the form it has in people's natural logic; see e.g., Braine, 1977) and represented as such for the purpose of reasoning. This formalization of natural language ex- pressions is not a straightforward matter, and its tortuous character has several facets. First, that there is no one-to-one correspondence between logical operators and natural language connectives has become an (em- pirical) truism. This situation has been confronted by the more recent research and theory on logical reasoning in two ways: documenting sources of discrepancies and the conditions in which they occur (e.g., Taplin & Staudenmayer, 1973; Staudenmayer, 1975; Neimark & Chap- man, 1975), and developing "natural logic" systems as substitutes for the formal representation provided by the standard propositional cal- culus (Braine, 1977). However, even in the latter case in which an alter- native formalism of greater psychological plausibility is postulated, the natural language input must be formalized accordingly.

Other modes of representation are possible as well, such as thematic or enactive mode including dynamic sequences of events, actions, and changes. To be sure, such a possibility is in need of operationalization, but no more so than the assumptions concerning static mental imagery, which are now so widely accepted. Finally, an interesting mode of rep- resentation of a problem is the one provided by an analogical process, whereby it is not the problem explicitly given that is represented, but some other (with which the subject is familiar, for example) that is felt to be analogous to it for some reason, perhaps some formal cue, perhaps some thematic cue.[8] Speculatively, one may wonder whether there exist "prototypes" available to represent certain logical relationships.

Which mode is used for representing a given problem can be assumed to depend jointly upon at least the three following factors:

1. The nature of the material; for example, an imaginal representation is certainly more available for some sentences than for others, irrespective of their being or not being part of a reasoning problem.
2. The form of the problem: If the statements are of a kind that the subject is able to recognize at some formal level, then the subject may encode these in a formal mode as outlined previously. If not, some other modality is used and the problem is operated upon in that modality.
3. The salience of cues in the sentence (or the problem) that cue its logical form. What is implied here is that some sentences may be more readily formalizable than others because of the specific way in which the logical relationships are expressed. For example, "if p then q" may be more readily formalized as implication than "p only if q".

One question of interest is whether those modes of processing are mutually exclusive for a given problem, and if they are not, as seems plausible to assume, what their functional interrelationships are. As mentioned previously, I think that we should not consider those modes of processing that rely on imagery or thematic content as extralogical; rather, they should be seen as another support for manipulations that, at a more abstract level, are monitored by some general logical knowledge (in those cases, of course, where the subject does reason logically; erroneous reasoning can occur whatever mode of processing is employed).

The framework just outlined permits one to define logical competence and logical development in a manner that is both relatively clear and suggestive of empirical questions; and to formulate more clearly the speculations discussed earlier in this chapter concerning the acquisition of patterns of deductive inference. In the remainder of this section, these two questions will be discussed in turn.

---

[8] The term "analogical" is used here in a different sense than the usage adopted by Johnson-Laird and Steedman (1978), who let this term refer to what has been termed here a "schmatized" or "prototypical" mode of representation.

Developmental Implications and Logical Competence Reconsidered

In terms of the framework proposed, the development of logical competence has at least three facets.

1. First, it involves an expansion of the logico–semantic network available in LTM, to include an appropriately rich and differentiated repertoire of logical relationships between propositions (such as the implication or disjunction relationships) or between lexical items (such as the entailment or antonymy relationships). Fascinating questions arise as to the developmental dependencies between these various acquisitions. Would implication develop from a more primitive notion of causality and come to be gradually differentiated from it? Could one identify primitive cognitive operations and uncover basic cognitive constraints that would explain the relative difficulty and developmental patterns of the various logical relationships? More generally, what are the relations, both developmental and functional, between lexical reasoning, that is, reasoning based on meaning relations between lexical items (e.g., "This book is either big or red; this book is blue; is it big?", where the inference is based on the fact that "blue" lexically negates "red"), and propositional reasoning, that is, reasoning involving inferences that rely on the form of the statements (although they can be drawn in other ways as well)? The speculation is that lexical reasoning may be both easier and developmentally prior to propositional reasoning. The question of particular interest, of course, is to investigate this claim with respect to specific logical relationships, regarding their lexical and propositional embodiments respectively. Space clearly does not permit these issues to be discussed here here with the seriousness they deserve, but they have to be at least acknowledged as pertaining to our general concern.

2. Logical competence is also defined by the greater availability of the formal mode for representing natural language expressions in working memory. This is related to two factors: the enrichment of the logico–semantic network, described in (1), and the increased range and generality of the cues that are used to identify the logical structure underlying natural language expressions. Thus, one aspect of logical development would consist in changes in the overall bias and in the distribution of availability of alternative modes of representation. As the formal repertoire of the child increases, as the range of surface cues pointing to each given logical relation expands, and as the cues increase in salience, a formal mode of representation and processing would become available for a wider range of inferential situations.

A qualification is needed here: Note that logical competence is said to be related to the availability of the formal mode, not necessarily to its use. Indeed, for meaningful material, it may be more efficient in many cases to carry out the inference with the full support of the meaning and imagery of the statements, than to abstract out the logical form of the problem, and a number of results in the empirical literature on reasoning in adults, points in that direction. Furthermore, as discussed previously, proper use of those representational media that are not ostensibly of a logical kind, must be monitored by some more abstract knowledge in order for the legitimate operations to be carried out. Therefore, the present tentative definition of logical competence does not regulate which modalities are used for processing a problem but rather which are available for potential use.

Finally, I want to stress again that the notion of competence proposed here encompasses not only the repertoire of logical relationships and patterns of deductive inferences available to an individual, but also the degree of mastery of the "translation" process through which the input from the linguistic environment is structured in logical terms and through which the mapping between the natural language input and the formal knowledge is achieved.

The view proposed here leads to interesting empirical questions concerning the way in which the content of the problems being reasoned about affects the reasoning process at various levels of mastery of a given rule of inference and at various developmental levels. The assumption is that problems whose structure is within the repertoire of the subject's logical knowledge, are more likely to be encoded and processed with reliance on formal cues. Therefore, the variability in performance due to content should decrease for problems whose form is within the child's competence. Thus, one question of interest is whether the effect of content factors—as reflected in latencies and error data for example—is reduced for problem types that are more fully mastered, what the asymptotic situation appears to be, and the pattern of age-related differences in problem types that appear to be mastered. Such an analysis may permit one to operationalize the notion of logical competence, which is otherwise so problematic, and to provide a developmental characterization of logical competence in which content factors play an intrinsic part.

3. The third aspect with regard to which logical competence may be defined, is the development of a sufficiently elaborate repertoire of patterns of deductive inference. Turning now to possible mechanisms that may account for this development, I proposed earlier in this chapter that acquisition of patterns of deductive inference may result in part from a concept-learning process whereby, by encountering instances of the given pattern and by picking up the essential function words or other relevant cues, the child eventually abstracts the structure of the argument. In terms of the framework proposed in this section, this con-

cept learning process can be formulated in a more specific way. When encountered, sentences or problems are encoded at a multiplicity of levels (including the syntactic–semantic encoding involved in language comprehension in general, as well as the modes of encoding in working memory discussed previously). For unmastered or difficult patterns, for which a formal mode of processing is not readily available, reasoning is likely to rely on empirical, factual information when available, or on an imaginal representation of the information when available, or on some kind of thematic processing of the information provided. Thus, initially, the operations leading to a conclusion are performed in a representational medium other than the formalized logical representation of the statements. However, after processing a variety of instances of a pattern, either the formal cues emerge through a process of abstraction from the previous content-bound procedures (the notion of reflective abstraction proposed by Piaget seems particularly illuminating in this regard. See, e.g., Piaget, 1970), or if these cues were present at some level of representation, they increase in salience because they are confirmed through feedback, even if they are not explicitly used. The fact that in the studies reported in the preceding section the subjects trained with meaningful material transferred it to nonsense problems as well, supports those notions, since formal cues must have been functional to mediate this generalization to problems that did not provide any thematic or imaginal support for the reasoning process.

Concluding Remarks

The theoretical framework outlined in this chapter is an attempt to integrate the view that logical reasoning relies, at some level, on a formal system of rules, with the recognition that a variety of representational media are available to represent and process verbally given information. It has been suggested that logical development consists both in an increased availability of the formal mode for an increasingly wide range of situations, and in elaboration of the logico-semantic network. It has also been argued that the increased availability of the formal mode involves not only an enrichment of the formal rules themselves but also an elaboration of the pattern recognition device through which the logical structure of a problem or sentence is abstracted from its natural language expression. One possible mechanism of acquisition of patterns of deductive inference has also been discussed. However, the qualification stressed earlier with regard to this acquisition process may be recalled, namely, that it should be seen as operating within the context of more general cognitive and developmental constraints and should not be mistaken as reflecting an empiricist epistemology.

In the first section of this chapter, in order to delineate the domain of discourse of this discussion, a distinction has been proposed both in terms of task analyses and in terms of the processes possibly involved between the reasoning situations of concern here and the "scientific" reasoning situations investigated by Inhelder and Piaget (1958). It was argued that, because of these differences, results obtained within one task domain are not immediately generalizable to the other. However, one fascinating set of questions concerns the very relationship between the competencies implicated in these respective situations. One specific question in this respect has been mentioned earlier in this chapter; namely, whether the translation processes involved in the two respective situations map the given information into the same representational format for logically equivalent problems. Developmental questions can be formulated concerning the relative accessibility of the formal mode in each of those two task domains. Finally, I believe that the framework discussed here is compatible in principle with a liberalized interpretation of Piaget's theory, in which the various facets of the notion of formal operations are distinguished and allowed not to be necessarily synchronous developmentally. As argued above, it seems that the heuristic aspect of formal operational thought is the one most characteristically implicated in scientific reasoning. Elaboration of those points is clearly beyond the scope and focus of this chapter; the aim of the present remarks is limited to opening up the issue for consideration.

References

Begg, I., & Paivio, A. Concreteness and imagery in sentence meaning. *Journal of Verbal Learning and Verbal Behavior*, 1969, *8*, 821–827.

Braine, M. D. S. On the relation between the natural logic of reasoning and standard logic. *Psychological Review*, 1977, *85*, 1–21.

Ennis, R. H. Conditional logic and primary school children: a developmental study. *Interchange*, 1971, *2*, 126–132.

Falmagne, R. J. Introduction. In R. J. Falmagne (Ed.), *Reasoning: Representation and process in children and adults*. Hillsdale, New Jersey: Lawrence Erlbaum, 1975. (a)

Falmagne, R. J. Overview: Reasoning, representation, process and related issues. In R. J. Falmagne (Ed.), *Reasoning: Representation and process in children and adults*. Hillsdale, New Jersey: Lawrence Erlbaum, 1975. (b) Pp 247–263.

Falmagne, R. J. The development of logical competence. Paper presented at the meeting of the Society for Research in Child Development, Denver, Colorado, 1975.(c)

Falmagne, R. J., Thompson, D., & Bennett, J. Acquisition of patterns of deductive inference in children. Paper presented at the Annual Meeting of the Eastern Psychologial Association, Boston, Massachusetts, 1977.

Falmagne, R., Thompson, D., Sherwood, V., & Bennett, J. Development of patterns of deductive inference. (in preparation).

Fodor, J. A., Bever, T. G., & Garrett, M. F. *The psychology of language: An introduction to psycholinguistics and generative grammer*, New York: McGraw-Hill, 1974.

Frege, G. The thought: A logical inquiry. *Mind*. 1956, *65*, 289–311. [Originally published in 1918.]

Haack, S. *Philosophy of logics*. Cambridge: Cambridge University Press, 1978.

Henle, M. On the relation between logic and thinking. *Psychological Review*, 1962, *69*, 366–378.

Hill, S. A. A study of logical abilities in children (doctoral dissertation, Stanford University). *Dissertation Abstracts*, 1961, *21*, 33–59.

Huttenlocher, J. Constructing spatial images: A strategy in reasoning. *Psychological Review*, 1968, *75*, 550–560.

Inhelder, B. & Piaget, J. *The growth of logical thinking from childhood to adolescence*. New York: Basic Books, 1958.

Johnson-Laird, P. N. Models of deduction. In R. J. Falmagne (Ed.), *Reasoning: Representation and process in children and adults*. Hillsdale, New Jersey: Lawrence Erlbaum, 1975. Pp. 7–54.

Johnson-Laird, P. N. Reasoning without Logic. (in preparation).

Johnson-Laird, P. N., & Steedman, M. The psychology of syllogisms. *Cognitive Psychology*, 1978, *10*, 64–99.

Katz, J. J. *Semantic theory*. New York: Harper and Row, 1972.

Kintsch, W. *The representation of meaning in memory*. Hillsdale, New Jersey: Lawrence Erlbaum, 1974.

Klahr, D., & Wallace, J. G. *Cognitive development: An information-processing view*. Hillsdale, New Jersey: Lawrence Erlbaum, 1967.

Klee, H., & Eysenck, M. W. Comprehension of abstract and concrete sentences. *Journal of Verbal Learning and Verbal Behavior*, 1973, *12*, 522–529.

Kodroff, J. K., & Roberge, J. J. Developmental analysis of the conditional reasoning abilities of primary-grade children. *Developmental Psychology*, 1975, *11*, 21–28.

Kosslyn, S. M. Information representation in visual images. *Cognitive Psychology*, 1975, *7*, 341–370.

Kosslyn, S. M. Can imagery be distinguished from other forms of internal representation? Evidence from studies of information retrieval times. *Memory and Cognition*, 1976, *4*, 291–297.

Kosslyn, M. S., & Pomerantz, J. R. Imagery, propositions and the form of internal representation. *Cognitive Psychology*, 1977, *9*, 52–76.

Kuhn, D. Conditional reasoning in children. *Developmental Psychology*, 1977, *13*, 342–353.

Lakoff, G. Linguistics and natural logic. In D. Davidson & G. Harman (Eds.), *Semantics of natural language*. Dordrecht: Reidel, 1972.

McCawley, J. D. Where do noun phrases come from? In D. D. Steinberg & L. A. Jakobovits (Eds.), *Semantics*. Cambridge: Cambridge University Press, 1971.

Marschark, M., & Paivio, A. Integrative processing of concrete and abstract sentences. *Journal of Verbal Learning and Verbal Behavior*, 1977, *16*, 217–231.

Neimark, E. D., & Chapman, R. H. Development of the comprehension of logical quantifiers. In R. J. Falmagne (Ed.), *Reasoning: Representation and process in children and adults*. Hillsdale, New Jersey: Lawrence Erlbaum, 1975. Pp. 135–152.

Neimark, E., & Slotnick, N. S. Development of the understanding of logical connectives. *Journal of Educational Psychology*, 1970, *61*, (6), 451–560.

Norman, D. A., Rumelhart, D. E., & the LNR Research Group. *Explorations in cognition*. San Francisco: Freeman, 1975.

Osherson, D. *Logical abilities in children*, Vol. 2. Hillsdale, New Jersey: Lawrence Erlbaum, 1974.

Osherson, D. *Logical abilities in children*, Vol. 3. Hillsdale, New Jersey: Lawrence Erlbaum, 1975.

Paris, S. G. Comprehension of language connectives and propositional logical relationships *Journal of Experimental Child Psychology*, 1973, *16*, 278–293.

Pea, R. Development of negation in early child language. In D. Olson (Ed.), *The social foundation of language and thought: Essays in honor of Jerome Bruner.* New York: W. W. Norton, 1980.

Peel, E. A. A method for investigating children's understanding of certain logical connectives used in binary propositional thinking. *British Journal of Mathematical and Statistical Psychology,* 1967, *20,* 81–92.

Piaget, J. Piaget's theory. In P. H. Mussen (Ed.), *Carmichael's manual of child psychology,* Vol. 1. New York: Wiley, 1970. Pp. 703–732.

Potter, M. C., Valian, V. V., & Faulconer, B. A. Representation of a sentence and its pragmatic implications: verbal, imagistic, or abstract? *Journal of Verbal Learning & Verbal Behavior,* 1977, *16,* 1–12.

Putnam, H. *Philosophy of logic.* New York: Harper Torchbooks, 1971.

Pylyshyn, Z. What the mind's eye tells the mind's brain: A critique of mental imagery. *Psychological Bulletin,* 1973, *80,* 1–24.

Revlis, R. Syllogistic reasoning: Logical decisions from a complex data base. In R. J. Falmagne (Ed.), *Reasoning: Representation and process in children and adults.* Hillsdale, New Jersey: Lawrence Erlbaum, 1975. Pp. 93–132.

Roberge, J. J. A reexamination of the interpretations of errors in syllogistic reasoning. *Psychonomic Science,* 1970, *19,* 331–333.

Roberge, J. J. Recent research on the development of children's comprehension of deductive reasoning schemes. *School Science and Mathematics,* 1972, *70,* 197–200.

Roberge, J. J., & Paulus, D. H. Developmental patterns for children's class and conditional reasoning abilities. *Developmental Psychology,* 1971, *4,* 191–200.

Russell, B. *Logic and knowledge.* Boston: Allen and Unwin, 1956.

Scribner, S. Modes of thinking and ways of speaking: culture and logic reconsidered. In P. N. Johnson-Laird & P. C. Wason (Eds.) *Thinking: Readings in cognitive science.* Cambridge: Cambridge University Press, 1977, Pp. 483–500.

Shaver, P., Pierson, L., & Lang, S. Converging evidence for the functional significance of imagery in problem solving. *Cognition,* 1974, *3,* 359–375.

Staudenmayer, H. Understanding conditional reasoning with meaningful propositions. In R. J. Falmagne (Ed.), *Reasoning: Representation and process in children and adults.* Hillsdale, New Jersey: Lawrence Erlbaum, 1975. Pp. 55–80.

Siegler, R. Three aspects of cognitive development. *Cognitive Psychology,* 1976, *8,* 481–520.

Suppes, P., & Feldman, S. S. Young children's comprehension of logical connectives. *Journal of Experimental Child Psychology,* 1971, *12,* 304–317.

Taplin, J. E. Reasoning with conditional sentences. *Journal of Verbal Learning and Verbal Behavior,* 1971, *10,* 218–225.

Taplin, J. E., & Staudenmayer, H. Interpretation of abstract conditional sentences in deductive reasoning. *Journal of Verbal Learning and Verbal Behavior,* 1973, *12,* 530–542.

Taplin, J. E., Staudenmayer, H., & Taddonio, J. L. Developmental changes in conditional reasoning: Linguistic or logical? *Journal of Experimental Child Psychology,* 1974, *17,* 360–373.

Wason, P. C., & Johnson-Laird, P. N. *Psychology of reasoning: Structure and content.* Cambridge, Massachusetts: Harvard University Press, 1972.

Wittgenstein, L. *Tractatus Logico-Philosophicus.* London: Routledge and Kegan Paul, 1922/1961.

9

Analysis of Understanding in Problem Solving

JAMES G. GREENO

Introduction

Pioneering studies of problem solving by German investigators (Duncker, 1945; Köhler, 1927; Wertheimer, 1945/1959) focused on the question of how problem solvers understand problem situations. The point was especially clear in discussions by Wertheimer, who distinguished problem solving based on understanding from simple use of algorithms. Until recently, studies of problem solving in the United States (e.g., Newell & Simon, 1972) have analyzed cognitive performance of problem solvers, rather than understanding. However, recent investigations have taken up various aspects of the process of representing and understanding problems (de Kleer, 1975; Hayes & Simon, 1974; Larkin, 1977; Novak, 1976; Simon & Simon, 1978).

An important goal of school instruction is that students understand the material they learn. In this chapter, I will discuss some issues in the theory of understanding that have arisen in our studies of problems that are used in the teaching of elementary arithmetic. Our main strategy in the preliminary stages of this work has been to use concepts and methods that have been developed for the theory of understanding language. While I do not expect that understanding of mathematics and language are necessarily the same, it seems worthwhile to try to look for possible analogies between the processes. Thus far, the effort has been encouraged by some insights that I believe have begun to provide some clarification of the theoretical issues that we need to address.

One idea that has developed in our preliminary analyses is a distinction between two aspects of understanding arithmetic. One aspect involves a close analogy to the process of understanding a sentence; I will refer to this as the "linguistic" aspect of understanding. The other aspect involves relationships between arithmetic and other knowledge; I will refer to this as the "conceptual" aspect of understanding. I do not intend to attach deep significance to these labels; concepts are involved in the processing of language, and language has an important role in processes that I call conceptual. However, the labels seem to capture some features of the distinction in an intuitively appealing way.

By the linguistic aspect of understanding arithmetic, I will refer to processes involved in the cognitive representation of arithmetic expressions. The conceptual aspect of understanding arithmetic is related to the kind of understanding people have in mind when they make statements such as the following: "A child who understands arithmetic can use it to solve verbal problems," or "A child who understands arithmetic can relate operations to general properties such as commutativity."

Two Aspects of Understanding Arithmetic

Linguistic Understanding

In the theory of language understanding, proposals of two kinds have been made concerning the process of representing sentences. In some systems, declarative representations of sentences are constructed, consisting of networks of related concepts (Anderson, 1976; Norman & Rumelhart, 1975; Schank, 1972). In other systems, procedural representations are constructed, consisting of programs that can be executed to verify the sentences, to find answers to questions, or to perform actions that are requested in the sentences (Winograd, 1972). In the domain of arithmetic, both these kinds of representations seem important.

Procedural representations are especially natural for arithmetic expressions, since these are most often used to specify computations. Figure 9.1 shows a hypothetical representation in the form of a procedure for answering questions such as, "What is 3 plus 5?" or "3 + 5 = ?" Several studies have been conducted to investigate the procedures used for answering simple addition and subtraction questions (Groen & Parkman, 1972; Groen & Poll, 1973; Groen & Resnick, 1977; Woods, Resnick, & Groen, 1975). The procedure shown in Figure 9.1 is apparently an accurate model of the representation that children construct after they have had a substantial amount of practice with addition. Similar procedures based on counting appear to provide good models of children's procedural representations of subtraction and missing addend questions.

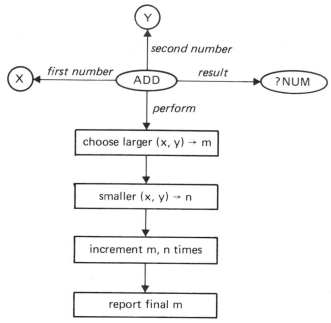

FIGURE 9.1. *Procedure for answering simple addition questions.*

A schema for constructing declarative representations of addition sentences is shown in Figure 9.2, using notation similar to that of Norman and Rumelhart (1975). Representations such as Figure 9.2 constitute hypotheses about important relations that an individual apprehends in understanding sentences. Norman and Rumelhart's notation focuses on analysis of verb meanings. One component of a schema such as Figure 9.2 represents the semantic cases associated with a verb. In sentences about actions, typical cases include the *agent, object,* and *instrument* of an action. In Figure 9.2 I have assumed that the semantic cases of addition are simply the two numbers that are added and their result. In addition to the basic case analysis, a schema includes a relational structure consisting of semantic components that show more specific relations among the concepts that occur as arguments of the case relations. The assumption in Figure 9.2 is that an addition relation includes a relation of equality as its major component, linking the result of the addition to a subordinate relation that connects the two addends. Results obtained by Case (1978) can be interpreted as indicating that an understanding of relations, perhaps in a form like Figure 9.2, is an important requisite for success in solving missing addend problems, such as "3 + ? = 7."

One consequence of these analyses is a greater appreciation of the

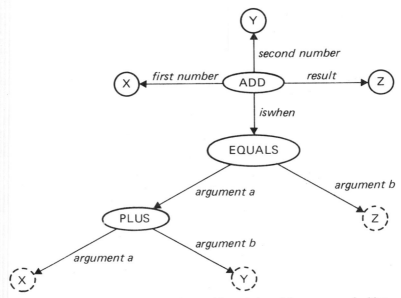

FIGURE 9.2. *Schema representing relational knowledge of the concept of addition.*

complexity of cognitive processes that are involved even in simple arithmetic tasks. When we think of children's understanding of arithmetic, we tend to consider more complex achievements, such as those that I will discuss in the next section. However, an analysis of the processes actually required even to perform simple computations shows that a considerable degree of understanding is required for these very common achievements.

Conceptual Understanding

Most educators and mathematicians hope that arithmetic concepts are understood by students in ways that go beyond the kinds of achievements I am calling linguistic understanding. To analyze conceptual understanding of arithmetic, we might consider a richer semantic system than the one in Figure 9.2. I will propose that there are at least two distinct kinds of semantic analysis required to deal with different problems used to test students' understanding of arithmetic.

Many problems involving conceptual understanding involve the relation between a formal language and a semantic model of the language. Consider the process of solving a word problem, such as "Sue had 3 marbles. Nancy gave her 5 more. How many does Sue have now?" This problem is solved by using a sentence in arithmetic, "3 + 5 = 8." The situation involving the girls and the marbles involves a model of arithmetic where the additive relation corresponds to changes in possession such as giving. Thus, we can view the solution of the word problem as a process of relating the formal language of arithmetic to one of its models.

Another kind of problem involving conceptual understanding requires students to relate arithmetic to more abstract concepts, such as commutativity. Questions about commutativity, inverse operations, and so on, require students to relate concepts in arithmetic to concepts in abstract algebra. In this case, abstract algebra is a formal language and arithmetic is a semantic model of that language. Thus, answering questions involving algebraic properties is the opposite case from solving a word problem, where arithmetic is the formal language to be related to one of its semantic models.

In the remainder of this chapter I will discuss each of these forms of conceptual understanding. My discussion of semantic interpretations of arithmetic will consist of a presentation of some preliminary results of research we are conducting on children's solution of word problems. My comments on arithmetic as a semantic model of a more abstract formal language will be brief and quite speculative, but will permit me to comment on a relationship between our studies of problem solving in arithmetic and some general features of Piagetian theory.

Solution of Word Problems

We have begun a program of research aimed toward developing an analysis of the processes involved in children's understanding and solution of simple arithmetic word problems.[1]

One of our projects involves development of a simulation model of the problem-solving process. Our approach is somewhat different from that usually taken regarding these problems. The most common approach views the problem as a translation from verbal text to equations. This approach was used by Bobrow (1968) in a computer program for solving verbal problems. The approach we are taking treats the problem primarily as a semantic process, involving generation of appropriate relations between quantities. For the problem,

Sue had 3 marbles. Nancy gave her 5 more. How many marbles does Sue have now?

the system produces a representation in which 3 is identified as a starting quantity, it is recognized that the situation involves increasing the quantity; and 5 is identified as the amount of the increase. The rep-

[1] I wish to acknowledge the collaboration of Joan Heller and Mary Riley in this work.

resentation is generated by a production system developed by Anderson (1976) that simulates understanding by generating propositional structures from English text. The selection of an arithmetic operation—addition, in the case of this problem—is based on direct associations between semantic structures and the operators. In this example, when the representation involves a quantity and an increase of that quantity, and the question asks for the resulting quantity, the system includes the knowledge that the result is obtained by addition.

The simulation of these semantic processes has required us to look rather carefully at the variety of verbal problems that are used in arithmetic instruction. This process of task analysis has led to an interesting finding. The semantic structures that correspond to a single operation, such as addition, are not homogeneous, even at a rather general level. There are three general kinds of situations in which students must decide to add: (a) increases in some quantity, as in "Sue had 3 marbles, Nancy gave her 5 more"; (b) combinations of two sets that remain distinct, as in "Sue has 3 marbles, Nancy has 5, how many do they have altogether?"; and (c) comparative information, as in "Sue has 3 marbles, and Nancy has 5 more marbles than Sue has. How many marbles does Nancy have?"

These three problems are all solved by adding the numbers given in the problems, but the semantic structures that determine that decision are quite different. Figure 9.3 shows a semantic network that represents an abstract relational structure of the kind specified by problems of type (a), where there is a starting amount, an event that causes an increase in that amount, and resulting amount that is not given in the problem. In these problems there is a further argument beyond the three numbers involved in the situation. This argument is the object whose starting quantity is specified in the question and whose quantity after the change is requested in the question. In the example problem mentioned earlier, Argument A would be the number of marbles owned by Sue, X would be 3, and Y would be 5. The semantic components shown in Figure 9.3 indicate a major relation of causation between an event and a result. The event consists of an increase in the amount of A, and Y is the amount of the increase. The result of this increase is indicated as a change from a state (involving quantity, hence $QSTATE$) where A's amount was X (the starting quantity) to a state where A's amount has become Z.

The semantic structure of problems of type (b), involving combinations of amounts, can be represented in the way shown in Figure 9.4. Here there are two objects shown as arguments. In the example of a type (b) problem given earlier, A would be the number of marbles owned by Sue and B would be the number of marbles owned by Nancy. The semantic components of a combination structure are quite different

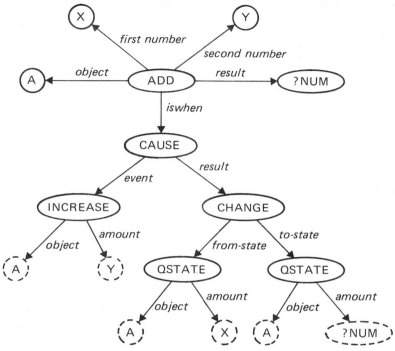

FIGURE 9.3. *Semantic schema for addition involving a change in a quantity.*

from those of a structure involving change in a quantity. Type (*a*) problems describe events in which a quantity changes its value. In type (*b*)
problems there is no actual change in quantity described, but a mental
operation of combination is applied to the two stated quantities to yield
a new quantitative state—the amount of their combination. This is represented in the semantic components shown in Figure 9.4 where a relation called "same-as" links the state in which an object formed by the
combination has an amount that is to be found with the relational
structure that represents the idea of combining the two states shown on
the left.

A similar analysis to Figures 9.3 and 9.4 can be given for problems of
type (*c*), which involve amounts associated with two objects, and the
difference between those amounts.

These semantic structures are more abstract than the ones that would
usually represent the sentences of these problems. For example, a sentence saying that Nancy gave Sue five marbles would usually indicate a
change in the possession of the marbles from Nancy to Sue (Gentner,
1975). The idea of an increase in a quantitative state is used for a variety
of changes in possession that have differing semantic structures, such as

giving, buying, and finding, as well as for other kinds of changes such as travelling a further distance, working for a longer time, and many other events. On the other hand, the structures in Figures 9.3 and 9.4 are less abstract than the general concept of addition, shown in Figure 9.2. We hypothesize that when children understand addition, they appreciate that the various situations involving increases in quantity, combinations, and comparisons of appropriate kinds all correspond to the relationship of addition, as represented in Figure 9.2.

In the model that we are developing, the problem solver first constructs an appropriate representation of the problem text. This is the process of understanding the problem. Then an appropriate arithmetic operation is selected for finding the answer. In all the problems listed here as examples, the appropriate operation is addition. However, note that if the unknown term is changed, problems with these same semantic structures require subtraction. For example, for the problem

Sue had 3 marbles, Nancy gave her some more, and now Sue has 5 marbles. How many did Nancy give to Sue?

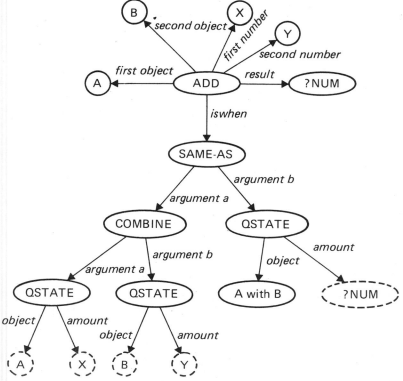

FIGURE 9.4. *Semantic schema for addition involving combination of two quantities.*

the semantic representation is a change involving an increase, as in Figure 9.3. However, the unknown term is the amount of the increase, rather than the result, and, therefore, the problem is solved by subtracting the numbers in the problem, rather than adding them.

When we test children's understanding of arithmetic by asking them to solve word problems, we are testing their ability to coordinate representations like those in Figures 9.3 and 9.4 with the procedures for adding and subtracting numbers. The structures that represent the semantic models of addition and subtraction are related to the operations of addition and subtraction in an interesting way. The addition and subtraction of numbers are more abstract than the situations that are the semantic models of those concepts. On the other hand, the mapping from semantic structures to the arithmetic operations is not simply many-to-one. When we group the semantic models into the three categories that seem natural to us, we find that some members of each of those categories correspond to addition, and other members of each category correspond to subtraction. The decision process required of a child in solving these problems is a relatively complicated one. Our present conjecture is that children's understanding of arithmetic would be facilitated if specific instruction were given involving semantic distinctions of the kind I have been discussing, but a test of that conjecture has not been conducted.

A second project that we are engaged in involves the process of generating the semantic structure that represents a problem, which is a problem in language processing. A problem text presents the information that a child needs to generate a semantic representation. However, the information may be in a form that makes it relatively easy for the representation to be constructed, or relatively difficult. We have begun to investigate factors that contribute to difficulty of the understanding process. We have some preliminary data consisting of observations of 17 first-grade children who were given a set of 14 problems orally. The problems were intended to produce a range of difficulty in comprehension, varying in a number of ways.

One of the easiest problems in the set we gave is the following:

Carol bought 6 popsicles. She ate 1. How many popsicles does she have left?

One of the most difficult problems was the following:

Joe had some books. He gave 5 to Sam. Now Joe has 4 books. How many did he have in the beginning?

The semantic structures of these two problems are identical at the level of the relationships that are involved. Both problems involve some starting quantity and an action that decreases that quantity. The problems differ in which components of the structure are given, and consequently, in the operation that is needed in order to solve the problem. If the difference in operation had any effect, it should have been to make the second problem easier, since children seem to have a general bias in the direction of adding the numbers of a problem if they are unable to determine the correct operation (Nesher & Teubal, 1975). Nonetheless, the greater complexity of the second problem made it much more difficult for the children in our study. Four of the 17 children solved it correctly, whereas 16 of the 17 children solved the first problem correctly.

There are several ways in which these two problems differ that probably contribute to the difference in their difficulty. First, there are more propositions in the second problem statement—four instead of three. Second, although the sequence of referring to the components of the structure is the same in both problems (starting quantity, then amount of decrease, then result), the difference in the unknown element leads to having the unknown quantity mentioned in the second problem as "some books," and this may present difficulties in comprehension. Effects of factors such as these can be understood in relation to a psycholinguistic analysis, such as that given by Kintsch (1974). Difficulty of comprehension of a passage is known to depend on the number of propositions represented in the passage. The difficulty of problems with indefinite quantities indicated by "some" may be partly due to easier integration of later propositions with statements that specify definite states, perhaps because definite propositions can be incorporated more directly into larger structures, while propositions with unspecified quantities must be kept available for later completion.

We will be conducting further studies to evaluate the relative importance of these and other linguistic factors in children's understanding of verbal problems. But this small example is probably sufficient to illustrate the major point I wish to make. The process of understanding a problem clearly includes a considerable component of extracting relevant information in the situation and arranging it in a coherent and correct cognitive representation.

The general purpose of these studies can be stated in relation to the general framework of concepts that I described earlier. When we ask a child to solve a verbal problem, we present a description of some situation that constitutes a model of an arithmetic relation. The goal of our research is a detailed theoretical description of the way in which children generate a semantic representation of the relevant information in the situation and then identify the appropriate relationship in the formal language of arithmetic in order to produce the answer to the problem.

Understanding Abstract Properties

Now I will consider another kind of schema involving arithmetic, but this time in relation to more abstract concepts in algebra. I think that someone who knows modern algebra has something like the schema in Figure 9.5. The person must know what "implies" means, and must understand about operators applying to members of a set. The diagram is simpler than it should be. Notably, it omits the universal quantifier, which is an important part of the concept. However, I hope that the gist of the idea is clear.

One function of this schema would be to enable parsing of a sentence such as, "addition is commutative over the real numbers," or if that proposition were already in memory, answering questions about the commutativity of addition. Such question-answering problems would require coordinating knowledge about arithmetic with knowledge about abstract algebra, which is a formal language that has arithmetic as one of its semantic models.

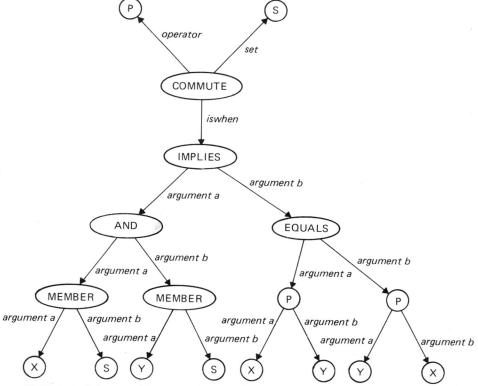

FIGURE 9.5. *Schema representing relational knowledge of the concept of commutativity.*

Now I need another distinction. When we say that a student understands the commutativity of addition, we do not necessarily mean that the student knows the language of abstract algebra and can apply it to arithmetic. We often mean only that the student's use of arithmetic correctly reflects the algebraic properties of arithmetic. For example, the counting procedure for addition in Figure 9.1 includes an operation that would not be appropriate if addition were not commutative. Students who use this procedure can be said to understand commutativity in the sense that the procedure they use is indifferent to the order of the numbers—and this indifference is precisely what commutativity means.

The distinction that I wish to emphasize might be called a difference between *explicit* and *implicit* conceptual understanding. I propose that for explicit conceptual understanding, a system must have knowledge of a formal language and a model of the language, and be able to relate the two appropriately.

Implicit conceptual understanding does not require that the system know a formal language, but simply that procedures that are used in reasoning in a domain have the properties that are specified in a formal language for which the domain is a model. For example, I would say that the counting procedure for addition in Figure 9.1 exhibits implicit conceptual understanding of commutativity, rather than explicit understanding of that property.

I suggest that there has been considerable confusion in discussions of children's mathematics learning because of a failure to distinguish between explicit and implicit conceptual understanding. During the 1950s and 1960s, it was recognized that children's understanding of arithmetic probably should include some connection with the general properties of arithmetic operators. Mathematicians have that general understanding, and for them it is explicit understanding. They, or in this case, we, have explicit knowledge of the formal system of abstract algebra, and we know how it is that arithmetic exemplifies general algebraic properties. I do not believe that most mathematicians wanted children to learn abstract algebra—though there were some efforts in that direction. What most people wanted, I believe, was that children should acquire implicit understanding of arithmetic in a way that would use the general principles expressed in the algebraic properties.

Unfortunately, the theoretical tools available at the time did not permit a careful analysis of this instructional goal. In order to state precisely what we mean by implicit understanding of a principle, we need a theory of procedures. Such a theory can be used to represent the procedures we wish children to acquire, and in that representation we can identify the constraints or invariances that correspond to the principles that are significant aspects of the understanding that is desired. Without such a theory of arithmetic procedures, the curriculum changes of the 1950s and 1960s involved a great deal of haphazard casting about, using problems that involve uncertain analogies to the desired principles that one hopes are understood, but often with no definite connection to the arithmetic procedures themselves. It often seems the case, then, that the attempts to make arithmetic meaningful do not succeed because their relationship to arithmetic is never firmly established. I believe that advances in the development of a theoretical framework for analyzing procedural knowledge will make possible a much sharper statement of what we want children to learn and understand in their study of arithmetic and other subjects.

There is an interesting implication of this idea regarding the kinds of theoretical analyses of children's cognition that have been developed by Piaget and his colleagues. Piaget's theory deals with the development of general principles in children's cognition. There are dozens of concepts that could be suggested as examples. One is the coordination of extension and intension of a set of objects, which is assumed to be required for a child to perform correctly in the class inclusion problem (Inhelder & Piaget, 1964). Piaget and his colleagues clearly have *not* asserted that children acquire the formal language of logic and set theory. If my distinction between explicit and implicit understanding is accepted, then the Piagetian assertion is that children acquire implicit understanding of the coordination of extension and intension.

Just as a theory of procedures is needed in order to analyze implicit understanding of general algebraic concepts in arithmetic, I believe that a theory of procedures is also needed for the ideas in Piagetian theory to be developed in a clear way. Piagetian ideas have been presented as a set of formal structures, and problems used to illustrate these ideas have been related to the formal structures by weak analogies, rather than by thorough analysis of the processes involved in performance of the problems.

In this regard, the developments are quite encouraging. Analyses of procedural components of children's cognitive performance have been proposed in several of the contributions to this volume, and these are representative of a growing body of theoretical analysis (for other examples, see Siegler, 1978). As this kind of work continues, I expect that we will understand much more clearly the nature of children's acquisition of general cognitive principles, because we will be learning about the cognitive procedures that children acquire.

References

Anderson, J. R. *Language, memory, and thought.* Hillsdale, New Jersey: Lawrence Erlbaum, 1976.

Bobrow, D. G. Natural language input for a computer problem-solving system. In M.

Minsky (Ed.), *Semantic information processing*. Cambridge, Mass.: MIT Press, 1968. Pp. 135–215.

Case, R. Piaget and beyond: Toward a developmentally based theory of instruction. In R. Glaser (Ed.), *Advances in instructional psychology*. Hillsdale, New Jersey: Lawrence Erlbaum, 1978. Pp. 167–228.

de Kleer, J. Qualitative and quantitative knowledge in classical mechanics. Artificial Intelligence Laboratory, Massachusetts Institute of Technology, Technical Report AI-TR-352, December 1975.

Duncker, K. On problem solving. *Psychological Monographs*, 1945, *58* (Whole No. 270).

Gentner, D. Evidence for the psychological reality of semantic components: The verbs of possession. In D. A. Norman & D. E. Rumelhart (Eds.), *Explorations in cognition*. San Francisco: Freeman, 1975. Pp. 241–246.

Groen, G. J., & Parkman, J. M. A chronometric analysis of simple addition. *Psychological Review*, 1972, *79*, 329–343.

Groen, G. J., & Poll, M. Subtraction and the solution of open sentence problems. *Journal of Experimental Child Psychology*, 1973, *16*, 292–302.

Groen, G. J., & Resnick, L. B. Can preschool children invent addition algorithms? *Journal of Educational Psychology*, 1977, *69*, 645–652.

Hayes, J. R., & Simon, H. A. Understanding written problem instructions. In L. W. Gregg (Ed.), *Knowledge and cognition*. Hillsdale, New Jersey: Lawrence Erlbaum, 1974. Pp. 167–200.

Inhelder, B., & Piaget, J. *The early growth of logic in the child*. London: Routledge & Kegan Paul, 1964.

Kintsch, W. *The representation of meaning in memory*. Hillsdale, New Jersey: Lawrence Erlbaum, 1974.

Köhler, W. *The mentality of apes*. New York: Harcourt Brace, 1927.

Larkin, J. H. Skilled problem solving in physics: A hierarchical planning model. Unpublished manuscript, University of California, Berkeley, September 1977.

Nesher, P., & Teubal, E. Verbal cues as an interfering factor in verbal problem solving. *Educational Studies in Mathematics*, 1975, *6*, 41–51.

Newell, A., & Simon, H. A. *Human problem solving*. Englewood Cliffs, New Jersey: Prentice-Hall, 1972.

Norman, D. A., & Rumelhart, D. E. *Explorations in cognition*. San Francisco: Freeman, 1975.

Novak, G. S. Computer understanding of physics problems stated in natural language. *American Journal of Computational Linguistics*, 1976, Microfiche 53.

Schank, R. C. Conceptual dependency: A theory of natural language understanding. *Cognitive Psychology*, 1972, *3*, 552–631.

Siegler, R. S. (Ed.). *Children's thinking: What develops?* Hillsdale, New Jersey: Lawrence Erlbaum, 1978.

Simon, D. P., & Simon, H. A. Individual differences in solving physics problems. In R. Siegler (Ed.), *Children's thinking: What develops?* Hillsdale, New Jersey: Lawrence Erlbaum, 1978. Pp. 325–348.

Wertheimer, M. *Productive thinking*. New York: Harper & Row, 1945. [Enlarged Edition, 1959.]

Winograd, T. Understanding natural language. *Cognitive Psychology*, 1972, *3*, 1–191.

Woods, S. S., Resnick, L. B., & Groen, G. J. An experimental test of five process models for subtraction. *Journal of Educational Psychology*, 1975, *67*, 17–21.

The Role of Invention
in the Development of
Mathematical Competence

LAUREN B. RESNICK

Introduction[1]

I intend in this chapter to address two closely related questions:
"How do people acquire new mathematical knowledge?" and "How can
we help them acquire it?" These questions, taken together, constitute
the core issues that a psychological theory of mathematics instruction
must address. They are questions that link those concerned with mathematics instruction forcefully and ineluctably to the expanding branch
of psychology concerned with the nature of understanding and the acquisition of complex intellectual capabilities.

I will begin by offering some tentative answers to these opening questions. I will then proceed to show why I believe what I do, and what
kinds of research are demanded by my responses. This process, if unorthodox as a chapter format, holds the clear advantage of keeping my
own and my readers' attention focused clearly on the central questions
throughout. If my reasoning seems faulty, the reader will not need to
wait until the end of the chapter to discover the context in which an argument must be judged.

My working answers are these. First, people acquire most new mathe-

---

[1] Portions of this paper are adapted from Resnick, L. B. and Ford, W. W. *The psychology
of mathematics for instruction.* Hillsdale, New Jersey: Lawrence Erlbaum, in press. Initial
work on this paper was done while I was a Fellow at the Center for Advanced Study in the
Behavioral Sciences and was supported in part by a grant from the Spencer Foundation
and in part by NIE Contract No. 400-76-0036 to the Learning Research and Development
Center, University of Pittsburgh.

DEVELOPMENTAL MODELS
OF THINKING

matical knowledge by constructing for themselves new organizations of concepts and new procedures for performing mathematical operations. I call this process *invention* because something new is constructed from material already available. People also, of course, acquire from outside certain new facts and information about mathematics operations or conventions of representation. I assume, however, that these externally given pieces of information take on significance—indeed are retained —only to the degree that they are incorporated by the learner into organized and interconnected systems of knowledge. That is the kind of answer one might expect from a structuralist such as Wertheimer or Piaget. It is also, I believe, the kind of answer on which modern information-processing psychology is prepared to elaborate. I shall in this chapter attempt to interpret in information-processing terms a number of concepts, such as structure, understanding, and invention, that have been traditionally associated with Gestalt or Genevan psychology.

With respect to the second question, we can help people acquire mathematical knowledge by facilitating the process of invention. That is, as educators we must contrive to put people in a position where they will be able to do the constructive work that makes new knowledge. Such facilitation of the thinking and performing of others is, in the broadest sense, what we mean by teaching. Defining teaching in this way means that it will not be enough to show learners the procedures used by skilled mathematicians, or even to drill them in those procedures—although practice in mathematical routines will often be called for in the course of instruction. It means, rather, that attention will have to be given to the kinds of representations and routines that the learner will be able to incorporate into existing knowledge structures, and that will invite the transformations and linkages involved in constructing knowledge. It also means that the possibility of instructing students in general strategies for learning and invention, as well as in the specific mathematical knowledge in question, will have to be considered.

Evidence for Invention

Although many mathematicians and some psychologists stress the importance of invention as a part of mathematical performance (see e.g., Hadamard, 1945; Peill, 1975), relatively few people believe that invention plays a central role in learning the simpler aspects of mathematics. My claim that invention characterizes even the learning of elementary school mathematics therefore obliges me to offer some evidence of the phenomenon before proceeding further. I can best do this by considering some studies of children's arithmetic performance on tasks normally associated with rote learning and drill. The presence of invention in the acquisition of these simple procedures constitutes strong evidence for the centrality of invention in much mathematics learning.

Efficient Addition and Subtraction

Let me begin by considering invention in relation to some of the earliest-learned and simplest arithmetic operations: addition and subtraction of very small numbers. There is increasing evidence that the way children perform these simple operations is not exactly the way they have been taught. Children apparently invent arithmetic procedures for themselves—procedures that not only yield correct answers, but that are also more efficient than the procedures taught. Furthermore, the invented procedures show signs of greater mathematical sophistication than those that were taught.

PROCEDURES FOR SIMPLE ADDITION

To set the stage for evidence of invention in young children, we first consider three models of addition performance that were hypothesized by Suppes and Groen (Groen & Parkman, 1972; Suppes & Groen, 1967). The models have in common the notion that there is some sort of "counter" in the head that can be set to an initial quantity and that can then "tick off" increments as counting proceeds. Figure 10.1 schematizes the process. First the counter is set to quantity a. Then the incrementing loop begins. Before each increment a test is made to see if the specified number of increments (x) has already been made. When the test yields a positive answer, processing exits from the incrementing loop and the counter can be "read."

To compute the answer to the problem $3 + 4 = ?$, several versions of the Figure 10.1 sequence are possible. One model suggests the following processing sequence: The counter is set to zero and incremented three

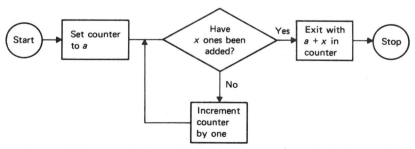

FIGURE 10.1. *Model of a mental counter that is set to a quantity* a *to which another quantity* x *is added by increments of one. (Adapted from Groen & Parkman, 1972, Figure 1.)*

times; then, without resetting, it is incremented four times. The final output, seven, can now be "read" on the counter. This is a reasonable way of adding and it is quite close to the procedure for adding that children are first taught in school.

The performance sequence suggested by a second model of addition is a bit more efficient. This model, too, assumes a counter in the head. However, the counter is set not at zero, as in the previous model, but at whatever the first number in the equation is. So, for the problem 3 + 4, the counter is set at the number three, and it then increments four times, again yielding a readout of seven. This is a more sophisticated procedure because the person doing it recognizes that the number three always stands for the same quantity. The quality of "threeness" need not be verified each time by counting to three.

A third way of doing addition is even more sophisticated and efficient than the second. According to this model, the counter is set first to whichever of the two numbers is *greater;* then the incrementing procedure is used for the other number. Thus, the problem 3 + 4 is solved by setting the counter to four and incrementing three times. This saves time because there is always a minimum of counting to be done. Besides being more efficient than the other models, this procedure indicates a higher level of mathematical understanding. The person using this procedure knows that, with respect to the final answer, 3 + 4 is always the same as 4 + 3; it makes no difference in which order the numbers are added. This is the mathematician's law of commutativity. The procedure is also a bit more complex in that it requires a decision as to which is the larger number, the one from which to begin counting.

Each of these models predicts a different pattern of response times to a set of addition problems. Assuming that the time to set the counter is always the same, under the first model solution of the problem would require the time needed to tick off both numbers on the counter. For example, solving the problem 2 + 7 would require the time needed to count to nine. Under the second model the counter would be set at two, and performance would take only as long as needed to count out the remaining seven. Under the third model, it would take a very small amount of time to decide which is the larger number[2] and set the counter to begin at seven, plus the time needed to count out the remaining two. Labeling the parts of the equation m, n, and o, so that $m + n = o$, we can tabulate the predicted performance times for the three models as follows:

---

[2] The model assumes that the quantity comparison takes a constant amount of time that does not alter the overall reaction time predicted by the model. Actually, there are data suggesting that such quantity comparisons are not all equally difficult (Moyer & Landauer, 1967). Deciding which number is smaller seems to be easier (quicker) the greater the difference between the two numbers (i.e., comparing 7 and 2 is easier than comparing 4 and 5).

MODEL A: *Reaction time = the sum of m + n*
MODEL B: *Reaction time = n*
MODEL C: *Reaction time = either m or n, whichever is smaller.*

In several experiments, first-grade children's patterns of latencies were compared with the predictions of the models under consideration. Figure 10.2 shows the predictions that would be made for each of the

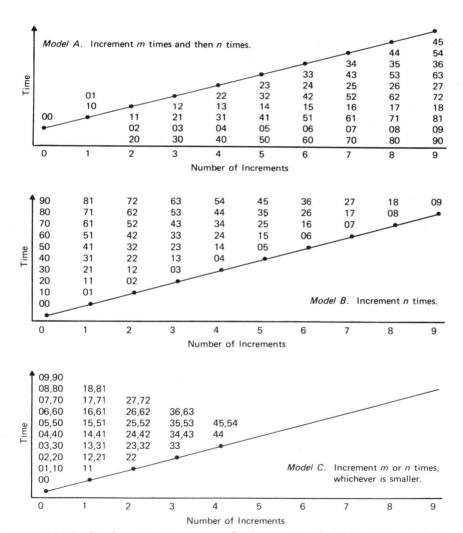

FIGURE 10.2. *Predicted reaction time patterns for three models of addition. Pairs of numbers listed above or below dots stand for single-digit addition problems (e.g., 0 + 0, 0 + 1, 1 + 0, etc.). Dots indicate the reaction times required to add particular pairs of numbers as hypothesized under the respective models.*

three models. In the figure, individual problems are designated by two numerals, so that 72 refers to 7 + 2 = ?, 45 refers to 4 + 5 = ?, and so on. The models differ in the amount of time predicted for each individual addition equation.

For virtually all the first-grade children studied (see Groen & Parkman, 1972), the data best matched the predictions of Model C. Figure 10.3 compares observed latencies (averaging all scores for first graders) to predicted latencies for this model. The data are judged to fit the prediction because the observed dots *as a whole pattern* do not deviate significantly from the predicted positions. Note, however, that a certain subset of problems, namely the "doubles" (2 + 2, 3 + 3, etc.), do not come out as predicted. Instead, these problems are all solved very quickly. This probably indicates that the counting model is not applied to these particular problems at all, but that their answers are already stored in long–term memory and are recalled directly.

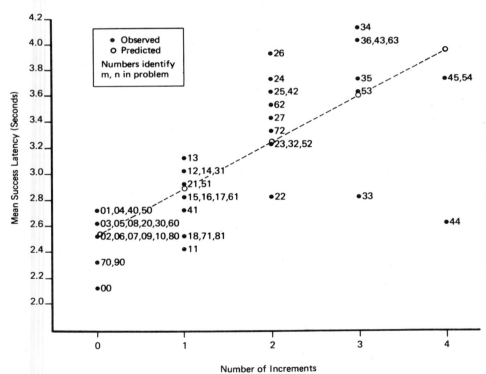

FIGURE 10.3. *Observed latencies for first-graders solving addition problems, compared with their predicted latencies. [Reprinted from Groen, G. J., & Parkman, J. M. A chronometric analysis of simple addition.* Psychological Review, *1972, 79(4), 320–343. Copyright 1972 by the American Psychological Association. Reprinted by permission.]*

TRANSITIONS IN COMPETENCE: A SUBTRACTION STUDY

If a similar kind of experiment is conducted with children at two different ages, it is possible to see how computation strategies change with age. In a study analyzing how children solve subtraction problems of the form $m - n = r$, Woods, Resnick, and Groen (1975) compared second and fourth graders. Two basic strategies for subtraction were hypothesized: Set the counter to m and count down (decrement) from there n times (Model A), or set the counter to n and count up (increment) until m is reached (Model B). Depending on the size of the difference between m and n, either Model A or Model B could be quicker. This suggested a third model: Do *either* the incrementing *or* the decrementing procedure, depending on which will be quicker (Model C, the "choice model"). Under Model C, $8 - 3 = ?$ would be solved by setting the counter to eight and *decrementing* three times; $8 - 5 = ?$ would be solved by setting to five and *incrementing* three times. The two problems would thus require the same amount of time.

The straight decrementing routine (Model A) is close to what we assume is usually taught in schools: Count out m blocks, then remove n blocks, and state how many remain, r. It seems likely that second graders, being relatively close to their first formal experience with subtraction, would follow this model. But somewhere along the line children probably discover that it is sometimes more efficient to count up from n to m in order to get to r, and for each particular problem they choose whichever is the quicker way to get a correct answer. Thus, by fourth grade we might expect greater use of the choice model (Model C). This is roughly what we found. One-fifth of the second-grade children had latency data of the pattern predicted by Model A, while the other four-fifths matched the Model C pattern. All of the fourth graders matched Model C. It seems reasonable to assume that the change from decrementing to choice is largely the children's own invention, based on their earlier observations of number relationships while they solved hundreds of addition and subtraction problems over months of schooling.[3]

CONTROLLING FOR INSTRUCTION: A PRESCHOOL ADDITION STUDY

The addition and subtraction studies described thus far used subjects who had already been in school for some time. On the basis of our knowledge of common school practice, we inferred that these children

---

[3] The regression line for the fourth graders also had a shallower slope than did that for the second graders. This indicates that by this age children were able to retrieve some of the subtraction facts from memory and so used the counting routine only when direct memory failed. The slopes for adults are typically even shallower, indicating even more direct memory solutions (cf. Groen & Parkman, 1972).

had not been directly taught the routines for adding and subtracting that we observed them using. To test more directly whether children actually invent more efficient computation routines than those they are taught, Groen and Resnick (1977) conducted a study in which we controlled what the children were originally taught by doing the teaching ourselves. To be sure the children could not have been exposed to prior teaching practices, we worked with preschool children.

The children were taught to solve single-digit addition problems of the form $m + n = ?$ (where m and n ranged from zero to five) by using the following algorithm: Count out m blocks, count out n more blocks, combine the two sets, and then count the combined set. After a number of practice sessions the blocks were removed and children gave their answers on a push-button timing device. Since practice continued over several weeks, it was possible to note when and if each child switched to the more efficient routine of setting a counter to whichever was more, m or n, and then incrementing by the smaller number (Model C in Figure 10.2). Half of the children studied made such a switch—a clear case of invention, since no instruction in the more efficient routine was offered. Thus, children who were taught a certain algorithm changed, after some practice but no additional direct instruction, to a faster and more efficient routine. The improved efficiency was the result, not of faster performance of the taught algorithm, but of the fewer steps in the new algorithm.

Each of these examples points to invention on the part of young children learning simple arithmetic. By the end of first grade, according to Groen and Parkman's (1972) data, children are performing a complex addition routine that implies an understanding of commutativity. That this is acquired without instruction—and is therefore an invention by the children—is strongly suggested by the Groen and Resnick (1977) experiment with preschool children, in which the exposure to instruction was controlled. The shift by fourth grade to a contingent or choice procedure for doing subtraction suggests a similar invention process at work. Furthermore, intuitive evidence in support of the invention interpretation of these performances comes from trying to directly teach the more sophisticated routines to young children. These routines, so easy and efficient to perform, turn out to be very difficult to communicate to children who do not already know them. The language required tends to confuse instead of enlighten children, and there is no simple physical demonstration that matches the sophisticated routines in a clear way. It may be that the reason these routines are not regularly taught in school is that teachers have discovered how difficult they are to teach. Yet children use these routines early in their arithmetic experience. We can only infer that the routines were constructed, or invented, by the learners themselves.

Systematic Errors in Arithmetic Routines

We have been discussing cases of successful, highly adaptive invention. But evidence for the ubiquity of invention in mathematics learning comes even more strongly from cases where invention leads to maladaptive performances. Such cases are widespread among children learning arithmetic. Surely no one teaches children wrong algorithms, yet children who are having difficulty with arithmetic often turn out, upon careful observation, to be using systematic routines that yield wrong answers. Probably these children were confused by some aspect of the teaching of the correct or conventional routine, or perhaps they forgot some part of the sequence of operations. To fill the gap, they developed a procedure for themselves. I call these responses inventions, although teachers, concerned with having their students compute correct answers, would normally just call them errors.

Evidence for these maladaptive inventions comes from several recent studies. Ginsburg (1977), basing his report on a variety of case studies and reviewing literature from many sources, gives the widest range of examples. Lankford (1972) reports his study of the behavior of seventh graders on a variety of typical computational problems. One hundred seventy-six pupils were interviewed individually, using as a basis for discussion a test made up of a series of quantity comparisons and 36 problems in addition, subtraction, multiplication, and division of whole numbers and fractions. In what were characterized as "diagnostic interviews," the experimenter asked the children to read the problems out loud and then compute the answers, verbalizing their thoughts while carrying out the procedures. The resulting data included calculations written on the test sheets and tape recordings of the students' verbalizations and the experimenter's occasional questions aimed at clarifying the students' thinking.

Lankford's analysis of the calculations made it clear that the students' computational strategies were highly individualistic and often did not follow the orthodox models of textbook and classroom. That is, there were many deviations from the algorithms taught in the classroom. Some of these unorthodox strategies were successful; others were not. Consider, for example, the range of ways different students wrote down the multiplication problem 19×20:

20	19	20	19	19	19	19	19	19
$\times 19$	$\times 20$	$\times 19$	$\times 20$	$\times 20$	$\times 20$	$\times 20$	$\times 20$	$\times 20$
180	00	180	00	3800	19	218	00	20
20	38	200	380		28	00	218	
380	380	380	380		299	218	2180	

Some of the students' deviant strategies produced correct answers. Others did not. Examination of individual patterns of incorrect computation made it obvious that the student's grasp of the number facts was not always at fault. Rather, errors resulted from the student's particular computational strategies.

Brown and his colleagues (e.g., Brown & Burton, 1978), in a more systematic and extended program of research than Lankford's (1972), also discovered instances of consistent error-producing algorithms in elementary school children. They describe the misunderstandings or mistaken strategies as "bugs" in the mental programs that are responsible for executing procedures or algorithms. Take as an example of the results of a "buggy" procedure the following problems as they were solved by a boy acknowledged to be having trouble with math:

7	9	17	87	365	679	923	27,493
+8	+5	+8	+93	+574	+794	+481	+1,509
15	14	25	11	819	111	114	28,991

Since some of the number pairs are added correctly, one might initially conclude that the wrong answers are due to random error. But a close inspection of the solutions reveals a systematic error of procedure that accounts for these specific errors and also predicts how this child would answer other similar problems. Notice the number of ones in his solutions. The bug in his procedure for column addition is that whenever the sum of a column is a two-digit number, he writes down the tens digit (which should be carried) and simply ignores the units digit. Presumably the first three sample problems are solved correctly either because the boy has memorized the number facts required or because he computes the answers using some other algorithm, such as counting.

The same bug, writing down the tens digit and ignoring the units digit, shows up in the boy's multiplication, along with another consistent procedural error:

68	734	543
×46	×37	×206
24	792	141

In the first problem, he multiplies 6×8 in the units column, and gets the correct answer of 48, but notates only the 4. Then he multiplies the two digits in the tens column, and writes down the 2 from the 24. The same bugs are seen in the other two problems as well, along with an incorrect rule for handling zeros. What appears to be very erratic computational behavior is actually strict adherence to an algorithm, albeit an incorrect one.

According to Brown and Burton (1978), "A common assumption among teachers is that students do not follow procedures well and that 'random' behavior is due to the student's inability to perform each of the steps correctly. Our experience has been quite the opposite. We have found students to be remarkably able procedure followers who are often following the wrong procedures [p. 4]." These "wrong procedures" are, in the present terms, inventions by the students designed to help them cope with the demands of the arithmetic class. That inventions may produce wrong answers does not detract from their status as inventions.

It can be seen, then, that inventions are not always mathematically correct ways of solving problems or performing computations. On the contrary, many very creatively invented algorithms lead to serious computational errors. Are there ways of teaching computation routines that will maximize the likelihood of fruitful inventions and minimize the chances of error-producing ones? This is a key question to which our attention is directed when we recognize the role of invention in mathematics learning. It is, however, a question to which little direct study has been addressed. To answer it we will need to learn a great deal more than we now know about the nature and range of invention in mathematics learning.

How Invention Happens

I turn now to the question of how invention works. How do people do it? This question is critical, for if we are going to put children and other learners in a position to make inventions we will have to know something about how they invent. For some help on this question it is possible to turn to the literature on problem solving.

Psychologists agree that the term "problem" refers to a situation in which an individual is called upon to perform a task not previously encountered and for which externally provided instructions do not specify completely the mode of solution. The particular task, in other words, is new for the individual, although processes or knowledge already available to the individual can be called upon for solution. Problem solving occurs when individuals discover, on their own, a new way to perform the task. Despite considerable theoretical diversity, psychologists agree that problem solving involves combining in some new way information or routines that the individual already has. Nothing new is learned, in the sense of being newly acquired; instead, a reorganization of information and skilled performance processes takes place (Resnick & Glaser, 1976). This is the same sense in which I have been using the term "invention."

The characterization of problem solving as a process of recombining or reorganizing already held information and procedures suggests several factors to be taken into account in understanding invention. I will consider three such factors here: (a) what the individual already knows —that is, the knowledge structures on which the invention will be based; (b) the form in which new information, including the demand to perform a specific task, is presented—especially its likelihood of cueing particular segments of already-held knowledge; and (c) general strategies for using one's knowledge in a complex and often incompletely specified task environment.

Knowledge Structures

MULTIPLICATION AND ADDITION

An exploration of the role of knowledge structures in mathematical invention can well begin by considering the kinds of knowledge likely to produce certain observed performances. We can then develop hypotheses concerning the kinds of knowledge structures that would foster adaptive inventions and block maladaptive ones. Consider, for example, the Brown and Burton (1978) example of the child who consistently completed the multidigit problems by writing the carry (tens) digit and omitting the units digit. What might he have understood about the structure of numerals, and of addition and multiplication, to have produced this response?

Here is a portion of a procedural rule that would produce his observed multiplication performance:

1. Examine the rightmost column. If no zeros, go to 2; if either digit is zero, go to 4.
2. Multiply the bottom right digit by the digit above it.
3. If the answer has only one digit, write it down in the column underneath; if the answer has two digits, ignore the digit on the right and write the remaining digit in the answer space in the column. Go to 5.
4. Where one digit is zero, write the other digit in the answer space in the column. Go to 5.
5. Now examine the next column. If no zeros, go to 2; if either digit is zero, go to 4.
   Repeat the procedure until no columns remain.

Clearly this is not an entirely ignorant individual. He knows, first of all, how to divide numerals into digits (this is evident in all steps of the procedure). He has an order—right to left—for processing the digits (evident in Steps 1 and 5). He knows that only one digit of a multidigit numeral can be written in a particular column (Steps 2 and 3). It is hard to say what else he may know about place value and the structure of the numeration system. He *may* know that the rightmost digits are called *units*, the next *tens*, and so forth, but this knowledge is not necessary to produce the solutions observed. If he possesses this information it does not appear to influence his solution behavior in any way. For the present purpose it is best to focus on the minimal knowledge structure capable of yielding solutions such as this individual produces.

Contrast this boy's procedure, and the knowledge apparently underlying it, with the algorithm he was probably taught:

1. Multiply the top right digit by the bottom right digit.
2. If the answer has only one digit, write it down in the column underneath.
3. If the answer has two digits, write down the units digit and hold in mind (or write down somewhere else) the carry digit.
4. Multiply the next left digit on the top by the bottom right digit.
5. Add the remembered "carry" amount to the result (i.e., complete the carrying).
6. If there are no more digits on top, write down the result.
7. If there is another digit to be multiplied, multiply it by the bottom right hand digit, then go to Step 2.
8. Now multiply the top right digit by the bottom left digit.
9. etc.

What are the differences between the two routines? What underlying knowledge supports performance of the second algorithm and might block performance of the first? One piece of knowledge essential to the taught algorithm is that in multiplying multidigit numbers, each digit in one number must be multiplied by each digit in the other. (The boy's algorithm only requires that the digits in the same column be multiplied.) This knowledge is necessary to produce Steps 4, 7, and 8 of the taught algorithm rather than the corresponding Step 5 of the child's actual routine. A second body of knowledge that underlies the taught routine is that there is a structure to multidigit numbers that dictates which digits should be written in which columns, and what should be done with the "extra" digit that cannot, for the moment, be written down. This structure—*place value*—can be represented in many ways. I explore here one possible representation: expanded notation.

In expanded notation a multidigit numeral is rewritten as the sum of its separate units, tens, and hundreds values: 35 becomes 30 + 5, 874 becomes 800 + 70 + 4. The expansion can obviously be extended to an indefinite number of place values. Writing numerals in expanded notation forces attention to the different values of each of the digits, and to the role of the position, or "place," of the numeral in assigning value. It is also possible to perform arithmetic operations on the expanded numerals. For example:

$$
\begin{array}{rl}
75 = & 70 + 5 \\
+\,39 = & 30 + 9 \\
\hline
& 100 + 14 = 100 + 10 + 4 = 114
\end{array}
$$

Figure 10.4 shows an algorithm for multidigit multiplication that incorporates knowledge of expanded notation. The knowledge structure that supports this algorithm is much richer concerning numerals, place value, and even the meaning of multiplication than the one held by Brown and Burton's (1978) subject. Like that child, a person performing

Algorithm

1. Interpret the numerals in expanded notation.

2. Set goal of multiplying the entire top value by the bottom units quantity.

3. Multiply the top units quantity by the bottom units quantity.

4. Write the product in expanded notation.

5. Multiply the top tens quantity by the bottom units quantity.

6. Write the product in expanded notation.

7. Continue multiplying by the bottom units quantity until all the quantities in the top value have been multiplied.

8. Now set goal of multiplying the entire top value by the bottom tens quantity.

9. Multiply the top units quantity by the bottoms tens quantity.

10. Write the product in expanded notation.

11. Continue multiplying by the bottom tens quantity until all quantities in the top value have been multiplied.

12. If there are more quantities in the bottom value, set new multiplication goal.

13. If there are no more quantities in the bottom value, add all of the expanded notation quantities that have been generated as products.

14. Express the sum in standard notation.

Example

```
68 =  60 + 8     8 x  6  =   48  =                        40 + 8
x46 = x40 + 6   60 x  6  =  360  =            300  +   60 + 0
                 8 x 40  =  320  =            300  +   20 + 0
                60 x 40  = 2400  = + 2000  +  400  +   00 + 0
                                     2000  + 1000  +  120 + 8
```

```
2000  = 2000 + 000 + 00  + 0
1000  = 1000 + 000 + 00  + 0
 120  =         100 + 20  + 0
   8  =                     8
        3000  + 100 + 20  + 8 = 3128
```

FIGURE 10.4. *Algorithm for multidigit multiplication using expanded notation, and an example.*

this algorithm would know that numerals are composed of digits, and would have an order for processing the digits. Unlike that child, however, this person would also understand that the position of a digit gives it part of its meaning: If it is in the rightmost position it is worth the amount shown, if it is in the next position it is worth ten times the amount shown, etc. This understanding is demonstrated in the procedures for expressing standard numerals in expanded notation and for expressing expanded quantities in standard notation. Furthermore, this person would understand that multiplying pairs of two-digit numbers requires that all the digits in one of the numbers be multiplied by all the digits in the other.

What kinds of performance would result if instruction in multiplication began with this expanded notation routine? We can only speculate, but I think that the routine would be easy to remember, making maladaptive inventions to fill in forgotten steps less likely. I think the routine would be memorable because it would make sense—assuming that the place value information represented in expanded notation was well established before multiplication itself was introduced. When the digits are understood to represent quantities that must be summed, it is easy to see why the 60 and the 8 must be multiplied both by 6 and by 40. For the same reason it is also easy to see why generating a series of quantities and then adding them up makes sense, so there would be no search for a "one-pass" solution such as Brown and Burton's boy tried. An individual who understood the place value of the digits would probably also not omit writing a digit, as this boy did. The routine as shown will not block all possible bugs. On the whole, though, the expanded notation routine is sensible, and its sensibleness is rooted in the very logic of expanded notation. For these reasons the procedure should be easy to remember, and the tendency to drop steps or to use other buggy algorithms should be reduced.

The expanded routine has a distinct drawback. It takes a long time and a considerable amount of paper to perform. It is not efficient; it is clearly not the routine any of us would like to have to use regularly. Nevertheless, it may be useful for propaedeutic purposes. Once fluent in the expanded routine, it seems likely that some children—particularly if they were challenged to find a quicker routine or one with fewer steps —might invent for themselves something like the standard routine or an equally efficient substitute. Chances are these children would be in the minority, although I may be underestimating the inventiveness of children. But I think even the noninventors would benefit from having learned the expanded routine. I believe they would learn the efficient routine more quickly once it was shown to them, would remember it more easily (because it mapped directly onto an expanded routine, each step of which was motivated by a supporting knowledge structure), and would be less inclined to introduce errors incompatible with the basic logic of the routine. Those are my predictions. Experiments systematically exploring the effect of this and other representations of place value on the acquisition of multiplication are now clearly called for.

Consider also how knowledge of expanded notation might influence the acquisition of addition and subtraction routines. If a child understands place value in the sense of being able to perform and explain the transformations from standard notation to expanded notation and vice versa, consider what he or she is likely to do with problems such as the first set in our Brown and Burton (1978) discussion (p. 222). Suppose these problems were simply presented, with no algorithm for solving double digit addition problems having previously been taught. I can imagine a child's realizing that the problems cannot be solved by simply writing down sums, then searching about for a transformation he or she already knows how to make on multidigit numerals. The search might produce something like the following:

$$\begin{array}{cc} 87 & 80 + 7 \\ +93 & 90 + 3 \\ \hline \end{array}$$

The display itself suggests an obvious next step, adding the columns:

$$\begin{array}{ll} 87 = & 80 + 7 \\ +93 = & +90 + 3 \\ \hline & 170 + 10 \end{array}$$

Now, if the child in question knows how to retranslate expanded numerals to standard ones, the answer is at hand:

$$\begin{array}{ll} 87 & 80 + 7 \\ +93 & +90 + 3 \\ \hline & 170 + 10 = 100 + 70 + 0 + 10 = 180 \end{array}$$

Could this invented expanded routine be transformed by yet another invention into a more efficient performance routine for addition? Perhaps. That, too, is a question for experiment and observation.

PROBLEMS IN AREA AND GEOMETRIC STRUCTURE

Let us consider now another type of problem in which underlying knowledge structure might also facilitate or inhibit discovery of an appropriate procedure for solution. The problem in question, how to find the area of a parallelogram, is famous from the work of Wertheimer (1945/1959). Wertheimer visited classrooms in which children were adept at applying a rule they had been taught for calculating the area of a parallelogram. They could quite easily construct the necessary perpendicular for the figures presented by the teacher and then compute the product of the base times the perpendicular (Figure 10.5a). Following this proud demonstration of competence, Wertheimer stepped to the blackboard and asked the children to find the area of a figure such as the one in Figure 10.5b. Unable to construct the perpendicular in the accustomed way, everyone, including the teacher, would typically object. They complained that the new figure was "unfair," that their rule would not work,[4] that they hadn't "had that one yet," and the like. Yet in each class one or two students expressed the idea, sometimes quite hesitantly, that the perpendicular might be drawn in a different

---

[4] The rule, of course, does work, even when the perpendicular falls outside the figure. This is not intuitively obvious, however, and was apparently not noticed by the children.

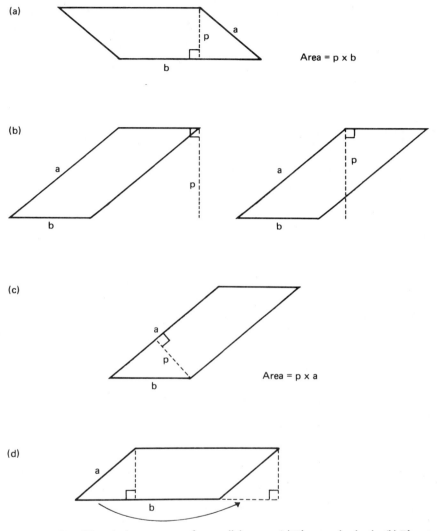

FIGURE 10.5. *Possible solutions to area of a parallelogram. (a) The standard rule. (b) The standard rule does not seem to work in some orientations. (c) Recognition of a different orientation makes the rule work. (d) The parallelogram transformed into a rectangle.*

direction, as in Figure 10.5c, or that the entire figure could be reoriented. Some even got to the mathematical heart of the matter by noting that however the parallelogram was oriented it could be transformed into a rectangle and the rule for finding the area of a rectangle (length × width) then applied (Figure 10.5d).

What knowledge about parallelograms and their areas would produce the kind of puzzled and ineffective behavior that Wertheimer initially observed? And conversely, what knowledge might produce the solutions that a few children invented? Most children—the nonsolvers —probably recognized a parallelogram only when the longer sides were parallel to the bottom of the page or to the floor (in the case of a blackboard). They did not use a more general definition that would recognize any four-sided figure with opposite sides parallel as a parallelogram. Area of a parallelogram was probably defined in terms of the specific procedure they had been taught, rather than a more generative concept.

Suppose, however, that a parallelogram is seen as a special kind of figure that is equivalent to a rectangle with a gap at one end and an extra piece at the other end. As in Figure 10.5d, the extra piece can be transferred over to the gap side to produce a complete rectangle. Figure 10.6 shows a representation of a knowledge structure that would include this definition. The structure is shown as a network of concepts linked by relational terms. Relational networks of this kind, although varying in representational detail, are common to current theories of human long-term or "semantic" memory. Such theories (e.g., Anderson & Bower, 1974) are explicitly concerned with accounting in information-processing terms for the role of structured and ordered knowledge in human thinking. They are thus attempts to apply associationist principles of human learning to some of the traditional problems and concerns of structuralist psychology. The knowledge structure represented by Figure 10.6 invites recognition that operations, including area measurement, that can be performed on rectangles can also be performed on parallelograms.

Figure 10.7 represents, in network form, the knowledge of area that Wertheimer advocated teaching to students so that they would avoid blindly applying algorithms. A person with this kind of knowledge structure for area understands that the area of a figure is equivalent to the number of equal size square units (square inches or square centimeters, depending upon one's measurement system) that can be superimposed on the figure. In the case of rectangles, this superimposition of square units can be performed quite directly, as in the top part of Figure 10.8.[5] The standard computational algorithm, length × width, is simply a way of determining how many squares would fit without going through the trouble of actually laying them out and counting.

Wertheimer believed that if children had been taught these "meaningful" conceptions of geometric figures and their areas they would not display the uncomprehending behavior that so many children did in his school investigations. He actually tried a number of experiments in which children were shown the square-units representation of area and

[5] Cubes were actually used in our experiments because they are easier for children to manipulate than two-dimensional squares.

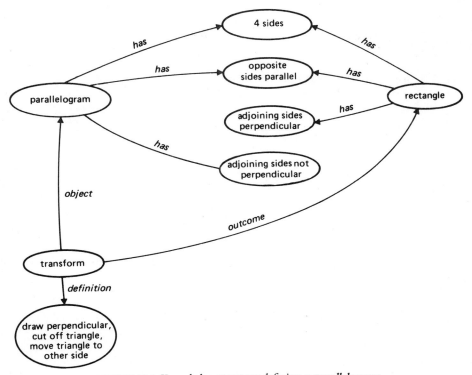

FIGURE 10.6. *Knowledge structure defining a parallelogram.*

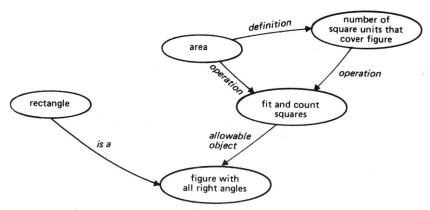

FIGURE 10.7. *Knowledge structure defining area.*

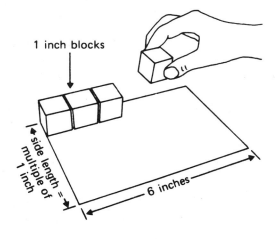

(a) *Measurement Training*

1 inch blocks

side length = multiple of 1 inch

6 inches

Area = number of blocks covering the figure.

(b) *Transformation Training*

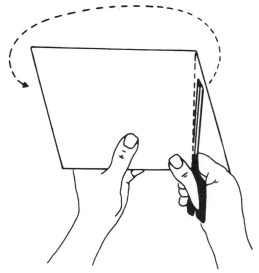

FIGURE 10.8. *Training in (a) measuring area, using blocks, and (b) transforming nonrectangles into rectangles. During transformation training, nonrectangular shapes other than the parallelogram are used.*

also were asked to work with figures in which the gap-extra relationship to rectangles was more evident. Despite his enthusiasm for the undertaking, no firm evidence concerning the effectiveness of these representations in producing greater understanding of the parallelogram area problem was ever, to my knowledge, reported.

Along with several colleagues (Resnick, Pellegrino, Lyons, Schadler, Mulholland, Glaser, & Blumberg, 1980), I set out several years ago to test whether these representations would produce a greater likelihood of inventing a solution to the area problem. We conducted a series of experiments in which 10- and 11-year-old children were taught two separate procedures. They were taught how to compare the areas of two rectangles by exactly covering the figures with inch-cube blocks and then counting the total number of blocks on each of the rectangles. They were also taught how to transform nonrectangular paper figures into rectangular ones by cutting them with scissors and replacing the pieces to form a rectangle, as in the bottom part of Figure 10.8. Following the training the children were presented with the problem of figuring out how to find the area of a parallelogram, a nonrectangular shape they had not seen in training.

Figure 10.9 suggests the kind of knowledge structures these children had probably built up by the end of their training on the measurement and transformation procedures. In the lower right segment of the diagram we see that they know a procedure for comparing the size of figures. They also know there is a limit on when to apply the procedure. They can apply it only when the figure to be measured is a rectangle (see arrows marked "allowable" object and "nonallowable" object). Connected to this *procedural* knowledge is *definitional* knowledge about the nature of rectangles and nonrectangles. When presented with rectangles, children possessing this segment of the knowledge structure would be able to measure them and to compare their areas. When confronted with a nonrectangle, these children would state that they could not apply the measurement procedure. This knowledge segment is coherent within itself and in good correspondence with the mathematical meaning of area. But for solving the area-of-a-parallelogram problem it is not adequately connected with other knowledge.

The additional piece of knowledge needed is shown in the top left portion of Figure 10.9. This is the knowledge structure that derives from having learned to transform nonrectangles into rectangles. As the figure shows, transformation training should result in a knowledge structure that includes the ability to distinguish between a rectangle and a nonrectangle, and the understanding that the area of a plane figure will not be changed by cutting up and reassembling the figure as long as all pieces are used in the process and no new pieces are added.

In the Resnick *et al*. (1980) experiments, children were taught these

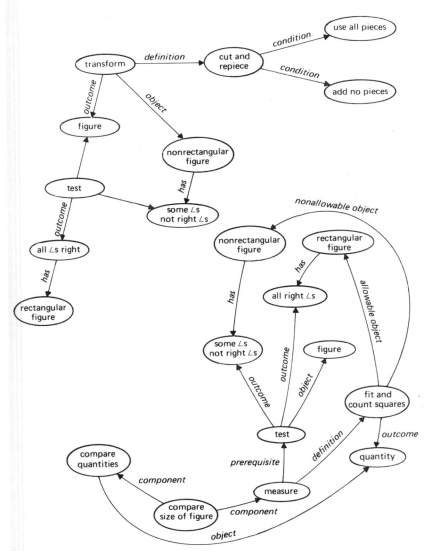

FIGURE 10.9. *Separate knowledge structures for comparing area and transforming figures.*

two separate procedures for measurement and transformation and thus presumably had in their minds something like the knowledge structures depicted in Figure 10.9. But in the experimental task, after the two separate procedures had been taught, children were required to try to find for themselves the solution to the area-of-a-parallelogram problem, a solution that required them to build or "invent" a connection between the measurement and transformation knowledge-structures. They were presented with two figures, at least one a nonrectangle, and were asked to find which was bigger.

Figure 10.10 shows the knowledge structure that we assume is needed to solve the parallelogram problem. It is a new structure formed when the knowledge concerned with transforming nonrectangles becomes connected with the knowledge concerned with measurement. Once this connection is made, an individual faced with the problem of comparing areas of nonrectangles will have two knowledge networks to probe. One network includes the fact that the *measurement* procedure *cannot* be applied; the other includes the fact that the *transformation* procedure *can*

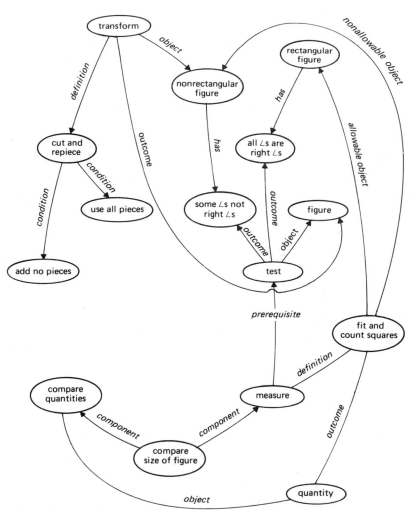

FIGURE 10.10. *Linked knowledge structures for comparing area and transforming figures.*

be applied. In this integrated knowledge structure, the outcome of the transformation procedure is a figure to which measurement can be applied. A person with this connected knowledge structure should be able to solve not only the area-of-a-parallelogram problem, but problems involving many other nonrectangular figures as well.

How well did the 10- and 11-year-olds do in forming this connection between knowledge structures? Across the various experiments, about 50% of the children succeeded in inventing the solution under the conditions just described. A few immediately saw the connection between measurement and transformation. More, however, needed to do some active searching. Eventually, sometimes after several attempts to fit blocks on the parallelogram, they too realized that transformation (cutting) needed to come first. They did this without any explicit suggestion from the experimenter; we can thus say they invented the solution— that is, they built for themselves the connection needed in their knowledge structure. The percentage of children who invented solutions in our experiments is probably higher than that in Wertheimer's original classes (he never actually reported percentages). Nevertheless, the numbers certainly do not suggest that if one has the right mathematical knowledge-structures one will *necessarily* be able to invent a solution to the area-of-a-parallelogram problem. Wertheimer, in other words, may have been partly right in suggesting that a good representation would help; but he had not accounted for the entire process of invention. To attempt to account more fully for invention, I turn now to a consideration of the second and third hypothesized factors in invention (see pages 223–234).

Form of New Information

About 50% of the children in our parallelogram experiments never did invent the connection between transformation and area measurement themselves. What distinguishes between those who did and those who did not invent? Part of the difference is likely to lie in the way the problem was presented—that is, in the form of the new information relevant to the problem and the extent to which this new information made contact with already stored knowledge. Across our experiments there was some variation in the figures presented during the problem-solving session—one or two figures were presented, a rectangle was or was not included, and the nonrectangle was either a parallelogram or an analogous figure in which the "gap-extra" relationship was especially evident. Figure 10.11 shows these variations.

In general, the absence of a rectangle or the presence of a gap-extra figure produced more solutions. The gap-extra figure probably cued the transformation procedure directly, an interpretation supported by the

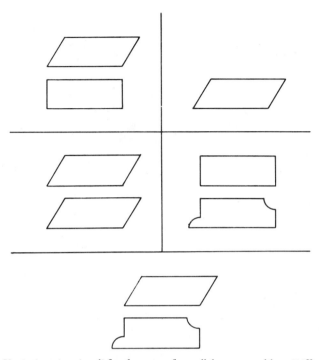

FIGURE 10.11. *Variations in stimuli for the area-of-parallelogram problem. Different sets of figures had the power to cue different learned routines.*

frequency and primacy with which transformation was mentioned in verbal protocols taken in later experiments. Analysis of the sequence of behaviors during problem solving suggests that the presence of the rectangle led most subjects immediately to employ the blocks-measurement routine on the rectangle. Many children, once they had measured one of the figures, found it difficult to switch goals and persisted in trying to place blocks on the parallelogram. In these cases characteristics of the physical task environment prompted specific solutions, apparently because they led to different conceptualizations of the problem.

Sometimes verbal instructions can also influence the conceptualization of a task, which in turn influences which cues in the environment are noticed and how the physical environment is searched for clues about which moves to make. An experiment in our laboratory by Magone (1977) illustrates quite dramatically the effects of task instructions on conceptualization. The task Magone studied, a familiar one in the classical problem-solving literature, is a variant of the two-string problem extensively studied by Duncker (1945) and Maier (1930). Two strings are hung from opposite sides of a room, and the subject is asked to tie them together. Upon trying to do this the subject discovers that the strings are hung so far apart that both cannot be reached at the same time. The subject is then told that any of the objects in the room may be used to help in tying the strings together.

There are three classes of solution to the problem. The one that Duncker and Maier liked best (because it is discovered less frequently than the others) is the *pendulum* solution: The subject hangs a weight from one of the strings, and starts the string swinging. He or she can then go over to pick up the other string, walk to the middle of the room, and wait for the first string to swing in. Another class of solution can be termed the *anchor* solution. In this solution the subject ties down or otherwise anchors one string at the center. Then the subject crosses the room to pick up the second string, brings it back to the first string, and ties the two together. The third, and in Magone's work the most frequent, class of solution is the *extension* solution. For this solution the subject either lengthens one of the strings so that it is possible to hold on to it while crossing to pick up the other; or extends his or her reach (using some kind of long, rigid rod with a hook at one end such as a cane) enough to be able to reach both strings at once. Irrespective of which class of solution the subjects employ, they can solve the two-string problem in either of two modes: top–down ("solution from above" in Duncker's terms), or bottom–up ("solution from below"). In the top–down solution mode, an idea for how to solve drives the process and leads the subject to search for objects that can perform particular functions. In bottom–up solutions, features of the objects suggest ways in which they might be used to solve the problem.

The Magone experiment was designed to place subjects in one or the other of these modes. Top–down subjects were given instructions of the form, "I would like you to tie these two strings together. One good way is to swing one string toward the other." They were then handed a fishing bob and told to use it to help in solving the problem. The suggested "good way" and first object were varied so that some subjects received pendulum, some anchor, and some extension instructions. Virtually every subject followed the initial instruction and solved the problem in the way suggested. Next, five additional objects (chair, ribbon, hanger, yardstick, umbrella) were uncovered and the subject was asked to use each object in turn to tie the strings together. What each subject did was to select from among the objects one that could be used for the class of solution just completed. Anchor followed anchor, pendulum followed pendulum, extension followed extension. This was repeated, usually for three more trials, until no objects were left that could be used for the original solution class. Only then did the subjects typically switch classes of solution.

Were the subjects perhaps just being obedient to our wishes and using the solution they thought we wanted, rather than following the dictates of their own representation of the problem? We have evidence that tells us that this is not the case. Another group of subjects was given instructions that varied slightly from the original top–down group's. They were told, "I would like you to tie the two strings together. One good way is to swing one string toward the other, although you may think of something else." This single additional phrase apparently gave subjects permission to analyze the problem for themselves and find their own solutions, for under this condition very few used the class of solution for which they had been prompted. Yet when they were shown the remaining objects and asked to solve the problem again using each object in turn, they now repeated the class of solution they had used on their first trials. In other words, they had formed a representation of the problem for themselves as requiring that a certain class of solution be used, and that representation directed subsequent problem-solving efforts for as long as it was workable.

That top–down solutions were not always at work is demonstrated by the performance of still a third group of subjects, who were given what we hoped would induce a bottom–up approach. No particular class of solution was suggested to this group, but instead they were given an object and asked to use it to tie the strings together. The object given them was suitable for either a pendulum, an anchor, or an extension solution. Once the first solution was completed, the remaining objects were uncovered and the subjects were asked to use each of them in succession, just as the preceding groups of subjects had been. The result of the initial focus on the object rather than on a specific type of solution was that subjects in this group tended to use the objects in a random order rather than searching for objects suitable for a given class of solution. The solution used on each trial was a function of the object; there was no tendency to repeat the solution used immediately before. Thus, these subjects did indeed appear to be solving in a bottom–up fashion, allowing the features of the objects to dictate their solutions.

From the present perspective, the important thing about this experiment is that, with exactly the same objects present, and exactly the same final goal, differences in initial representation were able to produce fundamentally different approaches to the problem, and therefore quite different sequences of solutions. Instructions that focused attention on a certain class of solution produced top–down solution styles in which objects were scanned for their applicability to that class of solution. Instructions that focused attention on the objects themselves produced bottom–up solution styles in which the features of the objects were allowed to suggest solutions. Even a very small change in instructions—such as suggesting a solution mode but also allowing that others might be equally good—was capable of producing at least modest changes in solutions, as evidenced by the differences in performance between the first and second groups.

Strategies for Invention

I have up to now discussed the role of knowledge structures and of the form in which a problem is presented in influencing the likelihood of invention. Each has implications for how mathematics teaching might best proceed. But the third of our assumed influences on invention—strategies of thinking that can be applied, more or less consciously, to enhance the likelihood of finding new solutions to puzzling problems—remains to be considered.

Whatever the power of well-structured presentations in enhancing mathematics learning, these presentations by a teacher or a text will always remain specific to the particular topic taught. Can an individual's power to learn mathematics be significantly enhanced by learning some strategies that are not specific to particular topics? That is the question we address when we consider, from an instructional point of view, the role of strategies in problem solving and invention.

To illustrate the power of nonspecific strategies in enhancing the likelihood of invention, let us return for a moment to our experiments on the area of a parallelogram (Resnick *et al.*, 1980). Two final experiments are of interest here. Both concerned the role of goal analysis and planning in problem solving. As in the other experiments, children were given the transformation and measurement training and then were presented with two figures, at least one a nonrectangle. This time, however, instead of asking the children to find which figure was bigger, the experimenter said nothing except, "What do you think I want you to do?" Each answer was recorded and the question was repeated until no new ideas were forthcoming. All the children thought of both measuring *and* transforming, and many thought of testing explicitly to see whether the figure was a rectangle. In other words, they formulated alternative goals in the course of "guessing" what the experimenter wanted. One might expect that this formulation in advance would lead them to recognize the connections between the measurement and transformation knowledge structures. And indeed, that is what happened, for when finally asked to find which figure was bigger, virtually every child went on to invent a solution.

This suggests that overt attention to the possible goals and subgoals in a problem-solving situation can dramatically improve the likelihood of discovering the solution. It is only a hint at the power of general strategies of thinking, but a hint that fits well with the speculative accounts of both mathematicians and psychologists. Mathematicians such as Polya (1945, 1957), for example, have suggested that there are strategies for analyzing mathematical problems that can sharply improve one's power to do mathematical work. A very similar proposal has been made by Wickelgren (1974), a psychologist who has written a book on strategies for solving the kinds of problems typically encountered by engineering students. His work relies more explicitly on information-processing theories of intellectual functioning than any earlier "how-to-do-it" work on problem solving.

Teaching Mathematics by Facilitating Invention: A Summary and Some Proposals for Investigation

With the foregoing perspective on factors that may contribute to the likelihood of invention, I can now return to the second of my opening questions: How can we help people acquire new mathematical knowledge by placing them in a position to invent? I have discussed three factors likely to affect invention. Each suggests some pedagogic actions that ought to enhance students' acquisition of mathematical knowledge.

First, the central role of prior knowledge in invention suggests that we should seek to present to students powerful and transparent representations of fundamental mathematical concepts. Powerful representations are those that apply to a large variety of specific cases. Having learned a powerful representation, one presumably has a tool for understanding and acting in situations beyond those initially presented. Transparent representations are ones that are easy to present and to understand, for individuals with some presumed body of prior knowledge. Discovering which representations have these dual characteristics of power and transparency poses a research problem of substantial scope. For example, is it the case, as I have proposed earlier in this discussion, that expanded notation is a powerful representation of place value that will permit invention of a variety of specific computational algorithms? And is it the case that expanded notation is transparent enough to be easily appreciated by children? These are, of course, questions for empirical research.

A research program aimed at enlightening invention-oriented teaching for even so limited a domain as the elementary school mathematics curriculum will be a very extended program indeed. It is unlikely that a few general principles will be adequate to the task of specifying effective instructional representation. Rather, this will require systematic study of the knowledge structures—procedural and conceptual—that are generated by different instructional representations in each major topic in the curriculum. Methods for uncovering children's knowledge structures will have to be found. Much can be learned, as Brown and Burton's (1978) work on buggy algorithms shows, from careful analysis of children's computational performance. But we will often want a more direct assessment of their underlying knowledge. Therefore, special procedures for inducing children to show us what they know will have to be devised. I expect that as we engage increasingly in the difficult process of trying to figure out what children know, experimental information-processing psychologists will become increasingly respectful of the clinical interview method that has been developed by Piaget and his Genevan colleagues. But experimental controls and "treatments"—particularly instructional treatments—will continue to be necessary for a tough-minded instructional psychology of mathematics.

In fact, a distinctive characteristic of the kind of research needed is its close tie to instructional interventions. The goal is to understand the way in which specific elements of instruction affect the course of cognitive development in mathematics. This requires, at a minimum, that research be conducted in a setting in which a great deal is known about what the children studied are being taught. In many cases, the search for optimum content and models of presentation will dictate experimental instruction—closely controlled presentations and response evocations, whose effects on both immediate and longer term knowledge structures can be examined. In this work, close attention must be given to details of presentation. If, as examples in this chapter suggest, verbal instructions and details of physical displays can affect the course of problem solving, then it is clear that casual presentation may vitiate the power of even the most carefully designed instructional routines and demonstrations.

I come next to the question of general strategies for problem solving and invention. The fundamental question to be addressed is whether there are general strategies for thinking that are teachable, and whether these strategies, once acquired, will indeed mediate speedier or more independent acquisition of a variety of mathematical knowledge. The question of general strategies for information processing is being increasingly addressed today by developmental psychologists (see Baron, 1977; Brown, 1978). Most of this research, however, focuses on strategies for memorizing and other short-term or laboratory-like tasks. It will be a substantially new venture to extend this line of investigation to strategies for thinking about a complex domain of learning and performance such as mathematics. As I have mentioned earlier, the possibility of teaching general strategies has already occurred to both mathematicians (Polya, 1945/1957) and psychologists (Wickelgren, 1974). The general strategies that these writers propose are based, in Polya's case, on a mathematician's intuitions concerning his field, and in Wickelgren's, on a psychologist's intuitive extension of a rather limited body of psychological theory. That both sets of proposals contain powerful suggestions for instruction I have little doubt. But neither has been subjected to serious empirical analysis; until this is done, we have no way of knowing which aspects of the intuitions presented in these books are the important ones. Furthermore, both of these writers are concerned with relatively sophisticated mathematical problem solving. There has been no comparable work, even at the intuitive level, on elementary and secondary school mathematics. Thus, there is room—even demand— for research that can be seen as a joining of the developmental psychologist's interest in the growth and functioning of certain simple, general strategies for information handling, and the mathematician's and information-processing psychologist's interests in complex strategies applicable to a specified domain of subject matter.

Finally, this raises the question of the general relationship between research that is fundamentally concerned with instruction and the more general theme of this volume, developmental models of thinking. I have tried, in the course of this chapter, to talk about "acquisition" rather than "learning" of mathematical knowledge. I have chosen the term "acquisition" as one that I hoped would be reasonably neutral with respect to the kinds of controversies that tend to divide developmental from learning psychologists. The view of instruction taken here, which explicitly recognizes the role of the individual's constructive intellectual processes in acquiring new knowledge, seems to me to be totally compatible with the conception of cognitive development held by many developmental psychologists—that is, that cognitive development is largely driven from within. In this view, instruction is simply a focusing of the environmental influence that all developmentalists agree plays an important role in cognitive development. Instruction is a matter of designing an environment—particularly an information-communicating environment—in such a way as to facilitate intellectual construction that might normally take place only with difficulty, or which might become misdirected altogether (as, for example, where buggy algorithms or other misconceptions take hold). Instruction, then, is not ranged against developmental processes of thinking, but rather is seen as a way of channeling those processes, and giving them an optimal opportunity within some domain of human intellectual functioning.

References

Anderson, J. R., & Bower, G. H. *Human associative memory.* (New York: Hemisphere, 1974.

Baron, J. Intelligence and general strategies. In G. Underwood (Ed.), *Strategies in information processing.* New York: Academic Press, 1977.

Brown, A. L. Knowing when, where, and how to remember: A problem of metacognition. In R. Glaser (Ed.), *Advances in instructional psychology*. Hillsdale, New Jersey: Lawrence Erlbaum, 1978.

Brown, J. S., & Burton, R. R. Diagnostic models for procedural bugs in basic mathematical skills. *Cognitive Science*, 1978, *2*, 155–192.

Duncker, K. On problem solving. *Psychological Monographs*, 1945, *58*(5), 1–113.

Ginsburg, H. *Children's arithmetic: The learning process*. New York: Van Nostrand, 1977.

Groen, G. J., & Parkman, J. M. A chronometric analysis of simple addition. *Psychological Review*, 1972, *79*(4), 329–343.

Groen, G. J., & Resnick, L. B. Can preschool children invent addition algorithms? *Journal of Educational Psychology*, 1977, *69*(6), 645–652.

Hadamard, J. *The psychology of invention in the mathematical field*. New York: Dover Publications, 1945.

Lankford, F. G. *Some computational strategies of seventh grade pupils* (Final report, Project Number 2-C-013). HEW/OE National Center for Educational Research and Development and the Center for Advanced Studies, University of Virginia, 1972.

Magone, M. E. *Goal analyses and feature detection as processes in the solution of an insight problem*. Unpublished master's thesis, University of Pittsburgh, 1977.

Maier, N. Reasoning in humans I. On direction. *Journal of Comparative Psychology*, 1930, *10*, 115–143.

Moyer, R. S., & Landauer, T. K. Time required for judgments of numerical inequality. *Nature*, 1967, *215*, 1519–1520.

Peill, E. J. *Invention and discovery of reality: The acquisition of conservation of amount*. New York: Wiley, 1975.

Polya, G. *How to solve it* (2nd ed.). New York: Doubleday Anchor Books, 1957. [Originally published in 1945.]

Resnick, L. B., & Glaser, R. Problem solving and intelligence. In L. B. Resnick (Ed.), *The nature of intelligence*. Hillsdale, New Jersey: Lawrence Erlbaum, 1976.

Resnick, L., Pellegrino, J., Lyons, L., Schadler, M., Mulholland, T., Glaser, R., & Blumberg, P. Wertheimer revisited: Information-processing analyses of invention in the area-of-a-parallelogram task. Unpublished manuscript. University of Pittsburgh, Learning Research and Development Center, 1980.

Suppes, P., & Groen, G. Some counting models for first-grade performance data on simple addition facts. In J. M. Scandura (Ed.), *Research in mathematics education*. Washington, D.C.: National Council of Teachers of Mathematics, 1967.

Wertheimer, M. *Productive thinking* (Enlarged ed.). New York: Harper & Row, 1959. [Originally published in 1945.]

Wickelgren, W. A. *How to solve problems: Elements of a theory of problems and problem solving*. San Francisco: Freeman, 1974.

Woods, S. S., Resnick, L. B., & Groen, G. J. An experimental test of five process models for subtraction. *Journal of Educational Psychology*, 1975, *67*(1), 17–21.

Piaget's Theory: Refinement, Revision, or Rejection?

HARRY BEILIN

Introduction

It is often said that the vitality of a field is indicated by the rapidity with which its theories are replaced by other ostensibly more satisfactory theories. Piaget's theory has been with developmental psychology for some 60 years despite almost continuous criticism, but appears in no immediate danger of being superceded. Its resistance to decline derives in part from periodic augmentation as new areas of application are explored, and from continual revision of the theory itself. Piaget prides himself, in fact, on being his own "greatest revisionist." Is the theory then impervious to further criticism, and even complete repudiation?

If one considers within developmental psychology, the contemporary alternatives to Piaget's theory one finds relatively few major adversaries, although there are a number of minor ones. When Piaget came on the scene his principal theoretical target was empiricism. His attack on it has been constant and continues even when the ostensible adversary no longer exists in the form Piaget and his colleagues characterize it (e.g., Inhelder, Sinclair, & Bovet, 1974). The alternative formulations, other than the contemporary forms of empiricism, such as social learning theory, are of such a nature that much of their essence has been or can be incorporated into Piagetian theory, as in the case of functionalism, exemplified in Bruner's (1966) work, and in information processing theory, exemplified by chapters in this volume.

Thus, if Piaget's theory were to be rejected out of hand for one reason or another, it is not clear what theory would substitute for it as an adequate explanatory alternative for the large domain of cognitive phenomena that Piaget and others have described.[1] Instead, what appears to be more reasonable, in light of the many objections raised to the theory, is either its refinement or revision. Inasmuch as the theory has undergone constant revision by Piaget himself, has he in fact satisfied the most significant objections to it? The thesis of this chapter is that in some instances he has not.

It would do well first, however, to highlight some recent changes in the theory to indicate how radical these have been. I will then detail some recent findings that suggest where further revisions are necessary, but which Piaget has been apparently reluctant to make.

Transformations and Correspondences

Some revisions in Piaget's theory are difficult to discern, principally because they entail changes that are not announced or are quite subtle. One recent change, however, is quite clear. It is striking in its implications and involves an important change in the theory.

The heart of the change relates to the role of transformations in cognition. For the 60 or so years in which Piaget has developed his concept of development, two hypotheses were central to the nature of his research (Piaget, 1976). First, that knowledge derives from action and not from perception or language. Second, that some actions are "internalized and organized into groups of operations." Behind these hypotheses lies the notion that knowledge deals with systems of transformations: "to know is to transform [Piaget, 1976]." Thus, all knowledge was said to be based on transformations: "All operational subject structures, on the one hand, and all causal structures in the domain of physical experience, on the other hand, suppose a combination of production and conservation. There is always some production; that is, some kind of transformation taking place. Similarly, there is always some conservation, something that remains unchanged throughout the transformation. Without any transformation we have only static identity. . . . Without any conservation we have only constant transformation. . . . In reality there is always both conservation and production [Piaget, 1972, p. 17]."

A significant change in Piaget's theory was made, however, in which knowledge was also said to be possible from seeking and establishing correspondences among objects and events, as well as from transformations (Piaget, 1976, 1977). The establishment of correspondences occurs through "instruments of comparison" at every level of development. At

[1] Although functionalist approaches such as those of Bruner, Olver, Greenfield and others (1966) posit theorylike proposals for restricted aspects of development, it is questionable as to whether they represent a theory of development as such.

the sensorimotor level for example, each assimilation into a scheme of action is a correspondence. An instance Piaget cites is of the child who sees a hanging object and hits it to make it swing. Seeing a later hanging object he establishes a correspondence between the presently perceived object and the one he had previously categorized and proceeds to hit the new one in the same fashion. Similarly, at the operational level, every direct operation, addition, for example, "corresponds to an inverse operation," in this case, subtraction. Thus, both at the level of sensorimotor action and of operations there are correspondences.

Piaget proposes three types of relations between correspondences and transformations. First, correspondences pave the way for transformations. One needs to know the primary state of objects in order to make comparisons between them. This has to precede transformations, which entail manipulation of these states. Then, there are interactions between correspondences and transformations, by virtue of which they provide aid to one another in their function. At the third level, new kinds of correspondence exist in transformations (i.e., the [logically] necessary correspondence that exists between every direct operation and its inverse). Where transformations were said to culminate in the achievement of reversibility, the cornerstone of logical thought, correspondences lead to the knowledge of reciprocals through the search for resemblances. The relations of transformations to correspondences, and reversibility to reciprocals, are not contradictory; rather, Piaget sees them as complementary.

A particular feature of correspondences is that they are very general and inhere in all structures, thus making it possible to compare structures through their correspondences. That is, common forms (morphisms) are extractable from structures, or analogical relations can be established between them (Piaget, 1977). To define the nature of these morphisms, Piaget relies on recent theoretical advances in mathematics, namely in category theory, to provide a model for the logical and mathematical characterization of correspondences in the child's thought (Piaget, 1977).

The use of category theory to define an aspect of the child's cognition had led to a general revision in Piaget's ideas concerning preoperational and concrete operational thought. It has resulted in a new formulation of the structure of groupings, particularly as they apply to classification and seriation, and has led to to a new theory of conservation based on commutability (Piaget, 1977). The logical groupings are no longer confined to the system of operational structures (and thus transformations), but encompass as well a set of correspondences (and thus comparisons).

The new theory of conservation starts with two conditions that have to be met before the subject can conserve:

1. A change in the form of an object or collection is understood to be the result of a position change of the components, in other words, in the identity of the components despite displacements.
2. In any change, what is added at the terminal point has been subtracted from the starting point (as in the separation of a piece from one side of a ball of clay that is then added to another side). These conditions express commutability of the parts in what Piaget has previously characterized as vicariance, occurring together with invariance in the total, irrespective of internal rearrangements. Thus, conservation is said to be founded on both commutability and on vicariance relationships.

To establish the commonality of structure (morphisms), rearrangements and displacements have to be combined. In the conservation case, the morphism is one of compensation (a loss in diameter made up by an addition in length), and shows true vicariance since segmentation of the whole does not occur. The fact that the total system enbodies an automorphism (the object compared with itself in two states), qualifies it as constituting a category (although one of primitive order), and is treated in a way similar to the groupings of classifications and seriation, which too are now treated as categories.

What is the significance of this new development that is both a revision and refinement in Piaget's theory?

First, Piaget is proposing the incorporation of a branch of mathematics (category theory), only developed since the 1960s, into the corpus of cognitive development theory. It supplements Piaget's use of the Bourbaki groups, those mathematical theories of structure that have a central place in his earlier theory of genetic epistemology. This development alone indicates that the theory, even at the level of mathematical and logical model building, is not complete–that new developments in mathematics and logic will continue to inform and enrich psychological theory as it relates to cognition and other aspects of development. Some of these developments that hold great promise may turn out to be more fruitful than others. The catastrophe theory of Thom (Saari, 1977), derived from topological theory, appeared for a while to be a promising tool for psychology. It still appears to have such potential, particularly as applied to Piagetian theory (see Saari, 1977); however, serious questions have been raised in some quarters about its application to biology and the social sciences (see Sussman & Zahler, 1977; Kolata, 1977). Nevertheless the application of category theory to cognitive development appears particularly promising because it suggests the possibility of establishing closer liason between Piaget's developmental hypotheses and those theoretical formulations that utilize matching and comparing processes more extensively, such as information processing models. The suggestion that correspondences and transformations are complementary logical and psychological systems encourages this view. Thus, one of the important implications of this development in Piaget's theory is that, even as it refines and further differentiates relations within the domain of operational and preoperational development, it simultaneously expands the theory's ability to articulate with other theories that up to now have been seen as based on different and ostensibly incompatible assumptions (e.g., the list matching processes of at least certain kinds of information processing models).

This new development in Piaget's theory is not without its difficulties, however. Implicit in this revision and expansion of Piaget's theory is, for example, a serious question concerning the role of action in cognitive development. As indicated earlier, transformations were seen by Piaget as basic to both the overt action of the sensorimotor period and to the implicit action of operational thought. Piaget attempts now to link correspondences, like transformations, to action by associating them with the act of comparison. "Acts" of comparison, however, can be perceptual, imaginal, or ideational without the implied action of alignment or overlapping that would indicate a motor act of comparison. It would thus correspond to some form of implicit or covert action, in the Piagetian sense of an operational "activity." The difficulty with this idea, as with the entire conception of operational activity, however, is that it is difficult to conceive of any animal life that is devoid of action in some sense. Thus, perception can be said to involve "action" and language can be said to involve linguistic "activity" as long as these processes are psychological in nature. If all psychological processes can be said to involve action, it is impossible to differentiate processes that involve action from those that do not. The Piagetian claim that knowledge derives only from action becomes vacuous. Theoretically then, no advantage appears to be gained by extending the definition of action to covert events. It renders Piaget's usage equivalent to neobehaviorists' making mediating behavior covert, for example. One difficulty in this tactic is that it becomes difficult, if not impossible, to empirically establish whether an internal event is similar to or different from an external action.

A specific example of the difficulty is evident in the instance of sensorimotor level correspondence cited previously. A correspondence is said to be made between a new object sighted and one previously known. This correspondence is clearly based on comparison in memory and results in some form of generalization. As Piaget puts it, "Anytime he assimilates a new object into a scheme that he's already capable of doing, that is a correspondence—whenever there is generalization from a new element of something already known [Piaget, 1976]." Clearly, this is not action in the usual sense. Again, if this is to be considered action, it is difficult to imagine what is not action. Thus, Piaget's formulation of correspondences and morphisms, as significant as it is, raises issues for the theory that, at the least, require further clarification.

Decalage

An issue often raised in respect to Piaget's theory, and one used as an argument against its internal consistency, is the matter of the decalages (or time lags) in the acquisition of particular concepts based on the same operational structures. The observed time lag, for example, in acquisition of the various conservations, or between the conservation of length and the seriation of lengths, is said to be inconsistent with the stage concept in that the structures that define a stage (e.g., those of concrete operations) cannot be acquired if various representations of the stage are clearly not in the child's repertoire at the same time. The problem is now clearly aggravated if the structures of operational conservation, for example, are dependent upon the prior achievement of the correspondences of conservation and related morphisms.

The decalage issue was addressed by Inhelder, Sinclair, and Bovet (1974, pp. 255–258), with a clarification and extension of the concept. The earlier view of stage acquisition emphasized the direct developmental relationship between the first notions of conservation (discontinuous quantities), for example, and later acquisitions (i.e., continuous quantities). The revised conception hypothesizes "the existence of corresponding, or parallel, processes starting from a common base and developing as a function of the growing complexity of the reality a child tries to assimilate [Inhelder et al., 1974, p. 247]." Although the stress in this quotation is on the growing complexity of reality, the obstacles that hinder the construction of conservation in the described learning experiments were said to be the lack of differentiation between arithmetical and physical quantification, both of which refer as much to the subject's thought processes (prelogical and spatial "modes of evaluation") as to the qualities of the objects, that is, the reality. In effect, what Inhelder et al. (1974) suggest is that to make the transition from one form of operational structure to another, in the case where operational structures are isomorphic (as in conservation) but the concept context differs (as with measurement and number), requires a "'strategy' model [p. 253]," that is, a solution method, applicable to a variety of problems. Such strategy application is interpreted within the Piagetian framework as the transfer of schemes from one problem to another.

Inhelder et al. (1974) also emphasize that the child has to be capable of dealing with concepts of different complexity, in addition to the basic schemes of a stage. For example, length has a one-dimensional quality;

a length, however, that is bent requires knowledge of a spatial framework with at least 2-dimensional characteristics.

The Inhelder *et al.* (1974) proposal concerning decalage embodies a number of elements. First is a distinction between horizontal and oblique decalage, in addition to the vertical decalage of progressive development (e.g., formal operations relative to concrete operations). Horizontal decalage refers to the "links between knowledge in adjourning areas [p. 255]," such as among the various types of conservation. The oblique decalages entail parallel processes that are linked and achieved at different times in the child's development (as between classification and seriation or conservation). Thus, a decalage that occurs in a parallel track from a common core affects acquisition differently from a linkage between adjourning areas. The former requires knowledge of complementary cognitive systems, in addition to the isomorphic operational structures of the stage.

Second are the problems of complexity implicit in both horizontal and oblique decalages. In these instances, complementary systems or types of knowledge have to be developed in addition to the basic operational structures. These involve different types of physical or logical knowledge depending on the particular conceptual context. Mass, number, and length, for example, require different types of specific knowledge, in addition to the operatory structures entailed in the conservation of each of the related quantitative concepts. Likewise, the logic of seriation requires different, if complimentary, fundamental logical relations from those of the logic of classification, even though they share isomorphic operatory structures common to the concrete operational period.

The observed decalages are, then, a function of the difficulty encountered by the child who lacks knowledge of either the complexity of a specific structure, such as number, which may not be differentiated from length, or, more general logical or mathematical knowledge, such as seriation or classification. The difficulties in assessing the existence of common structures are compounded by problem variables themselves which affect performance (e.g., whether the problems entail language use or not).

The third element to define the decalage is the presence or absence of strategies for problem solution. Inhelder *et al.* (1974) imply that such strategies come from existing schemes applied to new situations. My own research, as well as those of others (Beilin, 1976), shows that these strategies need not be exclusively endogenous in origin, that is, derived from the subjects own available schemes, but may have their origin externally, such as from an experimenter in a research study or from a teacher in school or from a parent or other model. Solution strategies may be of two types: (*a*) algorithms, that entail fixed solution procedures specific to particular inputs or stimulus information; and (b) heuristics, general solution procedures that may be applied to varieties of inputs that share general structural properties. The Genevans favor the use of the latter strategies and, as indicated, limit their use to the application of existing schemes.

The strategy-based regulatory system proposed by Inhelder et al. (1974) adds a significant functional aspect to an otherwise structural model of stage development. This reemphasis by them on the functional aspect of development is an important extension of Piagetian theory. However, in my view, the notion that the heuristics basic to change are restricted to available schemes is too restrictive for the theory, and I will suggest later in this chapter how it may be extended without doing violence to Piaget's theory.

Learning and Development

In at least one sense, Piaget's view of learning is very contemporary. For him, learning is an aspect of the process of adaptation. Piaget has carried on a very long intellectual debate with empiricists over interpreting the effects of experience and the nature of the processes of acquisition and change. The empiricist position has been that exogenous factors, those external to the individual, account for the nature of the child's behavior and his disposition to behave in particular ways. Piaget conceives that change in the child's behavior occurs as an adaptation to the disequilibria created when external or internal demands are in conflict with the child's (internal) cognitive schemes. The adaptive responses to conflict are incorporated into the child's existing cognitive repertoire if appropriate cognitive schemes exist to which such generalized features of action can be assimilated. In turn, every such assimilation is accompanied by a change in existing structure reflecting an accommodation to the nature of the incorporated patterns or "objects." This system of active exchange and change is under the control of a self-regulating mechanism that is assumed to be part of the individual's innately-given biological structures.

This particular conception of learning-as-adaptation differs from the empiricist conception in a number of ways. Among the most significant is the notion that the effects of experience (natural or experimental) are lasting only when the effects of experience can be assimilated to appropriate existing structures, whether simple as in the case of sensorimotor adaptation, or more elegant, as in the logical structures of formal operational thought. Experience has no significant learning consequence if it occurs when no appropriate structure is evident. In empiricist theories, this view is replaced by one that holds that every experience affects the subject's behavior, although the nature and extent of that influence is not necessarily independent of the subject's prior experience (in the form of habits, dispositions to respond, etc.).

Another feature of Piaget's adaptational conception of cognitive learning is the stress on the action basis of cognitive change. This emphasis, as already indicated, underlies all of Piaget's ideas concerning the origin of cognitive structure, denying in turn the possibility of perception and language as the source of cognitive operations. The other side of the coin is the view that knowledge is the result of the constructive activity of the subject. The empiricist subject is, on the contrary, relatively passive; the principal sources of cognition and cognitive change deriving instead from external forces, and internal processes (such as memory and imagery) that involve no active exchange with objects. Thus, learning takes place when the subject actually engages the world of objects, events, or abstract forms that are external, or the representations of objects, events, and abstract forms when they are internal.

Has Piaget's conception of adaptive change stood up well both theoretically and experimentally? No categorical answer is possible. The conception is so broad, abstract, and complex that it is difficult, in fact, to establish how this aspect of Piaget's theory is to be tested empirically. There is one area, however, in which it may be said that a continuing series of tests has been made. These are in the so-called training studies. In general, the rationale behind these studies has been: (a) If Piaget's thesis is *correct* concerning the limiting effect on experience by the presence of absence of cognitive schemes, and (b) if such schemes *cannot* be assumed to be present in particular children, then (c) providing relevant experience should lead to no assimilation (i.e., learning), whereas, (d) if there are such structures in place, the effects of experience in the form of experimental training will be demonstrable in new patterns of behavior. On the other hand, if Piaget's theory is *not correct*, then (a) providing experience through training, when no relevant cognitive (Piagetian) structures are presumed to be present, will (b) lead to new patterns of response of the kind the training was designed to instill.

Interestingly enough, the first series of training studies was undertaken by the Genevans themselves. The intent of these studies was to show that the effects of practice or the demonstrations of appropriate responses (reflecting empiricist views) would not lead to effective learning, relative at least to Piagetian conflict-generating (i.e., "equilibration") procedures based on the Genevan "clinical method." Almost at the same time, other training studies were being undertaken with other intentions, principally in the United States and the Soviet Union (see Beilin, 1971; 1978, for reviews). One, less important intent, was to show that the natural ages of operational acquisition suggested by Piaget were in fact too conservative and that sophisticated cognitive functioning was possible at earlier ages. The second intent was evident in a series of experimental studies designed to assess the effectiveness of various methods of training relative to the Piagetian equilibration methods. These studies were designed to test Piagetian assumptions concerning cognitive change as a function of cognitive conflict between schemes. Although these two research approaches were at first independent, they began to merge when successful nonPiagetian training studies were pointed out (e.g., Beilin, 1971) to have been carried out on children (5 years and older) who could be presumed to have some elements of relevant cognitive structure present. Other studies (Beilin, 1978) in turn have been conducted with very young (i.e., 4-year-old) children where the presence of such structures are less likely presumed.

What the training studies show, despite considerable Genevan skepticism, is that cognitive (operational) acquisitions are demonstrable with almost every training method employed, based on nonPiagetian as well as Piagetian assumptions. This fact, which has significant theoretical consequences, demonstrates for one thing, that cognitive change is not the sole consequence of cognitive conflict or disequilibrium. What the studies also show is that training can instate cognitive structure when no existing relevant cognitive (operational) structures can be said to be present, that is, in very young preoperational children.

The considerable interest in training studies outside Geneva prompted the Genevans to undertake their own studies again, although this time with a new approach to training. Studies (Inhelder *et al.*, 1974) were designed to determine what training (based on Piagetian assumptions—with the "clinical method" now characterized as the "method of critical exploration") could show about the transition mechanisms in cognitive development. These studies have been criticized by Lefebvre-Pinard (1976). They are critical of Inhelder *et al.* for their neglect of investigations (also based on equilibration methods) that show training effects more powerful than those demonstrated by the Genevans. Pascual-Leone (1976a, 1976b) in turn defends the Genevans on the ground that their intentions were different from those of the other investigators.

Nonetheless, the larger issue remains as to why so many nonequilibration (nonPiagetian) training methods lead to operational level performance, even with preoperational level children. One possibility is that Piaget's theory is incorrect with respect to assimilation. It is premature to draw this conclusion, however, inasmuch as it would have to be shown first that training studies in principle provide a decisive test of the theory. Second, the data have to be conclusive. On one hand, the data do appear to be conclusive, at least for the many studies that demonstrate operational level achievement as a function of a variety of training methods, with operational level performance defined by the strongest criteria, in fact, the criteria proposed by Piaget himself (Piaget, 1964). With the training of clearly preoperational children, on the other hand, although there are such data, they are far from conclusive. Nevertheless, some of the latter studies, although they involve few subjects, are well controlled and provide clear cut results (cf. Beilin, 1978). There are a much larger number of studies, however, which suggest the opposite conclusion, namely that:

1. The *differential* effects of age on training are considerable, that is, older and more advanced operational subjects show superior training effects to younger and transitionally-operational subjects who, in turn, are superior to preoperational subjects.
2. In absolute terms, a number of studies show no training effects with younger preoperational subjects, even when they do show training effects with older subjects (e.g., Bruner *et al.*, 1966).

There is also a theoretical and methodological issue that is not easily resolved. According to Piaget (Beilin, 1975), the logical structures of the concrete–operational and formal–operational periods have their origin in the elementary schemes of sensorimotor intelligence. The reversibility feature of the concrete and later operations, for example, is anticipated in the so-called empirical reversibility ("empirical return") of sensorimotor schemes. (Empirical reversibility is evident when a sensorimotor-level child is capable of returning an object moved from point A to point B back to point A as directed.) In instances such as this, it could be argued (if one were attempting to save this aspect of Piagetian theory) that *some* relevant structure, however primitive, does exist in young preoperational children, even sensorimotor-level children, and training if successful at these levels, entails assimilation to these primitive schemas or schemes. Saving Piagetian theory this way, however, substantially vitiates the power of the theory of stages that is fundamental to the theory, and does possible violence to the adaptational implications of assimilation. On the other hand, if one entertains a distinction between natural and experimental or "forced" development, then one may posit, as I will now, that in natural conditions of development, the assimilation constraints exercised by existing schemes will be consistent with the findings reported by Genevans and others. Training studies that are based on nonforced equilibration methods will generally operate under the same constraints. "Brute" or forced methods, such as those used in verbal rule instruction (Beilin, 1975, 1976), and possibly even some types of equilibration training will force assimilation to the simplest available structures, but these will have only limited generalization value with the youngest children. However, the more developed preoperational schemes (one-way mapping of constituent structures) of older, and transitionally-operational children, will provide a more stable base for the assimilation of forced strategies or solution algorithms, or lead to the forced restructuring of incomplete or unintegrated structures. In these circumstances, the training data obtained with preoperational children need not, necessarily, do violence to Piaget's theory. Instead the theory can be modified to accommodate the research evidence that bears upon this aspect of the theory.

What of the other body of data, much larger and persuasive than that obtained from preoperational level subjects, which shows that almost every training method leads to operational-level performance? In this case, the same proposal offered previously may hold, namely that all methods other than the equilibration method represent brute or forced training methods that result, for the most part, in unstable acquisitions. The research evidence, however, contradicts this, for many of these studies show operational acquisitions to be quite stable with the strongest criteria satisfied (e.g., delayed post-testing, counter-suggestion, and nonspecific-transfer tests).

In this instance as well, I do not believe that Piaget's theory requires rejection although, clearly, the claim cannot be made that cognitive change is explained solely by cognitive conflict within an equilibration model. Again, as the theory is very general, it is not clear that these studies provide a decisive test of the theory; by the same token, however, these studies cannot be taken as definitive evidence in favor of the theory. Nevertheless, the nonGenevan training studies cannot be denied as having some bearing on the understanding of the nature of assimilation, accommodation, and adaptation, even if the Genevans choose for the most part to ignore them.

As I see it, the training studies tell us something significant about the effect of experience on cognitive change. If the effect of training is such that many different types of experience can lead to the same result (for example, conservation) then the effect of experience is nonspecific. That is, no specific element in training or experience can be said to be both a necessary and sufficient source of change that would lead to conservation (or other cognitive operations). Even though Piaget's theory makes much of the interaction between subject and object, as well as of the nonmaturational and noninnate elements in development, he rarely if ever specifies what in experience other than "action" (i.e., the child's own action on the world) leads to cognitive change. If the effects of experience are necessary (change does not take place without experience, presumably even in natural conservation development), then they, in addition to providing the contents of cognition, act as facilitators in the restructuring of existing structures. In other words, cognitive structures derive largely from endogenous elements and influences, some innately given, some constructed, but all from internal elements. Thus, what is assimilated is essentially "content" (e.g., information about the physical properties of objects or events); *structure*, however, is internally constructed. Nor is it confined to structuring by action, or implicit action, inasmuch as Piaget never really defines action (Beilin, 1977). When he implies what action might include, it is apparent that "action" when not merely motor activity, includes all "mental activity," which suggests the same differentiation between action and nonaction as the differentiation between the living and nonliving, as already indicated. Thus, structuring may result from perception, action, or language. The effects of such experience could lead then automatically to accommodative activity that results in organization of the products of that experience. (It has to be understood that while the experience referred to is nonspecific—it still has to be relevant or connected to the structure one seeks to construct.) Externally-constructed experience, as provided, for example, in algorithmic training procedures, may be incorporated as a whole into the existing cognitive system, but only if it articulates and can be integrated into existing schematic organization. Thus, one is led by these research data to the view that constructed, operational schemes are a function of the press of nonspecific or only broadly connected experience that leads to internal accommodative restructuring and integrating activity, or to the employment of innately given or newly constructed organization that integrates newly assimilated contents. These new organizations, at whatever level, are not confined to actions carried out solely by the subject but may have their source in perception, imagery, and language as well as in action. Naturally-acquired structure thus has its origin in accommodative activity, whereas assimilation is designed to introduce new contents from experience into the child's cognitive repertoire.

Language and Thought

Piaget's views on language have undergone a number of subtle changes over the long period of time he has expressed them, but on the general relation between language and thought he has remained constant: Language is subordinate to cognition; it is not the source of cognition, which is to be found in action.

Piaget's early research (in the 1920s) on language was designed to show that the child's knowledge and use of language was an ideal vehicle for the analysis of the child's thought. Parenthetically, there are many researchers these days who are interested in communication competence who overlook the fact that Piaget did not assert that the young child was incapable of socially-centered thought. Instead, in early development there was more egocentrism than socio-centrism;

further development provided a progressive shifting toward more socially centered communication. Nevertheless, Piaget (1962) later reinterpreted the nature of egocentric language and thought under the impetus of Vygotsky's (1962) criticism. His reinterpretation was based on the progressive decentration of the child's language, thus deemphasizing egocentricity, which Piaget recognized as an unfortunate choice of term.

Piaget continues his insistence, however, on the fact that language is not sufficient as a source of cognitive structure, although in some instances, particularly in the case of formal operations, it might be necessary for thought. The evidence for this assertion has been primarily indirect. One argument offered is that cognitive capacities manifest themselves at ages prior to the emergence of language. A second argument is that, although a child might have the necessary linguistic components of a particular type of thought in place (e.g., classification), the child might still not be able to order or otherwise appropriately organize the relations among the linguistic elements themselves. Such would be the case with class-inclusion problems in which the child might have all the lexical and syntactic structures related to a class inclusion (flowers to roses) and still not know the logically necessary class-inclusion relation (more flowers than roses).

More direct evidence of the relation between language and thought was sought when Sinclair, a linguist by training, joined the Genevan group. She first conducted a series of studies (1967) on conservation, which showed that conservers were distinguished from nonconservers both lexically and syntactically. This in itself did not establish a priority in cognitive functioning, but she attempted then to train nonconservers in the linguistic elements characteristically used by conservers. Although a number of nonconserving subjects acquired some of the appropriate language of conservers, it did not materially affect their conservation performance. These data were offered as stronger evidence of the reliance of language on the development of prior cognitive structure. Sinclair (1971, 1973) has also argued that the origin of linguistic structure is to be found in previously developed cognitive structure, principally in response to the Chomskyan (1975) claim that universal linguistic structure derives from an innately-given, abstract, linguistic rule system. Her argument is that language does not develop for a long time (1 ½ to 2 years), too long to assume that it reflects an autonomous innately given system. Further, language is not achieved all at once; once it starts to develop, it is constructed over a span of a few years. In addition, prior to the beginning of language development, a series of structures and processes are elaborated in sensorimotor intelligence (recursiveness, subject-object differentiation, prediction, etc.) that provide the logical forms that language requires for its construction. These claims have had considerable influence in the language acquisition literature (Bloom, 1970; Brown, 1973; Slobin, 1973; McNeill, 1974; Beilin, 1975, etc.).

In spite of the effect of Piaget's and Sinclair's ideas on the theory of language acquisition, it is not unreasonable to ask whether their views on the relation between language and cognition bear continued acceptance in light of contradictory evidence.

First, a now-considerable body of data from a variety of investigations (reviewed in Beilin, 1976) shows that conservation can be trained by linguistic means when the training is based on verbal–rule instructional methods. In these studies, training provides the child who fails to give a correct conservation response, with a conservation strategy embodied in a verbal rule (e.g., "nothing was added or taken away so the number remains the same"). Over a series of trials, the child learns to apply the algorithm and in some instances is even able to transfer it. Thus, it cannot be maintained as Piaget and Sinclair do that a cognitive operation is incapable of linguistic instatement. What these findings suggest is that the relation between cognition and language is more complex than suggested by Piagetian theory and that it is possible to conceive that the source of cognitive operations may be linguistic just as well as in action. As indicated earlier in this chapter, it is difficult, if not impossible, to unambiguously define in Piagetian theory what is meant by "action." If it were necessary to extend Piagetian theory in order to maintain action as the source of cognition, then it would not be beyond reason to consider linguistic activity as simply another type of action and not require that it be considered as a distinct modality.

A second body of evidence comes from a series of studies (Beilin, 1975) in which an attempt was made to show that specific logical operations (for example, reversibility, logical conjunction, and disjunction) are indeed necessary for the acquisition of a variety of linguistic structures. The linguistic structures studied were lexical and syntactical (the number and time lexicons, the passive construction, and the logical connectives). While the experiments showed general, and sometimes specific, relations between knowledge of cognitive and linguistic structures, there was no one-to-one mapping between them, as suggested by Piagetian theory. What these data do imply is, first, that language and nonlinguistic cognition are in the same general cognitive domain. Second, each system has properties that are unique to that system. Thus, some facts of (nonlinguistic) cognition cannot be accounted for by linguistic explanations (Piaget cites many of these), and some linguistic structures cannot be accounted for by knowledge of cognitive structure (Chomsky, 1975, cites a number of these). What then establishes the commonality between linguistic and cognitive structure? I have previously suggested (Beilin, 1975) that the common source is a more abstract logical system of which the logical structures of cognition and the logical structures of language are derivatives. Knowledge of the nature of that logical system at this point can only be specified as a goal of analysis and research.

A Final Comment

Piagetian theory has shown itself to be very adaptive: Piaget has radically altered aspects of his theory to accommodate new experiments and new data. What this chapter has shown is that there are other bodies of data that suggest further revision and/or refinement of the theory, particularly with respect to the definition of action and the almost exclusive reliance of cognitive constructions on action, the role of language in cognitive development, and the consequences of nonequilibration training on the construction of operations. This does not exhaust the issues that confront Piaget's theory. Nevertheless, it remains surprisingly robust for a psychological theory that has been developing for some 60 years.

References

Beilin, H. The training and acquisition of logical operations. In M. F. Rosskopf, L. P. Steffe, & S. Taback (Eds.), *Piagetian cognitive-development research and mathematical education.* Washington, D.C.: National Council of Teachers of Mathematics, 1971. Pp. 81–124.

Beilin, H. *Studies in the cognitive basis of language development.* New York: Academic Press, 1975.

Beilin, H. Constructing cognitive operations linguistically. In H. W. Reese (Ed.), *Advances in child development and behavior.* Vol. 11. New York: Academic Press, 1976. Pp. 67–106.

Beilin, H. Language and thought: Thistles among the sedums. Invited address. Jean Piaget Society. Philadelphia, June, 1977.

Beilin, H. Inducing conservation through training. In. G. Steiner (Ed.), *Psychology of the 20th Century.* Vol. 7. *Piaget and Beyond.* Zurich: Kindler, 1978. Pp. 260–289. (In German.)

Bloom, L. *Language development: Form and function in emerging grammars.* Cambridge, Mass.: MIT Press, 1970.

Brown, R. *A first language: The early stages.* Cambridge, Mass.: Harvard University Press, 1973.

Bruner, J., Olver, R. R., Greenfield, P. M., and others. *Studies in cognitive growth.* New York: Wiley, 1966.

Chomsky, N. *Reflections on language.* New York: Pantheon Books, 1975.

Inhelder, B., Sinclair, H., & Bovet, M. *Learning and the development of cognition.* New York: Harvard University Press, 1974.

Kolata, G. B. Catastrophe theory: The emperor has no clothes. *Science,* 1977, *196,* 287.

Lefebvre-Pinard, M. Les experiences de Geneve sur l'apprentissage: Un dossier peu concaincant (Meme pour un Piagetian). *Canadian Psychological Review,* 1976, *17,* 1C 109.

McNeill, D. Semiotic extension. Paper presented at the Loyola Symposium on Cognition, 1974.

Pascual-Leone, J. On learning and development, Piagetian style: I. A reply to Lefebvre-Pinard. *Canadian Psychological Review,* 1976, *17,* 270–288. (a)

Pascual-Leone, J. On learning and development, Piagetian style: II. A critical historical analysis of Geneva's research programme. *Canadian Psychological Review,* 1976, *17,* 289–297. (b)

Piaget, J. Comments on Vygotsky's critical remarks concerning *The Language and Thought of the Child* and *Judgment and Reasoning in the Child.* Cambridge, Massachusetts: MIT Press, 1962.

Piaget, J. Development and learning. In R. E. Ripple & V. N. Rockcastle (Eds.), *Piaget rediscovered: A report of a conference on cognitive studies and curriculum development.* Ithaca, New York: School of Education, Cornell University, 1964. Pp. 7–20.

Piaget, J. Problems of equilibration. In C. F. Nodine, J. M. Gallagher & R. H. Humphreys (Eds.), *Piaget and Inhelder: On equilibration.* Philadelphia: Jean Piaget Society, 1972. Pp. 1–20.

Piaget, J. On correspondences and morphisms. *Jean Piaget Society Newsletter.* 1976, *5* (3). (Unpaged)

Piaget, J. Some recent research and its link with a new theory of groupings and conservations based on commutability. In R. W. Rieber & K. Salzinger (Eds.), The roots of American psychology: Historical influences and implications for the future. *Annals of the New York Academy of Sciences,* 1977, *291,* 350–357.

Saari, D. G. A qualitative model for the dynamics of cognitive processes. *Journal of Mathematical Psychology,* 1977, *15,* 145–168.

Sinclair-de-Zwart, H. *Acquisition du langage et dèveloppment de la pensèe.* Paris: Dunod, 1967.

Sinclair, H. Sensorimotor action patterns as a condition for the acquisition of syntax. In R. Huxley & E. Ingram (Eds.), *Language acquisition: Models and methods.* New York: Academic Press, 1971. Pp. 121–135.

Sinclair-de Zwart, H. Language acquisition and cognitive development. In T. E. Moore (Ed.), *Cognitive development and the acquisition of language.* New York: Academic Press, 1973. Pp. 9–25.

Slobin, D. Cognitive prerequisites for grammar. In C. Ferguson and D. Slobin (Eds.), *Studies in child language development.* New York: Holt, Rinehart & Winston, 1973. Pp. 175–225.

Sussman, H. J., & Zahler, R. S. Catastrophe theory: mathematics misused. *The Sciences,* 1977, *17,* 20–23.

Vygotsky, L. S. *Thought and language.* Cambridge, Massachusetts: MIT Press, 1962.

12

Constructive Problems for Constructive Theories: The Current Relevance of Piaget's Work and a Critique of Information-Processing Simulation Psychology

J. PASCUAL-LEONE

Introduction[1]

I will start by making two claims about cognitive psychology which I hope you will accept. The first claim is that the modern purpose of cognitive psychology is to develop a theory or general model of the subject's psychological organism which has both generative and psychogenetic constructive power. By generative constructive power I mean the model's ability to simulate the processes that generate the subject's performance. By psychogenetic constructive power, I mean the ability of the model to simulate the organism's developmental process of change. It is, I hope, apparent that these constructive requirements impose the need to define the basic constructs of the organism as recursive operators whose interactions generate performance. The psychogenetic process is, then, the change in the organism's repertoire of operators, which results from the interactions between cognitive learning and development.

My second claim is that scientific theories and their constructs *reflect*

[1] Preparation of this chapter was facilitated by Grants A0234 of the National Research Council of Canada and S76-0694R1 of The Canada Council. The author's address is Department of Psychology, York University, 4700 Keele Street, Downsview, Ontario, Canada.

DEVELOPMENTAL MODELS
OF THINKING

the structural invariants of their data base, as filtered by the data analyses chosen by their developers (i.e., by the school of scientists who developed the theories). Notice that, to satisfy the requirements of my first claim, this epistemological function of *reflection* must be understood as signifying that the theories or constructs in question can simulate the psychogenetic or generative processes which caused the performances represented in the data (c.f. Pascual-Leone, 1973, 1976a, 1976d). Since theories reflect their data base, as filtered by the methods of the school they come from, a direct comparison of theories should not be carried out unless mediated by a comparison of their respective data bases and the methods used by their sponsoring schools.

My plan in this chapter is to compare the data bases, methods, and theories of Piagetian and information-processing–artificial-intelligence (AI) researchers, and to mention a few experimental results bearing on issues raised by this comparison. One purpose of this comparison is to determine whether two of Piaget's main theoretical conclusions, the concepts of *general stages* and of *equilibration*, can be disregarded, as many researchers—among them the Carnegie-Mellon school—are now doing, or whether these two descriptive concepts must be accepted as descriptively adequate for Geneva's data base and methods. In this last case, stages and equilibration become problems that any adequate constructive theory must face up to. The implications of this last case, which I believe to be true, can be clarified by examining two possible objections to it. First, if the concepts of general stages and equilibration are descriptively real, how is it that the Carnegie-Mellon school and so many others find them unnecessary? Second, if they are at least descriptively valid (i.e., stand for structural invariants in the data), why has no one purified and perfected the data extraction procedures so as to quantify and demonstrate unambiguously those structural invariants?

A second purpose of the comparison of Piaget's and the information-processing–AI's data bases and methods is to suggest how these approaches complement each other, thus correcting their respective deficiencies, and how in fact both lack one methodological and data base dimension (i.e., the proper consideration of human differences). This issue is important because the development of valid organismic constructs may not be possible unless the data base utilized includes from the outset not only *psychogenetic data* à la Piaget and *step-by-step generative data* in the information-processing–AI manner, but also *cognitive-style* or human differences *data* which go beyond a mere recognition of difference in strategies among people.

I wish I could discuss these issues and then proceed to illustrate concretely my point on stages by summarizing experiments already available which show stage-bound quantitative changes related to some form of "working memory" or "mental energy" (M energy, possibly activation of the reticular system by the prefrontal cortex which in turn activates other specific areas in the cortex), whose measure increases with age in a stagewise manner (Burtis, 1976; Case, 1972; DeAvila, 1974; Goodman, 1979; Logan, 1974; Parkinson, 1975; Pascual-Leone, 1970, 1978a; Pulos, 1979; Todor, 1977). I would also like to illustrate my point on equilibration by discussing data which suggest that subjects' performance is not just a function of M and their repertoire of *habitual* structures (i.e., structures permanently stored in the repertoire of long-term memory) but is also a function of many other organismic factors, so that the performance outcome is quite often a truly novel synthesis jointly brought up by all the (often conflicting) active factors—a synthesis that current computer systems could not simulate. Unfortunately, space limitations do not permit the presentation of these experimental results. I will therefore content myself with a succinct reference to some of the results illustrating the relevance for human cognition of the field factors or field effects, F factor for short, such as the phenomena that human performance investigators classify as S–R compatibility—the F factor which Gestaltists first discovered and then converted into an explain-it-all *deus-ex-machina*. These factors cannot be handled by current AI theories, although their role, together with M, is central for understanding the generative and psychogenetic constructivity of humans.

These are the conclusions of my chapter, which I will argue in support of in as much detail as space permits. The points I want to cover are as follows:

1. I shall examine critically Piaget's data base and methodology in order to illustrate the empirical invariances underlying the Piagetian notions of stage and equilibration.
2. I shall compare the Piagetian data base and methods with those of information-processing–AI approaches, in particular Carnegie-Mellon's, to determine why these approaches reject the descriptive value of the notions of general stage and equilibration.
3. I shall give a very brief answer to the question, "If stages and equilibration are descriptively valid notions, how can one obtain data that exhibit stage patterns and/or the equilibration phenomena in an unambiguous quantitative manner?"

On the Data Base and Methods of Piaget's Team

It is well known that Geneva typically groups the results from a given task across subjects of a given age-group, and then compares these results (often the frequency of performance patterns found) across ages. Tasks with different content but similar structure are often compared developmentally to verify that it is the hypothesized similar structure, and not content characteristics, which determines the developmental trace in the data.

Four characteristics of Geneva's methodology must be emphasized:

P1. The data are usually obtained cross-sectionally and, most commonly, through the use of problem-solving (as opposed to learning) designs. Even when learning designs are used, the emphasis remains on self-discovery without direct external facilitation (cf. Pascual-Leone, 1976b; Pascual-Leone & Bovet, 1966, 1967).

P2. Tasks are not broken down into steps on time-ordered sections, as is the case in the information-processing–AI tradition, but are examined as a whole, the data being the final pattern of performance obtained when no feedback is given.

P3. Geneva's emphasis on the developmental trace of the performance patterns often leads, or used to lead,[2] to the selection for further study of those tasks which elicit performances with an interesting (e.g., stage wise) developmental trace.

P4. The data are used to infer and/or test the characteristic Piagetian notions (e.g., psycho-Logical structures) that, in a qualitative manner, are intended to account for the empirical invariances found *across situations as a whole for each age-group* (Piaget's epistemic subject). In other words, the tasks' structural type and the subjects' age-group type are held constant, the subjects and tasks are varied, and the dependent variable is the developmental trace of the obtained patterns of performance.

A tacit, but nonetheless characteristic method of Piaget's structuralism is the search for *genetic–epistemological sequences*. Call *psychogenetic* a sequence of tasks empirically obtained by ordering the tasks in terms of the developmental trace exhibited by the performance score (or proportion of correct performances) they elicit from different age-group samples. Call *psycho-Logical* a *sequence* of tasks obtained by ordering the tasks' corresponding theoretical structuralist (or process-structural) models, according to *psycho-Logical inclusion relations*—that is, Task B is psycho-Logically ordered after Task A whenever its structuralist model (or underlying constructive process) psycho-Logically includes or presupposes the model (or constructive process) of A. Using this terminology, a *genetic–epistemological sequence* can be concisely defined: It is the congruent pairing of a psychogenetic sequence and a psycho-Logical sequence.

Performances (tasks) related in this manner are expected by Geneva to exhibit the processing organismic constraints of the subjects. This ex-

[2] This was my experience from 1960 to 1964 when I was a research assistant with Piaget and Inhelder in Geneva. This practice could be different now.

pectation is based on the assumption (later adopted by modern information-processing approaches) that the organism is a psycho-Logical machine of some sort which develops according to a psychological (and psycho-Logical) Differentation–Integration principle. As such, its performance and patterns of growth (development, learning) could in principle be predicted by theoretical task analyses based on a suitable psycho-Logic. Piaget's research program attempts to infer this organismic psycho-Logic using a two-way genetic-epistemological method:

1. Using "unlearned" psychogenetic sequences of tasks, obtained from many different content areas, infer a psycho-Logic that generates sequences equal to observed psychogenetic sequences.
2. Verify the thus obtained psycho-Logic by constructing new tasks and predicting their psychogenetic sequence.

By "unlearned" I mean a psychogenetic sequence that is cross-sectionally reliable using concept-attainment or problem-solving tasks in which intratask or prior learning of the solution for any of the tasks has been avoided.

As with all methodologies, Geneva's methodology tacitly serves to screen out some facets or aspects of the organismic functioning and to emphasize or bring into focus some others. For instance, the emphasis on problem-solving (see P1) ensures that little intratask learning or learning due to repeated task presentations occurs.

Also, Geneva's preference for tasks with reliable and "interesting" developmental traces (stagewise curves or clear inflexion points in the psychogenetic trace—P3) is likely to lead to the exclusion of tasks for which learning and passively acquired past experience, as opposed to active problem solving, are most important. (This is because, for subjects of the same cultural background, the amount of passively acquired learning should increase continuously with age, making it unlikely that interesting stagewise traces will appear in tasks where learning facets are important.)

This minimization of the role of concrete past experiences (which Piaget calls "specific" learning) is accentuated by Geneva's methods of scoring and data analysis which emphasize very molar qualitative patterns of performance that refer to the task as a whole (P2) and are invariant across contents (i.e., concrete situations).

Piaget's methods, which thus minimize learning and maximize conceptual problem solving, while generating a large family of often interrelated genetic–epistemological sequences, have thereby produced a data base and a descriptive theory that greatly clarify the notion of developmental intelligence (i.e., the progressive change that children's problem-solving ability undergoes as it approaches that of sophisticated adults). And, although Piaget's preference for *qualitative* logical models[3] has, in fact, obscured the quantitative aspect of developmental intelligence, his data base has actually made it possible to infer it (Halford, 1970; McLaughlin, 1963; Nassefat,1963; Pascual-Leone, 1963, 1969, 1970). In Geneva's data, developmental intelligence appears, I claim, as a psychogenetically increasing ability to cope with problems and to observe empirically abstract invariants—invariants whose *dimensionality* (or *rank*) increases with age.

I use the term *dimensionality* or *rank* of a problem-solving strategy (or an invariant) to mean the minimal number of organismically distinct semantic dimensions (conditions) that must be considered jointly for the problem to be solved (or the invariant detected). A classic example, well analyzed by Piaget although he *did not* explicitly examine the issue of dimensionality, is that of conservations (Inhelder, Sinclair, & Bovet, 1974; Piaget, 1941, 1956b, 1977; Piaget & Inhelder, 1962). I will analyze conservation of substance, weight, and volume with plasticine, in order to illustrate this notion.

The dimensionality of the substance problem, for the usual identity–reversibility or historical strategy, involves three conditions plus the formulation of the executive problem, which I will designate by the letter e (cf. Pascual-Leone, 1969, 1972, 1976b; Pascual-Leone, Goodman, Ammon, & Subelman, 1978). A representation of this conservation of substance–equivalence task appears in Figure 12.1, and a brief description of the $(3 + e)$ dimensions of this problem follows.

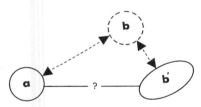

FIGURE 12.1. *The conservation of substance-equivalence task.*

1. The first semantic dimension of this problem is the relation existing between the two original balls of plasticine a and b (value: equal amount versus unequal).
2. The second semantic dimension is the actual transformation T (e.g., rolling a ball on the table), which produces the "sausagelike" piece b' out of b.
3. The third semantic dimension is the relevant type (or class) of transformation to which T belongs (value: quantity-preserving transformation as opposed to quantity-changing ones).

[3] Geneva's theoretical classification of psychogenetic sequences of tasks in terms of vertical, horizontal, and oblique decalages (Inhelder, Sinclair, & Bovet, 1974; Piaget, 1941, 1956a) is not helpful in clarifying the two key issues, stages and equilibration, in terms of modern information-processing theorizing. I will thus omit its discussion here, referring instead to papers where it is available (Pascual-Leone, 1970, 1972; 1976c; Scardamalia, 1977).

A quantity-preserving transformation is recognized by the psychological organism as a spatial rearrangement of the particles ("molecules") of an object which changes its surface appearance (its *perceptual facet*) but does not remove or add "molecules" to the object (preserves the object's quantitative identity). This concept of a quantity-preserving transformation is psychogenetically and structurally interrelated with the organism's representation of the substance (i.e., quantitative identity) of an object as a (naive) "molecular" aggregate of particles, each particle defined by an invariant quantum of surface-mass (mass for which weight and volume are not yet invariant); and such that the whole object is the sum of all the surface–mass quanta. Constructively the substance of an object emerges in the organism as the invariant generated under quantity-preserving transformations.

e. Finally, the *e* dimension or *executive problem*—to estimate whether or not the amounts of substance found in *a* and *b'* are equal. The quantity of substance of an object is first defined by the organism as the object's value under the concrete operation "perceptual exploration of the object's surface, and estimation (in length of scan-paths, exploration time cost, or some other cumulative recording mechanism) of this amount."

Later, after the problems (contradictions) created by this formulation in the context of conservation tasks are solved, quantity of substance comes to be defined in terms of a transperceptual cognitive invariant acquired via logical–structural (L) learning. This transperceptual invarient is constituted by a *habitual* (i.e., habitlike) representation of the distal object in question in terms of its various facets, and of the identify-preserving transformations (e.g., displacements of matter in the case of substance conservation) that transform one facet (aspect) of the object into another.[4] Substance conservation problems are generally solved at about 7 years of age.

[4] Notice that, as Piaget and Inhelder have suggested in different contexts (Piaget & Inhelder, 1948, Chap. XVI; Piaget, Inhelder, & Szemiska, 1948), young children's extensive measurement is *not* numerical but is possibly based on some form of extensive imaginal estimation which, in Piaget's theory of imagery as internalized action (imitation), could well be some form of cumulative recording of exploratory scanpaths. Notice further that a truly accurate estimation of the object's surface facet in terms of scanpaths would require very systematic eye–object exploratory procedures that are only found in older children. This deficiency of the eye exploration technique in estimating substance has been elegantly shown by Norman Anderson (Anderson & Cuneo, 1978) with his methods of functional measurement. Using suitably modified Piagetian conservation tasks, Anderson has shown that 5- and 6-year-olds estimate substance using an additive rule of integration of the two surface-dimension values of width and height. A truly multiplicative rule does not appear until 11 or 12 years while a mixed (additive or multiplicative) rule is found at 8 years of age. This limitation of young children in reliably estimating the substance of an object by its appearance (its surface facet) explains why young children in a substance

Consider now the weight conservation task, which uses the same situation to compare the weights of a and b'. There are several possible strategies and all, as far as I know, have the same rank, although they make use of different actual dimensions. The *identity-reversibility weight strategy*, often discussed by Piaget (1941; Piaget & Inhelder, 1962), requires a fourth dimension in addition to dimensions (1), (2), and (3) of substance equivalence as well as different executive structures. Namely:

4. A (naive) "molecular" representation of matter as constituted by an aggregate of surface-mass particles endowed with their own weight, so that the weight of the object is the sum of these particle weights.

e. The executive problem (which corresponds to the e dimension) is to estimate whether a and b' weigh the same and thus to anticipate the outcome of placing a and b' on the two plates of the balance. The weight of an object is first defined by the organism as its value under the concrete operations "its pressure on the hand" (kinesthetic weight) or "its pressure on the balance plate."

Note that the procedure by which the balance scale translates the relative weight of two objects into a position of the scale marker (values: equal weight, more weight, less weight) has been taught by the tester in advance and thus is chunked with the weight scheme (i.e., 4).

Conservation of weight problems are spontaneously solved at about 9 to 10 years of age, but not sooner.

Consider now the version of conservation of volume with plasticine which Piaget and Inhelder (1962) have called "displacement volume." There are several different strategies for solving this task, all, I believe, of the same rank or dimensionality. I will describe an identity-reversibility strategy since it is similar to those described for substance and weight. Note, however, that when this task is spontaneously solved (at age 11 or 12), children might alternatively adopt a compensation strategy (an integrated comparison of the spatial dimensions of both objects using, for example, a multiplicative rule).

The identity-reversibility strategy for displacement of volume (as well as other strategies for this task) has a dimensionality of $5 + e$. The dimensions in question are: (1), (2), and (3), the same three conditions described for the problem of substance, modified by the condition (4) (i.e., a naive "molecular" conception of matter as an aggregate of particles each endowed with weight and the three-dimensional boundaries of a solid body). The volume of the object is the sum of the volumes of its particles. Volume is construed as the object's value under the concrete

---

equivalence task must in fact resort to the identity-reversibility or "historical" strategy (their memory that $a = b$ and their judgment that b was transformed into b' by means of a quantity-preserving transformation) to solve equivalence conservation problems.

operation "amount of space it occupies that other objects cannot share."

5. A (naive) rule stating that when an object is placed in water, its tendency to sink is related to its weight but the amount of water it displaces is a function of its volume. This rule is needed because the phrasing of the problem question (i.e., which object will raise the water level higher when placed inside the container?) does not explicitly mention volume *and also* because there is an error factor, often exhibited by 10-year-olds, which induces them to believe that the amount of water displaced by the object is a function of its weight.

e. The executive problem in displacement-of-volume conservation is to state which of two objects, when completely immersed in their respective (identical) containers, will raise the water level higher. Notice, again, that the connection between the volume of the objects and the amount of water displaced is not explicitly stated.

The same functional relation between the psychogenetic difficulty of these tasks and the "rank" or dimensionality of their problem-solving strategies can be found in many Piagetian tasks: Problems with dimensionality of $3 + e$ are usually spontaneously solved at 7 or 8 years (if the subjects' background and cognitive style are adequate); problems of rank $4 + e$ are similarly solved at 9 or 10 years; problems of rank $5 + e$ are solved at 11 or 12 years. This intriguing linear relation extends from age 3 or 4 to 15 or 16 years. I hypothesized in 1963 (Pascual-Leone, 1963, 1970) that this growing dimensionality of the tasks found in Geneva's genetic–epistemological sequences was an expression of a situation-free organismic factor whose power increases with age; that is, a central mental "energy" or effort M that subjects can use to extend their field of focal attention (Piaget's centration). The sort of quantitative structural problem analysis required to discover the dimensionality of developmental tasks can be easily dismissed (as Piaget in fact did in 1963 when I proposed to him these theoretical results—Pascual-Leone, 1963) because the method must begin by assuming the strategy (and the structures) used by the subject, and also because the method's abstractness (its distance from the step-by-step concreteness of performance in data protocols) makes it appear, and sometimes become, unreliable. Although its discussion is beyond the scope of this chapter, I might point out that in the last 10 years I have developed a process–structural method of problem analysis that incorporates consideration of organismic factors—a method I call *metasubjective task analysis*—which I believe remedies the deficiencies of dimensionality analysis (see page 276 for an abbreviated illustration).[5]

[5] The adjective "metasubjective" comes from *metasubject*, my term (after Freud's term "metapsychology") for the subject's highly active psycho-Logical organism that is causally responsible for his performances. The prefix "meta," also used in cognition with a

Now, since more explicit experimental work has confirmed the dimensionality predictions for conservation tasks (e.g., Case, 1977; Parkinson, 1975; Pascual-Leone, 1976b), as well as for other Piagetian tasks (e.g., Case, 1974; DeRibaupierre, 1975; Parkinson, 1975; Pascual-Leone, 1969; Pascual-Leone & Smith, 1969; Scardamalia, 1977; Toussaint, 1976) it is appropriate to ask why Piagetian tasks (and often problem-solving tasks in the Gestaltist tradition) are amenable to this type of dimensionality analysis which predicts their stage-level or developmental difficulty. This question may in fact help in understanding the actual significance of Piagetian stages and their necessary connection with the notion of equilibration.

A first hint as to why dimensionality analysis often succeeds with Piagetian tasks is provided by an examination of the error patterns exhibited by subjects of different ages, as well as by the experimental analyses of the tasks. Both methods show, as is already known, that Piagetian tasks usually present *misleading situations* (e.g., Pascual-Leone, 1963, 1969, 1972, 1973, 1974, 1976b, 1976c; Pascual-Leone & Bovet, 1966; Pascual-Leone & Smith, 1969) that can be contrasted with the "facilitating" type of situation represented by typical learning tasks. The situations are misleading because they elicit powerful *error factors* (in Harlow's, 1959, sense) that produce erroneous strategies or responses. Two of the most common kinds of error factors are (*a*) overlearned (*strong habitual*) schemes or structures, developed in other situations where they were relevant, which are irrelevantly elicited in the new situation by salient yet misleading cues; and (*b*) the organismic disposition to produce performances or responses (i.e., percepts, behaviors, cognitive judgments) that are congruent with the dominant features of their perceptual and/or cognitive field of activated figurative schemes. This field factor (*F* factor), often manifested in the form of an "S–R compatibility" disposition (cf. Fitts & Seeger, 1953; Fitts & Posner, 1967; Pascual-Leone, 1969, 1974, 1976b), is misleading in many Piagetian tasks, as the typical errors of young children attest.

In the conservation tasks, these two error factors are quite strong (cf. Pascual-Leone, 1972, 1976b, 1976c; Pascual-Leone, *et al.*, 1978). In substance conservation, for instance, they appear as

1. A habitual scheme that equates amount of perceptual surface with amount of substance. This habitual scheme results from a Logical–structural learning factor (*L* learning) of the organism which internalizes the empirical probabilistically invariant relation usually

---

different (much less appropriate) meaning, is necessary here because the subject's processes can only be described by constructs that presuppose the fiction of an "ideal observer" who could "see" them inside the organism—a fiction that artificial intelligence models do not necessitate, but that computer simulation models still require.

found between the visible surface and the expectable substance of objects. This empirical L structure is in fact an instance of the preoperational structures Piaget calls "unidirectional functions." It constitutes an empirical rule, unwittingly developed and generally true in everyday life, which is as misleading in conservation tasks as it is in the packaging of supermarket products.

2. An F factor that induces subjects to assimilate the conceptual structure of the problem (i.e., the real quantity) to its perceptual structure (i.e., the perceptual quantity). This tendency to organize conceptualizations (e.g., the conservation judgment) in congruence with the perceptual organization of their data is a cognitive manifestation of the well-known S–R compatibility disposition (which in my neoPiagetian theory is explained as due to an organismic factor F, somewhat analogous to the Gestaltist authoctonous Field factor or Prägnanz—see Attneave, 1972; Pascual-Leone, 1976b; Pascual-Leone & Goodman, 1979; Prentice, 1959).

Similar error factors operate in conservation of weight and volume (e.g., the well-known weight–volume illusion). In addition, conservation of weight has a special error factor already mentioned previously: an overlearned and F-facilitated tendency to equate the weight of an object with its kinesthetic pressure on, for example, the hand—an error factor that will induce the child to consider more compact objects (e.g., a ball a) as being heavier (than a sausage b'). The same kinesthetic-weight error factor is often responsible for children's belief that an object (e.g., a long "sausage") which extends over the edge of the balance plate will not weigh as much.

Special error factors are also found in displacement of volume, for example, the F-facilitated one mentioned previously, which would equate the amount of water displaced with weight.

These error factors turn conservation tasks (and many other Piagetian and Gestaltist problem-solving situations) *into mental teasers or (unconscious) cognitive conflicts, where the correct solution (strategy X) to the problems must assert itself, if it can, against the strong interference provided by error-factor-facilitated wrong solutions (strategies Y).*[6]

---

[6] Notice that this internal contradiction generated by Piagetian situations, that is, their eliciting both error strategies and correct strategies, explains the possibility of finding "interesting" (e.g., stagewise or nonmonotonic) developmental traces, including the paradoxical decreasing-developmental traces, well-known to Geneva, which Bower (1974) and others have recently made popular (e.g., Bever, 1970; Mounoud & Bower, 1974; Strauss & Stein, 1978). This is because the strength of the error factors may well (and often does) increase concurrently with the growth of process mechanisms responsible for the correct solution. From an historical–epistemological viewpoint, this relation should of course be phrased the other way around: Geneva's theory-guided search for tasks presenting "interesting" developmental traces (an empirical invariant which underlies the concept of stages) led to the accumulation of tasks whose organismic-process structure presents internal contradictions.

The existence of these conflict situations and their powerful error factors raise the issue of the mechanism that allows strategy X to assert itself against strategies Y, when subjects spontaneously and for the first time solve the problem. This mechanism cannot be "simple" discrimination learning (e.g., Gibson, 1969) or even logical–structural cognitive learning, as Piaget's conception of operational learning or Klahr and Wallace's (1976) production-system model of conservation acquisition would suggest. That is, the orthodox interpretations, according to which cognitive *competences*, such as conservations, are spontaneously acquired *when and if the appropriate logical structures*, such as the grouping of "correspondences" (Piaget, 1977) or the specific production systems (Klahr & Wallace, 1976), *are acquired*, actually beg the question. They merely displace the psychogenetic problem from the spontaneous acquisition of problem-solving strategies—strategies whose dimensionality as empirical invariants is psychogenetically ordered—to the spontaneous acquisition of a transition rule (or "dynamic" model) for passing from a fully developed system of structures (whether "grouping," "group," or production system) to another fully developed system of structures. This move, which just makes the problem "deeper" in the Chomskyan sense (and thus more complicated) is somewhat reminiscent of Harlow's (1959; Harlow & Harlow, 1949) attempt to explain learning and development with the notion of "learning to learn."[7]

Instead of asking (as Tolman and the early Piaget did) about the origin of performance (or its development or its learning), we now ask about the "origin" of the ORIGIN of performance. In Piaget's formulation, the ORIGIN is, for each stage level, the corresponding psycho-Logical model; the "origin" is the equilibration process of the "regulatory" mechanisms—the still unknown mechanisms that productively resolve conflicts among schemes (often from different stage levels) and that I mentioned previously and described elsewhere in more detail (Pascual-Leone et al., 1978; Pascual-Leone & Goodman, 1979).

One merit of Piaget's formulation is that it highlights (in the qualitative psycho-Logical style which is Piaget's trademark) the two main descriptive–structural aspects of the data (stages and equilibration) *and* their interrelationship (i.e., the fact that descriptive stages usually appear in the context of equilibration processes—that is, in cognitive-conflict situations). In other words, Geneva has contributed (although it has not formulated) two major puzzles or problematic empirical laws:

1. The *psychogenetic* ordering of tasks is often predictable from the tasks' *dimensionality or rank*. (This is the factual basis of the descriptive stage theory.)

---

[7] I need not emphasize that this notion—contributed under various guises by Hunt, (1961), Gagné (1968), Gelman (1968), etc.—is still the basic "transition rule" proposed by modern behaviorists to explain away the psychogenetic problem.

2. Tasks whose developmental trace is both "interesting," in Geneva's sense, and robust (replicable across subjects and across content variations) present the structural characteristics of cognitive-conflict situations. (This is the factual basis of the descriptive equilibration theory.)

There are two problems (deficiencies) with the classic Piagetian formulation: First is the attempt to make one descriptive–structural model, equilibration, the cause (i.e., the generative *and* psychogenetic constructive model) of the other descriptive–structural model, the stages, when in fact both coexist as structural aspects of the data base. Second is the attempt to make the stage models (i.e., the abstract categorical descriptions of molar empirical invariances) into causal determinants of performance (cf. Pascual-Leone, 1976c).

Symptoms of these deficiencies are numerous. One illustration is the lack of distinction within classic Piagetian theory between the enduring or *habitual structures* (*schemes*, that is, the subject's repertoire of permanently stored information units) and the *ephemeral structures* which the observer reads in the subjects' performance as empirical invariants. The latter do not represent habitual structures, but rather *performatory structures* which result from the organisms' novel or truly novel (see page 283) syntheses of performances—creative acts (equilibration processes). Clear examples of these syntheses are often found in the Piagetian data in children's typical errors and in the "compromise" performances that often result from conflicts among strategies (e.g., Inhelder & Chipman, 1976; Inhelder, Sinclair, & Bovet, 1974; Pascual-Leone, 1969, 1976b). Similar equilibration processes are also found (and this is often disregarded) in the spontaneous generative construction of correct performances for logical–structural tasks such as conservations or inclusion of classes when they are solved for the first time. On this first occasion, the generative-construction mechanism causing the performatory synthesis cannot be a learned habitual structure (as is tacitly or explicitly assumed in AI models) because situation-specific structures cannot be learned without experience. To assume the contrary involves a *learning paradox* (cf. Pascual-Leone, 1972, 1973, 1976d; Pascual-Leone *et al.*, 1978).

To resolve this paradox one must either conclude that these generative–construction mechanisms are innate habitual structures, and assert, as Beilin (1971) did some years ago, that Piaget's is a neomaturationist theory, or, alternatively, one must infer that these mechanisms are little understood situation-free organismic factors of which the F, L, and M factors mentioned previously are but three illustrations (cf. Pascual-Leone, 1969, 1973, 1976a, 1976b, 1976c, 1976d; Pascual-Leone & Goodman, 1979; Pascual-Leone *et al.*, 1978).

Piaget's (1971) strong reply to Beilin and his many other frequent disclaimers indicate that Geneva's intuitive theory (tacitly) adopts the organismic-factors alternative: These are Geneva's fuzzy "regulatory mechanisms." This conclusion, however, suggests the theoretical artificiality of separating the ORIGIN (the psycho-Logical models defining stages) and the "origin" of performance (the regulatory mechanisms, that is, equilibration or the "transition rule"). This is because regulatory mechanisms are necessary to explain not only psychogenetic constructivity, but generative constructivity as well.

To illustrate the crucial point just made about regulatory mechanisms (i.e., equilibration, situation-free organismic factors), I will refer again to the acquisition of substance conservation, conducting, in a summary fashion, a step-by-step process-structural *and* organismic analysis of this task. This summary also serves as an abbreviated illustration of the sort of *metasubjective* (i.e., process-structural and organismic) *task analysis* that I mentioned earlier (cf. Pascual-Leone, 1976a, 1976b, 1976d, 1978b).

Children who are faced with the conservation task for the first time may be led, by the saliency of the here-and-now situation, to compare a and b' directly (see Figure 12.1). This is expression, we could say, of a perceptual–analytical executive which I described previously (dimension e of substance conservation). Its manifestation is the child's comparison of a and b' in terms of *one* of their dimensions, width or length. Up to 9 or 10 years, children are not able to carry out the comparison of a and b' on both dimensions simultaneously (see Footnote 4); this limitation may be caused by the child's insufficient M power (Pascual-Leone, 1963, 1969, 1976b, 1973). Since young children (4-, 5-, and 6-year-olds) carry out the comparison using only one (simple or compound) perceptual dimension (width or length, or an additive combination of both), the misleading organismic factors L and F mentioned above will tend to apply and produce a wrong response (i.e., $a < b'$ or $b' < a$).

As Piaget has emphasized (1956b, 1975), older children (6- or 7-year-olds) may tend to decenter (a decentration executive!) and focus again on the comparison of a and b' using *the other* perceptual dimension. Since the application of L and F factors to one or the other perceptual comparison yields contradictory results ($a < b'$ versus $b' < a$), subjects with sufficient M power and "memory retrieval structures" for simultaneously recalling the two results (which may well happen spontaneously at the age of 6 years by virtue of already acquired remembering executives) should experience great "cognitive dissonance" or "horror" of contradictions vis-à-vis them.[8] This "horror" of contradiction, found

[8] Theoretically an M power of $e + 2$ available to 5- and 6-year-olds, should make it possible to retrieve two independent events (results) and compare them. In fact, a variety of Piagetian tasks show that 6 years of age is the time when children experience for the first time a great need for internal consistency, which suggests their comparison of two independent, past acts. White and Pillemar (1979) have in fact proposed that flexible memory-retrieval strategies require an M power of at least $e + 2$. They explain in this manner the very common infantile amnesia found prior to 5 years of age.

at all ages (think of babies' "fear of strangers"), must be an expression of another situation-free organismic factor, that is, a disposition to maintain the *principle of internal consistency*. (This aspect of equilibration, the organismic pursuit of *Law*fulness, has often been emphasized by Piaget.) The innate aversive properties of internal inconsistency (which this "Law" disposition creates) would prompt the child's psycho-Logical system to abandon ("lose faith" in) the perceptual–analytical executive and attempt solution of the problem using a different executive (cf. Case, 1977; Minsky & Papert, 1972; Piaget, 1975; Pascual-Leone, 1969, 1976b). In this conjuncture, an "historical" (i.e., identity-reversibility) executive could take over; that is, an executive "suggesting" to recall the events that occurred prior to the problem situation in order to see whether they help to decide between the contradictory alternatives. Notice that this is a very general executive which preoperational children already possess in their repertoire. This historical executive, together with suitable retrieval structures could, *if the subject has enough M power for "retrieving" all the relevant schemes simultaneously*, generate a cognitive map or problem representation such as the one of Figure 12.1. The main relevant schemes of this cognitive map are the dimensions (1), (2), and (3) of the substance conservation problem which I discussed previously. Dimension (1), the original equality of substance between a and b (i.e., $a = b$) appears as a double arrow in Figure 12.1. *This scheme, $a = b$* (which results from the perceptual estimation of a and the match of this estimate with b), *must be kept alive as the child "retrieves" or computes the equality of substance between b and b'* (i.e., $b = b'$). This last computation requires applying a quantity-preserving transformation *type* or classifier CLASS T (this is dimension 3 of the task) onto the actual transformation-event T which led to the change of b into b' (this is the task's dimension 2). The result of this classification (type-coding) of T by CLASS T leads to the inference that $b = b'$.

This analysis suggests that an M power of $e + 3$ is necessary for the generative construction and maintenance of the cognitive map of Figure 12.1 (cf. Pascual-Leone, 1969, 1972, 1976b; Pascual-Leone et al., 1978). Since such an M power is available only at the age of 7 years (e.g., Pascual-Leone, 1970, 1978a), 6-year-olds could not usually generate the cognitive map of Figure 12.1 — in them, one of the double arrows would be missing. Note that this state of affairs explains the "empirical-reversibility" type of erroneous response occasionally given by 6-year-olds. (An example of these "empirical-reversibility" responses could be the following child's reply: "If you roll b' back into b, it will be the same amount as a but it is more now because b' is longer." In this child's cognitive map, the quantity-preserving transformation classifier CLASS T (i.e., task dimension 3) would not have been activated for lack of sufficient M power).

Children who can spontaneously generate a cognitive map such as

Figure 12.1 *still must infer* the relation holding between *a* and *b'* in terms of quantity, in order to solve the problem. A habitual structure (a learned rule) inferring $a = b'$ from $a = b$ and $b = b'$ (or some pragmatically equivalent rule) would explain the subject's access to the conserving response at this point. Such explanation assumes that this rule can be acquired spontaneously *before* successful solution of the conservation problem.

A quantification rule of this sort is in fact implicit in Piaget's model of conservation—his new "infralogical grouping of correspondences" (Piaget, 1975, 1977)—and it is explicit in Klahr and Wallace's (1976, p. 131) semantically similar production-system model for "estimated" quantity (productions PD.CON 7 and PD.CON 4 of production system PS. QC 5). Unfortunately, a rule of this sort cannot be acquired *prior* to solution of the continuous-quantity conservation problem because of its abstractness: As an empirical semantic–pragmatic invariant, this type of rule could only be abstracted after continuous-quantity conservation responses have been otherwise produced and have been empirically confirmed via validation of the expectancies implied by them. Geneva (e.g., Inhelder, Sinclair, & Bovet, 1974) as well as Klahr and Wallace (1976) assume that a rule of this sort is first learned in the context of discrete-quantities conservation (e.g., conservation of the amount of marbles in a row when the density of the row is changed by spreading the marbles out) and is later extended or "generalized" to continuous quantities. The problem is that this account ignores the existence of *error factors*, the misleading *L* structure and *F* factor described previously that turn the conservation problem into a mental teaser. Since the strength of these error factors is much greater in a continuous-quantity task than in a discrete-quantity task (and even more so if the number of "discrete" objects used is small, so that the "subitizing quantifier" of Klahr and Wallace can apply), the *spontaneous* "generalization" of the quantification rule from discontinuous to continuous quantities cannot be hypothesized. Interference from the error factors *should* prevent the *spontaneous* generalization of this rule.

Since the hypothesis of a quantification rule leads to a *learning paradox* (i.e., to a hypothetical spontaneous generalization that contradicts the empirical laws of learning), some unlearned (situation-free) organismic factor(s) *other than learning* must be the cause of the children's *spontaneous* inference that $a = b'$.

I have proposed (e.g., Pascual-Leone, 1969, 1972, 1974, 1976b; Pascual-Leone et al., 1978; Parkinson, 1975) that the organismic factor in question is the *F* factor mentioned previously. Indeed, *if* the cognitive map of Figure 12.1 is maintained (*M* centrated) by the child and *if* he feels compelled to give an answer to the question "Is there as much amount in *a* as in *b'*? (perhaps because he likes to please the experimenter—an affective factor discussed later), he may experience the cognitive-map terms $a = b$ and $b = b'$ as a mental stimulus-situation (S) which (much as in the Heider-inspired theory of balance graphs—for example, Flament, 1963; Zajonc, 1960) induces, via the F factor's S–R compatibility disposition, the tendency to respond (R) with a relation $a = b'$ that is congruent with the relation found in both terms of the cognitive map (which is the S component).

Consider the two important points which this abbreviated metasubjective task analysis illustrates:

1. The regulatory mechanisms of equilibration (i.e., in my conceptualization, the situation-free organismic factors L, F, M, affective factors, etc.), are necessary to explain the generative construction of the subject's problem-solving process—the very process that the psycho-Logical models which define stages are supposed to account for.

2. The only executive processes we need to assume, in subjects who for the first time spontaneously solve a stage-characteristic task, are (relative to the complexity of the required performance) exceedingly simple, general, or global. In fact, these necessary executives may lack the systemic closure of Geneva's algebraic models and of computer-simulation programs. This generality and lack of computational closure make it possible to understand why the learning paradox mentioned previously does not apply to the human organism. This assumption of very simple, general, or global executives leaves unexplained, however, the manner in which the subject's relatively complex performance is produced, and why the organism does not get jammed instead. This explanation is provided by *other* situation-free organismic factors that, *in (hidden) interaction among themselves and with the executives*, step-by-step construct serendipitously the subject's spontaneous and new performance (De Ribaupierre & Pascual-Leone, 1979; Pascual-Leone *et al.*, 1978; Pascual-Leone & Goodman, 1979).

Summing up this section, contrary to common belief, the data base and methods of Geneva, when closely examined, indicate that stages and equilibration are approximative valid *descriptive* models. Their lack of step-by-step representation and other idiosyncracies make them nonetheless too global or even inapplicable for many purposes.

Inhelder's recommendation (e.g., Inhelder, Sinclair, & Bovet, 1974) that a "dynamic" theory is needed to supplement Piagetian structuralist theory, is an acknowledgment of these conclusions. Her description of the problem, however, is misleading, for it maintains the illusion that Piaget's own equilibration models[9] are more than descriptive (i.e.,

---

[9] There are at least two, related but different, models of equilibration offered by Piaget. The one proposed originally (Piaget, 1956b) focused on the *growing power for synthesizing* a correct performance in the presence of strong misleading situational factors. The more recent one (Piaget, 1975) focuses on the *cognitive conflict* itself: conflict among schemes or scheme systems.

data to be explained). She leaves the impression that they are *explanatory* foundations of the to-be-developed "dynamic" theory. The solution to the Piagetian problem is, I suggested previously, a constructive theory that, in addition to schemes and structures (or productions and production systems!), contains organismic factors which can explain the processes of equilibration and the why and how of general stages.

A Comparison with the AI NeoPiagetian Approach of Carnegie–Mellon

The conclusion that situation-free organismic factors exist—a conclusion demanded by the Piagetian data—runs counter to modern AI theorizing about humans, which the Carnegie-Mellon school has pioneered (e.g., Newell & Simon, 1972; Simon, 1969). For my purposes here, the Carnegie-Mellon theorizing can be summarized in four points:

T1. Humans are just information-processing machines with limited processing resources. Consequently, their processing work is carried out in a serial or step-by-step manner.

T2. The psychological organism of humans contains little more than situation-specific programs—the AI translation of an old but still prevalent empiricist prejudice (e.g., Dawes, 1975; Simon, 1969; Simon & Newell, 1971).

T3. Information is represented in the organism by means of semantic –pragmatic conditionals or productions. Productions could in fact be considered an explication of the Piagetian notion of schemes (cf. Pascual-Leone, 1970, 1976a; Pascual-Leone & Smith, 1969) were it not that Piaget's very active assimilatory function is missing (schemes, unlike productions, tend to apply under *minimal* conditions of satisfaction).

T4. Productions are released if and when a match to their conditions is found in STM. Short-term memory is a situation-free organismic resource (possibly the exception to T2) which has a double function: It serves as a short-term store and as what I would call a "field of activation," that is, the imaginary "place" where the outputs of productions (or the environmental input) are in a state of activation capable of releasing other, matching, productions.[10]

Consistent with these types of presuppositions, information-processing AI researchers have applied themselves to studying and simu-

[10] This "field of activation" would correspond in Piagetian theory to the set of activated figurative schemes in the repertoire. Note that in my neoPiagetian theory I define the "field of activation" differently, that is, as the total set of schemes activated in the repertoire at a given moment. My "field of activation" includes (among others) figurative, operative, and executive schemes.

lating the step-by-step performances of subjects in specific tasks. Subject types (human differences) are not controlled nor are they systematically compared. Further, performance comparisons across types of tasks are not carried out in any systematic manner, certainly not as thoroughly as in Piaget's psychogenetic method of tracing and comparing the developmental patterns of systematically varied types of problems. This type of methodology and data base (I refer to human information-processing researchers in general) has not and could not expose the organismic empirical invariants (the stages and equilibration problems) described previously. The epistemological reasons are clear: "Fine-grained" step-by-step data repeatedly obtained from a single task with one or more subjects (such that no subject is ever tested across tasks) must *necessarily* generate structural invariants which reflect constraints belonging to the type of task—for no developmental or human differences organismic constraint is allowed to emerge as an empirical invariant (cf. Pascual-Leone & Goodman, 1979; Pascual-Leone & Sparkman, 1980).

A consequence of this methodological straitjacket is that theoretical presuppositions (T2), (T3), and (T4) are never properly tested and are taken by many as true by fiat. Just as behaviorism succeeded for some 30 years in repressing the gestaltists' empirical problem of the field factor, instead of facing it directly (hence this problem is still haunting us), so information-processing psychology may, by fiat, manage to repress Piaget's empirical problems of stages and equilibration. That would be unfortunate, indeed, because properly modified information-processing psychology could well succeed in clarifying them. To advance this line of positive thinking, I will outline how the problems of stages and equilibration might be solved within an information-processing framework, and at the same time comment on Klahr and Wallace's (1976) proposed solution.

The problem of stages, as I suggested earlier, has as its underlying (idealized) structural invariant a family of interrelated genetic–epistemological sequences; that is, the equivalence of the two orderings of tasks generated, respectively, by dimensionality analyses (or, better, by metasubjective task analyses) and by empirical psychogenetic sequences of tasks. To accept this formulation is to be compelled to infer, for the sake of parsimony, that stages are manifestations, *in suitable problem-solving situations*, of a limited and developmentally growing mental resource which I will call M without prejudging its nature. This M problem, raised by Piaget's problem of stages, has an obvious relation to (T4), in particular to the size of STM. The relationship is not simple, however, because mental-processing or mental-monitoring (i.e., M) constraints may only be clearly evident in the context of suitably misleading *problem-solving* situations (such as Piaget's tasks). This may be so because learning and field factors interact with M to hide (or change) its manifestations (e.g., Case, 1977; De Ribaupierre & Pascual-Leone, 1979; Parkinson, 1975; Pascual-Leone, 1969, 1970, 1976b; Pascual-Leone & Bovet, 1966, 1967; Pascual-Leone & Smith, 1969; Pascual-Leone & Goodman, 1979). To clearly separate the role of learning and the role of M, roles that are too often confounded (e.g., Chi, 1977; Simon, 1972, 1974; Trabasso & Foellinger, 1978; Brainerd, 1979; Klahr, this volume), it is probably necessary to remove the straitjacket of the one-task-at-a-time methodology and to make a clear theoretical distinction between the *"field of activation"* (see T4) and the *boosting* ("rehearsal") function of M (cf. Bernback, 1970, Pascual-Leone, 1963, 1970; Pascual-Leone & Smith, 1969). This distinction is necessary because the "field-of-activation" state can also be produced by "learning" (i.e., habitual structures), field factors, or affective factors, independent of M. This point is well illustrated in a major change that Klahr and Wallace (1976) have introduced in their theoretical formulations: Instead of a single STM facility, they now have five (echoic, iconic, auditory, visual, semantic). This change brings the notion of STM closer to the Piagetian (or neoPiagetian) notion of a field of activated figurative schemes classi-fied by content, and ensures that Klahr and Wallace's repertoire of pro-ductions (LTM) corresponds to the operative schemes and structures of Piagetians. This move clearly disambiguates STM and removes the pos-sibility of harshly interpreting M as being *just* STM. Should informa-tion-processing psychologists come to accept the need for a mental en-ergy (mental-effort mechanism) monitored by an executive and capable of bringing a scheme (figurative or operative) to a state of activation dominance[11], they would have to define a new activation-boosting oper-ator which is content-free and which applies on the different STM con-tents to assign a dominance weight to the conditions therein.

Consistent with their clear although tacit rejection of the M energy notion, Klahr and Wallace (1976) propose cognitive learning as the "transition rule" for cognitive development. I hope that my analysis of the Piagetian methodology, and the example of conservation discussed previously, made clear that learning (or chunking) are unlikely candi-dates for explaining the descriptive–structural fact of Piaget's stages, for they lead to either a neomaturationism or to a learning paradox. In any event, their approach is truly neoPiagetian, although for reasons different from mine and which I do not quite like. As does Geneva, they break the problem down into two issues: the ORIGIN of performance, and the "origin" of the ORIGIN. The ORIGIN (fittingly, with a computer-lan-guage capitalization) is the production-system model for the task in

---

[11] In the current Carnegie-Mellon theory, the degree of dominance of a production would probably be related to its ordinal number (its try-next number) in the list of pro-ductions being used.

question. The "origin" (which the Carnegie-Mellon group would also like to capitalize) is a "deeper" system of situation-free productions (their Tiers 2 and 3) which are still in a very programmatic state as models. That "deeper" system plays the role of Geneva's regulatory mechanisms, sharing with them the characteristic fuzziness of "deep" organismic constructs (cf. Pascual-Leone, 1976a). An "a priori" reduction of organismic processing systems to known AI systems (cf. Newell & Simon, 1976; Pascual-Leone & Goodman, 1979; Weizenbaum, 1976) shows in Klahr and Wallace's insistence that these regulatory mechanisms *are productions*. This insistence arbitrarily preempts possible solutions to the stage and equilibration problems that production systems may not be able to accommodate.

To give some concrete basis to this suggestion, I would point out that Klahr and Wallace do not discuss those aspects in the Piagetian data which justify the admittedly fuzzy Piagetian model of equilibration. I refer in particular to three salient types of data, which I will call "truly novel performances," "cognitive-conflict situations," and "motivational or affective paradoxes."

The concept of a truly novel performance (cf. Pascual-Leone, 1973, 1976a) becomes clearer when contrasted with simple transfer of learning (i.e., learned performance) and with novel performances. A *learned performance* is, for instance, a learning set, once it has been overlearned. Learned performances are explicitly represented in the subject's repertoire by means of one structure. A *novel performance* is a problem-solving act that involves the application of some already available *situation-specific* procedures which conjointly, by virtue of their combinatorial possibilities, generate the performance. In other words, a novel performance is not explicitly represented in the subject's repertoire (LTM) by any given structure but is *implicitly represented* in the constructive possibilities that the repertoire of structures as a generative system can produce. Novel performances are of course the type of performances that information-processing–AI science has so clearly demonstrated against the behavioristic attempt to reduce everything to learned performances. *Truly novel performances* are performances that are neither implicitly nor explicitly represented in the repertoire, but which result from the interactions between the structures found in the repertoire and the situation-free system of organismic factors—perhaps the biogenetic hardware of the human system, whether or not this system can be best modeled by Carnegie-Mellon's production systems. An alternative definition of truly novel performances, which is less metatheoretical and perhaps more congenial to the experimental and AI minds, can be phrased as follows: These are performances that result from the interaction (integration) of several productions or production systems (schemes or structures) which together codetermine the performance, but such that *no pre-existent*, learned or innate, integration mechanism of the situation-specific production type (e.g., a suitable goal organization in the productions or a special high-level goal production system) that might monitor the performance in question is likely to exist.

These definitions of learned, novel, and truly novel performances are unavoidably metasubjective definitions (i.e., they assume an ideal observer who can "see" beyond the subject's performance and inside his psychological organization). Since this ideal observer's metasubjective characterization is easily accomplished for computers but difficult for humans, to prove that a given performance is truly novel one must in fact disprove the more parsimonious assumptions that it is either learned or merely novel. Excellent examples of truly novel performances are in fact found among the so-called "compromise" (displacement, substitution, etc.) or error performances described by psychoanalysts, ethologists, Piagetians, and others, in the context of both "cool" problem-solving and affect-controlled behavior. Some other quite clear but more subtle cases are found (as suggested previously) in the generative construction of correct performances in misleading Piagetian situations, such as conservations (cf. Pascual-Leone, 1972, 1973, 1976b). This aspect of conservations is neglected by Klahr and Wallace.

To illustrate now the case of truly novel performances, let me use the Piagetian water level task, a task that I and my collaborators have studied quite thoroughly. This task also serves as an additional example of a cognitive-conflict situation. The water level task (WLT) or conservation of the horizontality of water (Piaget & Inhelder, 1948) uses an empty bottle (rectangular in my example) and/or a paper outline of this bottle. Items are generated by successively placing the bottle in various positions. The subject is instructed to imagine that the bottle is half-filled with water, and asked to indicate on the bottle (or draw on the outline) the expected surface line of the water, when the water is resting.

Figure 12.2 presents some of the reliable error types that have been found in children and/or field-dependent adults who tackle the task. Errors 1 and 4 could easily be interpreted from an empiricist viewpoint as learned performances because, in the normal environment, bottles are usually standing on their base or occasionally on their side, causing the water to move to these positions. It could therefore be said (and some other evidence supports this view) that 1 and 4 represent learned error factors, overgeneralizations of ecologically frequent perceptual configurations (figurative schemes) made possible by the subject's failure to consider the position of the bottle relative to its support. A similar interpretation might even be applied to error pattern 5, by considering it a novel-performance combination of 1 and 4.

The learned performance interpretation, however, is not sufficient because a host of experiments show that the angle of deviation of the subject's water line from the horizontal (his WLT score), which is largely

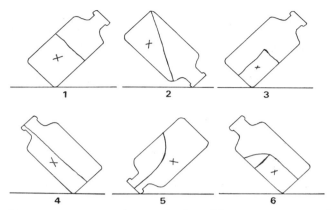

FIGURE 12.2. *Incorrect responses on the water level test. The instructions are to draw the water line as it would appear in a bottle half full of water, and to mark the water with an x. Some of these errors are examples of truly novel behavior.*

determined by responses such as #1, #4, and #5 (the commonest error responses), is predictable from performance in a number of completely different tasks that have nothing to do with water in bottles (Pascual-Leone, 1969, 1974).

One such task, the copy-the-stripe task (CST) (Pascual-Leone, 1969) is illustrated in Figure 12.3. In the CST, subjects must copy onto a paper outline of a bottle the vertical or horizontal stripes they see through a real bottle presented with a striped background placed behind it. Figure 12.3 illustrates what the subjects see, including the distortion of the stripes produced by refraction through the glass of the bottle.

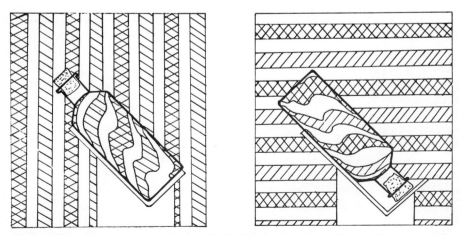

FIGURE 12.3. *A drawing of the stimulus display for the copy-the-stripe test. The instructions are to draw the stripes as they appear through the actual bottle, on a provided bottle outline. The cross-hatched lines represent black stripes; simple hatched lines represent gray stripes.*

There are several items depicting different bottle positions, and the CST score is the sum of item deviation scores of the subject's (normalized) stripe copies from the corresponding vertical or horizontal stripes. The responses of both children and adults tend to deviate in the direction of the bottom of the bottle—thus covarying with the bottle position. Clearly the CST is not a conceptual *but* a perceptual–motor task that contains a strong operative F factor (an S–R compatibility disposition) compelling subjects to draw the stripes (this is the R pattern) parallel to the dominant features of the bottle (this is the frame or S display). Performance in the CST is *very* highly correlated with WLT at all ages, and both tasks load heavily on the same factor-analytic (varimax or oblimax) rotated factor. This factor, incidentally, is Witkin's field-dependence–independence cognitive-style dimension—a structural dimension that is not content specific. Even more important for experimental psychologists are the following data: When, after having copied the stripes on the bottle outlines of CST, subjects are asked to use *the same paper outlines* for the problem questions of WLT, their water-line responses are affected in statistically significant and predictable ways by the misleading F factor constituted by the CST stripes they have just drawn.

All these (and a host of other) facts clearly point to the conclusion that Responses 1, 4, and 5 are not simply examples of learned or novel performances; their generative processes must also contain truly novel determinants since they are affected by organismic (F) factors, which are not task-related and cannot be learned. In addition, these performances are predictable from completely different tasks which, like WLT itself, exhibit strong cognitive-style organismic differences.

These conclusions are further confirmed by WLT error patterns such as 2, 3, and 6 in Figure 12.2. Pattern 2 seems to be an odd but common "compromise" performance between 1 and 4 (i.e., between the subject's knowledge that water "falls" to the lower part of the bottle and the F-determined "attraction" of the salient upper and lower corners of the bottle). One reaches this conclusion: (*a*) by questioning the subjects; (*b*) from the finding that, developmentally, 2 tends to appear *after* 1 and 4; and (*c*) from the curious fact that using two treatment conditions (bottles with a water stopper and without a stopper) and two styles of subjects (field-independent and field-dependent), field-dependent subjects (but not field-independent) exhibit Error 2 and related responses significantly more often in the no-stopper condition than in the stopper condition.

Finally, Patterns 3 and 6, never found in young children, were produced in 1964 by a field-dependent Brooklyn College physical-education student, of excellent academic standing and above-normal IQ. The response patterns were reliable, for he filled a whole set of eight tilted bottle outlines with them. I was so shocked with his responses that hesitantly I asked, pointing to the neat right angle: "Are you sure that it will be this way?" He blushed[12], reflected briefly, and said: "No, it will be that way!" proceeding carefully to smooth out the angle from the sharp configuration of 3 to a round one similar to 6.

There is another, more complex, type of truly novel performance that leads to *correct* solutions in misleading problem situations. In misleading situations, there are often error factors (such as these of WLT) which induce potent misleading strategies for coping with the task. These misleading strategies enter into conflict with the correct strategy (i.e., the one that eventually leads to the correct solution of the task). Since the correct strategy (Strategy A) must overcome the potency of the error factors (Strategy B) and Strategy A cannot be overlearned *prior to* solving this type of task (the contrary implies a learning paradox), the strength to overcome B that A exhibits the first time the task is spontaneously solved must come from some situation-free organismic factor. This factor is, I claim, M. A dimensionality analysis as well as a more careful metasubjective task analysis of WLT shows that the M demand of the various developmentally ordered WLT items corresponds to the known M capacity of children at the age when the WLT items in question are passed. Furthermore, experiments show that the requisite M capacity is a necessary (but not sufficient) condition for subjects to be able to pass the WLT items. Again, I must emphasize that M has already been measured in a variety of ways using very different sorts of tasks (for references see Pascual-Leone & Goodman, 1979; Pascual-Leone *et al.*, 1978).

The implications of these results (i.e., the existence of truly novel performances and of cognitive-conflicts) for information-processing– AI approaches, are, I believe, far reaching. Artificial intelligence researchers have repeatedly argued that their approach is superior because they prove the *sufficiency* of the strategies they propose (e.g., Klahr & Wallace, 1976; Newell & Simon, 1972, 1976; Pylyshyn, 1978). However, "sufficiency" is unwittingly used by them in two senses: One, which is legitimate, is to the effect that the simulation shows that the strategy being simulated works with the computer; the other sense, which is questionable, is that the strategy being simulated works with human systems.

---

[12] It is not uncommon for intelligent, field-dependent adults, when confronted in this oblique manner with their cognitive blunders, to react with symptoms of embarrassment – an emotional defense mechanism so often found in the affective domain. This conduct suggests that somehow they "know" their response to be wrong but cannot figure out the right answer. This is clear indirect evidence that they are experiencing a cognitive conflict: Two strategies, one correct, one incorrect, are competing, and the wrong one succeeds in controlling the output. Kurt Goldstein (1940) already noticed this sort of conduct in normal adults who use "concrete" thinking. Unlike brain-damaged patients whom they may initially resemble in their performance, normal "concrete-thinking" adults will react with symptoms of embarrassment when confronted with their errors and will often, with some help, produce the correct performance.

The equation of computers (as currently programmed) and human systems cannot be done by dictum (cf. Newell & Simon, 1976). Rather, it must be demonstrated experimentally by showing that the same computer-based information-processing simulation (IPS) can in fact exhibit in its output all the peculiarities of human performances, such as truly novel performances and cognitive (or affective) conflicts. Failure to prove this raises the issue of whether the computer-based model is humanly sufficient, for factors may exist in humans that prevent the computer-based strategy from succeeding.

To help formulate this equilibration problem in terms of AI research problems, consider cognitive-conflict situations in terms of their functional structure. These situations (such as WLT, CST, ambiguous linguistic sentences, or Witkin's embedded figures task and rod-and-frame task) elicit two incompatible alternative strategies–one relevant (A) and the other irrelevant (B); furthermore, Strategy B is initially stronger *and* shares with A many of the same "STM" elements, in the sense that they match elements of the conditions of both B-productions and A-productions. In terms of the IPS concept, the problem of cognitive-conflict situations corresponds, at least in part, to the issue of how an IPS which begins dealing with a task in terms of problem space B' can, in the course of its information-processing, change its task representation to problem space A'. This issue of how problem spaces (alternative task representations) can be *spontaneously* generated and changed is one that AI researchers seem to have neglected (Pascual-Leone, 1977, 1978b; Pascual-Leone & Goodman, 1979; Pylyshyn, 1978).

Similar unsolved issues which are intimated by Piaget's fuzzy notion of equilibration are the relations between affect and cognition. The fact that cognitive styles (affect-related organismic variables) are important for predicting subjects' performance in Piagetian tasks already points in this direction. But there is even more: The Piagetian tasks which present an interesting developmental trace (stages) often require, motivationally speaking, delayed reward and informational uncertainty. The friendly experimenter presents a problem and the child strives to satisfy the experimenter by solving the problem *to his own* satisfaction, because the experimenter will not express an opinion on the results. If this motivational structure of the Piagetian method is changed and, for example, the experimenter is unfriendly or provides informational feedback (conveys by means of reinforcement or some other means his view of how the problem should be solved), the task often loses or changes its stage-wise developmental trace, while becoming (respectively) harder or easier. Hundreds of more or less successful learning experiments with Piagetian tasks, where this motivational structure has been changed, prove the dependency of the Piagetian empirical stages on the motivational structure of the task. A case in point is the extinction experiments with conservation tasks (e.g., Robert & Charbonneau, 1977) where the presence of an affectively appealing human model can dramatically change the subject's performance. These results do not disprove the reality of stages in Piagetian situations, but show that different results are obtained in other situations. To my mind, they show (as the role of misleading L and F factors also do) the inadequacy of approaches which distinguish between the ORIGIN of the performance (i.e., rational–structural solving procedures) and the "origin" of the ORIGIN.

More appropriate, in my opinion, would be to represent the organism as a system constituted by a repertoire of highly active situation-specific program-demons (the schemes and structures) which usually, combined in compatible clusters, rush to synthesize performance according to the pecking order of their assimilatory strength (dominance weight); this assimilatory strength being affected by a number of situation-free organismic resources or factors, such as the M, L (i.e., overlearned logical structures of *any* operational level), C (i.e., concrete content schemes or structures), and A (purely affective schemes), factors that I, somewhat obliquely, suggested previously. With this view of the organism, the distinction between "origin" and ORIGIN vanishes, and empirical stages, equilibration, etc., become manifestations, conditioned by appropriate situations, of dynamic formulas (or relative strength) of organismic factors (i.e., M, L, C, F, A, . . .) as the alternative strategies they boost compete to determine performance (cf. Pascual-Leone, 1969; Pascual-Leone & Goodman, 1979; Pascual-Leone *et al.*, 1978).

Some Methods for Studying Stages and Equilibration in a Quantitative Manner

IF, as I claim and Piaget's data suggest, there are organismic factors or resources that are not elicited by the specific situational content but, rather, are mobilized in any situation by the *generic* pattern and the *type* of schemes and structures in the repertoire currently activated; *if* these mobilized organismic resources in turn can affect the subject's performance by differentially changing the assimilatory strength of activated scheme clusters; and, finally, *if* these organismic factors represent underlying dimensions of variation in human differences (development included)—human difference variations which are in fact the data base (the empirical invariants) leading to the factors' discovery, *then* the methods for studying these organismic factors must necessarily combine within the same study (or series of studies) four ingredients: (*a*) *Piagetian designs*, (*b*) experimental manipulation (variation) of *types* of tasks, (*c*) human-difference (psychometric) control and manipulation of the types of subjects used in the studies, and (*d*) the use of a *constructive-*

rationalist (and inductive–hypothetico-deductive) *method* for designing or choosing the tasks and/or subject types to be utilized.

By *Piagetian designs* I mean studies where the tasks' structural type and the subjects' age-group type are held constant or treated as independent variables; subjects and tasks are varied, and the dependent variable(s) is (are) the developmental trace(s) of the obtained patterns of performance. The first, descriptive–structural goal of these Piagetian or neoPiagetian studies is the induction of empirical equivalence-classes of tasks in terms of the developmental traces they generate—classes of tasks which serve to validate or correct the theoretically based psycho-Logical types of tasks. Notice that the Piagetian structuralist design generalizes to any human-difference dimension provided that there is a psychometric measure (or measures) permitting reliable ordering of subjects along a "continuum" and that this "continuum" is used in lieu of the subjects' chronological age in Piaget's traditional designs. Notice further that traditional correlational designs and methods are not equivalent to these neoPiagetian designs; while nonmonotonic relations or interactions among variables would decrease the power of the correlational design, they would be revealed by the neoPiagetian methods.

By *constructive-rationalist method* I mean some form of metasubjective task-analytic procedure capable of yielding metasubjective simulation models of the organismic processes (strategies) which underlie any type of performance in a *type* of task by a *type* of subject (cf. Pascual-Leone, 1978b; Pascual-Leone & Goodman, 1979; De Ribaupierre & Pascual-Leone, 1979). These metasubjective models (to which the information-processing/AI schools have contributed so much insight) may in fact serve to characterize *types of tasks* in terms of the strategies and organismic resources they mobilize in different types of subjects, allowing *subject types* to be defined in terms of their performance in theoretically understood types of tasks. Complex experimental manipulations and/or factor-analytic structures can then often be predicted using appropriately these known types of subjects and of tasks (e.g., Burtis, 1976; de Ribaupierre & Pascual-Leone, 1979; DeAvila, 1974; Goodman, 1979; Parkinson, 1975; Pascual-Leone, 1969; Pulos, 1979).

Using this sort of methodology, organismic factors appear as constructs inferred across types of problems (tasks) *and* across types of subjects, and which are capable of (constructively) explaining these data in terms of organismic rules. This methodology is based on a simple epistemological principle: The principle that it is impossible to understand the effects of human differences on cognitive performance without a theory of what that cognitive performance consists of; *and* conversely, it is impossible to formulate a theory of what cognitive performance consists of without varying the parameters of performance by choosing groups of individuals with different cognitive abilities. Insofar as human differences are poorly understood, they can be studied by observing the performance of different groups on a selected set of cognitive problems (types of task); insofar as a cognitive problem (type of task) is poorly understood, it can be studied by watching the performance of selected (known) types of subjects on that problem (type of task). Often neither human differences nor the cognitive problems (types of task) will be completely understood prior to the experiment and it is necessary to design experiments which allow the *conjoint* assessment of both these terms. In fact the conjoint assessment of both human differences and cognitive-task types is the best way (if not the only one) of experimentally studying metasubjective factors. The conjoint assessment is done by selecting both a series (two or more) of types of tasks (e.g., different type-versions of a given problem-paradigm) and a series (two or more) of subject types (e.g., different age group and/or cognitive styles), and pairing all tasks with all subject types in one experiment. In addition to traditional statistical analysis, the new methods of conjoint measurement (Krantz, Luce, Suppes, & Tversky, 1971) and of functional measurement (Anderson, 1977; Anderson & Cuneo, 1978) are appropriate for the type of methodology that attempts the conjoint assessment of two or more types of factors.[13]

My students and I have been using this kind of methodology with considerable success for the last 13 years (e.g., Burtis, 1976; DeAvila, 1974; De Ribaupierre, 1975; Goodman, 1979; Parkinson, 1975; Pascual-Leone, 1969, 1970, 1978a; Pulos, 1979, Scardamalia, 1977; Toussaint, 1976). Although many particulars of the methods would unavoidably change with the type of metasubjective theory being sought, I am certain that this methodology could, in a short time, eliminate data-base barriers and theoretical prejudices which separate, in developmental psychology, Piagetians, information-processing–AI researchers, and psychometricians.

Concluding Remarks

Even though I have often intimated in this chapter that my students and I have been working on a theory that, we believe, throws considerable light on stages, equilibration, and other empirical–structural

---

[13] Notice that in some of these designs, strict conjoint measurement structures may not be found because of interactions between the types of tasks and the types of subjects being used. These breakdowns of measurement structures are of great interest, for they are aspects of the data which an adequate metasubjective theory must process–structurally explain or predict. In fact, provided that the constructive-rationalist method assigns a metasubjective characterization to both the subject types and the tasks, and if suitable independent variables exist for selecting particular types of subjects, the subjects –tasks interactions can be eliminated by restricting the sample to a known subject type, thus allowing predicted conjoint measurement or functional measurement structures to emerge.

problems, this chapter's real aim was to outline problematic issues and suggest methodological approaches. Let me "key-word" some of these issues with my pet checklist of *problems* for cognitive psychologists: constructive versus descriptive theories; psychogenetic versus generative constructivity; purely structural versus process-structural versus metasubjective theories; the dimensionality of tasks and the problems of metasubjective task analysis and stages; specific executive (or "control") processes versus hidden interactions among organismic factors; learned, novel, and truly novel performances; cognitive conflict situations; learning and motivational paradoxes; neoGestaltist F factor or S–R compatibility in abstract cognition; are there equilibration processes?; making Piaget's theory functional and/or AI theories organismically valid.

Acknowledgments

I am grateful to Dr. P. J. Burtis, Dr. D. Goodman, S. Skakich and J. Johnson for their advice and help. I would like to acknowledge the written comments of Dr. H. Spada and Dr. R. Kluwe, which motivated several improvements in this chapter.

References

Anderson, N. Note on functional measurement and data analysis. *Perception and Psychophysics*, 1977, *21* (3), 201–215.

Anderson, N., & Cuneo, D. O. The height + rule in children's judgments of quantity. *Journal of Experimental Psychology: General*, 1978, *107*, 335–378.

Attneave, F. Representation of physical space. In A. W. Melton & E. E. Martin (Eds.), *Coding processes in human memory*. Washington, D.C.: Winston, 1972. Pp. 283–306.

Beilin, H. Developmental stages and developmental processes. In D. R. Green, M. P. Ford, & G. P. Flamer (Eds.), *Measurement and Piaget*. New York: McGraw-Hill, 1971. Pp. 172–197.

Bernback, H. A. A multiple-copy model for post-perceptual memory. In D. A. Norman (Ed.), *Models of human memory*. New York: Academic Press, 1970. Pp. 103–116.

Bever, T. G. The cognitive basis for linguistic structures. In J. Hayes (Ed.), *Cognition and the development of language*. New York: Wiley, 1970. Pp. 279–362.

Bower, T. G. R. *Development in infancy*. San Francisco: Freeman, 1974.

Brainerd, C. J. Markovian interpretations of conservation learning. *Psychological Review*, 1979, *86*, 181–213.

Burtis, P. J. A developmental study of chunking. Unpublished doctoral dissertation, York University, 1976.

Case, R. Validation of a neo-Piagetian mental capacity construct. *Journal of Experimental Child Psychology*, 1972, *14*, 287–302.

Case, R. Structures and strictures: Some functional limitations on the course of cognitive growth. *Cognitive Psychology*, 1974, *6*, 554–573.

Case, R. Responsiveness to conservation training as a function of induced subjective uncertainty, M-space, and cognitive style. *Canadian Journal of Behavioural Science,* 1977, *9,* 12–25.

Chi, Michelene T. H. Age differences in memory span. *Journal of Experimental Child Psychology,* 1977, *23,* 266–280.

Dawes, R. The mind, the model and the task. In F. Restle, R. M. Shiffrin, N. J. Castellan, H. R. Lindman, & D. B. Pisoni (Eds.), *Cognitive Theory.* (Vol. 1) Hillsdale, New Jersey: Lawrence Erlbaum, 1975. Pp. 119–129.

DeAvila, E. Children's transformation of visual information according to non-verbal syntactical rules. Unpublished doctoral dissertation, York University, 1974.

De Ribaupierre, A. Cognitive space and formal operations. Unpublished doctoral dissertation, University of Toronto, 1975.

De Ribaupierre, A. & Pascual-Leone, J. Formal operations and M power: A neo-Piagetian investigation. In D. Kuhn (Ed.), *Intellectual development beyond childhood* (Source books on New Directions in Child Development). San Francisco: Jossey-Bass, 1979. Pp. 1–43.

Fitts, P. M., & Posner, M. T. *Human performance.* Belmont, California: Brooks/Cole, 1967.

Fitts, P. M., & Seeger, C. M. SR compatibility: Spatial characteristics of stimulus and response codes. *Journal of Experimental Psychology,* 1953, *46,* 199–210.

Flament, C. *Applications of graph theory to group structure.* Englewood Cliffs, New Jersey: Prentice-Hall, 1963.

Gagne, R. Contributions of learning to human development. *Psychological Review,* 1968, *75,* 177–191.

Gelman, R. Conservation acquisition: A problem of learning to attend to relevant attributes. *Journal of Experimental Child Psychology,* 1968, *7,* 167–187.

Gibson, E. J. *Principles of perceptual learning and development.* New York: Appleton-Century-Crofts, 1969.

Goldstein, K. *Human nature in the light of psychopathology.* Cambridge, Massachusetts: Harvard University Press, 1940.

Goodman, D. Stage transitions and the developmental traces of constructive operators: A neo-Piagetian investigation of cognitive growth. Unpublished doctoral dissertation, York University, 1979.

Halford, E. S. A theory of the acquisition of conservation. *Psychological Review,* 1970, *77,* 302–317.

Harlow, H. F. Learning set and error factor theory. In S. Koch (Ed.), *Psychology: A study of science.* Vol. 2. New York: McGraw-Hill, 1959, Pp. 492–537.

Harlow, H. F., & Harlow, M. K. Learning to think. *Scientific American,* 1949, *181,* 36–39.

Hunt, J. McV. *Intelligence and experience.* New York: Ronald Press, 1961.

Inhelder, B., Blanchet, A., Sinclair, A., & Piaget, J. Relation entre les conservations d'ensembles d'éléments discrets et celles des quantités continués. *Anneé Psychologique,* 1975, *75,* 23–60.

Inhelder, B., & Chipman, H. H. (Eds.), *Piaget and his school.* New York: Springer-Verlag, 1976.

Inhelder, B., Sinclair, H., & Bovet, M. *Apprentissage et structures de la connaissance.* Paris: Presses Universitaires de France, 1974.

Klahr, D., & Wallace, J. F. *Cognitive development: An information-processing view.* Hillsdale, New Jersey: Lawrence Erlbaum, 1976.

Krantz, D. H., Luce, R. D., Suppes, P., & Tversky, A. *Foundations of measurement.* New York: Academic Press, 1971.

Logan, R. A quantification of the development of processing capacity. Unpublished M. A. thesis, York University, 1974.

McLaughlin, G. H. Psycho-Logic: A possible alternative to Piaget's formulation. *British Journal of Educational Psychology,* 1963, *33,* 61–67.

Minsky, M., & Papert, S. Research at the laboratory in vision language, and other problems of intelligence. Artificial Intelligence memo No. 252, MIT, 1972.

Mounoud, P., & Bower, T. G. R., Conservation of weight in infants. *Cognition*, 1974/75, *3*, 29–40.

Nassefat, M. *Etude quantitative sur l'évolution des opérations intellectuelles*. Neuchâtel: Delachoux & Niestle, 1963.

Newell, A., & Simon, H. A. *Human problem solving*. Englewood Cliffs, New Jersey: Prentice-Hall, 1972.

Newell, A., & Simon, H. A. Computer science as empirical inquiry: Symbols and search. *Communications of the A.C.M.*, 1976, *19*(3), 113–126.

Parkinson, G. M. The limits of learning: A quantitative investigation of intelligence. Unpublished doctoral dissertation, York University, 1975.

Pascual-Leone, J. Les mécanismes schématiques de la pensée. Institut des Sciences de l'Education. Unpublished manuscript, Université de Genève, 1963.

Pascual-Leone, J. Cognitive development and cognitive style: A general psychological integration. Unpublished doctoral dissertation, University of Geneva, 1969.

Pascual-Leone, J. A mathematical model for the transition rule in Piaget's developmental stages. *Acta Psychologica*, 1970, *32*, 301–345.

Pascual-Leone, J. A theory of constructive operators, a neoPiagetian model of conservation, and the problem of horizontal decalages. Paper presented at the annual meeting of the Canadian Psychological Association, Montreal, 1972.

Pascual-Leone, J. Constructive cognition and substance conservation: Towards adequate structural models of the human subject. Unpublished manuscript, York University, 1973.

Pascual-Leone, J. A neo-Piagetian process-structural model of Witkin's psychological differentiation. Extended version of paper presented at the Symposium on Cross-Cultural Studies of Psychological Differentiation, at the annual meeting of the International Association for Cross-Cultural Psychology, Kingston, Canada, 1974.

Pascual-Leone, J. Metasubjective problems of constructive cognition: Forms of knowing and their psychological mechanisms. *Canadian Psychological Review*, 1976, *17*, (2), 110–125. (a) [Errata for this paper appeared in *Canadian Psychological Review*, 1976, *17*(4), 307.]

Pascual-Leone, J. On learning and development, piagetian style. I. A reply to Lefebvre-Pinard. *Canadian Psychological Review*, 1976, *17*(4), 270–288.(b)

Pascual-Leone, J. On learning and development, piagetian style. II. A critical historical analysis of Geneva's research programme. *Canadian Psychological Review*, 1976, *17*(4), 289–297. (c)

Pascual-Leone, J. A view of cognition from a formalist's perspective. In K. F. Riegel and J. A. Meacham (Eds.), *The developing individual in a changing world*. (Vol. I). The Hague: Mouton, 1976. Pp. 89–100. (d)

Pascual-Leone, J. Review of Klahr and Wallace's *Cognitive development, an information processing view*. *Child Development Abstracts and Bibliography*, 1977, *51*, 251–252.

Pascual-Leone, J. Compounds, confounds, and models in developmental information processing: A reply to Trabasso and Foellinger. *Journal of Experimental Child Psychology*, 1978, *26*, 18–40. (a)

Pascual-Leone, J. Computational models for metasubjective processes. Commentary to Z. W. Pylyshyn's "Computational models and empirical constraints." *The Behavioral and Brain Sciences*, 1978, *1*, 112–113. (b)

Pascual-Leone, J., & Bovet, M. C. L'apprentissage de la quantification de l'inclusion et la théorie opératoire. *Acta Psychologica*, 1966, *25*, 334–356.

Pascual-Leone, J., & Bovet, M. C. L'apprentissage de la quantification de l'inclusion et la théorie opératoire. Partie II: Quelques resultatas experimentaux nouveaux. *Acta Psychologica*, 1967, *26*, 64–74.

Pascual-Leone, J. & Goodman, D. Intelligence and experience: A neo-Piagetian approach. *Instructional Science*, 1979, *8*, 301–367.

Pascual-Leone, J., Goodman, D., Ammon, P., & Subelman, I. Piagetian theory and neo-Piagetian analysis as psychological guides in education. In J. M. Gallagher & J. A. Easley (Eds.), *Knowledge and development* (Vol. 2). New York: Plenum, 1978. Pp. 243–289.

Pascual-Leone, J., & Smith, J. The encoding and decoding of symbols of children: A new experimental paradigm and a neo-Piagetian model. *Journal of Experimental Child Psychology*, 1969, *8*, 328–355.

Pascual-Leone, J., & Sparkman, E. The dialectics of empiricism and rationalism: A last methodological reply to Trabasso. *Journal of Experimental Child Psychology*, 1980, *29*, 88–101.

Piaget, J. Le mechanisme du developpement mental et les lois du groupement des opérations. *Archives de Psychologie* (Genève), 1941, *28*, 215–285.

Piaget, J. Les stades du développement intellectuel de l'infant et de l'adolescent. In P. Osterrieth, J. Piaget, R. de Saussure, J. M. Tanner, H. Wallon, & R. Zazzo (Eds.), *Le problème des stades en psychologie de l'infant*. Paris: P.U.F., 1956, Pp. 33–49. (a)

Piaget, J. Logique et équilibre dans les comportements du sujet. In L. Apostel, B. Mandelbrot, & J. Piaget (Eds.), *Logique et équilibre*. Paris: P.U.F., 1956. Pp. 27–117. (b)

Piaget, J. Closing remarks. In D. R. Green, M. P. Ford, & G. P. Flamer (Eds.), *Measurement and Piaget*. New York: McGraw-Hill, 1971. Pp. 210–213.

Piaget, J. L'équilibration des structures cognitives (problème central du développement). *Etudes d'Epistemologie génétique*. Vol. 33. Paris: P.U.F., 1975.

Piaget, J. Some recent research and its links with a new theory of groupings and conservation based on commutability. *Annals of the New York Academy of Science*, 1977, *291*, 350–371.

Piaget, J., & Inhelder, B. *La représentation de l'espace chez l'infant*. Paris: P.U.F., 1948. (English translation: *The child's conception of space*. London: Routledge & Keagan Paul, 1956).

Piaget, J., & Inhelder, B. *La developpement des quantités physiques chez l'infant*. Neuchâtel: Delachaux & Niestle, 1962.

Piaget, J., Inhelder, B., & Szeminska, A. *La géométrie spontanée de l'infant*. Paris: P.U.F., 1948.

Prentice, W.C.H. The systematic psychology of Wolfgang Köhler. In S. Koch (Ed.), *Psychology: A study of a science* (Vol. 1). New York: McGraw-Hill, 1959. Pp. 427–455.

Pulos, S. Developmental cognitive constraints on structural learning. Doctoral dissertation, York University, 1979.

Pylyshyn, Z. Computational models and empirical constraints. *The Behavioral and Brain Sciences*, 1978, *1*, 93–127.

Robert, M., & Charbonneau, C. Extinction of liquid conservation by observation: Effects of model's age and presence. *Child Development*, 1977, *48*, 648–652.

Scardamalia, M. Information-processing capacity and the problem of horizontal decalage: A demonstration using combinatorial reasoning tasks. *Child Development*, 1977, *48*, 28–37.

Simon, H. A. *The sciences of the artificial*. Cambridge, Massachusetts: MIT Press, 1969.

Simon, H. A. On the development of the processor. In S. Farnham-Diggory (Ed.), *Information processing in children*. New York: Academic Press, 1972. Pp. 3–22.

Simon, H. A. How big is a chunk? *Science*, 1974, *183*, 482–488.

Simon, H. A., & Newell, A. Human problem solving: The state of the theory in 1970. *American Psychologist*, 1971, *26*, 145–159.

Strauss, S. & Stein, D. U-shaped curves in language acquisition and the learning of physical concepts. *Die Neueren Sprachen*, 1978, *3/4*, 326–340.

Todor, J. I. Cognitive development: Cognitive style and motor ability. Paper presented at the 9th Canadian Symposium for Psycho-motor Learning and Sports Psychology.

Banff, Alberta, September 1977.

Toussaint, N. A. Mental processing capacity, anticipatory and retroactive abilities, and development of concrete-operational structures. *Canadian Journal of Behavioural Science*, 1976, *8*, 363–374.

Trabasso, T. & Foellinger, D. B. Information processing capacity in children: A test of Pascual-Leone's model. *Journal of Experimental Child Psychology*, 1978, *26*, 1–17.

Weizenbaum, J. *Computer power and human reason*. San Francisco: Freeman, 1976.

White, S. H., & Pillemar, D. B. Childhood amnesia and the development of a socially accessible memory system. In J. F. Kihlstrom & F. J. Evans (Eds.), *Functional disorders of memory*. Hillsdale, New Jersey: Erlbaum, 1979. Pp. 29–73.

Zajonc, R. B. Balance, congruity, and dissonance. *Public Opinion Quarterly*, 1960, *24*, 280–296.

Subject Index